Abortion Bibliography

for 1979

Abortion Bibliography

for 1979

The Whitston Publishing Company
Troy, New York
1982

TABLE OF CONTENTS

PREFACE

Abortion Bibliography for 1979 is the ninth annual list of books and articles surrounding the subject of abortion in the preceeding year. It appears serially each fall as a contribution toward documenting in one place as comprehensively as possible the literature of one of our central social issues. It is an attempt at a comprehensive world bibliography.

Searches in compiling this material have covered the following sources: *Abstracts on Criminology & Penology; Abstracts on Police Science; Access; Air University Library Index to Military Periodicals; Alternative Index; American Humanities Index; American Reference Books Annual; Applied Science & Technology Index; Art Index; Bibliographic Index; Biological Abstracts; Biological & Agricultural Index; British Humanities Index; Business Periodicals Index; Canadian Education Index; Canadian Periodicals Index; Catholic Periodical & Literature Index; Communication Abstracts; College Student Personnel Abstracts; Completed Research in Health, Physical Education, & Recreation; Criminal Justice Abstracts (form: Crime & Delinquency Literature); Criminal Justice Periodical Index; Cumulative Book Index; Cumulated Index to Nursing Literature; Current Index to Journals in Education; Dissertation Abstracts International: A. Social Sciences & Humanities; Dissertation Abstracts International: B. The Sciences & Engineering; Education Index; Environment Abstracts; Environment Index; Essay & General Literature Index; Government Reports Announcements and Index; Hospital Literature Index; Human Resources Abstracts; Humanities Index; Index Medicus; Index to Legal Periodicals; Index to Jewish Periodicals; International Bibliography of the Social Sciences; International Nursing Index; Journal of Human Services Abstracts; Library of Congress Catalog: Subject Catalog;*

Library of Congress Catalogs: Films & Other Materials for Projection; Media Review Digest; Monthly Periodical Index; PAIS; Philosophers Index; Popular Periodical Index; New Periodicals Index 1978; Nursing Literature (now—Nursing and Allied Health Literature); Masters Abstracts; Index to Periodical Articles Related to Law; Population Sciences: Index of Biomedical Research; Psychological Abstracts; Readers Guide to Periodical Literature; Religion Index One: Periodicals (form: Index to Religious Periodical Literature); Sage Urban Studies Abstracts; Social Sciences Index; Social Work Research & Abstracts (form: Abstracts for Social Workers); Sociological Abstracts; The Wall Street Journal Index; and *Women's Studies Abstracts.*

The bibliography is divided into two sections: a title section in alphabetical order; and a subject section. Thus, if the researcher does not wish to observe the subject heads of the compiler, he can use the title section exclusively. The subject heads have been allowed to issue from the nature of the material indexed rather than being imposed from Library of Congress subject heads or other standard lists.

The Book section includes Government Publications and Monographs.

The Subject Head Index includes page numbers.

Since Whitston's *Population Bibliography* series has ceased with the publication of the 1976 [1979] supplement, the *Abortion Bibliography* series, with this ninth annual listing, has begun to include subjects peripheral to but closely allied with the subject of abortion which traditionally had been covered in that earlier series: Birth Control, Contraceptives and Contraception, Sterilization, and the like. We hope that this added inclusion will enhance and prove useful to the coverage of the subject of Abortion.

LIST OF PERIODICALS CITED

AJR Information: Association of Jewish Refugees in Great
    Britain
AORN Journal: Association of Operating Room Nurses
Acres USA
Acta Biologica et Medica Germanica
Acta Chirurgiae Orthopaedicae et Traumatologiae Cechoslovaca
Acta Endocrinologica
Acta Europaea Fertilitatis
Acta Haematologica
Acta Hepatogastroenterologica
Acta Medica Academiae Scientiarum Hungaricae
Acta Medica Iranica
Acta Neurologica Scandinavica
Acta Obstetrica y Ginecologica Hispana-Lusitana
Acta Obstetricia et Gynecologica Scandinavica
Acta Orthopaedica Scandinavica
Acta Poloniae Pharmaceutica
Acta Virologica
Acta Zoologica Sinica
Adolescence
Advances in Experimental Medicine and Biology
Advances in Internal Medicine
Advances in Planned Parenthood
Advertising Age
Africa Report
Agenda
Air Force Times
Akusherstvo i Ginekologiia
Albany Law Review
Alberta Counsellor
Alter-Jornal de Edtudos Psicodinamicos

America
American Atheist
American Baby
American Bar Association Journal
American Druggist
American Economic Review
American Family Physician
American Heart Journal
American Indian Journal
American Journal of Clinical Nutrition
American Journal of Clinical Pathology
American Journal of Community Psychology
American Journal of Diseases of Children
American Journal of Epidemiology
American Journal of Human Genetics
American Journal of Law and Medicine
American Journal of Medicine
American Journal of Mental Deficiency
American Journal of Nursing
American Journal of Obstetrics and Gynecology
American Journal of Opthalmology
American Journal of Orthopsychiatry
American Journal of Pharmaceutical Education
American Journal of Psychiatry
American Journal of Psychology
American Journal of Public Health
American Journal of Sociology
American Pharmacy
American Philosophical Quarterly
American Sociological Review
Anaesthesia
Anaesthesiologische und Intensivmedizinische Praxis
Anesthesia and Analgesia
Angiologia
Angiology
Annales de Cardiologie et d'Angeiologie
Annales de Medecine Interne
Annales de la Nutrition et da l'Alimentation
Annales Medico-Psychologiques
Annali Sclavo
Annals of Clinical and Laboratory Science
Annals of Human Biology

Annals of Internal Medicine
Annals of Ophthalmology
Annals of the Rheumatic Diseases
Archiv fur Geschwulstforschung
Archiv fur Gynaekologie
Archives d'Anatomie et de Cytologie Pathologique
Archives of Andrology
Archives of Dermatology
Archives of Gynecology
Archives of Ophthalmology
Archives of Oto-Rhino-Laryngology
Archives of Sexual Behavior
Archives of Surgery
Archives of Toxicology
Archivio per la Scienze Mediche
Arizona Medicine
Arizona Nurse
Arizona State Law Journal
Arkhiv Patologii
Atherosclerosis
Atlantis
Atlas
Audiovisual Instruction
Australasian Nurses Journal
Australian and New Zealand Journal of Obstetrics and
    Gynaecology
Australian and New Zealand Journal of Psychiatry
Australian Family Physician
Australian Law Journal
Auxiliaire

Bangladesh Development Studies
Biochemical and Biophysical Research Communications
Birth and the Family Journal
Birth Defects
Boletin de la Oficina Sanitaria Panamericana
Bollettino Chimico Farmaceutico
Brain/Mind
Brigham Young University Law Review
British Journal of Cancer
British Journal of Criminology

British Journal of Hospital Medicine
British Journal of Law and Society
British Journal of Obstetrics and Gynaecology
British Journal of Pharmacology
British Journal of Surgery
British Journal of Urology
British Medical Journal
Bruxelles-Medicale
Bulletin de L'Acadamie de Chirurgie Dentaire
Bulletin der Schweizerischen Akademie der Medizinischen
    Wissenschaften
Bulletin of the New York Academy of Medicine
Bulletins et Memoires de la Societe Francaise d'Ophthalmologie
Business Insurance
Business Week

California Nurse
Canadian Business Review
Canadian Forum
Canadian Historical Review
Canadian Journal of Genetics and Cytology
Canadian Journal of Public Health
Canadian Journal of Surgery
Canadian Medical Association Journal
Canadian Nurse
Canadian Psychiatric Association Journal
Canadian Psychological Review
Cardiovascular Nursing
Casopis Lekaru Ceskych
Catholic Digest
Catholic Lawyer
Catholic Trustee
Cell and Tissue Research
Center Magazine
Ceskoslovenska Dermatologie
Ceskoslovenska Farmacie
Ceskoslovenska Gastroenterologie a Vyziva
Ceskoslovenska Gynekologie
Chatelaine
Chelsea Journal
Chemical and Engineering News

Chemical Marketing Reporter
Chest
Chicago Studies
Child Development
China Quarterly
Christian Century
Christianity and Crisis
Chronicle of Higher Education
Circulation
Civil Liberties Review
Clearing House Review
Clinica Terapeutica
Clinical and Experimental Immunology
Clinical Endocrinology
Clinical Obstetrics and Gynecology
Clinical Pharmacology and Therapeutics
Clinical Toxicology
College Student Journal Monograph
Columbia
Commerce
Commonweal
Communities
Community Dentistry and Oral Epidemiology
Comparative Education
Comparative Politics
Comparative Studies in Society and History
Comprehensive Psychiatry
Concordia Theological Quarterly
Congressional Monitor
Congressional Quarterly Weekly Report
Connecticut Medicine
Conservation Foundation Letter
Conservative Digest
Consumer Reports
Contemporary Literature
Contemporary Ob/Gyn
Contemporary Psychoanalysis
Contemporary Review
Contraception
Cornell Veterinarian
Cosmopolitan
Counseling Psychologist

Country Women
Crime Control Digest
Criminal Justice and Behavior
Criminal Law Reporter: Court Decisions and Proceedings
Criminal Law Reporter: Supreme Court Proceedings
Criminal Law Reporter: Text Section
The Criminal Law Review
Critical Care Update
Cross Currents
The Crown Agents Quarterly Review
Current Medical Research and Opinion
Current Practice in Obstetric and Gynecologic Nursing

Danish Medical Bulletin
Demography
Dental Student
Deutsche Medizinische Wochenschrift
Deutsche Zahnaerztliche Zeitschrift
Deutsche Zeitschrift fuer Verdauungs-und Stoffwechsel-
    krankheiten
Developmental Medicine and Child Neurology
Diabetes Care
Diabetes Forecast
Dimensions in Health Service
Dissertation Abstracts International
La Documentation Catholique
Drake Law Review
Draper Fund Report
Drug and Cosmetic Industry
Drug and Therapeutics Bulletin
Drug Topics
Drugs
Duodecim

East African Medical Journal
East West
Econometrica
Economic Development and Cultural Change
The Economist
Editor and Publisher

Editorial Research Reports
Educational Digest
Emergency Medicine
Endocrinologie
Endocrinology
Endokrinologie
Endoscopy
Engage/Social Action
Equine Veterinary Journal
Essence
Ethics
Ethics in Science and Medicine
European Journal of Cancer
European Journal of Obstetrics, Gynecology and Reproductive
    Biology
Experientia

FDA Consumer
Family Circle
Family Coordinator
Family Health
Family Law Quarterly
Family Planning Perspectives
Far Eastern Economic Review
Farmakologiya i Toksikologiya
Farmatsiia
Federal Probation Quarterly
Federation Proceedings
Fel'dsher i Akusherka
Feminist Studies
Fertility and Sterility
Financial Post
Folia Haematologica
Folia Medica
Food Process
Food Research Institute Studies
Fordham Law Review
Forest Industries
Fortschritte der Medizin
Foundations
Frontiers

Furrow

Gallup Opinion Index
Geburtshilfe und Frauenheilkunde
George Mason University Law Review
Georgetown Law Journal
Georgia Law Review
Gigiyena i Sanitariya
Gigiyena Truda i Professional'nyye Zabolevaniya
Ginecologia y Obstetricia de Mexico
Ginekologia Polska
Glamour
Good Housekeeping
Guardian
Gynaekologische Rundschau
Gynecologic and Obstetric Investigation
Gynecologic Investigation
Gynecologic Oncology

HNO: Hals-, Nasen-, Ohren-Heilkunde
Haematologica
Harefuah
Harper's Bazaar
Harvard Educational Review
Hastings Center Report
Health and Social Service Journal
Health and Social Work
Health Bulletin
Health Education
Health Visitor
Helvetica Paediatrica Acta
Hereditas
Heresies
Histopathology
History and Theory
Homiletic and Pastoral Review
Hormone and Metabolic Research
Hospital and Community Psychiatry
Hospital Progress
Hospital Topics

Hospitals: Journal of the American Hospital Association
Howard Law Journal
Human Behavior
Human Ecology
Human Events
Human Genetics
Human Organization
Human Pathology
Humanist
Humanitas

IACP Law Enforcement Legal Review
IPPF Medical Bulletin (International Planned Parenthood Federation)
Image
Improving Human Performance Quarterly
Indian Journal of Experimental Biology
Indian Journal of Medical Research
Indian Journal of Pathology and Microbiology
Indian Pediatrics
Infection and Immunity
Infirmiere Canadienne
Infirmiere Francaise
Inquiry
The Insiders' Chronical
International and Comparative Law Quarterly
International Dental Journal
International Family Planning Perspectives
International Journal for Vitamin and Nutrition Research
International Journal of Andrology
International Journal of Epidemiology
International Journal of Fertility
International Journal of Gynaecology and Obstetrics
International Journal of Health Education
International Journal of Sociology of the Family
International Nursing Review
International Surgery
Internist
Investigative Urology
Irish Medical Journal
Israel Journal of Medical Sciences

JAMA: Journal of the American Medical Association
JOGN: Journal of Obstetric, Gynecologic and Neonatal Nursing
Japanese Journal of Pharmacology
Jewish Digest
Jewish Spectator
John Marshall Journal of Practice and Procedure
Johns Hopkins Medical Journal
Josanpu Zasshi
Journal de Gynecologie, Obstetrique et Biologie de la Reproduc-
    tion
Journal de Pharmacie de Belgique
Journal for the Scientific Study of Religion
Journal for Special Educators
Journal of the American College Health Association
Journal of the American Dental Association
Journal of the American Dietetic Association
Journal of the American Medical Women's Association
Journal of the American Optometric Association
Journal of the American Podiatry Association
Journal of Antimicrobial Chemotheraphy
Journal of Applied Social Psychology
Journal of Biomedical Materials Research
Journal of Biosocial Science
Journal of Clinical Endocrinology and Metabolism
Journal of Clinical Pathology
Journal of College Student Personnel
Journal of Comparative Family Studies
Journal of Consulting and Clinical Psychology
Journal of Cross-cultural Psychology
Journal of Dental Research
Journal of Developing Areas
Journal of Development Studies
Journal of Divorce
Journal of Economic Entomology
Journal of Economic History
Journal of the Egyptian Medical Association
Journal of Endocrinology
Journal of Family History
Journal of Family Law

Journal of Family Welfare
Journal of Geography
Journal of Homosexuality
Journal of Hygiene
Journal of the Indian Medical Association
Journal of Interdisciplinary History
Journal of International Medical Research
Journal of the Kentucky Medical Association
Journal of Marriage and the Family
Journal of Medical Genetics
Journal of Medical Philosophy
Journal of Medical Primatology
Journal of Neurology, Neurosurgery and Psychiatry
Journal of Nurse-Midwifery
Journal of Nursing Administration
Journal of Occupational Medicine
Journal of Oral Pathology
Journal of Parasitology
Journal of Perinatal Medicine
Journal of Periodontology
Journal of Personality and Social Psychology
Journal of Pharmaceutical Studies
Journal of Political Economy
Journal of Population
Journal of Postgraduate Medicine
Journal of Practical Nursing
Journal of Psychiatric Nursing
Journal of Psychology
Journal of Religion and Health
Journal of Reproduction and Fertility
Journal of Reproductive Medicine
Journal of the Royal College of General Practitioners
Journal of School Health
Journal of Sex and Marital Therapy
Journal of Sex Education and Therapy
Journal of Sex Research
Journal of Social History
Journal of Social Issues
Journal of Steroid Biochemistry
Journal of Toxicology and Environmental Health
Journal of Tropical Medicine and Hygiene
Journal of Urology

Journal of Voluntary Action Research
Journalism Quarterly
Judicature
Jugoslavenska Ginekologija i Opstetricija
Juvenile Justice Digest
Juvenile Law Digest

Kango
Kango Kenkyu
Kansas Law Review
Kansenshogaku Zasshi
Katilolehti
Kenya Nursing Journal
Klinicheskaya Meditzina
Klinika Oczna
Korean Central Journal of Medicine
Krankenpflege

Labour Research
Ladies Home Journal
Lakartidningen
Lamp
Lancet
Law Enforcement News
Law Quarterly Review
Legal Aspects of Medical Practice
Legal Medical Quarterly
Life Sciences
Ligament
Lijecnicki Vjesnik
Linacre Quarterly
Liquorian
Local Population Studies
Loyola Law Review

MMW: Muenchener Medizinishe Wochenschrift
Ms Magazine
McCalls
Maccleans

Mademoiselle
Majority Report
Market Research Society. Journal
Marketing
Marquette Law Review
Maryland Nurse
Maternal and Child Health/Family Planning
Maternal-Child Nursing Journal
Media Report to Women
Medical Care
Medical Instrumentation
Medical Journal of Australia
Medical Journal of Malaysia
Medical Letter on Drugs and Therapeutics
Medical Self-Care
Medical Ultrasound
Medical World News
Medicinski Pregled
Meditsinskaia Sestra
Meditsinskaia Tekhnika
Medizinische Klinik
Medizinische Welt
Menninger Clinic. Bulletin
Mennonite Review
Mental Retardation
Mercer Law Review
Midstream
Milbank Memorial Fund Quarterly
Military Medicine
Minerva Anestesiologica
Minerva Ginecologia
Minerva Medica
Modern Law Review
Modern Packaging
Morphologiai es Igazsagugyi Orvosi Szemle
Mother Jones
Mythlore

NAT News (National Association of Theatre Nurses)
Nation
National Catholic Reporter

National News
National Review
National Underwriter Life and Health Insurance Edition
Naturwissenschaften
Nederlands Tijdschrift voor Geneeskunde
Neurologia i Neurochirurgia Polska
Neurology
New Age
New Direction for Women
New England Journal of Medicine
New Horizons
New Humanist
New Jersey Monthly
New Law Journal
New Leader
New Mexico Law Review
New Scientist
New Society
New Statesman
New Times
New York Review of Books
New York State Journal of Medicine
New York Times
New York University Law Review
New York University Review of Law and Social Change
New Zealand Journal of Laboratory Technology
New Zealand Law Journal
New Zealand Medical Journal
New Zealand Nursing Forum
New Zealand Psychologist
Newsweek
Nigerian Medical Journal
North Dakota Law Review
Not Man Apart
Nouvelle Presse Medicale
Nouvelle Revue Theologique
Now
Nurses Drug Alert
Nursing
Nursing Clinics of North America
Nursing Journal of India
Nursing Mirror and Midwive's Journal

Nursing Research
Nursing Times

OECD Observer: Organization for Economic Cooperation and
    Development
Observer
Obstetrical and Gynecological Survey
Obstetrics and Gynecology
Off Our Backs
Office
Oklahoma Law Review
Organizational Behavior and Human Performance
Origins
Orvosi Hetilap
Osservatore Romano
Our Sunday Visitor

Pacific Sociological Review
Paper Trade Journal
Paraplegia
Pathologica
Pediatria Polska
Pediatrics
Pediatriia Akusherstvo i Ginekologiia
Pediatriya, Akusherstvo i Ginekolohiya
People
Perception
Perceptual and Motor Skills
Personalist
Perspectives in Biology and Medicine
Philosophy and Public Affairs
Phylon
Pielegniarka i Polozna
Planta Medica
Plastics World
Playboy
Point of View
Policy Studies Journal
Politicks
Politics Today

Polski Tygodnik Lekarski
Population
Population and Development Review
Population Bulletin
Population et Famille
Population Reports
Population Studies
Populi
Praxis
Prevention
Problemy Endokrinologii i Gormonoterapii
Product Marketing
Professioni Infermieristiche
Progress in Clinical Cancer
Progressive
Prostaglandins
Prostaglandins and Medicine
Przeglad Lekarski
Psychology
Psychosomatics
Psychotherapie und Medizinische Psychologie
Psychotherapy and Psychosomatics
Public Health Reports
Public Health Reviews
Public Interest
Public Opinion Quarterly

Quest

RN
Radiology
Rain
Recent Results in Cancer Research
La Recherche
Redbook
Relations
Research Communications in Chemical Pathology and Pharma-
    cology
Research Quarterly
Respiratory Technology

Review of Economics and Statistics
Review of Religious Research
Revista Chilena de Obstetricia y Ginecologia
Revista de: Chirurgie Oncologie Radiologie orl Oftalmologie,
    Stomatologie, Oftalmologia
Revista de Gastroenterologia de Mexico
Revista de Sanidad e Higiene Publica
Revista Paulista de Medicina
Revue de l'Infirmiere et de l'Assistante Sociale
Revue Medicale de Liege
Revue Roumaine de Medicine. Serie Endocrinologie

SPM: Salud Publica de Mexico
St. Louis University Law Journal
Sairaanhoitaja
San Francisco Review of Books
Santa Clara Law Review
Saturday Evening Post
Saturday Review
Scandinavian Journal of Haematology
Schweizer Archiv fur Neurologie, Neurochirurgie und Psychiatrie
Schweizerische Medizinische Wochenschrift
Science
Science Digest
Science Forum
Science News
Scientific American
Score
Semaines des Hopitaux de Paris
Seven Days
Signs
Social Biology
Social Casework
Social Forces
Social Policy
Social Problems
Social Psychiatry
Social Science and Medicine
Social Service Review
Social Thought
Social Work

Social Work in Health Care
Society
Sociological Quarterly
Soins
South African Medical Journal
Southern California Law Review
Southern Illinois University Law Journal
Southern Medical Journal
Soviet Law and Government
Soziologenkorrespondenz
Spectator
Spokeswoman
Srpski Arhiv za Celokupno Lekarstvo
Steroids
Stomatologie der DDR
Stomatologiia
Storefront
Studies in Family Planning
Suffolk University Law Review
Surgery Clinics of North America
Surgery, Gynecology and Obstetrics
The Surgical Technologists
Sykepleien

Teratology
Texas Medicine
Texas Monthly
Theological Studies
Theology Today
Thesis Theological Cassettes
Thrombosis and Haemostasis
Thrombosis Research
Tidsskrift for den Norske Laegeforening
Tijdschrift vor Ziekenverpleging
Time
Times Educational Supplement
Toxicology
Tradition
Transactions of the Medical Society of London
Transactions of the Pacific Coast Obstetrical and Gynecological
    Society

Transfusion
Tropical Doctor
Tulane Law Review

US Catholic
US News and World Report
USA Today
Ugeskrift for Laeger
Undercurrent
Union Medicale du Canada
University of Baltimore Law Review
University of Cincinnati Law Review
University of Detroit Journal of Urban Law
University of Florida Law Review
University of Miami Law Review
University of Missouri-Kansas City Law Review
University of Pittsburg Law Review
Urban Life
Urologic Clinics of North America
Urology

Verhandlungen des Deutschen Gesellschaft fur Innere Medizin
Veterinariia
Veterinarni Medicina
Veterinarno-Meditsinski Nauki
Veterinary Pathology
Veterinary Record
Viata Medicala
The Village Voice
Virchows Archiv. Abt. A. Pathologische Anatomie-Pathology
Virginia Law Review
Virginia Medicine
Virologie
Vital Health Statistics
Voprosy Okhrany Materinstva i Detstva

WHO Bulletin
WHO Chronicles
WHO Technical Report Series

Wall Street Journal
Washburn Law Journal
Washington University Law Quarterly
Water and Sewage Works
Wayne Law Review
Weekend Magazine
Weekly
Well-Being
West Indian Medical Journal
West Virginia Medical Journal
Western Journal of Medicine
Western State University Law Review
Westminster Theological Journal
Wiadomosci Lekarskie
Wiener Klinische Wochenschrift
Wiener Medizinische Wochenschrift
Win Magazine
Wisconsin Law Review
Wisconsin Medical Journal
Women Lawyers Journal
Women's Rights Law Reporter
Women's Studies International Quarterly
Working Women
World Health
World Review of Nutrition and Dietetics

Yale Journal of Biology and Medicine
Yonsei Medical Journal
Youth and Society

Zahnaerztliche Mitteilungen
Zahnaerztliche Munden und Kieferheilkunde mit Zentralblatt
Zdravookhraneniye Rossiiskol Federatzii
Zeitschrift fur Aerztliche Fortbildung
Zeitschrift fur die Gesamte Innere Medizin
Zeitschrift fur Rechtsmedizin
Zeitschrift fur Gastroenterologie
Zeitschrift fur Geburtschilfe und Perinatologie
Zeitschrift fur die Gesamte Innere Medizin und ihre Grenzge-
    biete

Zentralblatt fur Allgemeine Pathologie und Pathologische
    Anatomie
Zentralblatt fur Gynaekologie
Zhurnal Mikrobiologii, Epidemiologii i Immunobiologii

SUBJECT HEADING INDEX

BOOKS, GOVERNMENT PUBLICATIONS, AND MONOGRAPHS

ABORTION. Notre Dame, Indiana: University of Notre Dame Press, 1977.

ABORTION IN PSYCHOSOCIAL PERSPECTIVE. New York: Springer Publishing Company, 1978.

Anastasio, Joseph Lee. "Contraceptive Sterilization as a Life Change Event: Its Effects Upon the MMPI and CPI Scales." University of the Pacific, 1979 (Ed.D. dissertation).

Andrade, Sally V. J. "Family Planning Attitudes and Practices as a Function of the Degree of Cultural Identification of Female Mexican-American College Students." The University of Texas at Austin, 1979 (Ph.D. dissertation).

Barr, S. J., et al. A WOMAN'S CHOICE. New York: Rawson, Wade Publishers, 1978.

BELLAGIO CONFERENCE ON POPULATION 1977. New York: Rockefeller Foundation, 1977.

Berger, Charlene. "Psychological Characteristics of Anglophone and Francophone Initial and Repeat Aborters and Contraceptors." Concordia University, 1978 (Ph.D. dissertation).

BIBLIOGRAPHY ON RESEARCH & EVALUATION REPORTS OF BANGLADESH FROM 1964; Research and Evaluation Reports of Official Family Planning Programme Under Erstwhile Pakistan Family Planning Council. Bangladesh: The Unit, 1977.

1

Blockwick, J. O. YOU, ME, AND A FEW BILLION MORE. Nashville: Abingdon Press, 1979.

Briggs, Michael, et al. ANNUAL RESEARCH REVIEWS: ORAL CONTRACEPTIVES, Volume 2, 1978. St. Albans, Vermont: Eden Medical Research, Inc., 1978.

Buckner, W. P., Jr., ed. MEDICAL READINGS ON HUMAN SEXUALITY. Medical Readings Inc., 1978.

Burgess, Rebecca B. "Effects of Attitudes About Premarital Sex on Contraceptive Risk-Taking Among Low-Income, Unmarried Teenagers." Emory University, 1979 (Ph.D. dissertation).

Canada. Statistics Canada Health Division. THERAPEUTIC ABORTIONS, 1977. Ottawa: Statistics Canada, 1979.

CHOOSING LIFE; SOME QUESTIONS AND ANSWERS ON ABORTION (News notes September 1979 no. 243). New York: Christophers, 1979.

Claeys, Godelieve. CONTRACEPTION; INTERNATIONAL SELECTIVE BIBLIOGRAPHY SYSTEMATICALLY CLASSIFIED 1965-1969. Belgium: Commission belge de bibliographie, 1978.

CONTRACEPTION? FACTS ON BIRTH CONTROL. Daly City, Califormia: Physicians Art Service, Inc., 1978.

Copp, Brian E. "Social and Psychological Factors in the Continuation of Contraceptive Behavior." The University of Chicago, 1979 (Ph.D. dissertation).

Corsa, L., et al. POPULATION PLANNING. Ann Arbor: University of Michigan Press, 1979.

Crews, Michael. "The Effect of Oral Contraceptive Agents on Copper and Zinc Balance in Young Women." V.P.I. and State University, 1979 (Ph.D. dissertation).

Denes, M. IN NECESSITY AND SORROW. New York: Penguin

Books, 1977.

DISCOVER NATURAL FAMILY PLANNING; YOU WILL
HAVE A LIFETIME TO BE THANKFUL. Collegeville,
Minnesota: St. John's University Human Life Center, 1979.

Dreyer, Nancy A. "A Study of Fibrinolytic Response and Indio-
pathic Thromboembolism With Special Reference to Oral
Contraceptive Use." The University of North Carolina at
Chapel Hill, 1978 (Ph.D. dissertation).

Dutkowski, Regina Theresa. "The Effect of Contraceptive
Steroids on Sister Chromatid Exchange and Nuclear Morphology." Fordham University, 1979 (Ph.D. dissertation).

Effendi, Sofian. "Occupation, Utility of Children, and Adoption
of Modern Contraceptives: A Field Study in Rural Yogya-
karta, Indonesia." University of Pittsburgh, 1978 (Ph.D.
dissertation).

Francke, L. B. THE AMBIVALENCE OF ABORTION. New
York: Random House, 1978.

FRONTIERS IN REPRODUCTION AND FERTILITY CON-
TROL: PART 2. Cambridge: MIT Press, 1977.

Gamble, George R. "Natality, Contraception and Family Patterns in a Caracas Barrio." The University of North Carolina
at Chapel Hill, 1978 (Ph.D. dissertation).

Garblik, Pauline. "Acceptance or Rejection of Sex-Role Stereo-
types as a Factor in Adolescent Female Sexual Behavior and
Use of Contraception." University of Cincinnati, 1978
(Ph.D. dissertation).

Gjorgov, Arne N. "Barrier Contraceptive Practice and Male Infertility as Related Factors to Breast Cancer in Married Women: A Retrospective Study." The University of North
Carolina at Chapel Hill, 1978 (Ph.D. dissertation).

Gordon, L. WOMAN'S BODY. WOMAN'S RIGHT. New York:
Penguin Books, 1977.

Halimi, G. THE RIGHT TO CHOOSE. Australia: University of Queensland Press, 1977.

Harmon, John D. "Rights, Obligations, and Social Freedom: The Case of Abortion." University of Wisconsin, 1978 (Ph.D. dissertation).

Harmon, Kathryn. "The Implementation of Federal Family Planning Objectives in the States." University of Iowa, 1978 (Ph.D. dissertation).

Hassouna, Taylor. "Policy Formulation and Implementation and the Diffusion of Contraceptive Technology in the Arab Republic of Egypt." University of Denver, 1978 (dissertation).

Kerr, Graham B. POPULATION AND FAMILY PLANNING IN AFGHANISTAN: Social Implications of the Data From Afghan Demographic Studies. Amherst, New York: SUNY at Buffalo, Council on International Studies, 1978.

Kessel, E., et al. AN ASSESSMENT OF IUD PERFORMANCE. Triangle Park, North Carolina: International Fertility Research Program, 1976.

Khoo, S. E. EFFECTS OF PROGRAM CONTRACEPTION ON FERTILITY. Honolulu: University Press of Hawaii, 1978.

McCarty, Dennis J. "Attitudinal and Normative Influences on Contraceptive Usage Intentions: A Test of the Fishbein Model of Intention." University of Kentucky, 1978 (Ph.D. dissertation).

Marcon, Mario J. "Consequences of Herpes Simplex Virus Type-2 and Human Cell Interaction During Abortive Infection." Wake Forest University, The Bowman Gray School of Medicine, 1978 (Ph.D. dissertation).

MODERN TRENDS IN INFERTILITY AND CONCEPTION CONTROL, Volume 1. Baltimore: Williams & Wilkins Company, 1979.

Moghissi, K. S. CONTROVERSIES IN CONTRACEPTION. Baltimore: Williams & Wilkins Company, 1979.

Mohr, J. C. ABORTION IN AMERICA. New York: Oxford University Press, 1978.

MORE THAN A CHOICE; WOMEN TALK ABOUT ABORTION. Somerville, Massachusetts: New England Free Press, 1978.

Mumford, Stephen D. VASECTOMY COUNSELING. San Francisco, California: San Francisco Press, 1977.

—. VASECTOMY: THE DECISION-MAKING PROCESS. San Francisco, California: San Francisco Press, 1977.

Nambudiri, C. N. S., et al. STRATEGY FOR FAMILY PLANNING IN THE INDIAN INDUSTRIAL SECTOR. New York: Sterling Publishing, 1977.

Nauful, Brenda. "Nursing Student's Attitudes Toward and Knowledge of Abortion Before and After a Supervised Clinical Experience With Patients Having Abortions." University of South Carolina, 1978 (dissertation).

Nickerson, J. E. COUNSEL FOR THE UNBORN BEFORE THE COURT OF REASON. Boston: Branden Press, 1978.

Noonan, J. T. A PRIVATE CHOICE. New York: Macmillan; Collier Macmillan, 1979.

Pasquariella, Susan K., ed. UNION LIST OF POPULATION/ FAMILY PLANNING PERIODICALS: A Serial Holdings List of 36 North American APLIC Member Libraries and Information Centers. Association for Population/Family Planning Libraries & Information Centers International, 1978.

Plattner, Sunya. "Conceptual Systems and Sex Role Attitudes and Beliefs and Their Effect on Short Term Abortion Outcome." University of Colorado at Boulder, 1979 (Ph.D. dissertation).

Powell, Dorian, et al. CONTRACEPTIVE USE IN JAMAICA: The Social, Economic and Cultural Context. Kingston, Jamaica: Institute of Social and Economic Research, University of West Indies, 1978.

Putka, John S. "The Supreme Court and Abortion: The Sociopolitical Impact and Judicial Activism." University of Cincinnati, 1979 (Ph.D. dissertation).

Scheidegger, Elisabeth. POPULATION AT DEVELOPMENT; BIBLIOG. SEL. D'OUVRAGES ET D'ARTICLES ECRITS EN FRANCAIS DE 1960 A 1974, AVEC REF. SPECIALE A L'AFRIQUE FRANCOPHONE. Geneva: International Institute for Labour Studies, 1977.

Siddiqui, Mohammad Khalid. "The Initiation of Contraception in Taiwan." The University of Michigan, 1979 (Ph.D. dissertation).

Simon, J. L. THE ECONOMICS OF POPULATION GROWTH. Princeton: Princeton Universtiy Press, 1977.

Somers, Ronald L. "Risk of Admission to Psychiatric Institutions Among Danish Women Who Experience Induced Abortion: An Analysis Based on National Record Linkage." University of California, Los Angeles, 1979 (Ph.D. dissertation).

Stevens, Ella. "Teaching Contraception Through Programmed Learning Modules." University of Michigan, 1978 (Ph.D. dissertation).

Strobino, Barbara A. R. "The Epidemiology of Recurrent Spontaneous Abortion." Columbia University, 1979 (Ph.D. dissertation).

THOU SHALT NOT KILL. New Rochelle: Arlington House, 1978.

United Nations. Department of Economic and Social Affairs. REVIEW AND APPRAISAL OF THE WORLD POPULATION PLAN OF ACTION. New York: United Nations, 1979.

United States. Bureau of Health Manpower. SURVEY REPORT ON MEDICAL, NURSING AND OSTEOPATHIC SCHOOL ADMISSIONS POLICY RELATING TO ABORTIONS/ STERILIZATION, AUGUST 22, 1978. Hyattsville, Maryland: HEW, 1978.

United States. Congress. House. Select Committee on Population. THE DEPO-PROVERA DEBATE: HEARINGS, AUGUST 8-10, 1978. Washington: GPO, 1978.

United States. Congress. House. Committee on Human Resources. ADOLESCENT HEALTH, SERVICES, AND PREGNANCY PREVENTION AND CARE ACT OF 1978: Hearings, June 14 and July 12, 1978, on S. 2910, to Establish a Program for Developing Networks of Community-Based Services to Prevent Initial and Repeat Pregnancies Among Adolescents, to Provide Care to Pregnant Adolescents, and to Help Adolescents Become Productive Independent Contributors to Family and Community Life. Washington: GPO, 1978.

United States. Department of Health Education and Welfare. FAMILY PLANNING SERVICE SITES, UNITED STATES. Washington: GPO, 1978.

United States. National Center for Health Statistics. Division of Vital Statistics. CONTRACEPTIVE UTILIZATION: UNITED STATES. Hyattsville: HEW, 1979.

United States. National Clearinghouse for Family Planning Information. CATALOG OF FAMILY PLANNING MATERIALS. Washington: GPO, 1979.

Wheeler, Kathryn J. "Psychological Variables Affecting Success in Contraceptive Planning." Northwestern University, 1978 (Ph.D. dissertation).

Wirth, John. "The Relationship of Static Muscle Strength and Endurance With the Use of Oral Contraceptives, Phase of the Menstrual Cycle, and Vitamin B-6 Status." University of Illinois at Urbana-Champaign, 1978 (Ph.D. dissertation).

Woods, J. ENGINEERED DEATH. Ottawa: University of Ottawa Press, 1978.

Zimmerman, M. K. PASSAGE THROUGH ABORTION. New York: Praeger, 1977.

PERIODICAL LITERATURE

TITLE INDEX

ACLU harasses pro-lifers. (ACLU suggests that the pro-life movement is part of a papal plot), by N. Thimmesch. CATHOLIC DIGEST 4:49, May, 1978.

ACLU's holy war. NATIONAL REVIEW 31:74+, January 19, 1979.

AECT's international window; Ghana national family planning program, by R. E. Wileman. AUDIOVISUAL INSTRUCTION 24:48-49, February, 1979.

AID investment of $1 billion in family planning/population is resulting in sharp birthrate declines. FAMILY PLANNING PERSPECTIVES 11(1):45-46, January-February, 1979.

AORN proposed standards for inhospital sterilization. AORN JOURNAL 29(6):1154+, May, 1979.

Ablactation after a major miscarriage and delivery, by M. Bulajić, et al. SRPSKI ARCHIV ZA CELOKUPNO LEKARSTVO 105(11):985-988, November, 1977.

Abnormalities among offspring of oral and nonoral contraceptive users, by H. E. Oritz-Pérez, et al. AMERICAN JOURNAL OF OBSTETRICS AND GYNECOLOGY 134(5):512-517, July 1, 1979.

Abortifacient effect of intrauterine contraceptive devices? by P. J. Keller, et al. GYNECOLOGIE INVESTIGATION

9(4):219-221, 1978.

Abortion. MOTHER JONES 3-1:14, January, 1978.

—. NEW SOCIETY 40(759):118-119, 1977.

—, by S. R. Isbister. QUEEN'S QUARTERLY 86:127-133, Spring, 1979.

Abortion [letter], by J. F. Cattanach. MEDICAL JOURNAL OF AUSTRALIA 1(5):182, March 10, 1979.

—, by K. Hume. MEDICAL JOURNAL OF AUSTRALIA 1(8):343, April 21, 1979.

—, by F. Long. MEDICAL JOURNAL OF AUSTRALIA 1(12): 572, June 16, 1979.

Abortion [review essay], by B. Hayler. SIGNS 5:307-323, Winter, 1979.

Abortion: alive issue. THE ECONOMIST 271:23, May 5, 1979.

Abortion alternative and the patient's right to know. WASH-INGTON UNIVERSITY LAW QUARTERLY 1978:167-210, Winter, 1978.

The abortion (Amendment) Bill. NEW HUMANIST 95:61-72, August, 1979.

Abortion and the abuse of the English language, by H. B. Gow. MADEMOISELLE 85:38-39, July, 1979.

Abortion and the arms race: the same sickness, by J. McGowan. NATIONAL CATHOLIC REPORTER 14:11, April 7, 1978.

Abortion and an attempt at dialogue, by J. Loesch. AMERICA 140:234-236, March 24, 1979.

Abortion and the Church, by E. Bryce. OUR SUNDAY VISI-TOR 67:12-14, January 21, 1979.

Abortion and the crimes amendment act 1977, by D. Kember. NEW ZEALAND LAW JOURNAL 1978:109-117, April 4, 1978.

Abortion and the duty to preserve life, by J. R. Connery. THEOLOGICAL STUDIES 40:318-333, June, 1979.

Abortion and government policy [argues that the exclusion of abortion services under programs of medical and social aid to the poor is discriminatory], by D. Callahan. FAMILY PLANNING PERSPECTIVES 11:275-279, September-October, 1979.

Abortion and Halakhah [letter], by R. Weiss; Reply by S. Carmy. TRADITION 17:112-115, September, 1979.

Abortion and intimacy, by M. F. Rousseau. AMERICA 140: 429-432, May 26, 1979.

Abortion and judicial review of statues, by E. Livneh. ISRAEL LAW REVIEW 12(1):15-31, January, 1977.

Abortion and the law. OUR SUNDAY VISITOR 67:9-11, January 21, 1979.

Abortion and maternal health: an American perspective, by L. Keith, et al. INTERNATIONAL SURGERY 63(5).31-35, July-August, 1978.

Abortion and mortality study. Twenty-year study in New York State exclusive of New York City, by R. A. McLean, et al. NEW YORK STATE JOURNAL OF MEDICINE 79(1):49-52, January, 1979.

Abortion and the NHS [letter], by J. R. Ashton. BRITISH MEDICAL JOURNAL 1(6164):689, March 10, 1979.

—, by W. Belton. BRITISH MEDICAL JOURNAL 1(6160): 415, February 10, 1979.

—, by C. Brewer, et al. BRITISH MEDICAL JOURNAL 1(6162):554-555, February 24, 1979.

—, by D. Flint. BRITISH MEDICAL JOURNAL 1(6162):555, February 24, 1979.

—, by A. Noble. BRITISH MEDICAL JOURNAL 1(6162): 554, February 24, 1979.

Abortion and the NHS: the first decade, by F. G. Fowkes, et al. BRITISH MEDICAL JOURNAL 1(6158):217-219, January 27, 1979.

Abortion and the NHS: the first decade [letter] , by R. Greenham, et al. BRITISH MEDICAL JOURNAL 1(6161):492, February 17, 1979.

Abortion and opinion, by C. Francome. NEW SOCIETY p. 678, March 22, 1979.

Abortion and the press, by M. Kenny. SPECTATOR p. 13, July 28, 1979.

Abortion and the "Right-to-Life": facts, fallacies, and fraud—II. Psychometric studies, by J. W. Prescott, et al. HUMANIST 38:36-43, November-December, 1978.

Abortion and the right to life: a rejoinder, by L. Robinson. CANADIAN FORUM 59:20-22, April, 1979.

Abortion and the status of women [letter] , by W. Blair. INQUIRY 9(1):28, February, 1979.

The Abortion and Sterilization Act in 1975—experience of the Johannesburg Hospital Pregnancy Advisory Clinic, by B. Bloch, et al. SOUTH AFRICAN MEDICAL JOURNAL 53(21):861-864, May 27, 1978.

Abortion anniversary, by C. Rice. AMERICA 140:65, February 3, 1979.

Abortion applicants: characteristics distinguishing dropouts remaining pregnant and those having abortion, by M. E. Swigar, et al. AMERICAN JOURNAL OF PUBLIC HEALTH 67(2): 142-146, 1977.

Abortion aquittal (note). OFF OUR BACKS 8-9:10, October, 1978.

Abortion attitude of nurses: a cognitive dissonance perspective, by P. J. Estok. IMAGE 10(3):70-74, October, 1978.

Abortion attitudes among university students in India, by P. D. Bardis. INTERNATIONAL JOURNAL OF SOCIOLOGY OF THE FAMILY 6(2):163-178, 1976.

Abortion attitudes in Trinidad, by S. Roopnarinesingh. WEST INDIAN MEDICAL JOURNAL 27(3):147-151, September, 1978.

Abortion: back to 1966? by M. Simms. NEW HUMANIST 95: 95-96, Autumn, 1976.

Abortion battle heats up, by R. S. Bingham. USA TODAY 108:38-41, November, 1979.

Abortion case hinges on parents' rights, Catholic league tells Supreme Court. OUR SUNDAY VISITOR 67:1, April 1, 1979.

Abortion: a changing morality and policy? by R. A. McCormick. HOSPITAL PROGRESS 60(2):36-44, February, 1979.

Abortion choices in the Philippines, by M. Gallen. JOURNAL OF BIOSOCIAL SCIENCE 11:281-288, July, 1979.

Abortion—a clarification, by T. G. A. Bowles, et al. NEW LAW JOURNAL 129:944-946, September 27, 1979.

Abortion clinics found unsafe by reporters. EDITOR AND PUBLISHER 111:15, December, 16, 1978.

Abortion clinics rush to diversify: abortion clinics add sex counseling, fertility help and simple surgery. BUSINESS WEEK p. 68, December 10, 1979.

Abortion clinics targets of "right-to-life" violence. SPOKES-WOMAN 8-10:5, April, 1978.

Abortion clinics under siege, by J. Barton. PROGRESSIVE 43: 27-29, March, 1979.

Abortion control act struck down; Supreme Court/fetal viability. ORIGINS 8:497+, January 24, 1979.

Abortion—controversy we can't seem to solve, by E. R. Dobell. REDBOOK 153(2):42, June, 1979.

Abortion counseling, by M. Kahn-Edrington. COUNSELING PSYCHOLOGIST 8(1):37-38, 1979.

Abortion counseling in a general hospital, by B. A. Kaminsky, et al. HEALTH AND SOCIAL WORK 4:92-103, May, 1979.

Abortion curbs promote needless surgery, by E. Cohn. POLITICKS 1:17-18, March 28, 1978.

Abortion debate: a call for civility, by J. C. Evans. CHRISTIAN CENTURY 96:300-301, March 21, 1979.

Abortion decision making: some findings from Colombia, by C. Browner. STUDIES IN FAMILY PLANNING 10(3):96-106, March, 1979.

Abortion decisions—how will the United States Supreme Court define "necessary"? by M. A. Duffy. WOMEN LAWYERS JOURNAL 64:3-16+, Winter, 1978.

Abortion: a dyadic perspective, by A. Rothstein. AMERICAN JOURNAL OF ORTHOPSYCHIATRY 47(1):111-118, 1977.

Abortion, ethics, and biology, by J. Wind. PERSPECTIVES IN BIOLOGY AND MEDICINE 21(4):492-504, 1978.

Abortion fight: crusade of many faces, by M. Winiarski. NATIONAL CATHOLIC REPORTER 14:5, March 3, 1978.

Abortion flap puts archidiocese on spot, N. Y. Times fans flames, priest charges, by F. Franzonia. OUR SUNDAY VISITOR 68:1, June 3, 1979.

Abortion for 'wrong' fetal sex: an ethical-legal dilemma [news],
by J. Elliott. JAMA 242(14):1455-1456, October 4, 1979.

Abortion funding cases: a comment on the Supreme Court's
role in American government, by M. J. Perry. GEORGE-
TOWN LAW JOURNAL 66:1191-1245, June, 1978.

Abortion funding conflict in temporary truce. OUR SUNDAY
VISITOR 68:2, November 4, 1979.

Abortion funding cutt-offs: the human cost, by M. M. Smith.
NOW 11(5&6):10, April, 1978.

Abortion harassment, by M. Stucky. McCALLS 106:62, March,
1979.

Abortion: here we go again [Britain]. THE ECONOMIST
272:25, July 14, 1979.

Abortion: historical and biblical perspectives, by J.A. Rasmussen.
CONCORDIA THEOLOGICAL QUARTERLY 43:19-25,
January, 1979.

Abortion: how early, how late and how legal, by V. Tunkel.
BRITISH MEDICAL JOURNAL 6184:253-256, July 28,
1979.

Abortion—the Illinois abortion act of 1975 was declared un-
constitutuional in part for the reason that some sections
were void and unenforceable because they conflicted with
rights guaranteed by the due process clause. JOURNAL
OF FAMILY LAW 17:797-805, August, 1979.

Abortion in the adolescent, by D. Lancaster. AUSTRALIAN
FAMILY PHYSICIAN 7(spec. no.):25-27, August, 1978.

Abortion in America: the origins and evolution of national
policy, 1800-1900 by James C. Mohr, a review by E. Farrell.
FRONTIERS 3(3):65-67, Fall, 1978.

Abortion—in brief. SPOKESWOMAN 9(6):6, December, 1978.

Abortion in the courts: a Laywoman's Historical Guide to the New Disaster Area, by K. B. Glen. FEMINIST STUDIES 4(1):1-26, February, 1978.

Abortion in Israel: social demand and political responses, by Y. Yisai. POLICY STUDIES JOURNAL 7:270-290, Winter, 1978.

Abortion in laboratory animals induced by Moraxella bovis, by J. O. Norman, et al. INFECTION AND IMMUNITY 24(2): 427-433, May, 1979.

Abortion in New South Wales—legal or illegal? by B. Lucas. AUSTRALIAN LAW JOURNAL 52:327-332, June, 1978.

Abortion in New Zealand public hospitals: a twenty-five year review, by R. A. Brown, et al. NEW ZEALAND PSY-CHOLOGIST 6(2):124-133, November, 1977.

Abortion in rural Thailand: a survey of practitioners, by T. Narkavonnakit. STUDIES IN FAMILY PLANNING 10:223-229, August-September, 1979.

Abortion in teenagers, by M. S. Hanson. CLINICAL OBSTE-TRICS AND GYNECOLOGY 21(4):1175-1190, December, 1978.

Abortion: is détente ahead? by A. Baron. POLITICS TODAY 6:7, January, 1979.

Abortion: is it murder? by W. F. Sayers. CATHOLIC DIGEST 4:18, June, 1978.

Abortion: is it right or is it murder? by D. L. Stern, et al. CHATELAINE 51:22, August, 1978.

Abortion: the issue no one wanted, so Catholics took it on, by M. Winiarski. NATIONAL CATHOLIC REPORTER 14:1+, February 24, 1978.

Abortion: its social and ethical issues: an invitation to responsi-bility and moral discourse, by B. C. Bangert. FOUNDA-

TIONS 22:198-217, July-September, 1979.

Abortion law and problems experienced by operating nursing
staff, by H. Twelftree. AUSTRALASIAN NURSES JOUR-
NAL 8(4):3-5, December, 1978.

Abortion law in Italy, by F. Havránek. CESKOSLOVENSKA
GYNEKOLOGIE 44(3):223, April, 1979.

Abortion law reform in the German Federal Republic, by K. C.
Horton. INTERNATIONAL AND COMPARATIVE LAW
QUARTERLY 28:288-296, April, 1979.

Abortion: listening to the middle, by E. A. Langerak. HAST-
INGS CENTER REPORT 9:24-28, October, 1979.

Abortion: major wrong or basic right, by R. Gordis. MID-
STREAM 24(3):44-49, 1978.

Abortion, medicaid, and the constitution. NEW YORK UNI-
VERSITY LAW REVIEW 54:120-160, April, 1979.

Abortion: myths and facts [Great Britain]. LABOUR RE-
SEARCH 68:197-198, September, 1979.

Abortion—parental consent—equal protection—due process—
U.S. Court of Appeals (7th Cir.). JUVENILE LAW DIGEST
11(3):84-88, March, 1979.

Abortion, poverty and the equal protection of the laws, by G. J.
Simson. GEORGIA LAW REVIEW 13:505-514, Winter,
1979.

Abortion, property rights, and the right to life, by L. H. O'Driscoll. PERSONALIST 58:99-114, April, 1977; Reply by
W. J. Boenmer, 60:325-335, July, 1979.

Abortion: a public health and social policy perspective, by B. M.
Sneideman. NEW YORK UNIVERSITY REVIEW OF LAW
AND SOCIAL CHANGE 7:187-213, Spring, 1978.

Abortion: public opinion pendulum swings back, by D. F. Phillips.

HOSPITALS 52(22):83-84+, November 16, 1978.

Abortion, religion and political life. COMMONWEAL 106:35-38, February 2, 1979.

Abortion restrictions approved by Congress, by M. M. Smith. NOW 11(1):5, January, 1978.

Abortion: review of Mennonite literature, 1970-1977, by G. Brenneman. MENNONITE REVIEW 53:160-172, April, 1979.

Abortion: reward for conscientious contraceptive use, by E. R. Allgeier, et al. JOURNAL OF SEX RESEARCH 15:64-75, February, 1979.

Abortion: a social-psychological perspective, by N. E. Adler. JOURNAL OF SOCIAL ISSUES 35(1):100-119, 1979.

Abortion: some observations on the contraceptive practice of women referred for psychiatric assessment in Dunedin, by D. J. Lord. NEW ZEALAND MEDICAL JOURNAL 88(626):487-489, December 27, 1978.

Abortion—termination of parental rights—physician-patient—right to privacy—U.S. Court of Appeals (8th Cir.). JUVENILE LAW DIGEST 11(2):44-46, February, 1979.

Abortion update. OFF OUR BACKS 8(4):13, April, 1978.

—, by J. E. Rodgers. MADEMOISELLE 85(2):64, February, 1979.

Abortion: women's choice in practice, by L. Owen. OBSERVER p. 39, May 6, 1979.

Abortion work: strains, coping strategies, policy implications, by C. Joffe. SOCIAL WORK 24:485-490, November, 1979.

Abortionist strangles bady (Dr. Wm. B. Wadill on trial for allegedly strangling baby after aborting it), by L. Jeffries. CATHOLIC DIGEST 4:16+, June, 1978.

Abortions, by W. Goodman. NEW LEADER 61:11-12, November 6, 1978.

Abortions don't hurt later pregnancies. SPOKESWOMAN 8(10):4, April, 1978.

Abortions in America [letter], by S. Shea. NEW ENGLAND JOURNAL OF MEDICINE 299(17):960-961, October 26, 1978.

Abortions in America: the effects of restrictive funding, by L. R. Berger. NEW ENGLAND JOURNAL OF MEDICINE 298: 1474-1477, June 29, 1978.

Abortions in clinics as safe as in hospitals. FAMILY PLANNING PERSPECTIVES 10:298, September-October, 1978.

Abortions—juveniles—parental or judicial consent. CRIMINAL LAW REPORTER: SUPREME COURT PROCEEDINGS 24(22):4221-4223, March 7, 1979.

Abortions performed before the sixteenth week of pregnancy. SPOKESWOMAN 8(11):4, May, 1978.

Acceptability of male sterilization in Bangladesh: its problems and perspectives, by A. R. Khan, et al. BANGLADESH DEVELOPMENT STUDIES 6:201-212, Summer, 1978.

Acceptability of a nonsurgical method to terminate very early pregnancy in comparison to vacuum aspiration, by A. S. Rosén, et al. CONTRACEPTION 19(2):107-117, February, 1979.

Acceptability of reversible versus permanent tubal sterilization: an analysis of preliminary data, by R. N. Shain. FERTILITY AND STERILITY 31(1):13-17, January, 1979.

L'accueil de l'entant a naitre; déclaration du Conseil permanent de l'Episcopat français aux catholiques de France. LA DOCUMENTATION CATHOLIQUE 76:442-443, May 6, 1979.

Accumulation of norethindrone and individual metabolities in human plasma during short- and long-term administration of a contraceptive dosage, by W. E. Braselton, Jr., et al. AMERICAN JOURNAL OF OBSTETRICS AND GYNECOLOGY 133(2):154-160, 1979.

The acquisition of basic sex information, by P. H. Gebhard. THE JOURNAL OF SEX RESEARCH 13(3):148-169, August, 1977.

Actinomyces and the IUD. EMERGENCY MEDICINE 11:48, August 15, 1979.

Action of oral contraceptive drugs on protein metabolism in rats, by M. T. Khayyal, et al. JOURNAL OF THE EGYPTIAN MEDICAL ASSOCIATION 60(7-8):633-638, 1977.

Acupuncture anesthesia in obstetrical surgery and nursing during delivery, by M. Isozaki, et al. JOSANPU ZASSHI 33(2):94-97, February, 1979.

Acute intermittent porphyria on withdrawal of oral contraceptives, by L. S. Gerlis. JOURNAL OF INTERNATIONAL MEDICAL RESEARCH 6(4):255-256, 1978.

Addressing the consent issue involved in the sterilization of mentally incompetent females. ALBANY LAW REVIEW 43:322-338, Winter, 1979.

Administration of 15-(S)-15-methyl prostaglandins F2 alpha in intrauterine fetal death, missed abortion and hydatidiform mole, by P. Husslein, et al. WIENER KLINISCHE WOCHENSCHRIFT 91(13):458-460, June 22, 1979.

Adolescent contraceptive use: current status of practice and research, by E. W. Freeman, et al. OBSTETRICS AND GYNECOLOGY 53(3):388-394, March, 1979.

Adolescent fertility: epidemic or endemic problem, by J. F. Jekel, et al. STUDIES IN FAMILY PLANNING 10:107-109, March, 1979.

Adolescent mourning reactions in infant and fetal loss, by N. H. Horowitz. SOCIAL CASEWORK 59:551-559, November, 1978.

Adolescent pregnancy: a review of the literature, by P. C. McKenry, et al. FAMILY COORDINATOR 28(1):17-28, January, 1979.

Adolescent pregnancy revisited, by J. E. Fielding. NEW ENGLAND JOURNAL OF MEDICINE 299:893-896, October 19, 1978.

Adolescent pregnancy: a study of pregnant teenagers in a suburban community in Ontario, by D. E. Guyatt. DISSERTATION ABSTRACTS INTERNATIONAL 39(4-A):2549, October, 1978.

Adolescent sexual behavior, by J. R. Faulkenberry, et al. HEALTH EDUCATION 10:5-7, May-June, 1979.

Adolescent sexuality: legal aspects, by L. Vick. AUSTRALIAN FAMILY PHYSICIAN 7(spec. no.):12-15, August, 1978.

Adolescents and knowledge of population dynamics and family planning, by V. Gupta, et al. JOURNAL OF FAMILY WELFARE 25:33-40, March, 1979.

Adolescents knowledge of childbearing, by J. Walter, et al. FAMILY COORDINATOR 28(2):163-171, April, 1979.

Adrenocorticotropic and steroid secretion in hirsute pregnant women with habitual abortion, by T. Despodova, et al. AKUSHERSTVO I GINEKOLOGIIA 17(6):417-423, 1978.

Advances in sterilization equipment, by M. F. McCann, et al. INTERNATIONAL JOURNAL OF GYNAECOLOGY AND OBSTETRICS 15(5):444-454, 1978.

Advantages and risks of different contraceptives, by B. Westerholm. LAKARTIDNINGEN 74(45):4123-4124, November 8, 1978.

Affective, attitudinal, and normative determinants of contraceptive behavior among university men, by W. A. Fisher. DISSERTATION ABSTRACTS INTERNATIONAL 39(9-B): 4613-4614, March, 1979.

Affirm government aid of abortions for indigents. AMERICAN BAR ASSOCIATION JOURNAL 64:1336, September, 1978.

Affirmative abortion funding proposals to be introduced, by M. M. Smith. NOW 11(2):4, February, 1978.

After initial risk-taking, most Canadian students use effective methods. FAMILY PLANNING PERSPECTIVES 11(1): 44, January-February, 1979.

Aftermath of abortion. Anniversary depression and abdominal pain, by J. O. Cavenar, Jr., et al. MENNINGER CLINIC. BULLETIN 42(5):433-438, 1978.

Age and sexual culture among homosexually oriented males, by J. Harry, et al. ARCHIVES OF SEXUAL BEHAVIOR 7(3):199-209, May, 1978.

Age structure, unwanted fertility, and the association between racial composition and family planning programs: a comment on wright, by M. Hout. SOCIAL FORCES 57(4) 1387-1392, June, 1979.

Air pollution in the operating room, by M. Bulligan. POINT OF VIEW 15:16-17, October, 1978.

Akron gets restrictive abortion measure, by J. Petosa. NATIONAL CATHOLIC REPORTER 14:20, March 10, 1978.

Akron, Ohio abortion ordinance outrageous, by M. M. Smith. NOW 11(5&6):5, April, 1978.

Akron ordinance challenged. OFF OUR BACKS 8(10):5, November, 1978.

Akron's pro-life experiment (provisions of a pro-life ordinance), by N. Thimmesch. CATHOLIC DIGEST 4:23, June, 1978.

The Alberta counsellor and medical care for minors, by L. Eberlein. ALBERTA COUNSELLOR 7(2):5-12, Summer, 1978.

Alive issue. THE ECONOMIST 271:23, May 5, 1979.

All in the Irish family way, by A. McHardy. GUARDIAN p. 9, August 7, 1979.

Allocution de. . .aux foyers des Equipes Notre-Dame, by R. Etchegaray. LA CODUMENTATION CATHOLIQUE 76: 271-273, March 18, 1979.

Alpha-fetoprotein concentration in maternal serum and abortion via VA and PGF2alpha, by H. A. Sande, et al. INTERNATIONAL JOURNAL OF GYNAECOLOGY AND OBSTETRICS 15(5):419-422, 1978.

Alpha-fetoprotein: a marker for threatened abortion, by H. A. Sande, et al. INTERNATIONAL JOURNAL OF GYNAECOLOGY AND OBSTETRICS 16(4):293-295, 1978-1979.

Altered plasma lipid and lipoprotein levels associated with oral contraceptive and oestrogen use. Report from the Medications Working Group of the Lipid Research Clinics Program, by R. B. Wallace, et al. LANCET 2(8134):112-115, July 21, 1979.

Alternative marital and family forms: their relative attractiveness to college students and correlates of willingness to participate in nontraditional forms, by L. D. Strong. JOURNAL OF MARRIAGE AND THE FAMILY 40(3):493-503, August, 1978.

An alternative test of the minority status and fertility relation, by H. H. Marshall, Jr., et al. PACIFIC SOCIOLOGICAL REVIEW 21:221-238, April, 1978.

An alternative to the use of high-dose estrogens for postcoital contraception, by L. H. Schilling. JOURNAL OF THE AMERICAN COLLEGE HEALTH ASSOCIATION 27(5):

247-249, April, 1979.

Alternatives to pregnancy prevention [letter] , by G. Hunt.
AMERICAN FAMILY PHYSICIAN 19(3):27, March, 1979.

Ambivalence of abortion, by L. B. Frank. SAN FRANCISCO
REVIEW OF BOOKS 4(2):20, June, 1978.

Ambulatory legal abortion, by J. Philip. UGESKRIFT FOR
LAEGER 140(44):2727, October 30, 1978.

American Association of Gynecologic Laparoscopists' 1976
membership survey, by J. M. Phillips, et al. JOURNAL OF
REPRODUCTIVE MEDICINE 21(1):3-6, July, 1978.

American Civil Liberties Union. SPOKESWOMAN 8(11):3,
May, 1978.

American letter: hunting season in American, by A. Brass.
BRITISH JOURNAL OF HOSPITAL MEDECINE 20(1):
86, July, 1978.

American shock tactics, by C. Doyle. OBSERVER p. 39, May
6, 1979.

American values and contraceptive acceptance, by J. R. Rzepka.
JOURNAL OF RELIGION AND HEALTH 18:241-250,
July, 1979.

Amore senza bambini gaining Italian favor, by E. Durie. AD-
VERTISING AGE 49:92, July 10, 1978.

An analysis of Bellotti v. Baird, by D. V. Horan. HOSPITAL
PROGRESS 60(8):18-20, August, 1979.

An analysis of the first 200 legal abortions at the Johannesburg
General Hospital, by T. Kopenhager, et al. SOUTH AFRI-
CAN MEDICAL JOURNAL 53(2):858-860, May 27, 1978.

Anatomic and chromosomal anomalies in 944 induced abortuses,
by T. Kajii, et al. HUMAN GENETICS 43(3):247-258,
September 19, 1978.

Anopheles stephensi; effect of gamma-radiation and chemo-
sterilants of the fertility and fitness of males for sterile male
releases, by V. P. Sharma, et al. JOURNAL OF ECONOMIC
ENTOMOLOGY 71:449-452, June, 1978.

Another abortion decision coming up, by G. Reed, et al. ORI-
GINS 8:510-512, January 25, 1979.

Another pregnancy vaccine is developed in Australia. SCIENCE
FORUM 10:32, October, 1977.

Another storm brewing over abortion. U.S. NEWS AND
WORLD REPORT 85:63, July 24, 1978.

Antecedents of adolescent parenthood and consequences at age
30, by D. Russ-Eft, et al. FAMILY COORDINATOR 28(2):
173-179, April, 1979.

Anti-abortion forces seek Akron's consent law as exploding
myths, by J. Petosa. NATIONAL CATHOLIC REPORTER
14:32, March 17, 1978.

Anti-abortion in England. OFF OUR BACKS 8(8):11, August,
1978.

Anti-abortion tactics subtle, blatant, by M. Winiarski. NATION-
AL CATHOLIC REPORTER 14:15, March 10, 1978.

Antibodies to leptospira in the sera of aborted bovine fetuses,
by W. A. Ellis, et al. VETERINARY RECORD 103:237-
239, September 9, 1978.

The antifertility action of alpha-chlorohydrin: enzyme inhibition by alpha-chlorohydrin phosphate, by P. M. Mashford,
et al. EXPERIENTIA 34(10):1267-1268, October 15,
1978.

The antifertility actions of a-chlorohydrin in the male, by A. R.
Jones. LIFE SCIENCES 23(16):1625-1646, 1978.

Antifertility effect in mice of medicinal plant of family Acantha-
ceae [letter], by M. Shamsuzzoha, et al. LANCET 2(8095):

900, October 21, 1978.

Anti-fertility effect of non-steroidal anti-inflammatory drugs, by R. Yegnanarayan, et al. JAPANESE JOURNAL OF PHARMACOLOGY 28(6):909-917, December, 1978.

Antifertility effects of Embelia ribes Burm, by S. D. Kholkute, et al. INDIAN JOURNAL OF EXPERIMENTAL BIOLOGY 16(10):1035-1037, October, 1978.

Antifertility effects of the fruits of Piper longum in female rats, by S. D. Kholkute, et al. INDIAN JOURNAL OF EXPERIMENTAL BIOLOGY 17(3):289-290, March, 1979.

Antifertility effects of the steroid 5 alpha-stigmastane-3 beta, 5, 6, beta-triol 3-monobenzoate on mice, by A. Pakraski, et al. CONTRACEPTION 19(2):145-150, February, 1979.

Antigenic cross-reactivity between human and marmoset zonase pellucidae, a potential target for immunocontraception, by C. A. Shivers, et al. JOURNAL OF MEDICAL PRIMATOLOGY 7(4):242-248, 1978.

Antimicrobial theapy in incomplete abortion [letter], by G. White. SOUTH AFRICAN MEDICAL JOURNAL 55(14). 533, March 31, 1979.

The anti-reproductive pharmacology of LH-RH and agonistic analogues, by A. Corbin, et al. INTERNATIONAL JOURNAL OF FERTILITY 23(2):81-92, 1978.

Antithrombin III and oral contraception with progestagen-only preparation [letter], by J. Conard, et al. LANCET 2(8140): 471, September 1, 1979.

The application of market research in contraceptive social marketing in a rural area of Kenay, by T. R. L. Black, et al. MARKET RESEARCH SOCIETY. JOURNAL 21:30-43, January, 1979.

Application of prostaglandins in obstetrics and gynecology, by F. J. Brunnberg. ACTA BIOLOGICA ET MEDICA GER-

MANICA 37(5-6):917-921, 1976.

Application of sterile technic. AUXILIAIRE 52(2):21-28, June, 1979.

Arachidonic acid in amniotic fluid after extra-amniotic instillation of rivanol for midtrimester abortion, by A. Olund, et al. PROSTAGLANDINS 16(6):989-994, December, 1978.

Arcus senilis-like degeneration of the cornea following a probable lipid metabolic disorder due to the use of contraceptives, by N. Zolog. REVISTA DE: CHIRURGIE ONCOLOGIE RADIOLOGIE ORL OFTALMOLOGIE, STOMATOLOGIE, OFTALMOLOGIA 23(1):69-72, January-March, 1979.

Are there really any gay male athletes? An empirical survey, by B. Garner, et al. THE JOURNAL OF SEX RESEARCH 13(1):22-34, February, 1977.

Are there two types of postpill anovulation? by S. Harlap. FERTILITY AND STERILITY 31(5):486-491, May, 1979.

Arrivals and departures: new patents (fertilty predictor), by E. Schlossberg. QUEST 2:106, January-February, 1978.

Artenal hypertension and oral contraceptives, by J. Lekieffre. ANNALS DE CARDIOLOGIE ET D'ANGEIOLOGIE 28(1): 35-39, January-February, 1979.

Artificial interruption of the early stages of pregnancy (regulation, menstruation, mini-interruption), by F. Havránek. CESKOSLOVENSKA GYNEKOLOGIE 44(5):374-378, June, 1979.

'Asexualization' proposed for convicted child molesters. JUVENILE JUSTICE DIGEST 7(1):5, January 12, 1979.

Ask a doctor [teenagers], by W. Gifford-Jones. CHATELAINE 52:10, September, 1979.

Ask a psychiatrist, by G. E. Robinson. CHATELAINE 52:16, July, 1979.

Aspects on ripening of the cervix and induction of labor by intra-cervical application of PGE2 in viscous gel, by U. Ulmsten. ACTA OBSTETRICA ET GYNECOLOGICA SCANDINAVI-CA (84):5-9, 1979.

Assessment of the promotion component in the postpartum/postabortion program, by J. M. Arredondo, et al. SPM 20(4):401-422, July-August, 1978.

Assessment of surveillance and vital statistics data for monitoring abortion mortality, United States, 1972-1975, by W. Cates, Jr., et al. AMERICAN JOURNAL OF EPIDEMOLOGY 108(3):200-206, September, 1978.

Assistance to the dying or protection of life? by A. C. Gokstad. SYKEPLEIEN 65(20):1290-1292, December 5, 1978.

Assistance to fertility regulation projects within the United Nations system, by R. K. Som. POPULATION BULLETIN (10):36-62, 1977.

Association of extrauterine fetal death with failure of prostaglandin E2 suppositories, by J. W. Orr, Jr., et al. OBSTETRICS AND GYNECOLOGY 53(3 suppl):56S-58S, March, 1979.

Atheist news: Bill Baird wins a big one. AMERICAN ATHEIST 21(7):6, July, 1979.

Attitude of patients and health workers as a factor influencing the utilization of reproductive health services in connection with birth control, by B. Nalbanski. AKUSHERSTVO I GINEKOLOGIIA 18(3):214-218, 1979.

Attitude toward abortion and attitude-relevant overt behavior, by E. H. Fischer, et al. SOCIAL FORCES 57:585-599, December, 1978.

Attitudes and experiences of sexual relations, by A. Lundstrom. INTERNATIONAL JOURNAL OF SOCIOLOGY OF THE FAMILY 8(2):231-234, July-December, 1978.

Attitudes of adolescent males toward abortion, contraception, and sexuality, by E. Vadies, et al. SOCIAL WORK IN HEALTH CARE 3(2):169-174, Winter, 1977.

Attitudes related to the number of children wanted and expected by college students in three countries, by H. G. Gough, et al. JOURNAL OF CROSS-CULTURAL PSYCHOLOGY 7:413-424, December, 1976.

Attitudes toward abortion and prenatal diagnosis of fetal ab-normalities: implications for educational programs, by R. R. Sell, et al. SOCIAL BIOLOGY 25:288-301, Winter, 1978.

Attitudes toward abortion have changed little since '75 [United States]. GALLUP OPINION INDEX pp. 20-24, May, 1979.

Attitudes toward and knowledge of abortion, by S. Snegroff. JOURNAL OF SEX EDUCATION AND THERAPY 4:22-26, Spring-Summer, 1978.

Attitudes towards family planning among the women of a Northern Australian Aboriginal community, by J. Reid, et al. MEDICAL JOURNAL OF AUSTRALIA 1(2 suppl):5-7, February 24, 1979.

The augmentary effect of intramuscular prostaglandins on ethacridine lactate, by V. B. Raote, et al. JOURNAL OF POSTGRADUATE MEDICINE 25(1):30-32, January, 1979.

Automatic sterilizer replaces autoclaves for ASTM humid-age test [urethane foams]. PLASTICS WORLD 37:35, September, 1979.

Avoid or achieve pregnancy naturally, by T. Guay. RAIN 4(9):6, July, 1978.

Awareness of unmarried girls regarding population problem, human reproduction and family planning, by P. Rasheed, et al. INDIAN PEDIATRICS 15(9):735-745, September, 1978.

B-scan ultrasonography in the diagnosis of oral-contraceptive related optic neuritis, by G. A. German. JOURNAL OF

AMERICAN OPTOMETRIC ASSOCIATION 50(2):243-244, February, 1979.

The baby—or the auto? by T. Blackburn. NATIONAL CATHOLIC REPORTER 16:2, November 2, 1979.

Babykillers' retort stops dialogue dead, by M. Winiarski. NATIONAL CATHOLIC REPORTER 15:3+, February 2, 1979.

Bacteriological quality control in human milk-banking, by A. Lucas, et al. BRITISH MEDICAL JOURNAL 1(6156):80-82, January 13, 1979.

Bacteriology of the tubes in postpartum salpingoclasia, by R. Velasco Almeida, et al. GINECOLOGIA Y OBSTETRICIA DE MEXICO 44(266):473-478, December, 1978.

Baird v. Bellotti (450 F Supp 997): abortion—the minor's right to decide. UNIVERSITY OF MIAMI LAW REVIEW 33: 705-722, March, 1979.

Barnyard sex, morality and birth control wee,, by Father Raby. CATHOLIC TRUSTEE 17(2):20-21, March, 1977.

Barrier contraception methods: the role of the pharmacist, by R. A. Hatcher. AMERICAN DRUGGIST 178:28+, August, 1979.

Barrier contraceptives: your questions answered, by D. Parti. MADEMOISELLE 85(8):85, August, 1979.

Barrier methods of contraception: they can be highly effective, by E. B. Connell. STUDIES IN FAMILY PLANNING 10(3):110-111, March, 1979.

Barrier methods: renewed interest, but more research needed, by D. Maine. FAMILY PLANNING PERSPECTIVES 11: 237-240, July-August, 1979.

Battle lines drawn again in Congress on federal financing. SPOKESWOMAN 9(2):6, August, 1978.

Battle over funding for abortion resumes, by J. M. Clarke. NOW 11(8):2, July, 1978.

Beal (97 Sup Ct 2366), Maher (97 Sup Ct 2376) and Poelker (97 Sup Ct 2391): the end of an era? JOURNAL OF FAMILY LAW 17:49-92, November, 1978.

Becoming close: intimate relations among college students, by G. Margolis. JOURNAL OF THE AMERICAN COLLEGE HEALTH ASSOCIATION 27(3):153-156, December, 1978.

Behavior of the male population with respect to family planning in Trujillo, Peru, by V. Villanueva Montoya, et al. BOLETIN DE LA OFICINA SANITARIA PANAMERICANA 85(4):290-299, October, 1978.

Behavior of satellite associations of acrocentric chromosomes in women with a history of obstetric-genetic abnormalities, by A. Midro, et al. GINEKOLOGIA POLSKA 50(3):251-257, March, 1979.

Beneficial effects of contraceptive doses and larege doses of medroxyprogesterone in the prevention and treatment of uterinehyperplasia, by J. Bonte. GYNAEKOLOGISCHE RUNDSCHAU 18(3-4):172-182, 1978.

Beneficial effects of nutrient supplementation in oral contraceptive usage, by E. B. Dawson, et al. AMERICAN JOURNAL OF CLINICAL NUTRITION 32:950, April, 1979.

Benign liver tumors and oral contraceptives, by C. W. Aungst. NEW YORK STATE JOURNAL OF MEDICINE 78(12):1933-1934, October, 1978.

Benign liver-cell-tumors and oral contraceptives, by W. Fabian, et al. MEDIZINISCHE KLINIK 74(17):662-666, April 27, 1979.

Beta-Thromboglobulin levels and oral contraception [letter], by M. Aranda, et al. LANCET 2(8137):308-309, August 11, 1979.

31

Beyond the pill, by E. Diozfalusy. WORLD HEALTH p. 22, August-September, 1978.

Binge eating associated with oral contraceptives, by R. A. Moskovitz, et al. AMERICAN JOURNAL OF PSYCHIATRY 136(5):721-722, May, 1979.

Biochemical changes in the uterus & uterine fluid of mated rats treated with Embelin—a non-steroidal oral contraceptive, by C. Seshadri, et al. INDIAN JOURNAL OF EXPERIMENTAL BIOLOGY 16(11):1187-1188, November, 1978.

The biocultural pattern of Japanese-American fertility, by D. L. Leonetti. SOCIAL BIOLOGY 25:38-51, September, 1978.

Bipolar coagulation. Technic of female sterilization by laporoscopy. Preliminary report of 100 cases, by L. C. Uribe Ramírez, et al. GINECOLOGIA Y OBSTETRICIA DE MEXICO 43(258):243-249, April, 1978.

Birth (and nonbirth) news. NEW AGE 4(4):15, September, 1978.

Birth control and abortion in Canada, 1870-1920, by A. McLaren. CANADIAN HISTORICAL REVIEW 59:319-340, September, 1978.

Birth control by injection? from the sea: a possible revolution, by P. Lee. SCIENCE DIGEST 85:61, March, 1979.

Birth control: clinics are major source of care for poor teenagers, and for more affluet, too. FAMILY PLANNING PERSPECTIVES 11:197-198, May-June, 1979.

Birth control denied to the mentally retarded, by M. S. Bass. THE HUMANIST 39:51-52, March, 1979.

Birth control for teenagers: diagram for disaster, by J. Ford, et al. LINACRE QUARTERLY 48:71-81, February, 1979.

Birth control guide. AMERICAN BABY 40:35-36+, November, 1978.

Birth control: how to choose what's best for you. McCALLS 106:65-67, October, 1978.

Birth control in the eighteenth and nineteenth centuries in some Hungarian villages, by R. Andorka. LOCAL POPULATION STUDIES (22):38-43, Spring, 1979.

Birth control in Tunisia. POPULATION 33:194-205, January-February, 1978.

Birth control news: once-a-month pill; prostaglandin pill, by M. Jeffrey. HARPER'S BAZAAR 111:24+, August, 1978.

Birth control practices and levels of development in India, by P. P. Karen, et al. JOURNAL OF GEOGRAPHY 77:229-237, November, 1978.

Birth control update, by J. Engel. CHATELAINE 51:27-29, January, 1978-1980; Correction, 152, May, 1978; Addendum, 112, July, 1978.

Birth control with caution. THE ECONOMIST 272:31, August 25, 1979.

Birth interval study in a culturally stable urban propulation, by S. O. Ayangade. INTERNATIONAL JOURNAL OF GYNAECOLOGY AND OBSTETRICS 15(6):497-500, 1978.

Birth intervals, survival and growth in a Nigerian village, by P. Doyle, et al. JOURNAL OF BIOSOCIAL SCIENCE 10(1): 81-94, January, 1978.

Birth pains. THE ECONOMIST 270:76, February 10, 1979.

Birth planning in China, by M. Chen. INTERNATIONAL FAMILY PLANNING PERSEPCTIVES 5:92-100, September, 1979.

Bishops gird for court clash over bill forcing employers to pay for abortion. OUR SUNDAY VISITOR 68:3, July 29, 1979.

Bishops, right to life hand-in-glove in New York, by M. Winiarski.

NATIONAL CATHOLIC REPORTER 14:1+, January 27, 1978.

Blessing and a cause: must she who lives by the pill also fear dying by it? by J. Webb. MACCLEANS 91:55-58+, April 17, 1978.

Board practice before and after the new abortion act of June 13, 1975. A comparison of boards in Oslo during 1971/1972, and 1975 and 1976, by O. M. Sejersted, et al. TIDSSHRIFT FOR DEN NORSKE LAEGEFORENING 98(29):1428-1432, October 20, 1978.

The Bohol Project and its impact, by N. E. Williamson. STUDIES IN FAMILY PLANNING 10(6-7):195, June-July, 1979.

Boll weevil; chemosterilization by fumigation and dipping, by A. B. Borkovec, et al. JOURNAL OF ECONOMIC ENTOMOLOGY 71:862-866, December, 1978.

Borderline cases in law and medicine, by G. Sorgo. ZEITSCHRIFT FUER RECHTSMEDIZIN 82(3):175-178, December 20, 1978.

Bourgeois abortion, by D. Vree. NATIONAL REVIEW 30:1351, October 27, 1978.

Bovine abortion associated with mixed Movar 33/63 type herpesvirus and bovine riral diarrhea rirus infection, by D. E. Reed, et al. CORNELL VETERINARIAN 69(1):54-66, 1979.

Breakage of falope-ring applicator forceps prongs [letter] , by T. H. Goh. BRITISH MEDICAL JOURNAL 1(6171):1148-1149, April 28, 1979.

A brief and better abortion. EMERGENCY MEDICINE 11:200+, October 15, 1979.

Brief reports decline of Down's syndrome after abortion reform in New York State, by H. Hansen. AMERICAN JOURNAL OF MENTAL DEFICIENCY 83(2):185-188, September, 1978.

The British Columbia Conference on the family—process and outcomes, by J. D. Friesen, et al. FAMILY COORDINATOR 28(2):260-263, April, 1979.

Budgeting against abortion. SEVEN DAYS 2(12):5, August, 1978.

Bureaucracy minimizes birth control. OFF OUR BACKS 8(1): 16, January, 1978.

Byron and Roe: the threshold question and juridical review, by P. J. Riga. CATHOLIC LAWYER 23:309-331, Autumn, 1978.

CA 7 strikes down provisions of two Illinois abortions statutes. THE CRIMINAL LAW REPORTER: COURT DECISIONS AND PROCEEDINGS 25(13):2284-2285, June 27, 1979.

California doctor charged with homicide: trial exposes consequences of abortion on demand (Dr. Waddill Jr. charged with strangling live aborted baby), by D. Duggan. HUMAN EVENTS 39:10+, March 10, 1979.

A call to responsible ecumenical debate on abortion and homosexuality, by National Council of Churches. ENGAGE/ SOCIAL ACTION 7:41-44, October, 1979.

Calls for constitutional conventions [United States] , by M. Leepson. EDITORIAL RESEARCH REPORTS pp. 187-204, March 16, 1979.

Can the birth of an unwanted child be grounds for a damage claim against a 3d party? Review of the facts, by H. Roesch. MEDIZINISCHE KLINIK 74(20:782-787, May 18, 1979.

Canada's abortion law: an obstacle to safer management of Canadian women, by C. Ringrose. LEGAL MEDICAL QUARTERLY 2(2):97-99, 1978.

Capitol Hill update. SPOKESWOMAN 9(3):3, September, 1978.

Capsules. . .a nosy contraceptive. TIME 114:68, August 20, 1979.

Carbohydrate metabolism in women receiving d-norgestrel for postcoital contraception, by F. Garmendia, et al. HORMONE AND METABOLIC RESEARCH 11(1):81-82, January, 1979.

Cardiovascular disease and oral contraceptives: a reappraisal of vital statistics data, by M. A. Belsey, et al. FAMILY PLANNING PERSPECTIVES 11(2):84-89, March-April, 1979.

Cardiovascular risks and oral contraceptives [editorial] . LANCET 1(8125):1063, May 19, 1979.

Caries prevalence and oral contraception, by S. Cebi, et al. COMMUNITY DENTISTRY AND ORAL EPIDEMIOLOGY 7(3):183-184, June, 1979.

Carter Defense appointments angers pro-life groups (appoints Dr. John H. Moxley's Asst. Sec. of Defense for Health Affairs; he discriminated against anti-abortion doctors at UCSD medical school). HUMAN EVENTS 39:3, July 21, 1979.

Carter launches new campaign to aid pregnant adolescents. JUVENILE JUSTICE DIGEST 7(14):6, July 27, 1979.

Case-control study of oral contraceptive pills and endometrial cancer, by R. I. Horwitz, et al. ANNALES DE MEDECINE INTERNE 91(2):226-227, August, 1979.

Case of abortion in rabbit due to aspergillus fumigatus infection, by B. R. Boro, et al. VETERINARY RECORD 103:287, September 23, 1978.

A case of intraligamentous tumor of the late post abortion, by K. Tshibangu, et al. JORURNAL DE GYNECOLOGIE, OBSTETRIQUE ET BIOLOGIE DE LA REPRODUCTION 7(1):73-76, 1978.

Case of premature labor with unusual course, by E. Jaworski. WIADOMOSCI LEKARSKIE 31(23):1705-1707, December 1, 1978.

Catholic Church hits the hustings, by R. Shrum. NEW TIMES

12(1):16, January 8, 1979.

Catholic left: can it live with feminism? by K. Lindsey. SEVEN DAYS 2(16):23, October 27, 1978.

Catholicism and family planning attitudes in Brazil, by A. H. Gelbard. DISSERTATION ABSTRACTS INTERNATIONAL 39(9-A):5743, March, 1979.

Catholics aren't the only pro-lifers, by M. Novak. CATHOLIC DIGEST 4:26, June, 1978.

Catholics' lawsuit suspends forced abortion payments. BUSINESS INSURANCE 13:1+, July 23, 1979.

The causes, diagnosis and treatment of perforations of the uterus by intrauterine devices, by A. Treisser, et al. JOURNAL DE GYNECOLOGIE, OBSTETRIQUE ET BIOLOGIE DE LA REPRODUCTION 7(4):837-848, 1978.

Central nervous system defects in early human abortuses, by J. E. Bell. DEVELOPMENTAL MEDICINE AND CHILD NEUROLOGY 21(3):321-332, June, 1979.

Central retinal vascular occlusion associated with oral contraceptives, by G. C. Stowe, ed, et al. AMERICAN JOURNAL OF OPTHALMOLOGY 86(6):798-801, December, 1978.

Central service guidelines present challenges for in-house backaging, by N. L. Belkin. HOSPITALS 52(21):146-148, November 1, 1978.

A certain point of view: 'Abortion, ethics, and the physicial', by S. Aberg. KATILOLEHTI 83(10):355-360, October, 1978.

Change in the classic gynecologie surgery: review of 3,300 pelviscopies in 1971-1976, by K. Semm. INTERNATIONAL JOURNAL OF FERTILITY 24(1):13-20, 1979.

Changes in the endometrium from the use of hormonal preparations and hormonal contraceptives, by G. Jellinek. ARKHIV

PATOLOGII 40(11):36-45, 1978.

Changes in laboratory tests after treatment with new contraceptive agent, by L. F. Cervantes, et al. GINECOLOGIA Y OBSTETRICIA DE MEXICO 43(258):285-297, April, 1978.

Changes in peripheral hormone levels after therapeutic abortion, by D. M. Saunders, et al. EUROPEAN JOURNAL OF OBSTETRICS, GYNECOLOGY AND REPRODUCTIVE BIOLOGY 8(1):1-4, 1978.

Changes in sexual behavior among unmarried teenage women utilizing oral contraception, by P. A. Reichelt. JOURNAL OF POPULATION 1(1):57-68, Spring, 1978.

Changing approaches to population assistance [since 1974; on the part of donor agencies, chiefly] , by M. Wolfson. PEOPLE 6(2):11-13, 1979.

Changing family roles: women and divorce, by P. Brown, et al. JOURNAL OF DIVORCE 1(4):315-328, Summer, 1978.

Changing views of abortion; study by T. C. Wagenaar, et al. HUMAN BEHAVIOR 7:58, March, 1978.

Characteristics of the action of oxidizing drugs in women with habitual abortion, by T. M. Shul'zhenko. PEDIATRIYA, AKUSHERSTVO I GINEKOLOHIYA (3):46-47, May-June, 1979.

Characteristics of women participating in the family planning program of the Direcction General de Atencion Medica Materna Infantil y Planificacion Familiar de la SSA, by S. Correu Azcona, et al. SPM 20(3):275-285, May-June, 1978.

The charge: gynocide; the accused: the U.S. government [distributuion under aid programs of contraceptives and contraceptive devices to developing countries which have been banned in the United States] , by B. Ehrenreich, et al. MOTHER JONES 4:26-31+, November, 1979.

Chemical inducers of ovulation: comparative results, by V. Ruiz-Velasco, et al. INTERNATIONAL JOURNAL OF FERTILITY 24(1):61-64, 1979.

Chemical sterilization of males—successful inhibition of spermatogenesis in langurs (Presbytis entellus entellus dufresne) after metopiron (SU-4885, Ciba) administration, by V. P. Dixit. ENDOKRINOLOGIE 72(3):291-298, November, 1978.

Chemical synthesis and bioassay of anordrin and dinordrin I and II, by P. Crabbé, et al. STEROIDS 33(1):85-96, January, 1979.

Chemosterilizatin of dermacentor variabilis say (acari: ixodidae); effects of metapa on the cytology and fertility of males treated as unfed adults, by R. L. Osburn, et al. JOURNAL OF PARASITOLOGY 64:719-726, August, 1978.

Chest pain, shock, arrhythmias and death in a young woman [clinical conference]. AMERICAN JOURNAL OF MEDICINE 66(5):853-861, May, 1979.

Childfree marriage—a theological view, by D. Doherty. CHICAGO STUDIES 18:137-145, Summer, 1979.

Child-parents: can we ignore the facts any longer? by M. Lalonde. INFIRMIERE CANADIENNE 21(1):10-11, January, 1978.

Children, magic, and choices, by D. Bisenieks. MYTHLORE 6(1):12-16, 1979.

Child's reaction to mother's abortion: case report, by J. O. Cavenar, Jr., et al. MILITARY MEDICINE 144(6):412-413, June, 1979.

China's answer doesn't lie in the coil, by J. Gittings. GUARDIAN p. 16, April 23, 1979.

Chinese birth controls penalise larger familes, by J. Mathews. GUARDIAN p. 7, May 2, 1979.

The Chinese experience [some of the ways in which China has established the small family norm, provided nationwide birth planning services and measured the results] , by P. Chen. PEOPLE 6(2):17-20, 1979.

Chinese say their pill works for men. MEDICAL WORLD NEWS 2-:13+, February 5, 1979.

Choice candidates. SEVEN DAYS 2(16):14, October 27, 1978.

The choice of childlessness: a workshop model, by M. G. Russell, et al. FAMILY COORDINATOR 27:179-184, April, 1978.

The choice of a combined oral contraceptive. DRUG AND THERAPEUTICS BULLETIN 17(1):1-4, January 5, 1979.

Choice of contraceptive pill, by P. Bergsjø. TIDSSKRIFT FOR DEN NORSKE LAEGEFORENING 99(16) 845-847, June 10, 1979.

Choice of hormonal contraception, by P. J. Keller. PRAXIS 68(13):408-411, March 27, 1979.

Choice of oral contraceptives, by P. Bergsjø. TIDSSKRIFT FOR DEN NORSKS LAEGEFORENING 99(16):845-847, June 10, 1979.

The choice of sterilizing procedure according to its potential reversibility with microsurgery, by B. Cantor, et al. FERTILITY AND STERILITY 31(1):9-12, January, 1979.

Choice rights and abortion: the begetting choicing right and state obstacles to choice in light of artificial womb technology. SOUTHERN CALIFORNIA LAW REVIEW 51: 877-921, July, 1978.

Cholestatic jaundice after administration of triacetyloleando-mycin: interaction with oral contraceptives? 10 cases [letter] , by J. P. Miguet, et al. NOUVELLE PRESSE MEDI-CALE 7(47):4304, December 30, 1978.

Cholestatic jaundice in women taking triacetyloleandomycin

and oral contraceptives simultaneously [letter] , by D. Goldfain, et al. NOUVELLE PRESSE MEDICALE 8(13):1099,
March 17, 1979.

Chorea complicating oral contraceptive therapy. Case report
and review of the literature, by W. A. Pulsinelli, et al.
AMERICAN JOURNAL OF MEDICINE 65(3):557-559,
September, 1978.

The Christian community and the welcoming of unborn human
life; pastoral instruction of the Permanent Council of the
Italian Episcopal Conference. OSSERVATORE ROMANO
11(572):6-9, March 11, 1979.

Chromosome abnormalities in oral contraceptive breakthrough
pregnancies [letter] , by S. Harlap, et al. LANCET 1(8130):
1342-1343, June 23, 1979.

Chromosome analysis in cases with repeated spontaneous abortions, by R. L. Neu, et al. OBSTETRICS AND GYNECOLO-
GY 53(3):373-375, March, 1979.

Chronic occlusion of the monkey fallopian tube with silicone
polymer, by R. H. Davis, et al. OBSTETRICS AND BYNE-
COLOGY 53(4):527-529, April, 1979.

Church and state, by E. Doerr. HUMANIST 39:62, March,
1979.

Church attendance and attitudes toward abortion: differentials
in liberal and conservative churches, by H. R. F. Ebaugh, et
al. JOURNAL FOR THE SCIENTIFIC STUDY OF RELI-
GION 17:407-413, December, 1978.

Church funding of anti-abortion lobby investigated. WIN
MAGAZINE 14(26):17, July 20, 1978.

Church v state, continued. THE ECONOMIST 270:42, January
13, 1979.

Cigarette smoking during pregnancy and the occurrence of spontaneous abortion and congenital abnormality, by D. U. Him-

melberger, et al. AMERICAN JOURNAL OF EPIDEMIOLO-
GY 108(6):470-479, December, 1978.

The circumstances surrounding pregnancy of a group of young
coloured mothers, by P. J. Van Regenmortel. HUMANITAS
4(2):203-206, 1977.

Civil liability arising from 'wrongful birth' following an unsuc-
cessfull sterilization operation, by G. B. Robertson. AMERI-
CAN JOURNAL OF LAW AND MEDICINE 4(2):131-156,
Summer, 1978.

Class action brought against hopsital to allow abortions, by W. A.
Regan. HOSPITAL PROGRESS 59(10):34+, October,
1978.

Class conflict over abortion, by P. Skerry. PUBIC INTEREST
(52):69-84, Summer, 1978.

Classical approaches to population and family planning, by L. P.
Wilkinson. POPULATION AND DEVELOPMENT REVIEW
4(3):439, September, 1978.

Classification of oral contraceptives and its practical application
to choice of prescriptions, by M. Renaud, et al. JOURNAL
DE GYNECOLOGIE, OBSTETRIQUE ET BIOLOGIE DE
LA REPRODUCTION 7(7):1291-1302, October-November,
1978.

Cleaning, disinfecting procedures help control spread of infection, by S. Crow. HOSPITALS 52(23):111-113, December
1, 1978.

Cleaning flexible fiberoptic endoscopes, by B. Y. Litsky. SCORE
3:4-5, March-April, 1979.

Cleaver: any man can. MOTHER JONES 3(3):10, April, 1978.

Clergy oppose abortion foes. NEW TIMES 11(11):26, November 27, 1978.

Cleveland abortion clinic firebombed. WIN MAGAZINE 14(9):

24, March 9, 1978.

Cleveland clinic bombed, by D. Holland. NATIONAL CATHO-
LIC REPORTER 14:2, March 3, 1978.

Clinical and exfoliative-cytology studies made prior and subsequent to the action of antiovulatory agents upon oral and
vaginal mucous membranes, by H. Ehrke, et al. ZAHNAER-
ZTLICHE MUNDEN UND KIEFERHEILKUNDE MIT ZEN-
TRALBLATT 67(1):5-9, 1979.

Clinical applications in the area of contraceptive development, by
K. J. Ryan. ADVANCES IN EXPERIMENTAL MEDICINE
AND BIOLOGY 112:737-742, 1979.

Clinical experience with implant contraception, by E. Coutinho.
CONTRACEPTION 18(4):411, October, 1978.

Clinical experience with a low dose and oral contraceptive con-
taining norethisterone and ethinyl oestradio, by E. M.
Morigi, et al. CURRENT MEDICAL RESEARCH AND
OPINION 5(8):655-662, 1978.

Clinical experience with a single silastic implant-D containing
norethindrone acetate in a Bombay hospital, by A. Mandlekar, et al. INDIAN JOURNAL OF MEDICAL RESEARCH
68:437-443, September, 1978.

Clinical observations, by S. L. Varnado. NATIONAL CATHO-
LIC REPORTER 14:9, April 28, 1978.

Clinical pharmacology of the steroidal oral contraceptives, by
J. L. Durand, et al. ADVANCES IN INTERNAL MEDICINE
24:97-126, 1979.

Clinical studies on the connection between preceding abruptio
placentae and abortus and subsequent complications during
the afterbirth phase, by R. Voigt, et al. ZEITSCHRIFT FUR
GEBURTSCHILFE UND PERINATOLOGIE 182(4):302-
306, August, 1978.

Clinical study of 425 couples soliciting vasectomies, by M. Días, et al. GINECOLOGIA Y OBSTETRICA DE MEXICO 43(259):317-323, May, 1973.

Clinical trial of a new suction system for uterine curettage. Preliminary report, by J. R. Ahued Ahued, et al. GINE- COLOGIA Y OBSTETRICIA DE MEXICO 43(260):387- 391, June, 1978.

Clinical uses of prostaglandins in human reproduction, by P. Bajaj. NURSING JOURNAL OF INDIA 69(9):197-199, September, 1978.

Clinically important drug interactions 1979, by F. E. Karch, et al. NURSES DRUG ALERT 3:25-40, March, 1979.

Les cliniques d'avortement: s'impliquer pour éduquer, by G. Durand. RELATIONS 38:308-311, November, 1978.

Cloprostenol and pregnancy termination [letter], by P. Boyd. VETERINARY RECORD 104(4):84, January 27, 1979.

Closer links between IPPF and WHO. IPPF MEDICAL BULLE- TIN 12:2-3, October, 1978.

Cohabitation: its impact on marital success, by J. M. Jacques, et al. FAMILY COORDINATOR 28(1):35-39, January, 1979.

Coital and contraceptive behavior of female adolescents, by P. A. Reichelt. ARCHIVES OF SEXUAL BEHAVIOR 8(2): 159-172, March, 1979.

Colautti v. Franklin (99 Sup Ct 675): the Court questions the use of "viability" in abortion statues. WESTERN STATE UNIVESRITY LAW REVIEW 6:311-323, Spring, 1979.

A collaborative study of the progesterone intraine device (pro- gestasert), by J. Newton, et al. CONTRACEPTION 19(6): 16, June, 1979.

Combined and national experience of postmenstrual IUD inser- tions of Nova-T and Copper-T in a randomized study, by

T. Luukkainen, et al. CONTRACEPTION 19(1):11-20, 1979.

Coming election [editorial], by A. DeValk. CHELSEA JOURNAL 5:51, March-April, 1979.

Coming out: similarities and differences for Lesbians and gay men, by C. de Monteflores, et al. THE JOURNAL OF SOCIAL ISSUES 34(3):59-72, 1978.

La communaute chrétienne et l'accueil de la vie humaine naissante; instruction pastorale du Conseil permanent de la Conférence épiscopale italienne. LA DOCUMENTATION CATHOLIQUE 76:262-271, March 18, 1979.

Communicating population and family planning, by R. R. Worrall. POPUALTION BULLETIN 31(5) 3-40, February, 1977.

Communications channels and family planning in Pakistan, by S. H. Syed. STUDIES IN FAMILY PLANNING 10(2):53-60, February, 1979.

Community-based and commercial contraceptive distribution: an inventory and appraisal, by J. R. Foreit. POPULATION REPORTS 19(1):29, March, 1978.

Community determinants of U.S. legal abortion rates, by J. A. Borders, et al. FAMILY PLANNING PERSPECTIVES 11:227-233, July-August, 1979.

Community linkages and outreach services in adolescent contraceptive clinic programs, by J. G. Greer, et al. PUBLIC HEALTH REPORTS 94:415-419, September-October, 1979.

Community nursing: roll down your stockings, by M. Tepper. NURSING MIRROR AND MIDWIVE'S JOURNAL 148(9):46, March 1, 1979.

Comparative clinical investigation of oral contraceptives with different doses, by M. Mall-Haefeli, et al. GEBURTSHILFE

UND FRAUENHEILKUNDE 39(7):553-557, July, 1979.

Comparative clinical trial of the progestins R-2323 and levonor-gestrel administered by subdermal implants, by F. Alvarez, et al. CONTRACEPTION 18(2):151-162, 1978.

The comparative efficacy and safety of intraamniotic prostaglan-din F2 alpha and hypertonic saline for second-trimester abortion. A review and critique, by D. A. Grimes, et al. JOURNAL OF REPRODUCTIVE MEDICINE 22(5):248-254, May, 1979.

Comparative electron-microscopic studies of benign hepatoma and icterus in patients on oral contraceptives, by M. Balázs. VIRCHOWS ARCHIV. ABT. A. PATHOLOGISCHE AN-ATOMIE-PATHOLOGY 38(1):97-109, December 12, 1978

Comparative electron microscopic studies on benign liver tumors and jaundice associated with contraceptive drugs, by M. Balázs. MORPHOLOGIAI ES IGAZSAGUGYI ORVOSI SZEMLE 19(1):1-9, January, 1979.

Comparative IUD study: Lippes Loop D, Dalkon Shield and TCu-200, by M. Medel, et al. INTERNATIONAL JOURNAL OF GYNAECOLOGY AND OBSTETRICS 16(2):157-161, 1978-1979.

Comparative studies on the termination of intact and disturbed pregnancies by intramuscular application of 15(s)-15-methyl-prostaglandin F2alpha, by H. Schridde, et al. GEBURT-SHILFE UND FRAUENHEILKUNDE 38(10):845-848, October, 1978.

Comparative studies on two combination oral contraceptives, one containing synthetic estrogen, the other 'natural' estrogens, by D. M. Saunders, et al. CONTRACEPTION 18(5):527-534, November, 1978.

A comparative study of rural and urban population undergoing tubal ligation, by N. N. Wig, et al. JOURNAL OF FAMILY WELFARE 24:34-43, June, 1978.

A comparative study of the tubal ring applied via minilaparotomy and laparoscopy in postabortion cases, by R. V. Bhatt, et al. INTERNATIONAL JOURNAL OF GYNAECOLOGY AND OBSTETRICS 16(2):162-166, 1978-1979.

Comparison of central nervous system malformations in spontaneous abortions in Northern Ireland and south-east England, by J. C. MacHenry, et al. BRITISH MEDICAL JOURNAL 1(6175):1395-1397, May 26, 1979.

A comparison of the clip and ring techniques for laparoscopic sterilization of postabortion and postpartum patients, by T. H. Lean, et al. INTERNATIONAL JOURNAL OF GYNAECOLOGY AND OBSTETRICS 16(2):150-156, 1978-1979.

Comparison of effects of different combined oral-contraceptive formulations on carbohydrate and lipid metabolism, by V. Wynn, et al. LANCET 1(8125):1045-1049, May, 1979.

Comparison of extra-amniotic instillation of rivanol and PGF2-alpha either separately or in combination followed by oxytocin for second trimester abortion, by A. Olund, et al. ACTA OBSTETRICIA ET GYNECOLOGICA SCANDINAVICA 57(4):333-336, 1978.

A comparison of the factors influencing husband and wife decisions about contraception, by H. M. Baum. DISSERTATION ABSTRACTS INTERNATIONAL 39(2-B):671, August, 1978.

A comparison of metal and plastic cannulae for vacuum aspiration, by M. R. Narvekar, et al. INTERNATIONAL JOURNAL OF GYNAECOLOGY AND OBSTETRICS 15(5):433-435, 1978.

A comparison of the predictive value of the pregnanediol/creatinine ratio and the human chorionic gonadatrophin titre in threatened miscarriage, by N. France. NEW ZEALAND JOURNAL OF LABORATORY TECHNOLOGY 32:85-86+, November, 1978.

Comparison of the sebaceous secretions of the skin of the forehead under the treatment with three oral contraceptives. Diane, Neogynon and Lyndiol, by D. Leis, et al. GEBURT-SHILFE UND FRAUENHEILKUNDE 39(1):54-57, January, 1979.

A comparison of socio-demographic and fertility characteristics of women sterilized in hospitals and camps, by S. Pachauri. INTERNATIONAL JOURNAL OF GYNAECOLOGY AND OBSTETRICS 16(2):132-136, 1978-1979.

A comparison of spontaneous and contraceptive menstrual cycles on a visual discrimination task, by J. Friedman, et al. AUSTRALIAN AND NEW ZEALAND JOURNAL OF PSYCHIATRY 12:233-240, December, 1978.

Comparisons: the United States and Britain, by E. F. Jones. FAMILY PLANNING PERSPECTIVES 11(2):136-137, March-April, 1979.

Compensation for damages in unsuccessful sterilization without occurring pregnancy, by H. J. Rieger. DEUTSCH MEDIZINISCHE WOCHENSCHRIFT 104(26):932-933, June 19, 1979.

Completeness and accuracy of reporting induced abortions performed in Hawaii's hospitals, 1970-74, by C. S. Chung, et al. PUBLIC HEALTH REPORTS 94:454-458, September-October, 1979.

Complication of abortion performed with plastic suction curet: intrauterine loss of the curet tip, by T. W. McElin, et al. AMERICAN JOURNAL OF OBSTETRICS AND GYNECOLOGY 132(3):343-344, October 1, 1978.

Complications and psychosomatic problems after tubal sterilization, by B. M. Berić, et al. FORTSCHRITTE DU MEDIZIN 97(7):304-306 February 15, 1979.

Complications from legally-induced abortion: a review, by D. A. Grimes, et al. OBSTETRICAL AND GYNECOLOGICAL SURVEY 34(3):177-191, March, 1979.

Complications of laparoscopic sterilization. Comparison of 2 methods, by M. S. Baggish, et al. OBSTETRICS AND GYNECOLOGY 54(1):54-59, July, 1979.

Complications of the new contraceptive preparations, by J. Clinch. IRISH MEDICAL JOURNAL 71(15):513-514, October 31, 1978.

Complications with use of IUD and oral contraceptives among Navajo women, by J. C. Slocumb, et al. PUBLIC HEALTH REPORTS 94(3):243-247, June, 1979.

Compulsory sterilization in the Breslau district in 1934-1944, by S. Kusperek. PRZEGLAD LEKARSKI 36(1):50-60, 1979.

Compulsory sterilization practices, by S. Tessler. FRONTIERS 1(2):52-66, 1975.

Conception control—a growing awareness. AMERICAN PHARMACY 19(8):14-15, July, 1979.

Concepts in emergency childbirth, by D. A. Zschoche. CRITICAL CARE UPDATE 6:32-35, October, 1979.

Concepts of family planning, by C. W. Hubbard. CURRENT PRACTICE IN OBSTETRIC AND GYNECOLOGIC NURSING 2:3-23, 1978.

A conceptual model for the identification, organization, and measure of influence of fertility policies and programs, by B. F. Pendleton. SOCIAL BIOLOGY 23(4):326-340, Winter, 1976.

Condom ads aim at the youth market, by T. Thompson. MARKETING 83:18, November 27, 1978.

Condoms. CONSUMER REPORTS 44(10):583, October, 1979.

—, by T. Thompson. MARKETING 84:6-7+, April 9, 1979.

Confusion about New Zealand abortion [letter] , by W. Savage.

BRITISH MEDICAL JOURNAL 2(6135):356, July 29, 1978.

Congress aborts medicaid. OFF OUR BACKS 8(1):13, January, 1978.

Congress acts on other anti-abortion measures. SPOKESWOMAN 9(4):5, October, 1978.

Congress bows to anti-choice pressure. SPOKESWOMAN 9(5):8, November, 1978.

Congress ends abortion funds deadlock. SPOKESWOMAN 8(7&8):5, January, 1978.

Consequences and psychological interactions associated with salpingoclasia, by E. Shapiro Ackerman, et al. GINECOLOGIA Y OBSTETRICIA DE MEXICO 43(259):333-338, May, 1978.

Consequences of induced abortion [letter], by J. Craft, et al. LANCET 1(8113):437, February 24, 1979.

Considerations in the management of patients taking oral contraceptives, by S. Kennon, et al. JOURNAL OF THE AMERICAN DENTAL ASSOCIATION 97(4):641-643, October, 1978.

Consistency between fertility attitudes and behavior: a conceptual model, by S. B. Kar. POPULATION STUDIES 32:173-186, March, 1978.

Consistency of reporting fertility planning status, by N. B. Ryder. STUDIES IN FAMILY PLANNING 10(4):115-128, April, 1979.

Constitutional Convention advances, by J. M. Clark. NOW 11(7):11, June, 1978.

Constitutional law—civil rights—section 1983—requirement of state action in discrimination suite against medical doctor. WISCONSIN LAW REVIEW 1978:583-605, 1978.

Constitutional law: a constitutional analysis of the new Oklahoma abortion statute. OKLAHOMA LAW REVIEW 32: 138-144, Winter, 1979.

Constitutional law—denial of state medicaid funds for abortions not 'medically necessary' does not violate the equal protection clause. HOWARD LAW JOURNAL 21:937-954, 1978.

Constitutional law—the fundamental right of parents to care, custody, and nurture of their children requires that parents have notice and an aopportunity to consult with their minor child before that minor may have access to contraceptives. UNIVERSITY OF DETROIT. JOURNAL OF URBAN LAW 56:268-288, Fall, 1978.

Constitutional law—substantive due process—children's rights— parents' right to be notified when their children are provided contraceptives by state funded family planning clinics. WAYNE LAW REVIEW 25:1135-1146, July, 1979.

Consultant report: incomplete abortions treated at Jahanshah Saleh Hospital in Tehran, Iran from May 14, 1973 to April 30, 1984, by Y. Behjatnia. ACTA MEDICA IRANICA 21(1):53-67, 1978.

Consultation: when abortion is demanded, by W. Greve, et al. PSYCHOTHERAPIE UND MEDIZINISCHE PSYCHOLOGIE 27(2):58-63, March, 1977.

Contamination of steril fluids [letter], by E. R. Tallet. BRITISH MEDICAL JOURNAL 2(6152):1645, December 9, 1978.

Contamination of ultrasonic equipment for the hand disinfection by chlorhexidine-resistant Alcaligenes faecalis, by T. Kim, et al. KANSENSHOGAKU ZASSHI 52(1):10-15, January, 1978.

Continued education course of the Swiss Society for Family Planning, Basel, 13—14 May 1977. Current contraception. GYNAEKOLOGISCHE RUNDSCHAU 18(3-4):157-266, 1978.

Continued pregnancy after curettage and incidental tubal fulguration by laparoscopy: a case report, by L. E. Savel, et al. INTERNATIONAL JOURNAL OF GYNAECOLOGY AND OBSTETRICS 16(1):39-39, 1978.

Continued used of contraception among Philippine family planning acceptors: a multivariate analysis, by J. F. Phillips. STUDIES IN FAMILY PLANNING 9(7):182, July, 1978.

Continuous low-dose progestagen oral contraceptives. DRUG AND THERAPEUTICS BULLETIN 17(1):4, January 5, 1979.

Contraception, by P. Senanayake. GUARDIAN p. 20, August 28, 1979.

—, by V. Lawrence. UNDERCURRENT 29:26, August, 1978.

Contraception after pregnancy, by E. J. Quilligan. JOURNAL OF REPRODUCTIVE MEDICINE 21(5 suppl):250-251, November, 1978.

Contraception and the adolescent female, by C. Polle. JOURNAL OF SCHOOL HEALTH 46(8):475-479, October, 1976.

Contraception and the Christian institution, by R. Slesinski. LINACRE QUARTERLY 46:264-278, August, 1979.

Contraception and its discontents: Sigmund Freud and birth control, by A. McLaren. JOURNAL OF SOCIAL HISTORY 12:513-529, Summer, 1979.

Contraception at the crossroads, by C. R. Garcia. CONTEMPORARY OB/GYN 13(1):81, January, 1979.

Contraception at Port Elizabeth clinics [letter], by A. A. Grodon. SOUTH AFRICAN MEDICAL JOURNAL 54(11): 424, September 9, 1978.

Contraception before and after pregnancy, by P. Conquy. SOINS 24(2):3-6, January 20, 1979.

Contraception before pregnancy: evolution between 1972 and 1975 in the Rhone-Alpes region, by B. Blondel, et al. JOURNAL DE GYNECOLOGIE, OBSTETRIQUE ET BIOLOGIE DE LA REPRODUCTION 7(4):767-778, 1978.

Contraception—a choice of methods, by W. E. Small. AMERICAN PHARMACY 19(8):16-22, July, 1979.

The contraception consultant, by M. C. Smith, et al. AMERICAN PHARMACY 19(8):23-24, July, 1979.

Contraception for teenagers, by N. Louden. MIDWIFE HEALTH VISITOR COMMUNITY NURSE 15:356+, September, 1979.

Contraception for the unmarried, by B. Bhasin. JOURNAL OF FAMILY WELFARE 25:35-43, December, 1978.

Contraception in the adolescent. Alternative methods, by G. Betheras. AUSTRALIAN FAMILY PHYSICIAN 7(spec. no.):37-38, August, 1978.

Contraception in the adolescent. Educational programmes, by K. Dunn. AUSTRALIAN FAMILY PHYSICIAN 7(spec. no.):21-24, August, 1978.

Contraception in the adolescent. Introduction, by J. Leeton. AUSTRALIAN FAMILY PHYSICIAN 7(spec. no.):3-5, August, 1978.

Contraception in the adolescent. Proceedings of a seminar held in Melbourne, March 10, 1978, by the Family Planning Association of Victoria. AUSTRALIAN FAMILY PHYSICIAN 7(spec. no.):3-38, August, 1978.

Contraception in the adolescent. Psychological aspects, by E. Koadlow. AUSTRALIAN FAMILY PHYSICIAN 7(spec. no.):16-20, August, 1978.

Contraception in the adolescent. Steps towards a situational ethic, by P. J. Hollingworth. AUSTRALIAN FAMILY PHYSICIAN 7(spec. no.):6-11, August, 1978.

Contraception in the cardiac patient, by R. Taurelle, et al. JOURNAL DE GYNECOLOGIE, OBSTETRIQUE ET BIOLOGIE DE LA REPRODUCTION 7(1):111-118, 1978.

Contraception in diabetic women, by G. Cathelineau. SEMAINE DES HOPITAUX DE PARIS 54(45-46):1462-1464+, December, 1978.

Contraception using 3-monthly injections of Depo-Provera, by C. Revaz, et al. GYNAEKOLOGISCHE RUNDSCHAU 18(3-4):183-192, 1978.

Contraception: what's best for you, by M. Josephs. HARPER'S BAZAAR (3206):122B, January, 1979.

Contraception with acting subdermal implants, by E. Coutinho, et al. CONTRACEPTION 18(4):315, October, 1978.

Contraception with the intrauterine pessary Progestasert, by K. W. Schweppe, et al. FORTSCHRITTE DU MEDIZIN 96(33):1685-1690, September 7, 1978.

Contraceptive acceptability research: its utility and limitations, by A. Keller. STUDIES IN FAMILY PLANNING 10:230-237, August-September, 1979.

Contraceptive-associated hepatic tumor, by K. T. Benedict, Jr., et al. AJR INFORMATION 132(3):452-454, March, 1979.

Contraceptive careers: toward a subjective approach to fertility regulating behaviour, by E. D. Boldt, et al. JOURNAL OF COMPARATIVE FAMILY STUDIES 8(3):357-367, Fall, 1977.

Contraceptive continuation in high-risk women, by M. D. Hoyos, et al. WEST INDIAN MEDICAL JOURNAL 27(4):196-200, December, 1978.

Contraceptive counseling for young girls, by A. Huber. FORT-SCHRITTE DU MEDIZIN 96(33):1638-1642, September, 1978.

Contraceptive development, by G. Bialy. CONTRACEPTION 19(4):353-363, April, 1979.

A contraceptive device updated. NEWSWEEK 94:69, September 3, 1979.

Contraceptive distribution in Bangladesh villages: the initial impact, by D. H. Huber, et al. STUDIES IN FAMILY PLANNING 10:246, August-September, 1979.

Contraceptive effectiveness warning issued; spermicide, Encare Oval. FDA CONSUMER 12:4, September, 1978.

Contraceptive effects of intravaginal application of acrosin and hyaluronidase inhibitors in rabbit, by C. Joyce, et al. CONTRACEPTION 19(1):95-106, January, 1979.

Contraceptive effects of native plants in rats, by M. O. Guerra, et al. CONTRACEPTION 18(2):191-199, August, 1978.

Contraceptive efficacy of Encare Oval [letter], by B. A. Harris, Jr. FERTILITY AND STERILITY 31(5):595, May, 1979.

Contraceptive evaluation, by H. Berendes. CONTRACEPTION 19(4):364-374, April, 1979.

The contraceptive habits of women applying for termination of pregnancy, by M. Wohlert, et al. UGESKRIFT FOR LAEGER 141(27):1863-1866, July 2, 1979.

Contraceptive hormones, vascular risk and abnormal precipitation of serium gamma-globulins, by V. Beaumont, et al. SEMAINE DES HOPITAUX DE PARIS 55(1112):585-591+, March, 1979.

Contraceptive knowledge: antecedents and implications, by R. O. Hansson, et al. FAMILY COORDINATOR 28(1):29-34, January, 1979.

Contraceptive methods: risks and benefits, by M. P. Vessey. BRITISH MEDICAL JOURNAL 2(6139):721-722, September 9, 1978.

Contraceptive PPIs called nearly useless. DRUG TOPICS 122: 34, May 9, 1978.

Contraceptive practice after clinic discontinuation, by P. S. Cosgrove, et al. FAMILY PLANNING PERSPECTIVES 10(6): 337-340, November-December, 1978.

Contraceptive practice before and after therapeutic abortion. II. Use-effectiveness of oral contraceptives and intrauterine devices, by P. Fylling, et al. FERTILITY AND STERILITY 32(1):24-27, July, 1979.

Contraceptive practice in France in 1978, by H. Leridon. FAMILY PLANNING PERSPECTIVES 11(3):153, May-June, 1979.

Contraceptive prevalence in Paraguay, by L. Morris, et al. STUDIES IN FAMILY PLANNING 9(10-11):272-279, October-November, 1978.

Contraceptive properties of endotoxin in rabbits, by M. J. Harper, et al. FERTILITY AND STERILITY 31(4):441-447, April, 1979.

Contraceptive research and population growth. FAMILY PLANNING PERSPECTIVES 10:294-297, September-October, 1978.

Contraceptive research funding: eroded by inflation, increasingly dependent upon government support. DRAPER FUND REPORT pp. 16-17, Summer, 1978.

Contraceptive risk taking among women entering a family planning clinic, by E. E. Hall. DISSERTATION ABSTRACTS INTERNATIONAL 38(10-B):5017, April, 1978.

Contraceptive risk-taking in White and Black unwed females, by H. Harari, et al. JOURNAL OF SEX RESEARCH 15: 56-63, February, 1979.

Contraceptive status in a community attached to a hospital in Delhi, by A. K. Madan, et al. JOURNAL OF FAMILY WEL-

FARE 24:44-49, June, 1978.

Contraceptive supply to single young persons. . .nurses attitudes, by D. Wills. NEW ZEALAND NURSING FORUM 7:5-6, June-July, 1979.

Contraceptive technology: coming into its own? by L. Lohr. AMERICAN PHARMACY 18(10):42-45, September, 1978.

Contraceptive tetrapeptide in hamster embryos [letter] , by H. A. Kent, Jr. FERTILITY AND STERILITY 31(5):595, May, 1979.

Contraceptive use and demographic trends in El Salvador, by L. Morris. STUDIES IN FAMILY PLANNING 10(2):43, February, 1979.

Contraceptive use-effectiveness and the American adolescent, by K. C. Lyle, et al. JOURNAL OF REPRODUCTIVE MEDICINE 22(5):225-232, May, 1979.

Contraceptive use in the United States, 1973-1976, by K. Ford. FAMILY PLANNING PERSPECTIVES 10(5):264, September-October, 1978.

Contraceptive workload in general practice in the Trent Region, by D. W. Cammock, et al. JOURNAL OF ROYAL COLLEGE OF GENERAL PRACTICIONERS 27(183):610-613, October, 1977.

Contraceptives, by S. Koslow. LADIES HOME JOURNAL 96: 82+, September, 1979.

Contraceptives: the barrier methods are back, by T. Gorman. DRUG TOPICS 123:62-65, April 6, 1979.

Contraceptives for women in their forties? by G. A. Hauser. GYNAEKOLOGISCHE RUNDSCHAU 18(3-4):193-212, 1978.

Contraceptives: your questions answered, by D. Partie. MADEMOISELLE 85:85-86+, August, 1979.

Contraindications in the interruption of pregnancy, by P. Drobnjak. JUGOSLAVENSKA GINEKOLOGIJA I OPSTETRICIJA 17(5-6):349-350, 1977.

The contribution of nurse practitioners to service delivery in family planning, by M. Flynn. LAMP 35:14-16, October, 1978.

Control of infection, sterilisation and bacteriology: the role of the microbiologist, by M. Thomas. NATIONAL NEWS 16(2):6-8, February, 1979.

Controlling the population explosion, by M. Potts. THE CROWN AGENTS QUARTERLY REVIEW pp. 1-6, Winter, 1978-1979.

Co-operative method of natural birth control, by M. Nofziger. UNDERCURRENT 29:41, August, 1978.

Coping with miscarriage, by M. Newton. FAMILY HEALTH 10:12+, October, 1978.

Coping with pregacy resolution among never-married women, by M. B. Bracken, et al. AMERICAN JOURNAL OF OR-THOPSYCHIATRY 48:320-334, April, 1978.

Copper intrauterine devices and the small intestine, by P. J. M. Watney. BRITISH MEDICAL JOURNAL 6132:255-256, July 22, 1978.

Corrective surgery of obstructive azoospermia, by H. Y. Lee. ARCHIVES OF ANDROLOGY 1(1):115-121, 1978.

The correspondence of data gathered from husband and wife: implications for family planning studies, by J. J. Card. SOCIAL BIOLOGY 25(3):196-204, Fall, 1978.

Cost-effectiveness evaluation of a home visiting triage program for family planning in Turkey, by R. L. Bertera, et al. AMERICAN JOURNAL OF PUBLIC HEALTH 69(9):950-953, September, 1979.

The cost per unit of family planning services, by W. C. Robinson. JOURNAL OF BIOSOCIAL SCIENCE 11(1):93-103, January, 1979.

Counseling clients in natural methods of family planning, by M. T. Curry. MARYLAND NURSE :26-29, Feburary, 1979.

Counseling, consulting, and consent: abortion and the doctor-patient relationship, by M. A. Wood, et al. BRIGHAM YOUNG UNIVERSITY LAW REVIEW 1978:783-845, 1978.

Counseling patients for contraception, by G. R. Huggins. CLINICAL OBSTETRICS AND GYNECOLOGY 22(2):509-520, June, 1979.

The couple to couple league, by J. Kippley. LIGUORIAN 67:17-21, January, 1979.

Couples want fewer children. SCIENTIFIC AMERICAN 241(4): 72A, October, 1979.

The Court, the Congress and the President: turning back the clock on the pregnant poor, by R. Lincoln, et al. FAMILY PLANNING PERSPECTIVES 9(5):207-214, September-October, 1977.

Court drives home final nail in coffin of unborn with Pennsylvania decision, by R. McMunn. OUR SUNDAY VISITOR 67:2, January 21, 1979.

Court kills law calling late abortions murder. MEDICAL WORLD NEWS 20:85-86, February 5, 1979.

Court labors over Roe v. Wade and gives birth to new standard. MERCER LAW REVIEW 30:761-768, Spring, 1979.

The court's dissenters; abortion control law, by B. White, et al. ORIGINS 8:506-509, January 25, 1979.

Courts: judicial immunity—courts of general jurisdiction. WASHBURN LAW JOURNAL 18:158-165, Fall, 1978.

59

The crime of precocious sexuality: female juvenile delinquency in the Progressive Era, by S. Schlossman, et al. HARVARD EDUCATIONAL REVIEW 48:65-94, February, 1978.

A critique of anthropological research on homosexuality, by T. K. Fitzgerald. JOURNAL OF HOMOSEXUALITY 2(4):385-397, Summer, 1977.

Crowding and human reproduction, by D. R. Johnson, et al. THE MILBANK MEMORIAL FUND QUARTERLY 54(3): 321-337, Summer, 1976.

Cruel and unusual tactics, by G. Lichtenstein. THE VILLAGE VOICE 24(17):1+, April 30, 1979.

Cruising the truckers: sexual encounters in a highway rest area, by J. Corzine, et al. URBAN LIFE 6(2):171-192, July, 1977.

Cultural cross fires; study by Carlos Velez of Mexican American women sterilized without consent at Los Angeles County-USC Medical Center, by D. Ainsworth. HUMAN BEHAVIOR 8:52-55, March, 1979.

Cultural factors affecting the use of family planning services in an Aboriginal community, by J. Reid. MEDICAL JOURNAL OF AUSTRALIA 1(2 suppl):1-4, February 24, 1979.

Curettage because of incomplete abortion in a 15-year-old girl, by W. Weissauer. ANAESTHESIOLOGISCHE UND INTENSIVMEDIZINISCHE PRAXIS 16:27-28, February, 1979.

Current concepts in contraception: a discussion. JOURNAL OF REPRODUCTIVE MEDICINE 21(5 suppl):243-271, November, 1978.

Current efforts to develop male hormonal contraception, by S. B. Schearer. STUDIES IN FAMILY PLANNING 9(8): 229-231, August, 1978.

Current status of sterilization, by C. Wood. AUSTRALIAN

FAMILY PHYSICIAN 8(5):486-490, May, 1979.

Current technics of birth control [news]. CASOPIS LEKARU
CESKYCH 118(13):415-416, March 30, 1979.

Current theories on the causes of miscarriage (review of the
literature), by N. G. Kosheleva. VOPROSY OKHRANY
MATERINSTVA I DETSTVA 24(1):65-68, January, 1979.

Curriculum and other choices: relationships with men's sex-role
beliefs, by M. J. la Plante. DISSERTATION ABSTRACTS
INTERNATIONAL 38(9-B):4537-4538, March, 1978.

Cyanamid attacked over sterilization of female workers.
CHEMICAL MARKETING REPORTER 215:3+, January
8, 1979.

Cyclic use of combination oral contraceptives and the severity
of endometriosis, by V. C. Buttram, Jr. FERTILITY AND
STERILITY 31(3):347-348, March, 1979.

Cytogenetic and histologic analyses of spontaneous abortions,
by M. Geisler, et al. HUMAN GENETICS 45(3):239-251,
December 29, 1978.

Cytogenetic investigation in 413 couples with spontaneous abor-
tions, by C. Turleau, et al. EUROPEAN JOURNAL OF
OBSTETRICS, GYNECOLOGY AND REPRODUCTIVE
BIOLOGY 9(2):65-74, 1979.

Cytohormonal assessment of ovarian function following tubal
ligation, by S. Khanna, et al. INTERNATIONAL JOURNAL
OF GYNAECOLOGY AND OBSTETRICS 16(5):373-376,
March-April, 1979.

DOD: lift abortion ban, kin limits. AIR FORCE TIMES 39:29,
July 2, 1979.

Dalkon Shield: a "primer" in IUD liability, by J. M. Van Dyke.
WESTERN STATE UNIVERSITY LAW REVIEW 6:1-52,
Fall, 1978.

Dare man "play God?", by S. J. Spiro. JEWISH SPECTATOR 43:13-16, Fall, 1978.

Dateline Europe [it was quite an innocent aid], by P. Wilson-Ferrill. MARKETING 83:15, October 30, 1978.

Dealing in divorce: is birth control to blame? study by R. T. Michael. HUMAN BEHAVIOR 7:37, November, 1978.

The decision for male versus female sterilization, by M. P. Clark, et al. FAMILY COORDINATOR 28(2):250-254, April, 1979.

The decision of parent or not: normative and structural components, by M. G. Ory. JOURNAL OF MARRIAGE AND THE FAMILY 40(3):531-539, August, 1978.

Decline of Down's syndrome after abortion reform in New York state, by H. Hansen. AMERICAN JOURNAL OF MENTAL DEFICIENCY 83:185-188, September, 1978.

Decoding the election game plan of the new right; Life Amendment Political Action Committee Inc., by L. C. Wohl. MS MAGAZINE 8:57-59+, August, 1979.

Decontamination of appartus for inhalation anesthesia and artificial ventilation of the lungs, by V. M. Iurevich. MEDITSINSKAIA TEKHNIKA (1):31-37, January-February, 1979.

Defense tries to prove that baby never lived outside mother's womb, by K. Granville. OUR SUNDAY VISITOR 67:2, April 22, 1979.

The definition of death: interview by D. Duggan, by M. DeMere. OUR SUNDAY VISITOR 67:6-7, January 28, 1979.

Demographic transition in Japan, 1920-1960 [summary of doctoral dissertation with reply by L. P. Cain], by C. Mosk. JOURNAL OF ECONOMIC HISTORY 38:285-286+, March, 1978.

Denial of state medicaid funds for abortions not 'medically

necessary' does not violate the equal protection clause: Maher v. Roe, by C. K. Barber. HOWARD LAW JOURNAL 21(3):937-954, 1978.

A dent in the shield, by A. Neustatter, et al. GUARDIAN p. 10, November 1, 1979.

Depo: the debate continues, by D. Maine. FAMILY PLANNING PERSPECTIVES 10:342-345, November-December, 1978.

Depo-provera and contraceptive risk: a case study of values in conflict, by C. Levine. HASTINGS CENTER REPORT 9:8-11, August, 1979.

Depo provera for third world women? OFF OUR BACKS 8(10):5, November, 1978.

Depot medroxyprogesterone acetate for contraception: a continuing controversy. INTERNATIONAL JOURNAL OF GYNAECOLOGY AND OBSTETRICS 16(5):433-441, March-April, 1979.

Depression and oral contraceptives: the role of pyridoxine. DRUG AND THERAPEUTICS BULLETIN 16(22):86-87, October 27, 1978.

Description of post-abortion sepsis with a fatal result in the novel 'Seobe' by Miloś Crnjanski, by B. Berić, et al. SRPSKI ARHIV ZA CELOKUPNO LEKARSTVO 105(10).917-923, October, 1977.

Desire for therapeutic abortion in the dependents of foreign workers. Outpatients psychiatric evaluation, by H. von der Mühlen. GEBURTSHILFE UND FRAUENHEILKUNDE 38(10):858-861, October, 1978.

The desire to have children, by W. Maier. GEBURTSHILFE UND FRAUENHEILKUNDE 38(12):1091-1092, December, 1978.

Despite Church opposition, Italy adopts new law providing free abortion for a variety of indications [news] . FAMILY

63

PLANNING PERSPECTIVES 10(4):241-243, July-August, 1978.

Despite data gathered. SPOKESWOMAN 9(3):4, September, 1978.

Despite media attack, pro-lifers march on (inability of media to cover anti-abortion advocates honestly), by C. Kincaid. NEW GUARD 19:10+, Spring, 1979.

Determinant factors in the illegal abortion trends in Chile, by T. Monreal. BOLETIN DE LA OFICINA SANITARIA PANA-MERICANA 86(3):206-218, March, 1979.

Determinants of abortion policy in the developed nations, by M. J. Field. POLICY STUDIES JOURNAL 7:771-781, Summer, 1979.

Determinants of genocide fear in a rural Texas community: a research note, by W. C. Farrell, Jr., et al. AMERICAN JOURNAL OF PUBLIC HEALTH 69:605-607, June, 1979.

The determination of antithrombin III. Comparison of six methods. Effect of oral contraceptive therapy, by H. Bouna-meaux, et al. THROMBOSIS AND HAEMOSTASIS 39(3): 607-615, June 30, 1978.

Determination of fertility behavior in a non-contracepting popu-lation, by V. Jesudason. JOURNAL OF FAMILY WEL-FARE 24:3-13, March, 1978.

Determination of selected coagulation parameters in induced abortion by means of 15-methyl-PGF2 alpha, by R. During, et al. FOLIA HAEMATOLOGICA 106(1):72-79, 1979.

Developing Asia's countryside, by P. C. Stuart. NEW LEADER 62:8-10, March 12, 1979.

Development of a dual-form abortion scale, by J. K. Bowers, et al. JOURNAL OF SEX RESEARCH 15:158-165, May, 1979.

Development of an estriol-releasing intrauterine device, by R. W. Baker, et al. JOURNAL OF PHARMACEUTICAL STUDIES 68(1):20-26, 1979.

The development of instruments to measure attitudes toward abortion and knowledge of abortion, by S. Snegroff. JOURNAL OF SCHOOL HEALTH 46(5):273-277, May, 1976.

Development of masturbation in college women, by R. Clifford. ARCHIVES OF SEXUAL BEHAVIOR 7(6):559-573, November, 1978.

Development of a reversible vas deferens occlusive device. VI. Long-term evaluation of flexible prosthetic devices, by E. E. Brueschke, et al. FERTILITY AND STERILITY 31(5):575-586, May, 1979.

Developments in criminal law and penal systems: Norway 1977-78, by J. Andenaes. THE CRIMINAL LAW REVIEW pp. 447-451, July, 1979.

Devices for washing out blood and blood substitute transfusion systems, by A. I. Salikova. MEDITSINSKAIA SESTRA 37(7):48-49, July, 1978.

Diagnosing marital and family systems: a training model, by R. E. Cromwell, et al. FAMILY COORDINATOR 28(1): 101-108, January, 1979.

Diagnostic/therapeutic preabortion interview, by P. D. Boekelheide. JOURNAL OF THE AMERICAN COLLEGE HEALTH ASSOCIATION 27:157-160, December, 1978.

Diary of my decision: why I had an abortion, by J. Maynard. REDBOOK 153:62+, September, 1979.

Did the Supreme Court impose its morality on us? by H. Gow. LIGUORIAN 67:35-38, January, 1979.

Differences in U.S. marital fertility, 1970-73, by planning status of births, by J. E. Anderson. PUBLIC HEALTH REPORTS 94(4):319-325, July-August, 1979.

The differential evaluation of "large" and "small" families in rural Colombia: implications for family planning, by M. Micklin, et al. SOCIAL BIOLOGY 22(1):44-59, Spring, 1975.

Differential fertility by intelligence: the role of birth planning, by J. R. Udry. SOCIAL BIOLOGY 25:10-14, Spring, 1978.

Differential impact of religious preference and church attendance on attitudes toward abortion, by W. A. Mc Intosh, et al. REVIEW OF RELIGIOUS RESEARCH 20:195-213, Spring, 1979.

Difficult birth. THE ECONOMIST 270:28+, January 6, 1979.

A difficult problem [editorial], by L. Valvanne. KATILOLEHTI 83(10):349-350, October, 1978.

Diffusion of contraception through a tailoress—a study, by K. Mahadevan. JOURNAL OF FAMILY WELFARE 25:64-68, March, 1979.

A direct evidence for the involvement of prostaglandin F2a in the first step of estrone-induced blastocyst implantation in the spayed rat, by M. Oettel, et al. STEROIDS 3(1):1-8, 1979.

The disappearance of HCG and return of pituitary function after abortion, by P. Lähteenmäki. CLINICAL ENDOCRINOLOGY 9(2):101-112, August, 1978.

Disinfectants, use and methods, by G. Piedrola Angulo, et al. REVISTA DE SANIDAD E HIGIENE PUBLICA 52(3-4):341-394, March-April, 1978.

Disinfection in hospitals, by G. Feier. VIATA MEDICALA/MEDICAL PRACTICE 27(4):85-88, April, 1979.

Disinfection in mycotic diseases, by V. M. Leshchenko. FEL'DSHER I AKUSHERKA 43(6):12-14, June, 1978.

Disinfection of C.P.R. training manikins. AUSTRALASIAN

NURSES JOURNAL 8(10):14-15, May, 1979.

Disinfection of effluents from municipal sewage treatment plants with peroxy acids, by R. Poffé, et al. ZENTRALBLATT FUER BAKTERIOLOGIE, PARASITENKUNDE, INFEKT-TONSKRANKHEITEN UND HYGIENE 167(4):337-346, November, 1978.

Disinfection of nitrous oxide inhalation equipment, by J. A. Yagiela, et al. JOURNAL OF THE AMERICAN DENTAL ASSOCIATION 98(2):191-195, February, 1979.

Disinfection of the oral mucosa before intraoral injections, by V. Beese, et al. STOMATOLOGIE DER DDR 28(10):688-691, October, 1978.

Disinfection of the return water at stations for the washing of long-distance trains, by V. A. Poliakova, et al. GIGIYENA I SANITARIYA (1):84-85, January, 1979.

Disinfection of the sewage from plants in the production of meat and bone meal, by K. N. Son, et al. VETERINARIIA (2): 22-23, 1979.

Disinfection of the skin of the abdomen, by J. Davies, et al. BRITISH JOURNAL OF SURGERY 65(12):855-858, December, 1978.

Disorders of the retinal vascular system in long-term use of oral contraceptives, by D. Fabiszewska-Górna, et al. KLINIKA OCZNA 81(2):157-159, 1979.

Disposition of chlordiazepoxide: sex differences and effects of oral contraceptives, by R. K. Roberts, et al. CLINICAL PHARMACOLOGY AND THERAPEUTICS 25(6):826-831, June, 1979.

Dispute over some herbicides rages in wake of Agent Orange, by P. Gunby. JAMA 241(14):1443-1444, April 6, 1979.

Dix ans apres Humanae Vitae, by G. Martelet. NOUVELLE REVUE THEOLOGIQUE 101:246-259, March-April, 1979.

Do Catholics have constitutional rights? Hyde Amendment challenge. COMMONWEAL 105:771-773, December 8, 1978.

Do intentions predict fertility? the experience in Taiwan, 1967-74, by A. I. Hermalin, et al. STUDIES IN FAMILY PLANNING 10:75-95, March, 1979.

Do-it-yourself abortions. NEW SCIENTIST 78:733, June 15, 1978.

Doctor knows best, by J. Chernaik. NEW SOCIETY pp. 779-780, June 28, 1979.

Doctors and the Islamic penal code [letter], by R. J. Brereton. LANCET 1(8117):672, March 24, 1979.

Does abortion affect later pregnancies? by D. Maine. FAMILY PLANNING PERSPECTIVES 11:98-101, March-April, 1979.

Does the cash register ring louder than freedom for rights of women? by F. Franzonia. OUR SUNDAY VISITOR 68:1, July 22, 1979+.

Does the First amendment bar the Hyde amendment? symposium on "McRae v. Califano" [a class-action lawsuit in which the plaintiffs contend that legislation prohibiting Medicaid payment for most abortions violates the establishment and free exercise religion clauses of the First amendment]. CHRISTIANITY AND CRISIS 39:34-43, March 5, 1979.

Does liberal abortion improve perinatal oucome? by A. G. Philip. JOURNAL OF PERINATAL MEDICINE 6(4):197-205, 1978.

The domestic sterilisation of feeding bottles, by A. Creagh, et al. IRISH MEDICAL JOURNAL 71(13) 452-454, September 29, 1978.

Down's syndrome in Nigeria: pregnancy wastage in mother of Down's syndrome, by R. A. Boroffice. NIGERIAN MEDI-

CAL JOURNAL 9(1):89-92, January, 1979.

Dr. Ira Lubell's cautious crusade is working: sterilization becomes the No. 1 birth control technique, by P. Burstein. PEOPLE 10(24):71, December 11, 1978.

Dreams and verbal reactions of nursing students to abortion, by A. Hurwitz, et al. CURRENT PRACTICE IN OBSTETRIC AND GYNECOLOGIC NURSING 2:232-237, 1978.

Drug-induced pulmonary disease, by E. C. Rosenow. JOURNAL OF PRACTICAL NURSING 29:23-26+, January, 1979.

Drug therapy today: what we know now about oral contraceptives, by M. J. Rodman. RN 42(9):133-146, September, 1979.

Drugs and pregnancy, by S. J. Yaffe. CLINICAL TOXICOLOGY 13(4):523-535, 1978.

Dystocia in heifers following induction of parturition using corticosteroids, by P. G. Jackson. VETERINARY RECORD 104(4):75, January 27, 1979.

EPA bans use of herbicide 2,4,5-T on eve of forest spraying season. PAPER TRADE JOURNAL 163:9, March 30, 1979.

EPA halts most use of herbicide, 2,4,5-T, by J. Smith. SCIENCE 203(4385):1090-1091, March 16, 1979.

The earlier the safer applies to all abortions [interview], by W. Cates, Jr. FAMILY PLANNING PERSPECTIVES 10(4): 243, July-August, 1978.

Early assessment of a tubal plastic (Bleier) clip, by L. Craft, et al. FERTILITY AND STERILITY 32(1):28-30, July, 1979.

Early experimental models of disinfection and sterilization, by S. Selwyn. JOURNAL OF ANTIMICROBIOL CHEMO-THERAPY 5(2):229-230, March, 1979.

Early repeated abortions and karyotypes. A cytogenic study of

80 consecutive couples, by G. Pescia, et al. JOURNAL DE GYNECOLOGIE, OBSTETRIQUE ET BIOLOGIE DE LA REPRODUCTION 8(1):35-38, January-February, 1979.

Early ultrastructural changes in the rat testis after ductuli efferentes ligation, by E. Anton. FERTILITY AND STERILITY 31(2):187-194, February, 1979.

East Asia review, 1976-7: Hong Kong, by P. Lam, et al. STUDIES IN FAMILY PLANNING 9(9):234-235, September, 1978.

—: Indonesia, by S. Surjaningrat, et al. STUDIES IN FAMILY PLANNING 9(9):235-237, September, 1978.

—: Korea (South), by D. W. Han, et al. STUDIES IN FAMILY PLANNING 9(9):238-241, September, 1978.

—: Malaysia, by N. L. Aziz. STUDIES IN FAMILY PLANNING 9(9):41-42, September, 1978.

—: an overview, by S. M. Keeny. STUDIES IN FAMILY PLANNING 9(9):253-254, September, 1978.

—: Philippines, by M. B. Concepción. STUDIES IN FAMILY PLANNING 9(9):243-245, September, 1978.

—: Singapore, by M. Loh. STUDIES IN FAMILY PLANNING 9(9):246-247, September, 1978.

—: Taiwan, by C. M. Wang, et al. STUDIES IN FAMILY PLANNING 9(9):247-250, September, 1978.

—: Thailand, by W. Kolasartsenee, et al. STUDIES IN FAMILY PLANNING 9(9):251-252, September, 1978.

An ecological analysis of the impact of the Supreme Court's 1973 abortion decision, by J. M. Richards. JOURNAL OF APPLIED SOCIAL PSYCHOLOGY 8(1):15-28, January-March, 1978.

An ecological analysis of urban therapeutic abortion rates, by

E. M. Nett. SOCIAL BIOLOGY 25(3):235-242, Fall, 1978.

Econometric model of pronatalist and abortion policies, by
S. P. Coelen, et al. JOURNAL OF POLITICAL ECONOMY
86:1077-1101, December, 1978.

An economic model of contraceptive choice: analysis of family
planning acceptors in Bogotá, by W. J. Kahley, et al. SO-
CIAL BIOLOGY 24(2):135-143, Summer, 1977.

The economical and political consequences of generative behaviour, by W. Maier. GEBURTSHILFE UND FRAUEN-
HEIKUNDE 39(5):410-412, May, 1979.

Ectopic pregnancy by transmigration of sperm after sterilisation with Hulka-Clemens clips, by G. A. Clarke, et al.
BRITISH MEDICAL JOURNAL 1(6164).659-660, March
10, 1979.

Ecotpic pregnancy following tubal sterilizations, by T. A. Athari,
et al. WEST VIRGINIA MEDICAL JOURNAL 74(9):229-
232, September, 1978.

Ecumenical war over abortion; McRae v. Califano lawsuit on the
Medicaid issue. TIME 113:62-63, January 29, 1979.

Education, income, and fertility in Pakistan, by M. A. Khan, et
al. ECONOMIC DEVELOPMENT AND CULTURAL
CHANGE 27:519-547, April, 1979.

Effect of antisera against eggs and zonae pellucidae on fertilization and development of mouse eggs in vivo and in culture,
by Y. Tsunoda, et al. JOURNAL OF REPRODUCTION
AND FERTILITY 54(2):233-238, 1978.

Effect of copper intra-Fallopian tube device on the biochemical
responses of rabbit Fallopian tube, by A. Kushwah, et al.
INDIAN JOURNAL OF EXPERIMENTAL BIOLOGY
16(8):928-929, August, 1978.

Effect of an estrogen-progestin contraceptive preparation on the
enzymatic activity of the pentosephosphate carbohydrate

metabolic pathway and nucleic acid metabolic indices, by
V. V. Korukhov, et al. FARMAKOLOGIYA I TOKSIKOLO-
GIYA 41(5):604-608, September-October, 1978.

Effect of family planning programme on reduction in fertility
in Haryana, 1965-75, by P. A. Kataraki. JOURNAL OF
FAMILY WELFARE 25:20-27, December, 1978.

Effect of the hippocampus on the luteinizing action of the
adenohypophysis and contraceptive activity of megestranol,
by I. V. Tomilina. FARMAKOLOGIYA I TOKSIKOLOGI-
YA 40(3):342-346, 1977.

Effect of hormonal contraception on the fibrin-stabilizing factor
(factor XIII), by M. Brandt, et al. ZENTRALBLATT FUR
GYNAEKOLOGIE 100(17):1089-1092, 1978.

The effect of hormones on the periodontal condition—clinical
studies on 300 female patients, by G. Klinger, et al.
STOMATOLOGIE DER DDR 29(1):7-11, January, 1979.

The effect of indomethacin on the instillation-abortion interval
in rivanol-induced mid-trimester abortion, by A. Olund.
ACTA OBSTETRICIA ET GINECOLOGICA SCANDINA-
VICA 58(1):121-122, 1979.

Effect of infant death on subsequent fertility in Korea and the
role of family planning, by C. B. Park, et al. AMERICAN
JOURNAL OF PUBLIC HEALTH 69:557-565, June, 1979.

Effect of intra-scrotal implants of prostaglandin E2 or F2a on
bloom steroids in the adult male rats, by S. K. Saksena, et al.
INTERNATIONAL JOURNAL OF ANDROLOGY 1(2):
180-187, 1978.

Effect of medical termination of pregnancy on haemoglobin
status, by K. Prema, et al. INDIAN JOURNAL OF MEDI-
CAL RESEARCH 69:605-608, April, 1979.

Effect of oral contraceptive drugs on carbohydrate metabolism
in alloxan diabetic rats, by M. T. Khayyal, et al. JOURNAL
OF THE EGYPTIAN MEDICAL ASSOCIATION 60(7-8):

625-632, 1977.

Effect of oral contraceptive steroids on vitamin A status of women and female rats, by M. S. Bamji, et al. WORLD REVIEW OF NUTRITION AND DIETETICS 31:135-140, 1978.

Effect of oral contraceptive theapy on gingival inflammation in humans, by K. L. Kalkwarf. JOURNAL OF PERIODON-TOLOGY 49(11):560-563, November, 1978.

Effect of oral contraceptives on antithrombin III measurement [letter], by J. T. Brandt, et al. AMERICAN JOURNAL OF CLINICAL PATHOLOGY 71(3):360, March, 1979.

Effect of oral contraceptives on folate economy—a study in female rats, by N. Lakshmaiah, et al. HORMONE AND ME-TABOLIC RESEARCH 11(1):64-67, January, 1979.

The effect of oral contraceptives on vitamin B12 metabolism, by A. M. Shojania, et al. AMERICAN JOURNAL OF OB-STETRICS AND GYNECOLOGY 135(1):129-134, September 1, 1979.

Effect of past abortions and the sequence of gestations on the course of the next pregnancy and labor as well as the state-at-delivery, maturity, dystrophia and mortality rate of the newborn infants, by R. Osuch-Jaczewska, et al. GINE-KOLOGIA POLSKA 50(2):127-133, February, 1979.

Effect of racemic and S(+) alpha-chlorohydrin-1-phosphate on glyceraldehyde-3-phosphate dehydrogenase in relation to its contraceptive action, by R. W. Fitzpatrick, et al. CON-TRACEPTION 18(5):477-483, November, 1978.

Effect of salt consumption, psychological stress and contraceptives on the course of blood pressure in rats with hereditary spontaneous hypertension (SH rats), by A. Samizadeh, et al. VERHANDLUNGEN DER DEUTSCHEN GESELLSCHAFT FUR INNERE MEDIZIN (84):803-806, 1978.

The effect of sexual hormones on skin graft survival, thymic morphology and serum levels of glycoproteins and albumin in mice, by J. Kaden, et al. ACTA BIOLOGICA ET MEDICA GERMANICA 37(8):1247-1253, 1978.

Effect of surveillance on the number of hysterectomies in the province of Saskatchewan, by F. J. Dyck, et al. NEW ENGLAND JOURNAL OF MEDICINE 296:1326+, June 9, 1977.

Effect of synthetic and natural sex steroids on X-chromatin, by A. Chakravarty, et al. INDIAN JOURNAL OF MEDICAL RESEARCH 68:785-789, November, 1978.

The effect of termination of pregnancy on maturity of subsequent pregnancy, by G. J. Ratten, et al. MEDICAL JOURNAL OF AUSTRALIA 1(11):479-480, June 2, 1979.

The effect of tobacco and alcohol on pregnancy course and child development, by K. Knorr. BULLETIN DER SCHWEIZERISCHEN AKADEMIE DER MEDIZINISCHEN WISSENSCHAFTEN 35(1-3):137-146, March, 1979.

Effect of treatment of habitual and spontaneous abortion using Gestanon on birth weight, by S. Andjelković. SRPSKI ARHIV ZA CELOKUPNO LEKARSTVO 106(1):53-55, 1978.

Effect of the venereal diseases epidemic on the incidence of ectopic pregnancy—implications for the evaluation of contraceptives, by J. Urquhart. CONTRACEPTION 19(5):455-480, May, 1979.

Effectiveness of abortion as birth control, by S. J. Williams, et al. SOCIAL BIOLOGY 22(1):23-33, Spring, 1975.

The effectiveness of non-physicians as providers of family planning services, by B. N. Bibb. JOGN 8(3):137-143, May-June, 1979.

Effectiveness of paraformaldehyde foam in continuous disinfection of poultry bedding and dried liquid waste of pigs, by A. Fiser. VETERINARNI MEDICINA 24(1):37-47, January, 1979.

Effectiveness of sex information dissemination by selected planned parenthood clinics, by G. D. Pippin. DISSERTATION ABSTRACTS INTERNATIONAL 39(7-A):4070, January, 1979.

The effects and side-effects of the intra-cervical application of prostaglandin F-2 alpha during early pregnancy, by S. Sievers, et al. GEBURTSHILFE UND FRAUENHEILKUNDE 38(10):800-804, October, 1978.

Effects of anesthesia [letter]. SCIENCE 203(4382):705, February 23, 1979.

Effects of antiprogesterone on pregnancy: I. Midpregnancy, by A. I. Csapo, et al. AMERICAN JOURNAL OF OBSTETRICS AND GYNECOLOGY 133(2):176-183, 1979.

Effects of a combined oestrogen-progestin preparation on gastric acid and pepsin secretion, serum gastrin concentration and biliary secretion of bile acids, phospholipids, and cholesterol in the cat, by B. H. Hirst, et al. BRITISH JOURNAL OF PHARMACOLOGY 65(1):87-95, January, 1979.

Effects of contraceptive pills in the field of otorhinolaryngology, by H. A. Kley, et al. ARCHIVES OF OTO-RHINO-LARYNGOLOGY 219(2):475-476, November 22, 1978.

Effects of cyclic AMP altering drugs on endotoxin-induced termination of pregnancy, by R. Shaw, Jr., et al. RESEARCH COMMUNICATIONS IN CHEMICAL PATHOLOGY AND PHARMACOLOGY 24(1):49-56, April, 1979.

The effects of familial support systems on Black mothers' child-rearing attitudes and behaviors, and on their children's competence, by C. A. Trufant. DISSERTATION ABSTRACTS INTERNATIONAL 39(1-B):450-451, July, 1978.

The effects of husband and wife education on family planning in rural Turkey, by N. H. Fisek, et al. STUDIES IN FAMILY PLANNING 9(10-11):280-285, October-November, 1978.

Effects of immunization with the beta-subunit of ovine luteinizing hormone on corpus luteum function in the rhesus monkey, by R. B. Thau, et al. FERTILITY AND STERILITY 31(2):200-204, February, 1979.

The effects of longacting paracervical block anesthesia on the abortifacient efficacy of intra-amniotic PGF2alpha and hypertonic saline, by M. I. Ragab, et al. ACTA OBSTETRICIA ET GYNECOLOGICA SCANDINAVICA 57(4):327-331, 1978.

Effects of manufacturing oral contraceptives on blood clotting, by L. Poller, et al. BRITISH MEDICAL JOURNAL 1(6180): 1761-1762, June 30, 1979.

Effects of a new oral progestagen on pituitary ovarian function, by L. Viinikka, et al. CONTRACEPTION 17(1):19, January, 1978.

The effects of a once-a-week steroid contraceptive (R2323) on lipid and carbohydrate metabolism in women during three months of use, by W. N. Spellacy, et al. FERTILITY AND STERILITY 30(3):289-292, September, 1978.

Effects of oral contraceptives and pregnancy on melanomas [letter], by A. B. Lerner, et al. NEW ENGLAND JOURNAL OF MEDICINE 301(1):47, July 5, 1979.

Effects of oral contraceptives of cancerogenesis of cervical epithelium, by H. J. Soost, et al. ARCHIV FUER GESCHWULSTFORSCHUNG 48(4):345-355, 1978.

Effects of oral contraceptives on laboratory test results. MEDICAL LETTER ON DRUGS AND THERAPEUTICS 21(13): 54-56, June 29, 1979.

Effects of oral contraceptives on nutritional status, by L. K. Massey, et al. AMERICAN FAMILY PHYSICIAN 19(1): 119-123, January, 1979.

Effects of oral contraceptives on zinc and copper levels in human plasma and endometrium during the menstrual cycle, by

E. J. Sing, et al. ARCHIVES OF GYNECOLOGY 226(4): 303-306, December 29, 1978.

The effects of student practice on several types of learning in a functional marriage course, by M. R. Jensen, et al. FAMILY COORDINATOR 28(2):217-227, April, 1979.

Effects of ultraviolet radiation as a sterilizing agent on synthetic dyes used in Poland for drug coloring. II. Azo dye derivatives of naphtionic acid, by Z. Wójcik, et al. ACTA POLONIAE PHARMACEUTICA 35(6):649-654, 1978.

The effects on sexual response and mood after sterilization of women taking long-term oral contraception: results of a double-blind cross-over study, by J. Leeton, et al. AUSTRALIAN AND NEW ZEALAND JOURNAL OF OBETETRICS AND GYNAECOLOGY 18(3):194-197, August, 1978.

Efficacy and acceptability of intravenously administered sulprostone, a tissue-selective prostaglandin-E2 derivative, for induction of first-trimeter abortion, by B. Schuessler, et al. CONTRACEPTION 19(1):29-38, January, 1979.

Efficacy of a group crisis-counseling program for men who accompany women seeking abortions, by R. H. Gordon. AMERICAN JOURNAL OF COMMUNITY PSYCHOLOGY 6(3):239-246, June, 1978.

Efficiency in the use of contraception in the voluntary family planning program of the Institute Mexicano del Seguro Social, by J. García Peña, et al. SPM 20(4):425-434, July-August, 1978.

Efficiency of cold sterilizing agent for endodontic procedure, by R. V. Suchde, et al. JOURNAL OF DENTAL RESEARCH 58(2):670, February, 1979.

Electronmicroscopic findings in a malignant hepatoma after oral contraceptives, by J. Hatzibujas, et al. ZEITSCHRIFT FUR GASTROENTEROLOGIE 16(10):616-624, October, 1978.

Electrophysiology of the rabbit oviduct following tubal microsurgery, by D. R. Archer, et al. FERTILITY AND STERIL-
ITY 31(4):423-427, April, 1979.

Electrosurgery in laparoscopy, by F. W. Harris. JOURNAL OF
REPRODUCTIVE MEDICINE 21(1):48-52, July, 1978.

The embryo and the soul [letter on R. Gordis's "Abortion"], by
J. Cooper; Reply by R. Gordis. MIDSTREAM 25:78-79,
January, 1979.

Embryonal rhabdomyosarcoma. A case report, by A. A. Visser,
et al. SOUTH AFRICAN MEDICAL JOURNAL 54(2):70-
71, July 8, 1978.

Emergence of countercyclical U.S. fertility, by W. P. Butz, et al.
AMERICAN ECONOMIC REVIEW 69:318-328, June, 1979.

Emotional distress in morning-after pill patients, by G. R. Huggins, et al. ACTA OBSTETRICIA ET GYNECOLOGICA
SCANDINAVICA 58(1):65-68, 1979.

Emotional reaction to interval and postpartum sterilization, by
A. Aribarg, et al. INTERNATIONAL JOURNAL OF GY-
NAECOLOGY AND OBSTETRICS 16(1):40-41, 1978.

The end of "Catholic" fertility, by E. F. Jones, et al. DEMO-
GRAPHY 16:209-218, May, 1979.

End-to-end tubal anastomosis using an absorbable stent, by
A. H. Ansari. FERTILITY AND STERILITY 32(2):197-
201, August, 1979.

Endocervical heterotopia by fetal implants during induced abortion [letter], by M. Trojani, et al. NOUVELLE PRESSE
MEDICALE 8(7):521, February 10, 1979.

Endocrinologic aspects of oral contraception, by A. B. Little.
JOURNAL OF REPRODUCTIVE MEDICINE 21(5 suppl):
247-249, November, 1978.

Endocrinology of reproduction in the female beagle dog and its significance in mammary gland tumorigenesis, by K. J. Gräf, et al. ACTA ENDOCRINOLOGICA (222):1-34, 1979.

Endometrial adenocarcinoma: in estrogen, oral contraceptive and nonhormone users, by J. G. Blythe, et al. GYNECOLO- GIC ONCOLOGY 7(2):199-205, April, 1979.

England: women's right to choose, by J. Rosiello. OFF OUR BACKS 8(3):3, March, 1978.

Enhanced retention of metals from nutritional supplementation in oral contraception users, by E. B. Dawson, et al. AMERI- CAN JOURNAL OF CLINICAL NUTRITION 32:949, April, 1979.

An epidemiologic study of breast cancer and benign breast neo- plasias in relation to the oral contraceptive and estrogen use, by B. Ravnihar, et al. EUROPEAN JOURNAL OF CANCER 15(4):395-405, April, 1979.

Epidemiological analysis and reproductive characteristics of in- complete abortion patients in Khartoum, the Sudan, by H. Rushwan. JOURNAL OF BIOSOCIAL SCIENCE 11(1):67- 75, January, 1979.

An epidemiological study of oral contraceptives and breast can- cer, by M. P. Vessey, et al. BRITISH MEDICAL JOURNAL 1(6180):1757-1760, June 30, 1979.

Epidemiology of hepatocellular adenoma. The role of oral con- traceptive use, by J. B. Brooks, et al. JAMA 242(7):644- 648, August 17, 1979.

Epididymal extravasation following vasectomy as a cause for failure of vasectomy reversal, by S. J. Silber. FERTILITY AND STERILITY 31(3):309-315, March, 1979.

Equal access to legal abortion [letter], by W. Pick. NEW ENG- LAND JOURNAL OF MEDICINE 301(6):335, August 9, 1979.

An erogonomic appraisal of the use and functional efficiency of condom urinals in the male patient with spinal cord paralysis, by S. D. Lawson, et al. PARAPLEGIA 16(3):317-321, November, 1978.

An estimate of the effect of abortions on the stillbirth rate, by R. J. Grandy. JOURNAL OF BIOSOCIAL SCIENCE 11(2): 173-178, April, 1979.

Estimation of births averted due to induced abortions, by K. B. Pathak, et al. JOURNAL OF BIOSOCIAL SCIENCE 10: 361-366, October, 1978.

Estrogen and progestogen binding site concentrations in human endometrium and cervix throughout the menstrual cycle and in tissue from women taking oral contraceptives, by B. M. Sanborn, et al. JOURNAL OF STEROID BIOCHEMISTRY 9(10):951-955, October, 1978.

Ethical issues in genetic intervention, by C. C. Sammons. SOCIAL WORK 23:237-242, May, 1978.

Ethics and amniocentesis for fetal sex identification, by J. C. Fletcher. NEW ENGLAND JOURNAL OF MEDICINE 301(10):550-553, September 6, 1979.

Ethnic differences in family planning acceptance in rural Guatemala, by J. T. Bertrand. STUDIES IN FAMILY PLANNING 10:238-245, August-September, 1979.

Ethylene oxide update. . .a sterilizing agent for heat- and moisture-sensitive items, by N. E. Danielson. SCORE 4:12-16, Summer, 1979.

Etiopathogenetic aspects and therapy of rental cortical necrosis. Report of a case, by G. Sorba, et al. MINERVA ANESTESIOLOGICA 45(1-2):55-66, January-February, 1979.

Evaluating abortion counselling, by R. J. Marcus. DIMENSIONS IN HEALTH SERVICE 56(8):16-18, August, 1979.

Evaluating acceptance strategies for timing of postpartum contraception, by R. G. Potter, et al. STUDIES IN FAMILY

PLANNING 10(5):151, May, 1979.

Evaluation of a balloon dilator before second-trimester abortion by vacuum curettage, by P. G. Stubblefield, et al. AMERICAN JOURNAL OF OBSTETRICS AND GYNECOLOGY 135(2):199-201, September 15, 1979.

Evaluation of the carcinogenic effects of estrogens, progestins and oral contraceptives on cervix, uterus and ovary of animals and man, by V. A. Drill. ARCHIVES OF TOXICOLOGY (2):59-94, 1979.

An evaluation of cytogenetic analysis as a primary tool in the assessment of recurrent pregnancy wastage, by M. T. Mennuti, et al. OBSTETRICS AND GYNECOLOGY 52(3):308-313, September, 1978.

Evaluation of 496 menstrual regulation and abortion patients in Calcutta, by D. Lilaram, et al. INTERNATIONAL JOURNAL OF GYNECOLOGY AND OBSTETRICS 15(6):503-506, 1978.

Evaluation of local contraceptives, by E. B. Connell. ZAHNAERZTLICHE MITTEILUNGEN 69(15):919, August 1, 1979.

An evaluation of male contraceptive acceptance in rural Ghana, by P. Lamptey, et al. STUDIES IN FAMILY PLANNING 9(8):222, August, 1978.

Evaluation of polymer flock and metal alloy intra-tubal device in pigtail monkeys, by R. M. Richart, et al. CONTRACEPTION 18(5):459-468, November, 1978.

The evaluation of sexual health services in a medical setting, by J. P. Held, et al. JOURNAL OF SEX AND MARITAL THERAPY 3(4):256-264, Winter, 1977.

Evaluation of soft contact lens disinfection in the home environment, by R. E. Pitts, et al. ARCHIVES OF OPHTHALMOLOGY 97(3):470-472, March, 1979.

Evaluation of various liver function and blood coagulation tests in early stages of treatment with oral contraceptives, by C. Del Vecchi-Blanco, et al. CLINICA TERAPEUTICA 87(3): 233-242, November 15, 1978.

Everything you've always wanted to know about contraceptives; excerpt from Ms. medical guide to a woman's health, by C. W. Cooke, et al. MS MAGAZINE 8:84+, September, 1979.

Examination of hormonal contraceptives by enzyme induction, by G. Klinger, et al. ZENTRALBLATT FUR GYNAE-KOLOGIE 101(5):302-305, 1979.

Examination of the hypophysis-thyroid system feedback in recent pregnancy and following its interruption, by W. Hartwig, et al. GINEKOLOGIA POLSKA 50(5):431-436, May, 1979.

Experience of abortion, by D. D. Miller, et al. AMERICA 140:510-512, June 23, 1979.

Experience report on Austria's first operating room using the ALLLO-PRO-laminar-flow-system, by A. Zängl, et al. WIENER MEDIZINISCHE WOCHENSCHRIFT 128(15): 489-491, August 15, 1978.

Experience with the conservative treatment of intrauterine adhesions in women suffering from abortion, by N. M. Pobedinskii, et al. AKUSHERSTVO I GINEKOLOGIIA (4):20-21, April, 1979.

Experience with early induced abortion, the socalled 'menstrual extraction' method, by P. Voskuijl, et al. NEDERLANDS TIJDSCHRIFT VOOR GENEESKUNDE 122(41):1551-1554, October 14, 1978.

Experience with midtrimester abortion, by I. R. Pahl, et al. OBSTETRICS AND GYNECOLOGY 53(5):587-591, May, 1979.

Experience with a new low dose oral contraceptive: norgestimate & ethinyl estradiol, by B. Rubio-Lotvin, et al. ACTA

EUROPAEA FERTILITATIS 9(1):1-6, March, 1978.

Experience with vasovasostomy: operative technique and results, by I. L. Jenkins, et al. BRITISH JOURNAL OF UROLOGY 51(1):43-45, February, 1979.

Experiences with early induced abortion, the so-called 'overtime treatment' [letter] . NEDERLANDS TIJDSCHRIFT VOOR GENEESKUNDE 123(2):57-58, January 13, 1979.

Experimental production of corynebacterium pyogenes abortion in sheep, by P. B. Addo, et al. CORNELL VETERINARIAN 69:20-32, January, 1979.

Experiments on prevention of the endotoxin-abortifacient effect by radiodetoxified endotoxin pretreatment in rats, by T. Csordás, et al. GYNECOLOGIC AND OBSTETRIC INVESTIGATION 9(1):57-64, 1978.

Experts still preach sterilization, by C. Douglas-Home. TIMES (London) December 14, 1979, p. 9.

An exploration of factors affecting referral of adolescent girls to a planned parenthood clinic, by S. E. Osterbusch. DISSERTATION ABSTRACTS INTERNATIONAL 38(11-A): 6943, May, 1978.

An extended expectancy-value approach to contraceptive alternatives, by J. B. Cohen, et al. JOURNAL OF POPULATION 1(1):22-41, Spring, 1978.

An extension of the waiting time distribution of first conceptions, by K. B. Pathak. JOURNAL OF BIOSOCIAL SCIENCE 10:231-234, July, 1978.

Extent of demand for exclusive private family planning clinics among urban middle classes, by G. Narayana. JOURNAL OF FAMILY WELFARE 24:52-57, December, 1977.

Extraamniotic induction of abortion with a new prostaglandin E-2 derivative, by U. Gethmann, et al. FORTSCHRITTE DER MEDIZIN 96(35):1771-1773, September 21, 1978.

Extra-amniotic prostaglandin for mid-trimester abortion. MEDI-CAL WORLD NEWS 19:32+, December 11, 1978.

FDA acts on Depo-Provera. SPOKESWOMAN 8(11):6 May, 1978.

FDA criticizes contraceptives ads. PREVENTION 30:204, October, 1978.

FDA revises birth pill warning. SPOKESWOMAN 8(9):7, March, 1978.

FDA says it is concerned. SPOKESWOMAN 9(2):8, August, 1978.

Factors associated with ex-nuptial birth, by D. M. Fergusson, et al. NEW ZEALAND MEDICAL JOURNAL 89(633):248-250, April 11, 1979.

Factors associated with high and low family planning acceptance in Karnataka State, by S. S. Yadav, et al. JOURNAL OF FAMILY WELFARE 24:3-19, December, 1977.

Factors associated with planned and unplanned nuptial births, by D. M. Fergusson, et al. NEW ZEALAND MEDICAL JOURNAL 88(617):89-92, August 9, 1978.

Factors involved in the acceptance of voluntary female sterilization among Indians in Natal, by M. E. Hampson. SOUTH AFRICAN MEDICAL JOURNAL 55(18):719-721, April 28, 1979.

Factors related to the intention to have additional children in the United States: a reanalysis of data from the 1965 and 1970 national fertility studies, by C. F. Lee, et al. DEMOGRAPHY 15(3):337-344, August, 1978.

The facts of life. CONGRESSIONAL MONTHLY 46:13, April, 1979.

Failure of laparoscopic sterilization [letter], by H. Puder. GE-BURTSHILFE UND FRAUENHEILKUNDE 38(12):1099,

84

December, 1978.

Failure of withdrawal bleeding during combined oral contraceptive therapy: 'amenorrhoea on the pill', by M. D. Gillmer, et al. CONTRACEPTION 18(5):507-515, November, 1978.

Failures following fimbriectomy: a further report, by K. G. Metz. FERTILITY AND STERILITY 30(3):269-273, September, 1978.

Faith and order's call to ecumenical debate, by R. J. Neuhaus. CHRISTIAN CENTURY 96:205-206, February 28, 1979.

Falope ring application via culdoscopy, by S. M. Lim, et al. INTERNATIONAL JOURNAL OF GYNAECOLOGY AND OBSTETRICS 16(5):430-432, March-April, 1979.

Familial dicentric translocation t(13;18)(p13;p11.2) ascertained by recurrent miscarriages, by A. Daniel, et al. JOURNAL OF MEDICAL GENETICS 16(1):73-75, February, 1979.

Familial porphyria cutanea tarda in a patient with retinitis pigmentosa, by D. Willerson, Jr., et al. ANNALS OF OPHTHALMOLOGY 11(3):409-411, March, 1979.

Families question planning, by G. Mkangi. GUARDIAN p. 19, June 11, 1979.

Family allowance and family planning in Chile, by S. J. Plank. AMERICAN JOURNAL OF PUBLIC HEALTH 68(10):989-994, October 1978.

Family health and family planning in medical education, by J. F. Martin. TROPICAL DOCTOR 9(2):85-88+, April, 1979.

Family planning, by H. Dutly. KRANKENPFLEGE 71(7):296-305, July, 1979.

Family planning agencies and the mentally retarded, by J. L. Cohen. THE JOURNAL FOR SPECIAL EDUCATORS 15:3-9+, Fall, 1978+.

Family planning and abortion policy in the United States, by K. H. Gould. SOCIAL SERVICE REVIEW 53:452-463, September, 1979.

Family planning and contraception. NOT MAN APART 8(6): 11, April, 1978.

Family planning and family health, by J. F. Martin. INTERNATIONAL NURSING REVIEW 25(6):172-174, November-December, 1978.

Family planning and the private primary care physician, by P. Tschetter. FAMILY PLANNING PERSPECTIVES 10(6): 350-353, November-December, 1978.

Family planning and sex education: the Chinese approach, by S. E. Fraser. COMPARATIVE EDUCATION 13:15-28, March, 1977.

Family Planning Association, by B. Górnicki. PEDIATRIA POLSKA 54(6):633-637, June, 1979.

Family planning availability and contraceptive practice, by G. Rodríguez. FAMILY PLANNING PERSPECTIVES 11(1): 51-70, January-February, 1979.

Family planning campaign halted; India, by A. S. Abraham. TIMES EDUCATIONAL SUPPLEMENT 3305:15, November 3, 1978.

Family planning course for nurses and midwives in the Philippines, by A. Cerdinio. IPPF MEDICAL BULLETIN 12(5): 2-3, October, 1978.

Family planning: a crucial programme, by A. B. Wadia. JOURNAL OF FAMILY WELFARE 24:58-65, December, 1977.

Family planning. Current problems with crucial reference to the preparation and education of obstetrical nursing staff, by L. B. Sassi. PROFESSIONI INFERMIERISTICHE 32(2):65-66, April-June, 1979.

Family planning democratized, by M. Manisoff. AMERICAN JOURNAL OF NURSING 75(10):1660-1666, October, 1975.

Family planning for the mentally ill [letter], by H. Grunebaum. AMERICAN JOURNAL OF PSYCHIATRY 136(4):461-462, April, 1979.

Family planning in big town conditions depending on the birthplace of the parents, by I. Dimitrov. FOLIA MEDICA 20(1):35-41, 1978.

Family planning in four Latin American countries—knowledge, use and unmet need: some findings from the world fertility survey, by J. W. Brackett. INTERNATIONAL FAMILY PLANNING PERSPECTIVES AND DIGEST 4:116-123, Winter, 1978.

Family planning in India: living with frustration, by J. Rowley. POPULI 5(4):7, 1978.

Family planning in Japan: a comparison between successful and unsuccessful couples, by C. M. Lu, et al. INTERNATIONAL JOURNAL OF HEALTH EDUCATION 21(3):174-182, 1978.

Family planning in the practice of midwifery in England and Wales, by S. M. Clark. JOURNAL OF NURSE-MIDWIFERY 24:11-17, May-June, 1979.

Family planning in Virginia: the role of public health, by H. D. Gabel. VIRGINIA MEDICINE 106(5):393-394+, May, 1979.

Family planning: the Irish solution, by C. Walter. SPECTATOR p. 12, March 31, 1979.

Family planning knowledge, attitude and practice in the rural areas of Sarawak, by C. K. Lam. JOURNAL OF BIOSOCIAL SCIENCE 11:315-324, July, 1979.

Family planning nursing in Britain, by M. Pollock. IPPF MEDI-

CAL BULLETIN 12:1-2, October, 1978.

Family planning policies: a 1979 people wallchart, by N. Fincancioglu, et al. PEOPLE 6:1 folded sheet insert no. 2, 1979.

Family planning program in Korea, by J. M. Yang. YONSEI MEDICAL JOURNAL 18(1):64-74, 1977.

Family planning services for indigent women and girls, by K. T. Sung. HEALTH AND SOCIAL WORK 3(4):152-172, November, 1978.

The family planning success story, by M. Potts. PEOPLE 6(2):14, 1979.

Family planning training: a network program and sample instructional materials, by K. Finseth, et al. IMPROVING HUMAN PERFORMANCE QUARTERLY 7(1):217-225, Spring, 1978.

Family planning visits to private physicians, by B. K. Cypress. FAMILY PLANNING PERSPECTIVES 11:234-236, July-August, 1979.

The family, sex and marriage in England 1500-1800 [critique of Lawrence Stone], by A. MacFarlane. HISTORY AND THEORY 18(1):103-126, 1979.

Family size, contraceptive practice and fertility intentions in England and Wales, 1967-1975, by A. Cartwright. FAMILY PLANNING PERSPECTIVES 11:128-131+, March-April, 1979.

Family type, family resources, and fertility among Iranian peasant women, by A. Aghajanian. SOCIAL BIOLOGY 25: 205-209, Fall, 1978.

Family violence explored in newly-released books, by J. R. Nash. LAW ENFORCEMENT NEWS 4(22):9, December 25, 1978.

Fanatical abortion fight. TIME 114:26-27, July 9, 1979.

Fatal air embolism during an attempt at criminal abortion, by M. Srch. CESKOLOVENSKA GYNEKOLOGIE 43(8):615-618, September, 1978.

"Fathers United" fights abortion (group in favor of father's rights in deciding on abortion), by J. Beck. CATHOLIC DIGEST 4:45, January, 1978.

Fay Wattleton has been appointed. NOW 11(3):2, March, 1978.

Feasibility of the randomized response technique in rural Ethiopia, by L. P. Chow, et al. AMERICAN JOURNAL OF PUBLIC HEALTH 69:273-276, March, 1979.

Features of liver damage caused by 17-alpha-alkyl-substituted anabolic steroids, by P. Lovisetto, et al. MINERVA MEDICA 70(11):769-790, March 3, 1979.

Febrile spontaneous abortion and the IUD, by R. J. Kim-Farley, et al. CONTRACEPTION 18(6):561-570, December, 1978.

Female sexual attitudes and the rise of illegitimacy: a case study, by C. Fairchilds. JOURNAL OF INTERDISCIPLINARY HISTORY 8:627-668, September, 1978.

Female sterilization, by J. F. Hulka. SOUTH AFRICAN MEDICAL JOURNAL 55(4):118-124, January 27, 1979.

Female sterilization in small camp settings in rural India, by R. Bhatt, et al. STUDIES IN FAMILY PLANNING 9:39-43, February-March, 1978.

Female sterilization using an elasticated silicone ring, by D. G. Cave. MEDICAL JOURNAL OF AUSTRALIA 1(12):577-578, June 16, 1979.

Feminism, socialism and abortion, by C. Roberts, et al. WOMEN'S STUDIES INTERNATIONAL QUARTERLY 1(1): 3-14, 1978.

Fertility and child mortality over the life cycle: aggregated and individual evidence, by T. P. Schultz. AMERICAN ECONOMIC REVIEW 68:208-215, May, 1978.

Fertility and demographic structures—hypothesis on evolution of fertility since 1940, by H. Leridon. POPULATION 33:441-447, March-April, 1978.

Fertility and possibilities of anticonception in adolescence, by F. Havránek. CESKOSLOVENSKA GYNEKOLOGIE 44(4):304-308, May, 1979.

Fertility awareness and sexuality, by W. May. LINACRE QUARTERLY 46:20-26, February, 1979.

Fertility awareness as a natural birth control, by C. Berry. MEDICAL SELF-CARE (4):24-29, 1978.

Fertility control and family planning in the United States of America, by R. W. Rochat, et al. BOLETIN DE LA OFICINA SANITARIA PANAMERICANA 85(2):115-127, August, 1978.

Fertility control: what's ahead?—symposium, by C. R. Garcia, et al. CONTEMPORARY OB/GYN 13(1):54, January, 1979.

Fertility desires and child mortality experience among Guatemalan women, by A. R. Pebley, et al. STUDIES IN FAMILY PLANNING 10(4):129-136, April, 1979.

Fertility effect of seasonal migration and seasonal variation in fecundability: test of a useful approximation under more general conditions, by J. Bongaarts, et al. DEMOGRAPHY 16:475-480, August, 1979.

Fertility effects of family planning programs: a methodological review, by J. D. Forrest, et al. SOCIAL BIOLOGY 25:145-163, Summer, 1978.

Fertility in psychiatric outpatients, by W. A. Burr, et al. HOSPITAL AND COMMUNITY PSYCHIATRY 30:527-531,

August, 1979.

Fertility preferences and social exchange theory, by L. J. Beckman. JOURNAL OF APPLIED SOCIAL PSYCHOLOGY 9:147-169, March-April, 1979.

Fertility regulating agents from plants. WHO CHRONICLES 33(2):58-59, February, 1979.

Fertility regulation in the male, by D. M. de Kretser. WHO BULLETIN 56(3):53-60, 1978.

Fertility related attitudes of minority mothers with large and small families, by M. W. Linn, et al. JOURNAL OF APPLIED SOCIAL PSYCHOLOGY 8:1-14, January-March, 1978.

Fertility rights, by M. Potts. GUARDIAN p. 11, April 25, 1979.

Fertility, schooling, and the economic contribution of children in rural India: an econometric analysis, by M. R. Rosenzweig, et al. ECONOMETRICA 45:1065-1079, July, 1977.

Festschrift in honour of C. A. Hoare on the occasion of his 85th birthday. JOURNAL OF TROPICAL MEDICINE AND HYGIENE 81(8):141, August, 1978.

Fetal diagnosis and abortion [30 min], by R. L. Shinn. THESIS THEOLOGICAL CASSETTES 10(1):   , February, 1979.

Fetal loss, twinning and birth weight after oral contraceptive use, by K. J. Rothman. NEW ENGLAND JOURNAL OF MEDICINE 297:468-471, September 1, 1977.

Fetal transplants could resolve abortion conflict, by R. McClory. NATIONAL CATHOLIC REPORTER 16:1+, October 26, 1979.

The fetus as parasite and mushroom; Judith Jarvais Thompson's defense of abortion, by G. Meilaender. LINACRE QUARTERLY 46:126-135, May, 1979.

Fetus display upsets abortion leaders' talk, by M. Winiarski.
NATIONAL CATHOLIC REPORTER 15:5, February 23,
1979.

Fetus papyraceus causing dystocia: inability to detect blighted
twin antenatally, by P. C. Leppert, et al. OBSTETRICS
AND GYNECOLOGY 54(3):381-383, September, 1979.

Fiberoptic bronchoscope-related outbreak of infection with
Pseudomonas [letter], by S. A. Hussain. CHEST 74(4):
483, October, 1978.

Fibrocystic breast disease in oral contraceptive users: a his-
topathological evaluation of epithelial atypia. NEW ENG-
LAND JOURNAL OF MEDICINE 299:381-385, August
24, 1978.

(15S)-15 methyl prostaglandin F2 alpha levels in amniotic fluid
and blood in second trimester abortions, by L. Weinstein, et
al. SOUTHERN MEDICAL JOURNAL 72(9):1159-1160,
September, 1979.

Fighting for the right to choose: the bishops' threat to Maltese
women, by J. Condon. NEW STATESMAN p. 295, August
31, 1979.

Filling family planning gaps, by B. Stokes. POPULATION RE-
PORTS (20):J369-J389, September, 1978.

Final sterilization rules issued. SPOKESWOMAN 9(6):5, December, 1978.

Final weapon in war on native peoples, by A. Carmen. WIN
MAGAZINE 14(43):4, December 28, 1978.

Finally resolving abortion issue. Congress votes money for colleges; 1979 appropriations, by A. C. Roark. CHRONICLE
OF HIGHER EDUCATION 17:17, October 16, 1978.

Fine structure and cytochemistry of the morphogenesis of round-
headed human sperm, by L. Castellani, et al. ARCHIVES OF
ANDROLOGY 1(4):291-297, September, 1978.

First trimester abortion by vacuum aspiration: interphysician variability, by E. R. Miller, et al. INTERNATIONAL JOURNAL OF GYNAECOLOGY AND OBSTETRICS 16(2):144-149, 1978-1979.

Fit for duty: pregnancy. Adaptation, by A. L. Brekken. AIR FORCE TIMES 40:34, October 8, 1979.

5-hydroxytryptamine (serotecin), copper and ceruloplasmin plasma concentrations in spontaneous abortion, by B. A. Bassiouni, et al. EUROPEAN JOURNAL OF OBSTETRICS, GYNECOLOGY AND REPRODUCTIVE BIOLOGY 9(2): 81-88, 1979.

$5 million lawsuit over experimental contraceptive. OFF OUR BACKS 8(11):7, December, 1978.

Five submit to sterilization to avoid losing their jobs, by P. Kassel. NEW DIRECTIONS FOR WOMEN 8:1+, January, 1979.

Focal nodular hyperplasia of the liver and contraceptive steroids, by F. B. St. Omer, et al. ACTA HEPATOGASTROEN-TEROLOGICA 25(4):319-321, August, 1978.

Focal nodular hyperplasia of the liver and oral contraceptives, by R. Kinch, et al. AMERICAN JOURNAL OF OBSTETRICS AND GYNECOLOGY 132(7):717-727, December 1, 1978.

Foetal remnants in the uterus and their relation to other uterine heterotopia, by S. P. Tyagi, et al. HISTOPATHOLOGY 3(4):339-345, July, 1979.

Follow-up observation of the so-called normophasic method of hormonal contraception, by H. Fritzsche, et al. ZEITSCHRIFT FUR AERZTLICHE FORTBILDUNG 73(3): 113-114, February 1, 1979.

Follow-up of 50 adolescent girls 2 years after abortion, by H. Cvejic, et al. CANADIAN MEDICAL ASSOCIATION JOURNAL 116(1):44-46, 1977.

Follow-up of vasectomy using medical record linkage, by M. J. Goldacre, et al. AMERICAN JOURNAL OF EPIDEMIOLOGY 108(3):177-180, 1978.

For whose benefit are mentally retarded people being sterilized? by D. Robillard. CANADIAN MEDICAL ASSOCIATION JOURNAL 120(11):1433-1434+, June 9, 1979.

"Forced pregnancy" group holds convention. NOW 11(9):12, August, 1978.

Former pill users: healthier babies? MEDICAL WORLD NEWS 19:32, June 12, 1978.

Fourth international conference on voluntary sterilization, by L. C. Landman. FAMILY PLANNING PERSPECTIVES 11:241-247, July-August, 1979.

The fractured conjugal family: a comparison of married and divorced dyads, by P. C. McKenry, et al. JOURNAL OF DIVORCE 1(4):329-339, Summer, 1978.

The French bishops on abortion, by J. O'Leary. FURROW 30:353-360, June, 1979.

Frequency of endocrine disorders in repeated spontaneous abortion, by A. M. D. Serban. REVUE ROUMAINE DE MEDECINE. SERIE ENDOCRINOLOGIE 16(1):55-60, 1978.

Frieman v. Ashcroft, 443 F Supp 1390. JOURNAL OF FAMILY LAW 17:153-157, November, 1978.

From China: new pill for men, by D. Fortino. HARPER'S BAZAAR (3211):129, June, 1979.

From generation to generaton: fathers-to-be in transition, by L. Barnhill, et al. FAMILY COORDINATOR 28(2):229-235, April, 1979.

From here to 2000: a look at the population problem, by J. F. Kantner. JOHNS HOPKINS MEDICAL JOURNAL 144(1): 18-24, January, 1979.

From one generation to the next: changes in fertility, family size prefernces, and family planning in an Indian state between 1951 and 1975, by K. Srinivasan, et al. STUDIES IN FAMILY PLANNING 9(10-11):258-271, October-November, 1978.

Frontlines: no abortions for soldiers (DOD hoped for defeat of recent anti-abortion legislation). MOTHER JONES 4:8, January, 1979.

Full story of Chicago abortion scandal untold, pro-life leaders say, by C. Anthony. OUR SUNDAY VISITOR 67:1, November 26, 1978.

Functional luteolysis in the pseudopregnant rat: effects of prostaglandin F2a and 16-aryloxy prostaglandin F2a in vitro, by A. K. Hall, et al. JOURNAL OF ENDOCRINOLOGY 81(1):157-166, 1979.

Furor in New York; for archdiocese, contract may dull abortion dilemma's horns, by F. Franzonia. OUR SUNDAY VISITOR 68:1, August 5, 1979.

Further results about pregnancy and childbirth after use of oral contraceptives, by G. K. Döring, et al. GEBURTSHILFE UND FRAUENHEILKUNDE 39(5):369-371, May, 1979.

The future of the pill, by M. Kenny. SPECTATOR p. 13, December 15, 1979.

Galactorrhea and pituitary tumors in postpill and non-postpill secondary amenorrhea, by C. M. March, et al. AMERICAN JOURNAL OF OBSTETRICS AND GYNECOLOGY 134(1): 45-48, May 1, 1979.

Gamma-rays + PVC + EO = OK, by R. B. Roberts. MEDICAL INSTRUMENTATION 13(2):107, March-April, 1979.

Gamma sterilization moves up, by W. C. Simms. MODERN PACKAGING 52:50-52, May, 1979.

Gastrointestinal complications of oral hormonal contraceptives, by B. Braendli, et al. MEDIZINISCHE KLINIK 74(12):425-436, March 23, 1979.

General theories of chemical disinfection and sterilization of sludge, by L. K. Wang, et al. WATER AND SEWAGE WORKS 125:30-323, July, 1978+.

Genetic causes and workup of male and female infertility. 1. Prenatal reproductive loss, by J. M. Opitz, et al. POSTGRADUATE MEDICINE 65(5):247-252+, May, 1979.

Genital actinomycosis and intrauterine contraceptive devices. Cytopathologic diagnosis and clinical significance, by B. S. Bhagavan, et al. HUMAN PATHOLOGY 9(5):567-578, September, 1978.

Gestation, birth-weight, and spontaneous abortion in pregnancy after induced abortion. Report of Collaborative Study, by W.H.O. Task Force on Sequelae of Abortion. LANCET 1(8108):142-145, January 20, 1979.

Gestational age at termination of pregnancy on medical indications [letter], by P. E. Polani, et al. LANCET 2(8139): 410, August 25, 1979.

Getting a second opinion; role of father in estranged husband-wife case, by S. Kimber. MACLEANS 92:25, September 3, 1979.

Going public: a study in the sociology of homosexual liberation, by J. A. Lee. JOURNAL OF HOMOSEXUALITY 3(1):49-78, Fall, 1977.

Going to the barricades, by C. Perozino. AMERICAN ATHEIST 21(10):14, October, 1979.

Gonadotropic activity of the immunoglobulins from placental, abortion and donor blood, by L. V. Minakova, et al. ZHURNAL MIKROBIOLOGII, EPIDEMIOLOGII I IM-MUNOBIOLOGII (3):66-71, March, 1979.

Gonorrhea, candidiasis and vaginal trichomoniasis in patients

requesting legal abortion, by O. C. Evjen, et al. TIDS-
SKRIFT FOR DEN NORSKE LAEGEFORENING 99(9-
10):470-471, March 30, 1979.

Goose-stepping against abortion. . .and some tripping attempts.
OFF OUR BACKS 8(3):13, March, 1978.

Gossypol—proposed contraceptive for men passes the Ames test
[letter], by A. de Peyster, et al. NEW ENGLAND JOUR-
NAL OF MEDICINE 301(5):275-276, August 2, 1979.

Government funding, abortions, and the public forum, by W. C.
Canby, Jr. ARIZONA STATE LAW JOURNAL 1979:11-
21, 1979.

Greening of the future: population control (motherwort,
zoapatle plants used as c.), by N. Vietmeyer. QUEST 3:32,
September, 1979.

Guide to birth control for trainable mentally retarded people, by
J. D. Treubaft. MENTAL RETARDATION 26(3).31-33,
July, 1976.

Guidelines for cleaning and disinfection of flexible fiberoptic
endoscopes (FFE) used in GI endoscopy. AORN JOURNAL
28(5):907+, November, 1978.

Guidelines for ecumenical debate on abortion and homosexuality; Faith and Order Commission of the National Council of
Churches. ORIGINS 8:517-519, February 1, 1979.

Guidelines to birth control counseling of the physically handicapped, by G. Szasz, et al. CANADIAN MEDICAL ASSO-
CIATION JOURNAL 120(11):1353-1368, June 9, 1979.

Gynecologic health problems: socially abused adolescent female,
by J. J. Rothbaid, et al. NEW YORK STATE JOURNAL OF
MEDICINE 76:1483-1484, September, 1976.

Gynecologic microsurgery: a déja vu of laparoscopy, by J. M.
Phillips. JOURNAL OF REPRODUCTIVE MEDICINE
22(3):135-143, March, 1979.

H-1 and X14 parvovirus antibodies in women with abortions or still-births, by S. Guglielmino, et al. ACTA VIROLOGICA 22(5):426-428, September, 1978.

HEW funds abortions, promiscuity, by C. Marshner. CONSERVATIVE DIGEST 5:28+, January, 1979.

HEW gets Hyde Amendment; regulations will cause 100,000 medical abortions this year, by J. D. Lofton, Jr. CATHOLIC DIGEST 4:48, May, 1978.

HEW makes mockery of Hyde Amendment (allows loose interpretation of rules by which Medicaid would fund abortions). HUMAN EVENTS 38:5, February 11, 1978.

HEW sets new sterilization rules. SPOKESWOMAN 8(7&8):8, January, 1978.

HEW sets rules for implementing Hyde ban. SPOKESWOMAN 8(9):6, March, 1978.

HEW sets sterilization funding rules. ARIZONA NURSE 32:4, March-April, 1979.

HLA-A,B compatibility in parents of offspring with neural-tube defects or couples experiencing involuntary fetal wastage, by B. Schacter, et al. LANCET 1(8120):796-799, April 14, 1979.

An habitual aborter's self-concept during the course of a successful pregnancy, by Y. Chao. MATERNAL-CHILD NURSING JOURNAL 6(3):165-175, Fall, 1977.

Habitual abortion. Analytic study of 57 cases, by F. Elizondo Elizondo, et al. GINECOLOGIA Y OBSTETRICIA DE MEXICO 43(259):311-316, May, 1978.

Happiness is never having to say it's permanent, by S. Henry. MACLEANS 92:39-40, April 30, 1979.

A hardening of the heart on abortion, by Bishop T. Kelly. ORIGINS 8:509-510, January 25, 1979.

The hate compaign against Catholics (Catholics accused of wanting to take away the right of decision in abortion), by M. J. Sobian. CATHOLIC DIGEST 4:27, June, 1978.

Health aspect, by Tager, et al. NEW AGE 4(3):56, August, 1978.

Health care system—related factors affecting population control, by D. N. Kakar. NURSING JOURNAL OF INDIA 70:157-159, June, 1979.

Health concerns, by J. Scheidler. OUR SUNDAY VISITOR 67: 6-8, January 21, 1979.

Health (family planning) bill 1978. IRISH MEDICAL JOURNAL 72(1):1-2, January 12, 1979.

The health impact of restricting public funds for abortion. October 10, 1977-June 10, 1978, by W. Cates, Jr., et al. AMERICAN JOURNAL OF PUBLIC HEALTH 69(9): 945-947, September, 1979.

Health problems of anaesthetists and their families [letter], by J. Nunn, et al. BRITISH MEDICAL JOURNAL 1(6170): 1079, April 21, 1979.

Healthy family systems, by L. R. Barnhill. FAMILY COORDINATOR 28(1):94-100, January, 1979.

Heil Mary! MOTHER JONES 3(9):9, November, 1978.

Hematological studies in induction abortion by extra-amniotic administration of sulproston, by R. C. Briel, et al. ARCHIV FUR GYNAEKOLOGIE 226(4):297-302, 1978.

Hemodialysis in the treatment of acute renal insufficiency in septic abortions, by G. I. Salashnyi, et al. KLINICHES-KAYA MEDITZINA 56(8):83-86, August, 1978.

Hemophilus influenza septicemia and midtrimester abortion, by E. Ogden, et al. JOURNAL OF REPRODUCTIVE MEDICINE 22(2):106-108, February, 1979.

Hepatic changes caused by contraceptive steroids, by M. Uribe, et al. REVISTA DE GASTROENTEROLOGIA DE MEXICO 42(3):139-147, September-December, 1977.

Hepatic lesions by oral contraceptives, by M. Lopez. PATHO-LOGICA 71(1012):253-258, March-April, 1979.

Hepatic neoplasms associated with contraceptive and anabolic steroids, by K. G. Ishak. RECENT RESULTS IN CANCER RESEARCH 66:73-128, 1979.

The hepatitis controversy. Environmental control of hepatitis B: how 'safe' is 'safe enough'? by W. C. Beck, et al. MEDI-CAL INSTRUMENTATION 13(1):55-58, January-February, 1979.

Hepatocarcinoma and oral contraceptives [letter], by R. Trias, et al. LANCET 1(8068):821, April 15, 1978.

Here we go again. THE ECONOMIST 272:25, July 14, 1979.

Heterosexual experience, marital status, and orientation of homosexual males, by N. McConaghy. ARCHIVES OF SEXUAL BEHAVIOR 7(6):575-581, November, 1978.

A hidden twin-pregnancy, by J. W. Bijlsma, et al. TROPICAL DOCTOR 9(1):41, January, 1979.

Hierarchy of birth planning values: an aid in genetic counseling, by B. D. Townes, et al. JOURNAL OF PSYCHIATRIC NURSING 17:37-41, September, 1979.

High court orders complex sterilization case to trial [forced sterilization of a deaf-mute woman]. MEDICAL WORLD NEWS 19:52+, October 13, 1978.

The high court, privacy and teenage seaxuality, by G. L. Beiswinger. FAMILY COORDINATOR 28(2):191-198, April, 1979.

High density lipoprotein cholesterole levels in peripheral vascular disease and in women on oral contraception, by J. M. Meerloo, et al. ATHEROSCLEROSIS 33(2):267-269, June, 1979.

High hepatoma risk for women on pill four years or more.
MEDICAL WORLD NEWS 19:13+, July 24, 1978.

High-risk pregnancy screening techniques: a nursing overview,
by F. Diamond. JOGN 7(6):15-20, November-December,
1978.

Higher education funds stalled in Congress, by E. K. Coughlin.
CHRONICLE OF HIGHER EDUCATION 17:17, October 2,
1978.

Histochemical and ultrastructural effects of enovid E on the endometrium of the baboon, by J. R. Dollar, et al. CELL AND
TISSUE RESEARCH 192(3):451-460, September 26, 1978.

A histological study of a microsurgical tube-to anastomosis, by
E. Cornier, et al. JOURNAL DE GYNECOLOGIA, OB-
STETRIQUE ET BIOLOGIE DE LA REPRODUCTION
7(8):1441-1446, December, 1978.

History of abortion: technology, morality, and law, by J. W.
Dellapenna. UNIVERSITY OF PITTSBURG LAW RE-
VIEW 40:359-428, Spring, 1979.

Holistic approach to contraception, by M. Kernis. COUNTRY
WOMEN 27:52, December, 1977.

Home remedy aggravates abortion woes [dangers and ineffective-
ness of penny-royal oil] . MEDICAL WORLD NEWS 20:72,
May 14, 1979.

Homocystinuria and oral contraceptives [letter] , by H. Gröbe.
LANCET 1(8056):158-159, January 21, 1978.

Hormonal considerations in early normal pregnancy and blighted
ovum syndrome, by M. O. Schweditsch, et al. FERTILITY
AND STERILITY 31(3):252-257, March, 1979.

Hormonal content of plasma and endometrium of women taking
oral contraceptives, by H. Porias, et al. OBSTETRICS AND

GYNECOLOGY 52(6):703-707, December, 1978.

Hormonal contraception today, by C. G. Nilsson. KATILOLEH-TI 84(2):76-81, February, 1979.

The hormonal levels in case of abortion during the first trimester, by M. Chartier. JOURNAL DE GYNECOLOGIE, OBSTE-TRIQUE ET BIOLOGIE DE LA REPRODUCTION 7(3 pt. 2):673-677, April, 1978.

Hormonal steroid contraceptives: a further review of adverse reactions, by E. G. McQueen. DRUGS 16(4):322-357, October, 1978.

Hormonal tissue concentration and oral contraceptives: the endometrium, by A. Carranco López, et al. GINECOLOGIA Y OBSTETRICIA DE MEXICO 45(270):329-347, April, 1979.

The hormonal treatment of paraphiliacs with depo-provera, by M. K. Spodak, et al. CRIMINAL JUSTICE AND BEHAVIOR 5(4):304-314, December, 1978.

Hormone level changes caused by abortion induced with prostaglandin F2 alpha in pregnancy interruption during the 1st trimester, by J. Sárdi, et al. ORVOSI HETILAP 120(24): 1429-1431, June 17, 1979.

Hospital coynseling in Khartoum: a study of factors affecting contraceptive acceptance after abortion, by H. E. Rushwan, et al. INTERNATIONAL JOURNAL OF GYNAECOLOGY AND OBSTETRICS 15(5):440-443, 1978.

Hot water as a tubal occluding agent, by T. S. Moulding, et al. CONTRACEPTION 19(5):433-442, May, 1979.

Hotline to health, by C. Fredericks. PREVENTION 30(6):42, June, 1978.

How dare they do this? by B. Baird. AMERICAN ATHIEST 21(5):24, May, 1979.

How images function, by N. Morton. QUEST 3(2):54-59, Fall.

How many children do couples really want? by L. C. Coombs. FAMILY PLANNING PERSPECTIVES 10(5):303, September-October, 1978.

How many girls do parents drive to abortion, by M. Finley. OUR SUNDAY VISITOR 68:5, November 4, 1979.

How safe is the pill? by R. Gray. WORLD HEALTH pp. 12-15, August, 1978.

Hulka-Clemens clips [letter], by B. A. Lieberman. BRITISH MEDICAL JOURNAL 1(6171):1148, April 28, 1979.

Human cervical mucus. V. Oral contraceptives and mucus rheologic properties, by D. P. Wolf, et al. FERTILITY AND STERILITY 32(2):166-169, August, 1979.

Human hexosaminidase isozymes. IV. Effects of oral contraceptive steroids on serum hexosaminidase activity, by H. M. Nitowsky, et al. AMERICAN JOUNAL OF OBSTETRICS AND GYNECOLOGY 134(6):642-647, July 15, 1979.

Human platelet aggregation curve and oral contraception, by C. M. Montanari, et al. ACTA HAEMATOLOGICA 61(4): 230-232, 1979.

Humanae Vitae—ten years after—wards; towards a more human civilization, by Bishop L. Moreira Neves. L'OSSERVATORE ROMANO 3(564):10-11, January 15, 1979.

Husband denied a say in abortion decision, by I. M. Kennedy. MODERN LAW REVIEW 42:324-331, May, 1979.

Husbands of abortion applicants: a comparison with husbands of women who complete their pregnancies, by F. Lieh-Mak, et al. SOCIAL PSYCHIATRY 14(2):59-64, 1979.

Hyde amendment battle starting all over again. SPOKESWO-MAN 8(12):6, June, 1978.

The Hyde amendment; a tradition, by M. Bourgoin. NATIONAL CATHOLIC REPORTER 15:18, July 27, 1979.

Hygienic analyses carried out in a public sauna, by W. Gräf, et al. ZENTRALBLATT FUER BAKTERIOLOGIE, PARASITEN-KUNDE, INFEKTIONSKRANHEITEN UND HYGIENE 167(4):362-374, November, 1978.

Hygienic assessment of the working conditions in centralized seed dressing, by L. N. Petrichenko. GIGIYENA TRUDA I PROFESSIONAL'NYYE ZABOLEVANIYA (1):35-36, 1979.

Hyperplastic changes and oral contraceptives in Anglo-Saxon countries, by C. Markuszewski. POLSKI TYGODNIK LEKARSKI 33(38):1519-1522, September 18, 1978.

Hypertension and oral contraceptives [letter], by M. G. Crane, et al. BRITISH MEDICAL JOURNAL 2(6145):1165, October 21, 1978.

IUD information. CONGRESSIONAL QUARTERLY WEEKLY REPORT 35:922, May 14, 1977.

IUD questionnaire. SPOKESWOMAN 9(2):8, August, 1978.

IUDs and oral contraceptives. A follow-up study of 504 women, by A. Bergqvist, et al. LAKARTIDNINGEN 76(3):125-128, 1979.

IUD's and pelvic infection; FDA labeling revisions, by A. Hecht. FDA CONSUMER 12:20-21, November, 1978.

IUDs—update and safety, effectiveness, and research. POPULA-TION REPORTS 7(3):1, May, 1979.

I had an abortion, by M. Grayson. COSMOPOLITAN 184:106+, March, 1978.

I was a rape victim. . .communication breakdown. NURSING MIRROR AND MIDWIVES' JOURNAL 147:21, November 9, 1978.

I would like to have a word with you, by S. Aberg. KATILO-LEHTI 83(10):351-354, October,1978.

Illinois abortion parental consent act of 1977: a far cry from permissible consultation. THE JOHN MARSHALL JOURNAL OF PRACTICE AND PROCEDURE 12:135-164, Fall, 1978.

Immediate and early postoperative complications and various psychosomatic problems following laparoscopic sterilization of women, by B. M. Berić, et al. JUGOSLAVENSKA GINEKOLOGIJA I OPSTETRICIJA 17(4):225-231, July-August, 1977.

Immediate postabortion intrauterine contraception in nulliparous adolescents, by J. A. Goldman, et al. ISRAEL JOURNAL OF MEDICAL SCIENCES 15(6):522-525, June, 1979.

Immediate sterility after vasectomy with the use of 0.1% ethacridine lactate, by D. S. Kamat, et al. JOURNAL OF POSTGRADUATE MEDICINE 24(4):218-220, October, 1978.

Immigration, social change and cohort fertility in Israel, by D. Friedlander, et al. POPULATION STUDIES 32:299-318, July, 1978.

Immune reactivity of women on hormonal contraceptives: dinitrochlorobenzene sensitization test and skin reactivity to irritants, by G. Gerretsen, et al. CONTRACEPTION 19(1): 83-89, January, 1979.

Immunological control of fertility: measurement of affinity of antibodies to human chorionic gonadotrophin, by Y. M. Thanavala, et al. CLINICAL AND EXPERIMENTAL IMMUNOLOGY 33(3):403-409, September, 1978.

Immunological procedure to regulate fertility, by V. C. Stevens. BOLETIN DE LA OFICINA SANITARIA PARAMERICANA 86(1):63-76, January, 1979.

Impact of family planning information on acceptance at a Ghanaian rural health post, by W. B. Ward, et al. INTERNATIONAL JOURNAL OF HEALTH EDUCATION 21(4): 273-281, 1978.

Impact of family planning nurse practitioners, by M. Manisoff. JOGN 8(2):73-77, March-April, 1979.

Impact of laparoscopic sterilization on birth prevention in Nepal, by B. R. Pande, et al. JOURNAL OF FAMILY WELFARE 25:13-19, December, 1978.

Impact of the Malaysian family planning program on births: a comparison of matched acceptor and non-acceptor birth rates, by J. T. Johnson, et al. POPULATION STUDIES 32(2):215, July, 1978.

The impact of midtrimester abortion techniques on patients and staff, by N. B. Kaltreider, et al. AMERICAN JOURNAL OF OBSTETRICS AND GYNECOLOGY 135(2):235-238, September 15, 1979.

The impact of physical disability on marital adjustment: a literature review, by Y. Peterson. FAMILY COORDINATOR 28(1):47-51, January, 1979.

Implications of oral contraceptive use on vitamin nutritional status, by M. S. Mabji. INDIAN JOURNAL OF MEDICAL RESEARCH 68(suppl):80-87, October, 1978.

Importance of being Sr. Marie Augusta a footnote by another hand, by R. G. Hoyt. CHRISTIANITY AND CRISIS 39: 122-125, May 14, 1979.

The importance of cytogenetic investigation of the couples with multiple spontaneous abortions and malformed offsprings, by D. Duca, et al. ENDOCRINOLOGIE 17(1):17-22, January-March, 1979.

Improvement in sterile supply, by D. Robinson. KENYA NURSING JOURNAL 7(1):9-10, June, 1978.

Improving contraceptive technology [eight articles]. DRAPER FUND REPORT pp. 3-30, Summer, 1978.

Improving management through evaluation: techniques and strategies for family planning programs, by M. E. Gorosh.

STUDIES IN FAMILY PLANNING 9(6):163-168, June, 1978.

In the courts. SPOKESWOMAN 9(2):6, August, 1978.

In defense of the pill, by J. W. Goldzieher. GINECOLOGIA Y OBSTETRICIA DE MEXICO 44(262):123-152, August, 1978.

In necessity and sorrow, by M. Denes. SPOKESWOMAN 8(12): 16, June, 1978.

In the states. OFF OUR BACKS 8(10):17, November, 1978.

In vivo evaluation of an effervescent intravaginal contraceptive insert by simulated coital activity, by W. H. Masters, et al. FERTILITY AND STERILITY 32(2):161-165, August, 1979.

'Incessant ovulation' and ovarian cancer, by J. T. Casagrande, et al. LANCET 2(8135):170-173, July 28, 1979.

Incidence of aerobic and anerobic infection in patients with incomplete abortion, by D. E. Kowen, et al. SOUTH AFRICAN MEDICAL JOURNAL 55(4):129-132, January 27, 1979.

Incidence of mycotic vaginitis in women using oral contraceptives, by A. Karwan-Płońska, et al. GINEKOLOGIA POLSKA 49(12):1093-1094, December, 1978.

Incidence of spontaneous abortion with and without previous use of contraceptive agents based on morphological studies, by G. Dallenbach-Hellweg. GYNAEKOLOGISCHE RUNDSCHAU 18(3-4):213-219, 1978.

Incidence of thyroid disease associated with oral contraceptives, by P. Frank, et al. BRITISH MEDICAL JOURNAL 2(6151): 1531, December 2, 1978.

Income and childlessness in Canada: a further examination, by J. E. Wolowyna. SOCIAL BIOLOGY 24:326-331, Winter,

1977.

Increased induced abortion rate in 1966, an aspect of a Japanese folk superstition, by K. Kaku. ANNALS OF HUMAN BIOLOGY 2(2):111-115, April, 1975.

Increased platelet aggregation and decreased high-density lipoprotein cholesterol in women on oral contraceptives, by M. L. Bierenbaum, et al. AMERICAN JOURNAL OF OBSTETRICS AND GYNECOLOGY 134(6):638-641, July 15, 1979.

Increased risk of thrombosis due to oral contraceptives: a further report, by M. G. Maguire, et al. AMERICAN JOURNAL OF EPIDEMIOLOGY 110(2):188-195, August, 1979.

Increasing anti-choice activity. SPOKESWOMAN 9(6):7, December, 1978.

Indian dilemma—coercive birth control or compulsory pregnancy, by T. Black, et al. CONTEMPORARY REVIEW 233: 232-236, November, 1978.

Indian experience with a single long-acting vaginal suppository for the termination of pregnancies, by S. Tejuja, et al. CONTRACEPTION 19(2):191-196, February, 1979.

Indian woman's sterilization suit starts, by P. Moore. NATIONAL CATHOLIC REPORTER 15:1+, January 19, 1979.

Indiana abortion clinic sues pro-life picketers, seeks $700,000 in damages, by C. Anthony. OUR SUNDAY VISITOR 67:1, January 28, 1979.

Indications for the sterilisation of the handicapped adolescent, by A. Animashaun. NIGERIAN MEDICAL JOURNAL 8(3): 253-254, May, 1978.

Indomethacin increases abortifacient effect of PGE2 in man, by J. Piotrowski, et al. PROSTAGLANDINS 17(3):451-459, March, 1979.

Induced abortion, by J. V. Larsen. SOUTH AFRICAN MEDI-

CAL JOURNAL 53(21):853-857, May 27, 1978.

Induced abortion after the 12th week of pregnancy. I., by P. E. Treffers, et al. NEDERLANDS TIJDSCHRIFT VOOR GENEESKUNDS 123(26):1103-1110, June 30, 1979.

Induced abortion and congenital malformations in offspring of subsequent pregnancies, by M. B. Bracken, et al. AMERICAN JOURNAL OF EPIDEMIOLOGY 109(4):425-432, April, 1979.

Induced abortion and contraceptive method choice among urban Japanese marrieds, by S. J. Coleman. DISSERTATION ABSTRACTS INTERNATIONAL 39(4-A):2381-2382, October, 1978.

Induced abortion and psychotherapy, by R. Mester. PSYCHOTHERAPY AND PSYCHOSOMATICS 30(2):98-104, 1978.

Induced abortion as a risk factor for perinatal complications: a review, by M. B. Bracken. YALE JOURNAL OF BIOLOGY AND MEDICINE 51(5):539-548, September-October, 1978.

Induced abortion. Report of a WHO scientific group. WHO TECHNICAL REPORT SERIES (623):1-65, 1978.

Induced abortions in France in 1976, by C. Blayo. POPULATION 34:307-342, March-April, 1979.

Induction of abortion with prostaglandins, by U. Haller. GYNAEKOLOGISCHE RUNDSCHAU 18(suppl 1):9-15, 1978.

Induction of hepatic drug metabolizing enzymes and pregnancy while taking oral contraceptives, by W. C. Buss. JOURNAL OF ANTIMICROBIOL CHEMOTHERAPY 5(1):4-5, January, 1979.

Induction of mid-term abortion by trichosanthin in laboratory animals, by M. C. Chang, et al. CONTRACEPTION 19(2):175-184, February, 1979.

Induction of second trimester abortion: comparison between

vaginal 15-methyl-PGF2alpha methyl ester and intra-amniotic PGF2alpha, by M. Mandelin, et al. PROSTAGLANDINS 16(6):995-1001, December, 1978.

Industrial sterilization, by C. Artandi. POINT OF VIEW 16:14-15, April 1, 1979.

The Infant Life (Preservation) Act after fifty years, by M. Simms. NEW HUMANIST 95:11-13, June, 1979.

Infections and perinatal mortality, by J. Pryse-Davies, et al. JOURNAL OF ANTIMICROBIOL CHEMOTHERAPY 5(A):59-70, May, 1979.

The influence of age, sex, and the use of oral contraceptives on the inhibitory effects of endothelial cells and PGI2 (prostacyclin) on platelet function, by A. Nordøy, et al. SCANDINAVIAN JOURNAL OF HAEMATOLOGY 21(3):177-187, September, 1978.

Influence of hormonal contraception on serum lipoproteins, by D. Pometta, et al. SCHWEIZERISCHE MEDIZINISCHE WOCHENSCHRIFT 108(50):2012-2015, December 16, 1978.

Influence of mineral intake and use of oral contraceptives before pregnancy on the mineral content of human colostrum and of more mature milk, by A. Kirksey, et al. AMERICAN JOURNAL OF CLINICAL NUTRITION 32(1):30-39, January, 1979.

Influence of oral contraceptives on ascorbic acid and triglyceride status, by N. K. Hudiburgh, et al. JOURNAL OF THE AMERICAN DIETETIC ASSOCIATION 75(1):19-22, July, 1979.

Influence of oral contraceptives on blood clotting (results after one year study), by S. Salahović, et al. LIJECNICKI VJESNIK 100(9):525-529, September, 1978.

Influence of oral contraceptives on immediate postabortal pituitary-ovarian function, by P. Lähteenmäki. ACTA OBSTETRICIA ET GYNECOLOGICA SCANDINAVICA 76:1-43,

110

1978.

The influence of others on teenagers' use of birth control, by
J. Cahn. DISSERTATION ABSTRACTS INTERNATIONAL
39(3-B):1537, September, 1978.

Influence of sterilization and temperature changes on the in vitro
characteristics of the pH electrode, by H. Rüttgers, et al.
ARCHIVES OF GYNECOLOGY 226(1-2):25-30, September 1, 1978.

The influence of traditional values and beliefs on family planning
decisions in Thailand, by D. M. Ebnet. DISSERTATION
ABSTRACTS INTERNATIONAL 38(10-A):6343, April,
1978.

Influence on haemostasis exercised by prostaglandin F2alpha in
missed abortion, by R. C. Briel, et al. GEBURTSHILFE
UND FRAUENHEILKUNDE 38(10):862-867, October,
1978.

Influences on family planning acceptance: an analysis of back-
ground and program factors in Malaysia, by J. T. Johnson.
STUDIES IN FAMILY PLANNING 10(1):15-24, January,
1979.

Informed consent for fertility control services [United States],
by E. W. Paul, et al. FAMILY PLANNING PERSPECTIVES
11:159-163+, May-June, 1979.

Inhibition of ovulation in women by chronic treatment with a
stimulatory LRH analogue—a new approach to birth control,
by S. J. Nillius, et al. CONTRACEPTION 17(6):537, June,
1978.

Initial consequences of the 1977 New Zealand abortion law, by
W. A. Facer, et al. NEW ZEALAND NURSING FORUM
6(2):9-12, December, 1978-January, 1979.

Initial results of laparoscopic tubal sterilization, by R. Burmucic,
et al. WIENER MEDIZINISCHE WOCHENSCHRIFT
128(23):724-726, December 15, 1978.

Injectable contraception. STOREFRONT 5(6):4, February, 1978.

Inner ear disturbance following long-term usage of hormonal contraceptives, by G. Okulicz. HNO 26(10):330-334, October, 1978.

Inquiry on abortion, views of J. T. Noonan, Jr., by B. J. Uddo. AMERICA 141:14-15, July 7, 1979.

Integration of health, nutrition, and family planning; the Companiganj project in Bangladesh, by C. McCord. FOOD RESEARCH INSTITUTE STUDIES 16(2):91-105, 1977.

Intelligent woman's guide to sex; diaphragm or pill, by J. Coburn. MADEMOISELLE 84:68, November, 1978.

Intentionally childless couple, by D. E. Bensen. USA TODAY 107:45-46, January, 1979.

Interaction of local anesthesia and chronic treatment of contraceptive medication in the rabbit, by P. Henry, et al. BULLETIN DE L'ACADAMIE DE CHIRURQU DENTAIRE 23(23): 53-58, 1977-1978.

Intergenerational occupational mobility and fertility: a reassessment, by F. D. Bean, et al. AMERICAN SOCIOLOGICAL REVIEW 44:608-619, August, 1979.

Interruption of early first trimester pregnancy by single vaginal administration of 15-methyl-pgf2 alpha-methyl ester, by K. Gréen, et al. CONTRACEPTION 18(6):551-560, December, 1978.

Interruption of pregnancy. TIJDSCHRIFT VOR ZIEKENVERPLEGING 31(25):1185-1186, December 12, 1978.

Interruption of pregnancy: the predicament indication and legal points of view, by J. Römer. FORTSCHRITTE DER MEDIZIN 96(35):1774-1776, September 21, 1978.

Interruption of the second and third trimester of a normal and missed pregnancy by extraamnial prostaglandin E administration combined with oxytocin infusion, by F. Havránek, et al. CESKOSLOVENSKA GYNEKOLOGIE 44(3):179-182, April, 1979.

Interval between pregnancies. LANCET 2(8095):879-880, October 21, 1978.

Intra-amniotic prostaglandin F2alpha termination of mid-trimester abortion, by J. M. Luwuliza-Kirunda. EAST AFRICAN MEDICAL JOURNAL 56(1):10-14, January, 1979.

Intra-hepatic cholestasis after taking a triacetyloleandomycin-estroprogestational combination [letter], by S. Claudel, et al. NOUVELLE PRESSE MEDICALE 8(14):1182, March 24, 1979.

Intramuscular 16-phenoxy PGE2 ester for pregnancy termination, by M. Toppozada, et al. PROSTAGLANDINS 17(3): 461-467, March, 1979.

Intranasal gonadotropin-releasing hormone agonist as a contraceptive agent, by C. Bergquist, et al. LANCET 2(8136): 215-217, August 4, 1979.

Intrauterine copper contraceptive. OFF OUR BACKS 8(10):5, November, 1978.

Intravascular spill of hyperosmolar urea during induced mid-trimester abortion, by B. M. Kovasznay, et al. OBSTETRICS AND GYNECOLOGY 53(1):127-130, January, 1979.

"Invasion of the fetus-snatchers" [national abortion summit meeting, Feb. 15, 1979, Washington, D.C.], by N. Borman. MAJORITY REPORT 8:1+, January 1, 1979+.

Investigation of the abortion decision process, by P. C. Shaw, et al. PSYCHOLOGY 16:11-20, Summer, 1979.

Investigation of hydroxyproline by hormonal contraception, by G. Klinger, et al. ZENTRALBLATT FUER GYNAEKOLO-

GIE 101(5):306-308, 1979.

Investigation of prostaglandins for abortion, by N. H. Lauersen. ACTA OBSTETRICIA ET GYNECOLOGIA SCANDINAVICA (81):1-36, 1979.

Investigation of a wrongful death: case of R. Jimenez, by E. Frankfort, et al. MS MAGAZINE 7:66-67+, January, 1979.

Investigation of hormones during early abortion induced by prostaglandin F2alpha and 15(S)-methyl-PGF2alpha, by B. Seifert, et al. ACTA BIOLOGICA ET MEDICA GERMANICA 37(5-6):955-957, 1976.

Involuntary sterilization: recent developments, by S. J. Vitello. MENTAL RETARDATION 16:405-409, December, 1978.

Ireland: difficult birth. THE ECONOMIST 270:28+, January 6, 1979.

Is abortion a religious issue? [letter], by G. M. Atkinson. INQUIRY 9(1):4+, February, 1979.

—. 1. Religious, moral, and sociologicological issues: some basic distinctions, by B. Brody. HASTINGS CENTER REPORT 8(4):13, August, 1978.

—. 2. Enacting religious beliefs in a pluralistic society, by F. S. Jaffe. HASTINGS CENTER REPORT 8(4):14-16, August, 1978.

—. 3. The irrelevance of religion in the abortion debate, by L. Newton. HASTINGS CENTER REPORT 8(4):16-17, August, 1978.

Is adultery biological? by M. North, et al. NEW SOCIETY 41(772):125-126, July, 21, 1977.

Is interruption of pregnancy indicated in osteo-articular tuberculosis? by C. Kopác, et al. ACTA CHIRURGIAE ORTHOPAEDICAE ET TRAUMATOLOGIAE CECHOSLOVACA 46(1):11-14, February, 1979.

Is the low fertility rate after vasovasostomy caused by nerve re-section during vasectomy? by R. Pabst, et al. FERTILITY AND STERILITY 31(3):316-320, March, 1979.

Is pregnancy good for teenagers? by R. Lincoln. USA TODAY 107(2398):34-37, July, 1978.

Is there an alternative to the family planning programme in India? by S. Mukerji. JOURNAL OF FAMILY WELFARE 25:19-33, September, 1978.

Is zero preferred? American attitudes toward childlessness in the 1970's, by J. Blake. JOURNAL OF MARRIAGE AND THE FAMILY 41:245-258, May, 1979.

Israel's abortion controversy, by R. G. Weisbord. CONGRES-SIONAL MONITOR 46:11-13, April, 1979.

Issues and opinions. I. Sterilization of the mentally retarded minor, by C. Cooper. JOURNAL OF NURSE-MIDWIFERY 23:14-15, Spring-Summer, 1978.

—. II. Sterilization and the mentally retarded: HEW's new regulations, by P. Urbanus. JOURNAL OF NURSE-MIDWIFERY 23:16, Spring-Summer, 1978.

It is now possible to reverse surgical sterilization of women. NOW 11(8):2, July, 1978.

Italy: abortion meeting. OFF OUR BACKS 8(4):7, April, 1978.

Italy: abortionist-rapist resisted. OFF OUR BACKS 8(4):7, April, 1978.

Italy: the best abortion law in the world, by J. Spivak. WALL STREET JOURNAL 193:22, February 28, 1979.

Italy: church v state continued. THE ECONOMIST 270:42, January 13, 1979.

Italy resists abortion. OFF OUR BACKS 8(10):6, November, 1978.

Italy's abortion law [letter], by G. Neri, et al. LANCET 2(8095): 895-896, October 21, 1978.

It's reigning again, by W. Stevens. OFF OUR BACKS 8(4):6, April, 1978.

It's time for a change? by P. Morris. NURSING MIRROR AND MIDWIVES' JOURNAL 148(19):5, May 10, 1979.

Jaundice by interaction of troleandomycin and contraceptive pills [letter], by R. Rollux, et al. NOUVELLE PRESSE MEDICALE 8(20):1694, May 5, 1979.

John Corrie's abortion bill [Great Britain], by T. Woodcraft. LABOUR MONTHLY 61:419-423, September, 1979.

Judge dismisses anti-abortion demonstrators' claims. NOW 11(7):10, June, 1978.

Judges—immunities—judicial act and jurisdiction broadly defined. MARQUETTE LAW REVIEW 62:112-123, Fall, 1978.

Judicial immunity or imperial judiciary. UNIVERSITY OF MISSOURI-KANSAS CITY LAW REVIEW 47:81-94, Fall, 1978.

Judicial immunity—tort liability of a state court judge in granting the sterilization of a minor without due process. HOWARD LAW JOURNAL 22:129-141, 1979.

Judicial immunity: an unqualified sanction of tyranny from the bench. UNIVERSITY OF FLORIDA LAW REVIEW 30: 810-819, Summer, 1978.

Jury: charges not proved, by P. Moore. NATIONAL CATHOLIC REPORTER 15:5, February 2, 1979.

A KAP study on MTP acceptors and their contraceptive practice, by M. Roy, et al. INDIAN JOURNAL OF PUBLIC HEALTH 22(2):189-196, April-June, 1978.

KNXT policymakers assigned news team to create "expose" that would inhibit abortions. MEDIA REPORT TO WOMEN 7:6, November 1, 1979.

Karolinska Hospital-study of laboratory personnel: every fifth pregnancy ends in miscarriage, by B. Kolmodin-Hedman, et al. VARDFACKET 3(5):54-55, March 8, 1979.

Karyotype studies in abortion, by J. Markowska, et al. GINE-KOLOGIA POLSKA 49(5):395-400, May, 1978.

Kentucky law makes abortion more painful. NEW TIMES 11(7):15, October 2, 1978.

Kentucky woman indicted for criminal abortion, manslaughter. NOW 11(9):12, August, 1978.

Keys to birth control still elude experts. CONSERVATION FOUNDATION LETTER p. 1, March, 1979.

Killing of Legionnaires' organism? JAMA 241(18):1877, May 4, 1979.

Knowledge about family planning in the urban area of Merida, Yucatan. Restricting factors, by T. E. Cando de Cetina, et al. SPM 20(3):355-360, May-June, 1978.

Knowledge, attitude and practice of family planning in a rural Ceylonese community, by P. L. R. Dias, et al. JOURNAL OF FAMILY WELFARE 25:28-34, December, 1978.

A laboratory model for the investigation of contact transfer of micro-organisms, by R. R. Marples, et al. JOURNAL OF HYGIENE 82(2):237-248, April, 1979.

The labs' search for safer birth control. BUSINESS WEEK (2581):40D, April 16, 1979.

Lactation for delaying re-establishment of menstruation and its possible role in family planning, by S. Rathee, et al. JOUR-NAL OF THE INDIAN MEDICAL ASSOCIATION 71(2): 30-33, July 16 1978.

Laminaria use in midtrimester abortions induced by intra-amniotic prostaglandin F2alpha with urea and intravenous oxytocin, by J. H. Strauss, et al. AMERICAN JOURNAL OF OBSTETRICS AND GYNECOLOGY 134(3):260-264, June 1, 1979.

Land tenure structures and fertility in Mexico, by A. De Vany, et al. REVIEW OF ECONOMICS AND STATISTICS 61:67-72, February, 1979.

Laparoscopic electrocoagulation and tubal ring techniques for sterilization: a comparative study, by S. Koetsawang, et al. INTERNATIONAL JOURNAL OF GYNAECOLOGY AND OBSTETRICS 15(5):455-458, 1978.

Laparoscopic sterilization with the band. JOURNAL OF THE KENTUCKY MEDICAL ASSOCIATION 76(10):505, October, 1978.

Laparoscopic sterilization with electrocautery: complications and reliability, by U. Bänninger, et al. GEBURTSHILFE UND FRAUENHEILKUNDE 39(5):393-400, May, 1979.

Laparoscopic sterilization with spring-loaded clip and tubal ring in postabortal cases—one-year follow-up, by S. D. Khand-wala, et al. INTERNATIONAL JOURNAL OF GYNAE-COLOGY AND OBSTETRICS 16(2):115-118, 1978-1979.

Laparoscopic tubal occlusion with silicone rubber bands, by T. Kumarasamy, et al. AUSTRALIAN AND NEW ZEALAND JOURNAL OF OBSTETRICS AND GYNAECOLOGY 18(3):190-193, August, 1978.

Laparoscopic tubal sterilization in unselected outpatients, by M. H. Saidi, et al. TEXAS MEDICINE 74(9):55-57, September, 1978.

Laparoscopy before insemination stirs debate. MEDICAL WORLD NEWS 20:11+, February 5, 1979.

Laparoscopy for the general surgeon, by T. C. Dickinson, et al. SURGERY CLINICS OF NORTH AMERICA 59(3):449-

457, June, 1979.

Large families penalized in attempt to cut back births, by C. Douglas-Home. TIMES p. 5, December 8, 1979.

Late complications following sterilization in women, by T. Sørensen, et al. UGESKRIFT FOR LAEGER 141(15): 998-999, April 9, 1979.

Late complications of laparoscopic sterilization, II., by W. D. Edgerton. JOURNAL OF REPRODUCTIVE MEDICINE 21(1):41-44, July, 1978.

Late manifestation of a burn of intestine cause laparoscopic tubal sterilization, by R.   . WIENER MEDIZINISCHE WOCHENSCHRIFT 129(6):157-158, March 30, 1979.

Late marriage and non-marriage as demographic responses: are they similar? by R. B. Dixon. POPULATION STUDIES 32: 449-466, November, 1978.

Latest contraceptive gamble, by A. Connell. SEVEN DAYS 2(7):27, May 5, 1978.

Law number 194 of 22 May 1978. Regulations for social protection of maternity and on voluntary interruption of pregnancy. Practical observations for complying with the law, by V. S. Pesce. MINERVA GINECOLOGIA 31(1-2):1-7, January-February, 1979.

Lawsuits, protests follow EPA suspension of 2,4,5-T. FOREST INDUSTRIES 106(5):80, May, 1979.

Learning about the population problem: children's attitudes toward family planning in India, by S. Iyengar. YOUTH AND SOCIETY 10(3):275-295, March, 1979.

Legal abortion—ambulatory or in hospital? A prospective analysis of the frequency of complications during ambulatory care or during hospital stay, by P. Saksø, et al. UGESKRIFT FOR LAEGER 140(44):2712-2714, October 30, 1978.

Legal abortion: are American black women healthier because of it? by W. Cates, Jr. PHYLON 38(3):267-281, September, 1977.

Legal abortion of advanced pregnancy—methods, by M. Bujalić. SRPSKI ARHIV ZA CELOKUPNO LEKARSTVO 105(9): 737-741, September, 1977.

Legal abortion. A prospective study by the Sociomedical Department of the University Clinic for Obstetrics and Gynecology of Basel, by M. Mall-Haefeli, et al. FORTSCHRITTE DER MEDIZIN 97(12):531-532+, March 29, 1979.

A legal and psychological study of pro and anti-abortion groups, by E M. Silverstein. DISSERTATION ABSTRACTS INTERNATIONAL 38(12-B):6174, June, 1978.

Legal aspects: the nurse and contraceptive practices among adolescents, by C. L. Sklar. INFIRMIERE CANADIENNE 21(1):16-19, January, 1978.

Legal briefs; questions and answers, by E. Elliot, et al. WORKING WOMEN 4:16, March, 1979.

Legal implications of sterilization of the mentally retarded, by C. Dowben, et al. AMERICAN JOURNAL OF DISEASES OF CHILDREN 133(7):697-699, July, 1979.

Legal in Spain. OFF OUR BACKS 8(2):8, February, 1978.

The legal position of the physician with reference to abortion, by W. Becker. MEDIZINISCHE KLINIK 73(37):1292-1297, September 15, 1978.

Legalized abortion in South Australia: the first 7 years' experience, by F. Yusuf, et al. JOURNAL OF BIOSOCIAL SCIENCE 11(2):179-192, April, 1979.

Legally speaking: when it comes to consent, empty gestures won't do, by W. A. Regan. RN 42(1):25-26, January, 1979.

Legislation to watch—and work for—in the 95th Congress [abortion, childcare, family planning, health, homemakers, welfare, congressional staffing, work], by S. Tenenbaum, et al. MS MAGAZINE 5:99-102, February, 1977.

Letter from Calcutta, by J. Sarkar. FAR EASTERN ECONOMIC REVIEW 103:90, March 30, 1979.

Liberalized abortion in Oregon: effects on fertility, prematurity, fetal death, and infant death, by J. D. Quick. AMERICAN JOURNAL OF PUBLIC HEALTH 68:1003-1008, October, 1978.

Life management practices with the profoundly retarded: issues of euthanasia and withholding treatment, by M. L. Hardman, et al. MENTAL RETARDATION 16:390-396, December, 1978.

Limitations of a single extra-amniotic injection of prostaglandins in viscous gel to induce midtrimester abortion, by I. Craft, et al. GYNECOLOGIC AND OBSTETRIC INVESTIGATION 9(5):256-261, 1978.

Limiting public funds for abortions: state response to Congressional action. SUFFOLK UNIVERSITY LAW REVIEW 13:923-959, Summer, 1979.

'Listeria monocytogenes' isolation from a urine specimen of a subject with repeated abortions, by V. M. Nicolosi, et al. ANNALI SCLAVO 20(5):692-695, September-October, 1978.

Live children and abortion of p mothers [letter], by R. Sanger, et al. TRANSFUSION 19(2):222-224, March-April, 1979.

Liver adenoma, causing fatal abdominal hemorrhage, after prolonged administration of oral contraceptives, by J. Lukács, et al. MORPHOLOGIAI ES IGAZSAGUGYI ORVOSI SZEMLE 18(3):228-311, July, 1978.

Liver and the pill, by J. Eisenburg. NATURWISSENSCHAFTEN 66(3):156, March, 1979.

Liver biopsy findings after intake of oral contraceptives, by K. Mölleken. ZENTRALBLATT FUER ALLGEMEINE PATHOLOGIE UND PATHOLOGISCHE ANATOMIE 123(3): 195-201, 1979.

Liver cell adenoma associated with oral contraceptive hormone therapy, by N. J. Nicolaides. MEDICAL JOURNAL OF AUSTRALIA 2(6):274-276, September 9, 1978.

Liver function studies under the effect of 4 sequential hormonal contraceptives, by E. Brügmann, et al. ZEITSCHRIFT FUR DIE GESAMTE INNERE MEDIZIN UND IHRE GRENZGEBIETE 33(22):826-829, November 15, 1978.

Liver function studies under the influence of hormonal contraceptives (sequential preparations), by E. Brügmann, et al. DEUTSCHE ZEITSCHRIFT FUER VERDAUUNGSUND STOFFWECHSELKRANKHEITEN 39(2):69-74, 1979.

Liver oncogenesis and steroids, by W. M. Christopherson, et al. PROGRESS IN CLINICAL CANCER 7:153-163, 1978.

Liver resection for hepatic adenoma, by R. Weil, 3d, et al. ARCHIVES OF SURGERY 114(2):178-180, February, 1979.

Liver tumor and prolonged oral contraception, by T. Espersen. UGESKRIFT FOR LAEGER 141(23):1581-1582, June 4, 1979.

Liver tumors and oral contraceptives, by J. J. Gonvers, et al. SCHWEIZERISCHE MEDIZINISCHE WOCHENSCHRIFT 108(48):1899-1901, December 2, 1978.

Liver tumors and oral contraceptives: pathology and pathogenesis, by T. D. Gindhart. ANNALS OF CLINICAL AND LABORATORY SCIENCE 8(6):443-446, November-December, 1978.

Liver tumors and oral contraceptives: a review of recent literature, by G. B. Feben. AUSTRALIAN FAMILY PHYSICIAN 8(6):641+, June, 1979.

Liver tumors as adverse effects of contraceptives, by H. Heiss-meyer, et al. VERHANDLUNGEN DER DEUTSCHEN GESELLSCHAFT FUR INNERE MEDIZIN (84):1612-1614, 1978.

Liver tumors associated with oral contraceptives, by W. J. Brit-ton, et al. MEDICAL JOURNAL OF AUSTRALIA 2(6): 223-227, September 9, 1978.

Local community health centers: a health program in perina-tology and fecundity, by L. Fontaine. INFIRMIERE CANA-DIENNE 21(4):34-38, April, 1979.

Longitudinal predictive research: an approach to methodological problems in studying contraception, by B. Mindick, et al. JOURNAL OF POPULATION 2(3):259, Fall, 1979.

A longitudinal study of success versus failure in contraceptive planning, by S. Oskamp, et al. JOURNAL OF POPULA-TION 1(1):69-83, Spring, 1978.

A look at community based planning, by E. Trainer. POPULI 6(2):9, 1979.

Lord Hale witches, and rape, by G. Geis. BRITISH JOURNAL OF LAW AND SOCIETY 5:26-44, Summer, 1978.

Lost cause, by E. Johnson. WEEKEND MAGAZINE 29:18-20, June 23, 1979.

Louisiana adopts strict abortion law. NOW 11(10):9, Septem-ber, 1978.

Louisiana Legislature has just enacted. SPOKESWOMAN 9(3):3, September, 1978.

Loving women: attachment and autonomy in Lesbian relation-ships, by L. A. Peplau, et al. THE JOURNAL OF SOCIAL ISSUES 34(3):7-27, 1978.

Low-level, progestogen-releasing vaginal contraceptive devices, by F. G. Burton, et al. CONTRACEPTION 19(5):507-516,

May, 1979.

Low temperature steam sterilisation, by R. J. Fallon. HEALTH AND SOCIAL SERVICE JOURNAL 89:543-544, May 4, 1979.

Luteal deficiency among women with normal menstrual cycles, requesting reversal of tubal sterilization, by E. Radwanska, et al. OBSTETRICS AND GYNECOLOGY 54(2):189-192, August, 1979.

Lysozyme in amniotic fluid during rivanol-induced second trimester abortion, by A. Olund. PROSTAGLANDINS 17(1):149-154, January, 1979.

MD's prosecution for abortion blocked [news], by L. V. Jowers. LEGAL ASPECTS OF MEDICAL PRACTICE 6(9):29, September, 1978.

Mad at Jimmy. CHRISTIANITY TODAY 23:64, October 20, 1978.

Major dailies blind to pro-life clout, by R. Shaw. OUR SUNDAY VISITOR 67:3, February 18, 1979.

Male adolescent contraceptive utilization, by M. L. Finkel, et al. ADOLESCENCE 13(51):443-451, Fall, 1978.

Male contraception, by N. B. Attico. PUBLIC HEALTH RE-VIEWS 7:55-81, January-June, 1978.

Male pill. SCIENTIFIC AMERICAN 240(6):104A, June, 1979.

—, by J. Seligmann, et al. NEWSWEEK 93:84, January 22, 1979.

Male pill; gossypol. SCIENTIFIC AMERICAN 240:104, June, 1979.

Male pill; gossypol pill developed in China, by J. Seligmann, et al. NEWSWEEK 93:84, January 22, 1979.

Malignant liver tumor after oral contraception, by H. Breining, et al. MEDIZINISCHE WELT 30(19):747, 750, May 11, 1979.

Malleability of fertility-related attitudes and behavior in a Filipino migrant sample, by J. J. Card. DEMOGRAPHY 15: 459-476, November, 1978.

Mammary neoplasia in animals: pathologic aspects and the effects of contraceptive steroids, by H. W. Casey, et al. RECENT RESULTS IN CANCER RESEARCH 66:129-160, 1979.

Management in threatened abortions, by P. Magnin. JOURNAL DE GYNECOLOGIE, OBSTETRIQUE ET BIOLOGIE DE LA REPRODUCTION 7(3 pt 2):663-664, April, 1978.

Management issues in the organization and delivery of family planning services, by R. A. Loddengaard, et al. PUBLIC HEALTH REPORTS 94:459-465, September-October, 1979.

Management of obstetric and gynecologic infections resulting from trauma, by W. J. Ledger. BULLETIN OF THE NEW YORK ACADEMY OF MEDICINE 55(2):241-247, February, 1979.

Management of threatened abortion in the first trimester, by P. Magnin. JOURNAL DE GYNECOLOGIE, OBSTETRIQUE ET BIOLOGIE DE LA REPRODUCTION 7(3 pt 2).683-685, April, 1978.

Manufacture of by-election news. NEW STATESMAN 95:515, April 21, 1978.

Many teenagers and their parents talk together about contraception and decisions on abortion [news]. FAMILY PLANNING PERSPECTIVES 10(5):298-300, September-October, 1978.

Many teens and parents talk about contraception and abortion. FAMILY PLANNING PERSPECTIVES 10:298-299, September-October, 1978.

Marriage and family enrichment: a new professional area, by R. M. Smith, et al. FAMILY COORDINATOR 28(1):87-93, January, 1979.

Marriage and family in a tudor elite: familial patterns of Elizabethan bishops, by J. Berlatsky. JOURNAL OF FAMILY HISTORY 3(1):6-22, Spring, 1978.

Marriage and fertility in the developed countries, by C. F. Westoff. SCIENTIFIC AMERICAN 239(6):51, 1978.

Marriage and parenting: our daughter's happiness depends on her being sterile. NEW HORIZONS 11(4):7-11, Summer, 1977.

Massachusetts NOW commemorates right to choose decision, by M. A. Hart. NOW 11(3):13, March, 1978.

A maternal death associated with prostaglandin E2, by S. P. Patterson, et al. OBSTETRICS AND GYNECOLOGY 54(1):123-124, July, 1979.

Maternal death caused by prostaglandin abortion. NURSES DRUG ALERT 3:94-95, August, 1979.

Maternal mortality study: abortion and mortality study: twenty year study in New York State exclusive of New York City, by R. McLean, et al. NEW YORK STATE JOURNAL OF MEDICINE 79:49-52, January, 1979.

—: teenage pregnancy and maternal mortality in New York State, by R. McLean, et al. NEW YORK STATE JOURNAL OF MEDICINE 79:226-230, February, 1979.

Maternal origin of a trisomy 7 in a spontaneous abortus, by J. del Mazo, et al. OBSTETRICS AND GYNECOLOGY 53 (3 suppl):18S-20S, March, 1979.

The mathematics of repeat abortion: explaining the increase, by C. Tietze, et al. STUDIES IN FAMILY PLANNING 9(12): 294-299, December, 1978.

May ovulation inhibitors be used without hesitation in the post-thrombotic syndrome? [letter], by H. Graeff, et al. MEDI-ZINISCHE WELT 30(14):507-508, April 6, 1979.

May spina bifida result from an X-linked defect in a selective abortion mechanism? by J. Burn, et al. JOURNAL OF MEDICAL GENETICS 16(3):210-214, June, 1979.

Maze of conflicting testimony faces jurors in murder trial of abortionist, by K. Granville. OUR SUNDAY VISITOR 68:2, May 13, 1979.

The McCormick Family Planning Program in Chiang Mai, Thailand, by G. B. Baldwin. STUDIES IN FAMILY PLANNING 9(12):300-313, December, 1978.

McRae case: theology and the constitution, by A. Neier. NATION 227:721+, December 30, 1978; Discussion, 228:34, January 20, 1979.

Meanwhile, back on the hill, by A. Brewer. POLITICKS 1:9, March 28, 1978.

Measurement of plasma human chorionic gonadotropin (hCG) and beta-hCG activities in the late luteal phase: evidence of the occurrence of spontaneous menstrual abortions in infertile women, by M. Chartier, et al. FERTILITY AND STERILITY 31(2):134-137, February, 1979.

Measuring the Thai family planning program's impact on fertility rates: a comparison of computer models, by S. E. Khoo. STUDIES IN FAMILY PLANNING 10(4):137-145, April, 1979.

Measuring tragedy; review article; with reply "Abortion and the 'right to life': a rejoinder", by L. Robinson, et al. CANADIAN FORUM 58:34-37+, April, 1978+.

The mechanism of prostaglandin action on the pregnant human uterus, by A. I. Csapo, et al. PROSTAGLANDINS 17(2): 283-299, February, 1979.

Media agendas and human rights: the Supreme Court decision on abortion, by J. C. Pollock, et al. JOURNALISM QUARTERLY 55(3):544-548+, Fall, 1978.

Media mating I. newspaper "personals" ads of homosexual men, by M. R. Laner, et al. JOURNAL OF HOMOSEXUALITY 3(2):149-162, Winter, 1977.

Medicaid abortion rules tightened. OFF OUR BACKS 8(8):12, August, 1978.

Medical consideration on timing of laparoscopic sterilization in first trimester therapeutic abortion patients, by H. M. Kwak, et al. YONSEI MEDICAL JOURNAL 19(2):105-110, 1978.

Medical contraindications in professional interruption of pregnancy, by N. Bregun-Dragić, et al. JUGOSLAVENSKA GINEKOLOGIJA I OBSTETRICIJA 17(5-6):341-347, 1977.

Medical termination of pregnancy: public opinion in an urban population, by S. X. Charles, et al. INTERNATIONAL JOURNAL OF GYNAECOLOGY AND OBSTETRICS 16(5):408-411, March-April, 1979.

Mediosocial reasons for limiting the birth rate, by I. V. Poliakov, et al. ZDRAVOOKHRANENIYE ROSSIISKOI FEDERATZII (3):17-21, 1979.

Medics; Dr. I. Lubell of the Association for Voluntary Sterilization, by P. Burstein. PEOPLE 10:71-72, December 11, 1978.

Megaloblastic anemia due to folic acid deficiency after oral contraceptives, by C. Barone, et al. HAEMATOLOGICA 64(2): 190-195, April, 1979.

Men and abortion, by P. Marchand. CHATELAINE 51(63): 168+, November, 1978.

Men and birth control, by K. Leishman. McCALLS 106:60, December, 1978.

Menstrual extraction: politics, by L. Punnett. QUEST 4(3):48-60, 1978.

—: procedures, by L. Rothman. QUEST 4(3):44-48, 1978.

Menstrual patterns and women's attitudes following sterilization by Falope rings, by L. M. Rubinstein, et al. FERTILITY AND STERILITY 31(6):641-646, June, 1979.

Menstrual regulation as a method for early termination of pregnancy, by M. Mandelin, et al. ACTA OBSTETRICIA ET GYNECOLOGICA SCANDINAVICA 58(2):169-173, 1979.

Menstrual regulation in Ibadan, Nigeria, by O. A. Ladipo, et al. INTERNATIONAL JOURNAL OF GYNAECOLOGY AND OBSTETRICS 15(5):428-432, 1978.

Mental birth control, by Jackson, et al. RAIN 5(3):14, December, 1978.

Metabolic and endocrine studies in women using norethindrone acetate implant, by S. M. Shahani, et al. CONTRACEPTION 19(2):135-144, February, 1979.

The metabolic clearance rate and uterine metabolism and retention of progesterone and 20 a-hydroxypregn-4-en-3-one during the secretion of uteroglobin in ovariectomized, steroid-treated rabbits, by R. B. Billiar, et al. ENDOCRINOLOGY 103(3):990-996, 1978.

Metabolic repercussions of oral contraception, by U. Gaspard. JOURNAL DE PHARMACIE DE BELGIQUE 33(5):312-324, September-October, 1978.

Methionine metabolism and vitamin B6 status in women using oral contraceptives, by L. T. Miller, et al. AMERICAN JORNAL OF CLINICAL NUTRITION 31:619-625, April, 1978.

Method for calculating costs of steam sterilization devised, by R. L. Sandler, et al. HOSPITALS 53(9):118-119, May 1, 1979.

A method for pasteurising human milk, by J. M. Birmingham. NURSING TIMES 74(49):suppl 5-6, December 7, 1978.

Mexico's birth-control effort catching on, by A. Riding. NEW YORK TIMES p. 2, April 29, 1979.

Microbial contamination of medical products and the effect of radiation sterilization, by V. Chýlková, et al. CASOPIS LEKARU CESKYCH 118(3):82-88, January 19, 1979.

Microsurgery after tubal ligation, by R. Henrion. NOUVELLE PRESSE MEDICALE 8(13):1089-1090, March 17, 1979.

Microsurgery: a new dimension in gynecology, by M. M. Oliphant, Jr. THE SURGICAL TECHNOLOGISTS 11:9-13, September-October, 1979.

Microsurgery of the fallopian tubes, by M. C. Ferreira. REVISTA PAULISTA DE MEDICINA 92(3-4):64-65, September-October, 1978.

Microsurgical techniques in reconstructive surgery of the fallopian tube, by J. F. Daniel. SOUTHERN MEDICAL JOURNAL 72(5):585-587, May, 1979.

Microsurgical techniques of anastomosis of the fallopian tubes, by R. N. Smith, et al. TRANSACTIONS OF THE PACIFIC COAST OBSTETRICAL AND GYNECOLOGICAL SOCIETY 45:111-115, 1978.

Microsurgical vasovasostomy clamp, by F. F. Marshall. UROLOGY 13(4):419, April, 1979.

Middle-class Americans frown on premarital sex but think teens should be offered contraception [news]. FAMILY PLANNING PERSPECTIVES 10(5):301-302, September-October, 1978.

Mid trimester abortion by single dose of betamethasone, by R. Baveja, et al. INDIAN JOURNAL OF MEDICAL RESEARCH 69:83-87, January, 1979.

Midtrimester bortion procedures [letter] , by W. Cates, Jr., et al. AMERICAN JOURNAL OF OBSTETRICS AND GYNECOLOGY 133(8):934-937, April 15, 1979.

Midtrimester abortion utilizing intraamniotic prostaglandin F2alpha, laminaria nd oxytocin, by A. J. Horowitz. JOURNAL OF REPRODUCTIVE MEDICINE 21(4):236-240, October, 1978.

Midtrimester abortion with prostaglandin and hypertonic saline—a comparative study, by R. V. Bhatt, et al. INTERNATIONAL JOURNAL OF GYNAECOLOGY AND OBSTETRICS 16(3):254-258, 1978-1979.

Migraine attacks and increased platelet aggregability induced by oral contraceptives, by S. Mazal. AUSTRALIAN AND NEW ZEALAND JOURNAL OF MEDICINE 8(6):646-648, December, 1978.

Mind & body, by L. Africano. WORKING WOMEN 4:28-29, August, 1979.

Minilaparotomy for female sterilization, by A. J. Penfield. OBSTETRICS AND GYNECOLOGY 54(2):184-188, August, 1979.

Ministat: a new oral contraceptive of the combined type with low estrogen contents, by R. Demol, et al. BRUXELLES-MEDICALE 59(4):225-232, April, 1979.

Minor tranquillisers and road accidents [letter] , by A. P. Presley. BRITISH MEDICAL JOURNAL 1(6173):1281-1282, May 12, 1979.

Minority status and family size: a comparison of explanations, by T. K. Burch. POPULATION STUDIES 33:375-378, July, 1979.

Minors and medical contraceptive services in Connecticut, by D. W. Schneider. CONNECTICUT MEDICINE 42(8):523-527, August, 1978.

Minors' right to litigate privacy interests without parental notice. WASHINGTON UNIVERSITY LAW QUARTERLY 1978: 431-449, Spring, 1978.

Miscarriage or premature birth: additional thoughts on Exodus 21:22-25, by H. W. House. WESTMINSTER THEOLOGICAL JOURNAL 41:105-123, Fall, 1978.

Mitotic chiasmata in human diplochromosomes, by E. Therman, et al. HUMAN GENETICS 45(2):131-135, December 18, 1978.

Model of fertility by planning status, by N. B. Ryder. DEMOGRAPHY 15:433-458, November, 1978.

Models of contemporary Dutch family building, by G. Santow. POPULATION STUDIES 33:59-77, March, 1979.

Modern contraceptive substances, their use and complications, by M. Kuprsanin. MEDICINSKI PREGLED 31(11-12):517-519, 1978.

Modified technique for microsurgical vasovasostomy, by A. Hamidinia, et al. INVESTIGATIVE UROLOGY 17(1):42-45, July, 1979.

The monthly injectable contraceptive: a two-year clinical trial, by S. Koetsawang, et al. INTERNATIONAL JOURNAL OF GYNAECOLOGY AND OBSTETRICS 16(1):61-64, 1978.

Morbidity in nursing infants depending on pregnancy pathology and previous abortions in the mothers, by A. V. Filyk. PEDIATRIJA, AKUSHERSTVO I GINEKOLOGIJA (6):24-25, November-December, 1978.

Mormon demographic history. I. Nuptiality and fertility of once-married couples, by M. Skolnick, et al. POPULATION STUDIES 32:5-20, March, 1978.

Morphologic studies on IUD-induced metrorrhagia: I. Endometrial changes and clinical correlations, by S. T. Shaw, Jr., et al. CONTRACEPTION 19(1):47-62, 1979.

Morphological and clinical liver changes after taking oral contraceptives, by K. Mölleken, et al. ZEITSCHRIFT FUR DIE GESAMTE INNERE MEDIZIN UND IHRE GRENZGEBIETE 34(2):79-81, January 15, 1979.

Mortality from abortion: the NHS record [letter] , by C. Brewer, et al. BRITISH MEDICAL JOURNAL 2(6136):562, August 19, 1978.

Mosaic autosomal trisomy in cultures from spontaneous abortions, by D. Warburton, et al. AMERICAN JOURNAL OF HUMAN GENETICS 30(6):609-617, November, 1978.

Mother and comforter [family planning in Israel] , by A. Sabiosky. NEW DIRECTIONS FOR WOMEN 7:12, August, 1978.

Motivation and family planning: incentives and disincentives in the delivery system, by F. O. Bicknell, et al. SOCIAL SCIENCE AND MEDICINE 10(11-12):579-583, November-December, 1976.

Movement of wild and released sterile adults of drosophila melanogaster in New Jersey, by R. T. Guest, et al. JOURNAL OF ECONOMIC ENTOMOLOGY 72:155-156, February, 1979.

Ms Magazine: some old fashioned anti-Catholicism, by M. Schwartz. OUR SUNDAY VISITOR 68:3, July 29, 1979.

Multinational comparative clinical evaluation of two long-acting injectable contraceptive steroids: norethisterone oenanthate and medroxyprogesterone acetate, by G. Benagiano, et al. CONTRACEPTION 17(5):395, May, 1978.

Multiple target involvement in pseudohypoaldosteronism, by S. Vaisrub. JAMA 242(2):177-178, July 13, 1979.

Multivariate analysis of interstate variation in fertility of teenage girls, by E. A. Brann. AMERICAN JOURNAL OF PUBLIC HEALTH 69:661-666, July, 1979.

The Muslim world [birth control and the status of women in several predominantly Muslim nations]. PEOPLE 6:3-30, November 4, 1979.

Must you have more than one child? by T. B. Brazelton. REDBOOK 152(5):58, March, 1979.

Myocardial infarction and other vascular diseases in young women. Role of estrogens and other factors, by H. Jick, et al. JAMA 240(23):2548-2552, December 1, 1978.

National board zeros in on reproductive rights. NOW 11(1):5, January, 1978.

A National Fertility Survey [VI]: the contraceptive methods used by Belgian and American couples: an application of dependency analysis, by P. Guilmot. POPULATION ET FAMILLE 3(33):61-130, 1974.

Native American peoples on the trail of tears once more: Indian Health Service and coerced sterilization, by M. Miller, et al. AMERICA 139:422-425, December 9, 1978.

Natural birth control, by N. Dorr. WELL-BEING 35:18, August, 1978.

—, by L. LeMole. EAST WEST 8(6):58, June, 1978.

Natural family planning: the contribution of fertility awareness to body-person integration, by H. Klaus. SOCIAL THOUGHT 5:35-42, Winter, 1979.

—: Father Bernard Häring's positions: an essay review, by W. May. SOCIAL THOUGHT 5:67-71, Summer, 1979.

—: in the U.S. the fight goes on for government funding, by F. Franzonia. OUR SUNDAY VISITOR 68:2, August 19, 1979.

—: the ovulation method, by N. Elder. JOURNAL OF NURSE-MIDWIFERY 23:25-30, Fall, 1978.

Natural family planning teachers, inc. WELL-BEING 33:5, June 15, 1978.

Natural oestrogens for oral contraception [letter] , by J. Serup, et al. LANCET 2(8140):471-472, September 1, 1979.

Natural prevention of genetic defects; spontaneous abortion or miscarriage in Down's syndrome. SCIENCE NEWS 114:379, November 25, 1978.

Necessity and the case of Dr. Morgentaler [Morgentaler v. Regina (1975) 53 D L R (3d) 161] , by L. H. Leigh. CRIMINAL LAW REVIEW 1978:151-158, March, 1978.

Necessity as a defense to a charge of criminal trespass in an abortion clinic. UNIVERSITY OF CINCINNATI LAW REVIEW 48:501-516, 1979.

The need for genetic counseling, by G. G. Wendt. INTERNIST 19(8):441-444, August, 1978.

Need now contraceptive method in next decade to make a major impact on population growth [news] . FAMILY PLANNING PERSPECTIVES 10(5):294-295, September-October, 1978.

The needs of adolescent women utilizing family planning services, by J. Cahn. JOURNAL OF SEX RESEARCH 13(3):210-222, August, 1977.

Neoplasia and dysplasia of the cervix uteri and contraception: a possible protective effect of the diaphragm, by N. H. Wright, et al. BRITISH JOURNAL OF CANCER 38(2):273-279, August, 1978.

Neural-tube defects: importance of a history of abortion in aetiology, by D. R. Evans. BRITISH MEDICAL JOURNAL 1(6169):975-976, April 14, 1979.

Neuro-ophthalmologic accidents caused by hormonal contraception, by M. Ardouin, et al. BULLETINS ET MEMOIRES DE LA SOCIETE FRASCAISE D'OPHTHALMOLOGIE 90:261-267, 1978.

New abortion statistics published. SPOKESWOMAN 9(5):9,
    November, 1978.

A new approach to tubal sterilization by laparoscopy, by R. F.
    Valle, et al. FERTILITY AND STERILITY 30(4):415-422,
    October, 1978.

A new category of ovulation inhibitors linear LH-RH analogues
    having more than ten residues, by T. Wasiak, et al. BIO-
    CHEMICAL AND BIOPHYSICAL RESEARCH COMMUNI-
    CATIONS 86(3):843-848, 1979.

A new conscience of the pro-life movement, by M. Weinberger.
    CONSERVATIVE DIGEST 5:18+, December, 1979.

New evidence on pill side effects. SPOKESWOMAN 9(5):6,
    November, 1978.

New federal abortion regulations, by M. M. Smith. NOW
    11(5&6):5, April, 1978.

New frontiers of contraception, by D. R. Mishell, Jr. JOURNAL
    OF REPRODUCTIVE MEDICINE 21(5 suppl):254-256,
    November, 1978.

A new gel for intracervical application of prostaglandin E2, by
    U. Ulmsten, et al. ACTA OBSTETRICIA ET GYNE-
    COLOGICA SCANDINAVICA (84):19-21, 1979.

New government rules may snuff out national scandal, Indian
    doctor hopes, by F. Franzonia. OUR SUNDAY VISITOR
    68:3, June 24, 1979.

New issues, new options: a management perspective on popula-
    tion and family planning, by D. C. Korten. STUDIES IN
    FAMILY PLANNING 10(1):13, January, 1979.

New Jersey update: Trojan war, by R. K. Rein. NEW JERSEY
    MONTHLY 3:40+, August, 1979.

A new long-acting injectable microcapsule system for the ad-
    ministration of progesterone, by L. R. Beck, et al. FER-

TILITY AND STERILITY 31(5):545-551, May, 1979.

A new method of crouptent cleaning/sterilizing, by N. Clarke.
RESPIRATORY TECHNOLOGY 14:23+, Fall, 1978.

New murder trial begins for California abortionist Waddill, by
L. Welborn. OUR SUNDAY VISITOR 67:1, March 4, 1979.

New poll finds majority support for abortion, sex education.
SPOKESWOMAN 9(1):9, July, 1978.

A new principle of injectable depot contraceptives. I. Drug
selection and studies in monkeys, by M. Hümpel, et al. CON-
TRACEPTION 19(4):411-419, April, 1979.

A new problem in adolescent gynecology, by M. J. Bulfin.
SOUTHERN MEDICAL JOURNAL 72(8):967-967, August,
1979.

New prostaglandin E2 analogue for pregnancy termination
[letter], by M. Bygdeman, et al. LANCET 1(8126):1136,
May 26, 1979.

New regulations governing DHEW sterilization funding now in
effect; stress informed consent [news]. FAMILY PLAN-
NING PERSPECTIVES 11(1):46-47, January-February,
1979.

New studies: pills don't increase diabetes danger: smoking
multiplies pill-associated stroke risk [news]. FAMILY
PLANNING PERSPECTIVES 11(2):120-122, March-April,
1979.

New York State report: prevention is key to teen pregnancy reduction. FAMILY PLANNING PERSPECTIVES 10:293-
294, September-October, 1978.

Newspaper's about-face on abortion astounds, delights Ohio
right-to-lifers, by J. McKenna. OUR SUNDAY VISITOR
67:3, February 18, 1979.

No going back. THE ECONOMIST 273:44, October 13, 1979.

No more chemicals, by T. Dejanikus. OFF OUR BACKS 8(5): 11, May, 1978.

No victory. NOW 11(11):6, October, 1978.

Nonprotective abortions OK o'seas if paid ahead, by R. Sanders. AIR FORCE TIMES 39:6, January 29, 1979.

Non-therapeutic sterilization—malpractice, and the issues of "wrongful birth" and "wrongful life" in Quebec law, by R. P. Kouri. CANADIAN BUSINESS REVIEW 57:89-105, March, 1979.

Normal, functional, and unhealthy? by D. A. Price. FAMILY COORDINATOR 28(1):109-114, January, 1979.

Normal intrauterine pregnancy after sterilization reversal in wife and husband [letter], by S. J. Silber, et al. FERTILITY AND STERILITY 31(1):90, January, 1979.

Norwich intro spurs new posture in marketing of contraceptives, by G. Zern. PRODUCT MARKETING 6:1+, December, 1977.

The nulliparous patient, the IUD, and subsequent fertility. BRITISH MEDICAL JOURNAL 6132:233, July 22, 1978.

Number of Americans choosing sterilization. SPOKESWOMAN 9(4):6, October, 1978.

Nun on trial for her baby's death: will Sister Maureen's tragedy shake the church? by C. Breslin. MS MAGAZINE 5:68-71, March, 1977.

Nurse-midwifery and family planning in the United States: data from the 1976-1977 American College of Nurse-Midwives' study, by S. H. Fischman, et al. ADVANCES IN PLANNED PARENTHOOD 13(3-4):78-86, 1978.

Nurse specialists in family planning: the results of a 3-year study, by J. Newton, et al. CONTRACEPTION 18(6):577-592, December, 1978.

Nursing care study. Surgical female sterilisation: it's all done with tubes and clips, by A. Bennett. NURSING MIRROR AND MIDWIVES' JOURNAL 148(10):42-44, March 8, 1979.

Nutrition and population in health sector planning, by C. E. Taylor. FOOD RESEARCH INSTITUTE STUDIES 16(2): 77-90, 1977.

Nutrition counseling at planned parenthood centers, by H. Smiciklas-Wright, et al. PUBLIC HEALTH REPORTS 94(3):239-242, June, 1979.

Nutrition during pregnancy, lactation, and oral contraception, by B. S. Worthington. NURSING CLINICS OF NORTH AMERICA 14(2):269-283, June, 1979.

OCs and resting blood flow [letter], by A. Singer. ANGIOLOGY 30(2):129-130, February, 1979.

OCs—update on usage, safety, and side effects. POPULATION REPORTS (5):A133-A186, January, 1979.

Objective versus subjective responses to abortion, by J. M. Robbins. JOURNAL OF CONSULTING AND CLINICAL PSYCHOLOGY 47:994-995, October, 1979.

Observations on abortion, by H. Wallot. UNION MEDICALE DU CANADA 108(3):301-302, March, 1979.

Observations on the effect of some oral contraceptives on the ovary of rat, by P. Ghosh, et al. JOUNRAL OF THE INDIAN MEDICAL ASSOCIATION 71(6):141-144, September 16, 1978.

Obstetrical complications in induced abortions, by M. Renkielska. GINEKOLOGIA POLSKA 49(5):389-393, May, 1978.

Obstructive azoospermia: respiratory function tests, lectron microscopy and the results of surgery, by W. F. Hendry, et al. BRITISH JOURNAL OF UROLOGY 50(7):598-604, December, 1978.

Occult pregnancy as a factor in unexplained infertility, by S. K. Block. JOURNAL OF REPRODUCTIVE MEDICINE 21(4): 251-253, October, 1978.

Occupational and environmental risks in and around a smelter in northern Sweden. V. Spontaneous abortion among female employees and decreased birth weight in their offspring, by S. Nordström, et al. HEREDITAS 90(2):291-296, 1979.

Occurrence of gonococcal perihepatitis after therapeutic abortion [letter], by D. Portnoy, et al. CANADIAN MEDICAL AS-SOCIATION JOURNAL 120(4):408, February 17, 1979.

Of many things; National Council of Churches' call for ecumenical debate, by J. O'Hare. AMERICA 140:inside cover, February 3, 1979.

Of two minds about abortion, by A. Hacker. HARPERS' BA-ZAAR 259:16-18+, September, 1979.

Off the pill; new slant on the old diaphragm [smaller, uniform-size diaphragm] : how to use the diaphragm, by V. Cava-Rizzuto. MAJORITY REPORT 8:8-9, September 30-October 13, 1978.

Office gynecology. Part II, by J. V. Kelly. ARIZONA MEDI-CINE 35(11):730-731, November, 1978.

Office termination of pregnancy by 'menstrual aspiration', by R. W. Hale, et al. AMERICAN JOURNAL OF OBSTETRICS AND GYNECOLOGY 134(2):213-218, May 15, 1979.

Oklahoma legislators. SPOKESWOMAN 8(10):8, April, 1978.

On abortion, by A. Amendola. AMERICAN ATHEIST 21(10) 10, October, 1979.

On the concept of the article 'test of sterility', by J. Sagáth, et al. CESKOSLOVENSKA FARMACIE 27(4):196-200, June, 1978.

On drawing policy conclusions from multiple regressions: some

queries and dilemmas, by R. B. Dixon. STUDIES IN FAMI-
LY PLANNING 9(10-11):286-288, October-November,
1978.

On the mechanism of action of 15-methyl-PGF2 alpha as an
abortifacient, by K. Gréen, et al. PROSTAGLANDINS
17(2):277-282, February, 1979.

On second thought. OFF OUR BACKS 8(5):19, May, 1978.

On social norms and fertility decline, by N. R. Crook. JOUR-
NAL OF DEVELOPMENT STUDIES 14:198-210, July,
1978.

On trial for abortion. SEVEN DAYS 2(14):6, September 29,
1978.

One culprit in unwanted pregnancies: the patients' doctor, by
S. J. Barr. MEDICAL WORLD NEWS 20:108, February 5,
1979.

Ongoing program of outpatient sterilizations, by R. E. Hassler.
WISCONSIN MEDICAL JOURNAL 77(11):113-114, No-
vember, 1978.

An open letter to Walter Cronkite (attack WC for his smear of
Catholic Church on abortion issue), by W. F. Gavin. HU-
MAN EVENTS 38:16+, March 11, 1978.

Opening debates range from abortions to estates. AMERICAN
BAR ASSOCIATION JOURNAL 64:1652, November, 1978.

Opinions of the United States Supreme Court: abortion. CRIM-
INAL LAW REPORTER: TEXT SECTION 24(14) 3043-
3051, January 10, 1979.

Optimum dosage of an oral contraceptive. A report from the
study of seven combinations of norgestimate and ethinyl
estradiol, by J. S. Lawson, et al. AMERICAN JOURNAL OF
OBSTETRICS AND GYNECOLOGY 134(3):315-320,
June 1, 1979.

Oral and intrauterine contraception: a 1978 risk assessment, by A. Rosenfield. AMERICAN JOURNAL OF OBSTETRICS AND GYNECOLOGY 132(1):92-106, September 1, 1978.

Oral contraception and depression, by J. L. Garrison. SOCIAL WORK 24:162-163, March, 1979.

Oral contraception and the detection of carriers in haemophilia B, by E. Briët, et al. THROMBOSIS RESEARCH 13(3): 379-388, September, 1978.

Oral contraception and the gingival mucosa, by C. Fruteau de Laclos, et al. LIGAMENT 13(119):17-20, January-March, 1976.

Oral contraception and multiple sclerosis, by A. Ghezzi, et al. ARCHIVIO PER LE SCIENZE MEDICHE 136(1):67-73, January-March, 1979.

Oral contraception in the adolescent, by E. Weisberg. AUSTRALIAN FAMILY PHYSICIAN 7(spec no):32-36, August, 1978.

Oral contraceptive estrogen and plasma lipid levels, by A. Hedlin, et al. OBSTETRICS AND GYNECOLOGY 52(4) 430-435, October, 1978.

Oral contraceptive pills and clinical otosclerosis, by L. Podoshin, et al. INTERNATIONAL JOURNAL OF GYNAECOLOGY AND OBSTETRICS 15(6):554-555, 1978.

Oral contraceptive use alters the balance of platelet prostaglandin and thromboxane synthesis, by A. E. Schorer, et al. PROSTAGLANDINS AND MEDICINE 1(1):5-11, July, 1978.

Oral contraceptive use and fasting triglyceride, plasma cholesterol and HDL cholesterol, by C. H. Hennekens, et al. CIRCULATION 60(3):486-489, September, 1979.

Oral contraceptive use and secondary amenorrhea, by M. Kissi, et al. OBSTETRICS AND GYNECOLOGY 53(2):241-244,

February, 1979.

Oral-contraceptive use in relation to myocardial infarction, by S. Shapiro, et al. LANCET 1(8119):743-747, April 7, 1979.

Oral contraceptives. POPULATION REPORTS (5):1, January, 1979.

—, by M. A. Barletta. AMERICAN DRUGGIST 178:35-36, August, 1978.

Oral contraceptives and birth defects [letter] , by I. D. Bross. NEW ENGLAND JOURNAL OF MEDICINE 300(1):47, January 4, 1979.

Oral contraceptives and cancer risk, by J. A. Gustafsson, et al. LAKARTIDNINGEN 76(17):1625-1627, April 25, 1979.

Oral contraceptives and cervix uteri cancer, by B. I. Nesheim. TIDSSKRIFT FOR DEN NORSKE LAEGEFORENING 98(29):1422-1423, October 20, 1978.

Oral contraceptives and depression, by H. Warnes, et al. PSY-CHOSOMATICS 20(3):187-189+, March, 1979.

Oral contraceptives and depressive symptomatology: biologic mechanisms, by B. L. Parry, et al. COMPREHENSIVE PSY-CHIATRY 20(4):347-358, July-August, 1979.

Oral contraceptives and diabetes mellitus, by S. J. Wingrave, et al. BRITISH MEDICAL JOURNAL 1(6155):23, January 6, 1979.

Oral contraceptives and endometriosis, by K. J. Karnacky. AMERICAN JOURNAL OF OBSTETRICS AND GYNE-COLOGY 135(2):279-280, September 15, 1979.

Oral contraceptives and HDL cholesterol, by O. Frankman, et al. LAKARTIDNINGEN 76(1-2):15-16, January 3, 1979.

Oral contraceptives and the liver, by A. G. de Pagter, et al. NEDERLANDS TIJDSCHRIFT VOOR GENEESKUNDE

123(21):881-887, May 26, 1979.

Oral contraceptives and liver tumours, by A. Marshall, et al. MEDICAL JOURNAL OF AUSTRALIA 2(6):240-241, September 9, 1978.

Oral contraceptives and myocardial infarction, by P. Dillon, et al. CARDIOVASCULAR NURSING 15(2):5-9, March-April, 1979.

Oral contraceptives and neoplasia, by G. R. Huggins, et al. FERTILITY AND STERILITY 32(1):1-23, July, 1979.

Oral contraceptives and the periodontium, by A. Fesseler. ZAHNAERZTLICHE MITTEILUNGEN 69(10) 634, May 16, 1979.

Oral contraceptives and platelet aggregation, by N. Shevde, et al. AMERICAN JOURNAL OF OBSTETRICS AND GYNE-COLOGY 132(3):303-306, October 1, 1978.

Oral contraceptives and the risk of neoplasms, by J. A. Gustafsson, et al. LAKARTIDNINGEN 76(17):1625-1627, April 25, 1979.

Oral contraceptives and stroke in young women: a clinico-pathologic correlation, by N. S. Irey, et al. NEUROLOGY 28(12):1216-1219, December, 1978.

Oral contraceptives and vitamins, by E. Heilmann. DEUTSCH MEDIZINISCHE WOCHENSCHRIFT 104(4):144-146, January 26, 1979.

Oral contraceptives as a possible cause of cerebral vascular disorders, by M. Jarema. NEUROLOGIA I NEUROCHIRUR-GIA POLSKA 13(1):81-86, January-February, 1979.

Oral contraceptives, hyperlipoproteinemia and ischemic heart disease, by V. N. Titov, et al. TERAPEUTICHESKI ARK-HIV 50(12):22-28, 1978.

Oral contraceptives, smoking, and other factors in relation to risk of venous thromboembolic disease, by D. B. Petitti, et al. AMERICAN JOURNAL OF EPIDEMIOLOGY 108(6) 480-485, December, 1978.

Oral contraceptives—an update, by D. Bartosik. AMERICAN FAMILY PHYSICIAN 19(5):149-150, May, 1979.

Oral contraceptives, venous thrombosis, and varicose veins. Royal College of General Practitioners' Oral Contraception Study. JOURNAL OF THE ROYAL COLLEGE OF GENERAL PRACTITIONERS 28(192):393-399, July, 1978.

Oral oestro-progestative contraception and cervical and vaginal cytology, by J. Favre, et al. SEMAINE DES HOPITAUX DE PARIS 55(7-8):384-388, February 18-25, 1979.

The oral toxicity of 1-amino-3-chloro-propanol hydrochloride (CL 88236) in rats, by R. W. James, et al. TOXICOLOGY 11(3):235-243, November, 1978.

Oregonians to battle anti-choice initiative. NOW 11(10):9, September, 1978.

Origins of trisomies in human spontaneous abortions, by T. Hassold, et al. HUMAN GENETICS 46(3):285-294, February 15, 1979.

Others don't see it that way. CRIME CONTROL DIGEST 13(2): 8-9, January 15, 1979.

Our bodies, ourselves and them, by K. Whitehorn. OBSERVER p. 43, July 15, 1979.

Our findings in patients examined before artificial abortion in 1973-1977, by M. Lisá, et al. CESKOSLOVENSKA DERMATOLOGIE 54(2):91-93, April, 1979.

Outcome of pregnancy for the fetus and the condition of newborn infant after threatened abortion, by N. G. Kosheleva. VOPROSY OKHRANY MATERINSTVA I DETSTVA 23(12):51-53, December, 1978.

Outpatient termination of pregnancy via intramural single-shot application of the prostaglandin derivative sh b 286 (sulproston), by H. Wiechell. GEBURTSHILFE UND FRAUEN-HEILKUNDE 39(5):401-403, May, 1979.

Ova harvest with in vivo fertilization, by L. B. Shettles. AMERICAN JOURNAL OF OBSTETRICS AND GYNECOLOGY 133(7):845, April 1, 1979.

Overall achievements in the training of physicians in medical termination of pregnancy in India, by M. D. Sharma. JOURNAL OF FAMILY WELFARE 25:3-12, December, 1978.

Overcoming the taboos of conception control, by W. E. Small. AMERICAN PHARMACY 19(8):7, July, 1979.

Ovulation recovery after hormonal contraception, by J. A. Portuondo, et al. ENDOSCOPY 11(2):114-115, May, 1979.

The ovum, its milieu and possibilities for contraceptive attack. Proceedings of a Symposium of the Society for the Study of Fertility and the World Health Organization, Cambridge, July 1978. JOURNAL OF REPRODUCTION AND FERTILITY 55(1):221-275, January, 1979.

P&G explores contraceptives, by L. Edwards. ADVERTISING AGE 49:3+, October 23, 1978.

P&G's contraceptive work could shake up market, by L. Edwards. ADVERTISING AGE 49:6, October 30, 1978.

Package primer; out of the closet and onto the shelf, by R. Glaxton. DRUG AND COSMETIC INDUSTRY 124:76, February, 1979.

Packwood and his pro-abortion backers (Gloria Steinem writes fundraising letter to help Sen. Robert Packwood battle his anti-abortion opponent forgetting that no such opponent now exists), by J. D. Lofton, Jr. HUMAN EVENTS 39:9+, July, 1978.

Pain of first-trimester abortion: its quantification and relations with other variables, by G. M. Smith, et al. AMERICAN JOURNAL OF OBSTETRICS AND GYNECOLOGY 133(5): 489-498, March 1, 1979.

Parental rights and teen-age sexuality counseling, by M. Schwartz. OUR SUNDAY VISITOR 67:4+, April 29, 1979.

Parents, children, and the supreme court, by G. J. Annas. HASTINGS CENTER REPORT 9:21-23, October, 1979.

Parkinsonism after traumatic childbirth, by R. P. Murphy. JOURNAL OF NEUROLOGY, NEUROSURGERY AND PSYCHIATRY 42(4):384-385, April, 1979.

Parliament and birth control in the 1920s, by M. Shinns. JOURNAL OF THE ROYAL COLLEGE OF GENERAL PRACTITIONERS 28(187):83-88, February, 1979.

Past and current contraceptive use in Pakistan, by N. M. Shah. STUDIES IN FAMILY PLANNING 10(5):164, May, 1979.

Patentex-Oval—a contraceptive agent for topical use, by J. Higier, et al. WIADOMOSCI LEKARSKIE 31(19):1349-1351, October 1, 1978.

Pathogenetic conditioning of the therapeutic effect of infecundin, by A. A. Kozhin. AKUSHERSTVO I GINEKOLOGIIA (8):40-43, August, 1978.

Pathologic effects of oral contraceptives, by G. D. Hilliard, et al. RECENT RESULTS IN CANCER RESEARCH 66:49-71, 1979.

Pathological and embryological studies on abortion cases related to the Seveso accident, by H. Rehder, et al. SCHWEIZERISCHE MEDIZINISCHE WOCHENSCHRIFT 108(42): 1617-1625, October 21, 1978.

Pathological aspects of the infertile testis, by T. W. Wong, et al. UROLOGIE CLINICS OF NORTH AMERICA 5(3):503-530, October, 1978.

Pathomorphological and histochemical characteristics of the fetus and placenta in missed abortion and labor, by M. M. Kliherman. PEDIATRIIA AKUSHERSTVO I GINEKOLOGIIA (6):51-54, November-December, 1978.

Pathomorphological studies of spontaneous and experimental abortions in cows and guinea pigs, by S. Savova-Burdarova, et al. VETERINARNO-MEDITSINSKI NAUKI 15(5):59-68, 1978.

Patient attitudes about two forms of printed oral contraceptive information, by M. Mazis, et al. MEDICAL CARE 16(12): 1045-1054, December, 1978.

Patient recall of induced abortion, by P. E. Slater, et al. EUROPEAN JOURNAL OF OBSTETRICS, GYNECOLOGY AND REPRODUCTIVE BIOLOGY 8(4):185-186, 1978.

Patients' evaluations of gynecologic services provided by nurse practitioners, by J. M. Wagener, et al. JOURNAL OF THE AMERICAN COLLEGE HEALTH ASSOCIATION 27:98-100, October, 1978.

Patients treated for gynecologic cancer after use of oral contraceptives and IUD, by M. Szegvári, et al. ORVOSI HETILAP 120(13):756-758, April 1, 1979.

Paton v. British Pregnancy Advisory Serv. Trustees [1978] 3 W L R 687. LAW QUARTERLY REVIEW 95:332-335, July, 1979.

Patterns of aggregate and individual changes in contraceptive practice. United States, 1965-1975, by C. F. Westoff, et al. VITAL HEALTH STATISTICS 3(17):iii-vi+, June, 1979.

Patterns of serum LH and FSH in response to 4-hour infusions of luteinizing hormone releasing hormone in normal women during menstrual cycle, on oral contraceptives, and in postmenopausal state, by D. M. de Kretser, et al. JOURNAL OF CLINICAL ENDOCRINOLOGY AND METABOLISM 46(2):227-235, February, 1978.

Paul and Judy Brown vow they'll change the constitution to stamp out abortion, by C. Crawford. PEOPLE 11(3):28, January 22, 1979.

Pedal surgical table and sterilizer box for storing and retrieving syringes, by V. Z. Voiko. STOMATOLOGIIA 58(1):77-78, January-February, 1979.

Penetrating electron radiation for the disinfection of manure, by I. S. Zharikov, et al. VETERINARIIA (12):63-64, December, 1978.

Pennsylvania abortion law ruled unconstitutional. IACP LAW ENFORCEMENT LEGAL REVIEW 83:3, May, 1979.

Peptide agents may spark contraceptive revolution. MEDICAL WORLD NEWS 20:4-6, September 17, 1979.

Peptide contraception:—antifertility properties of LH-RH analogues, by A. Corbin, et al. INTERNATIONAL JOURNAL OF GYNAECOLOGY AND OBSTETRICS 16(5):359-372, March-April, 1979.

Perceived contribution of children to marriage and its effects on family planning behavior, by P. L. Tobin, et al. SOCIAL BIOLOGY 22(1):75-85, Spring, 1975.

Perception of parental sex guilt and sexual behavior and arousal of college students, by P. R. Abramson, et al. PERCEPTUAL AND MOTOR SKILLS 45(1):337-338, August, 1977.

Perils of personhood, by R. Weiss. ETHICS 89:66-75, October, 1978.

Perlaparoscopic tubarlc electrocoagulation, by A. Herruzo. ACTA OBSTETRICA Y GINECOLOGICA HISPANA-LUSITANA 27(1):43-62, January, 1979.

Permanent control of female fertility by surgical methods, by A. de la Cruz Colorado. GINECOLOGIA Y OBSTETRICIA DE MEXICO 45(270):319-328, April, 1979.

Permissible scope of parental involvement in the abortion decision of an unmarried minor. GEORGE MASON UNIVERSITY LAW REVIEW 2:235-263, Winter, 1978.

Personal and moral concepts: a study of women's reasoning and decision-making abortion abortion, by J. G. Smetana. DISSERTATION ABSTRACTS INTERNATIONAL 39(7-B): 3595-3596, January, 1979.

Personality and attitude-activism correspondence, by P. D. Werner. JOURNAL OF PERSONALITY AND SOCIAL PSYCHOLOGY 36:1375-1390, December, 1978.

Personality and the use of oral contraceptives in British university students, by R. Priestnall, et al. SOCIAL SCIENCE AND MEDICINE 12(5A):403-407, September, 1978.

Personality, sexuality, and demographic differences between volunteers and nonvolunteers for a laboratory study of male sexual behavior, by G. M. Farkas, et al. ARCHIVES OF SEAXUAL BEHAVIOR 7(6):513-520, November, 1978.

Perspectives on the abortion decision. NEW MEXICO LAW REVIEW 9:175-186, Winter, 1978-1979.

Peruvian experience of the practice of tubal ligation, by J. O. Dalrymple, et al. TROPICAL DOCTOR 8(4):198-200, October, 1978.

The pharmacological activity of a new prostaglandin analogue, 13-dehydro-a-ethyl prostaglandin F2a, by H. Shu, et al. ACTA ZOOLOGICA SINICA 24(4):314-321, 1978.

Pharmacological and clinical application of progestational hormone depot preparations, by J. Andor. GYNAECOLOGISCHE RUNDSCHAU 18(3-4):163-171, 1978.

Pharmacology of the new steroid contraceptives, by V. V. Korkhov. AKUSHERSTVO I GINEKOLOGIIA (2):5-8, 1979.

Philippa Foot and the doctrine of double effect, by R. Weatherford. PERSONALIST 60:105-113, January, 1979.

The philosophy of existentialism and a psychology of irreversible homosexuality, by J. P. Cangemi, et al. COLLEGE STUDENT JOURNAL MONOGRAPH 8(3):1-11, September-October, 1974.

Physical sensations during stressful hospital procedures: a preliminary study of saline abortion patients, by K. Aby-Nielsen. JOGN 8(2):105-106, March-April, 1979.

Physician behavior as a determinant of utilization patterns: the case of abortion, by C. A. Nathanson, et al. AMERICAN JOURNAL OF PUBLIC HEALTH 68:1104-1114, November, 1978.

Physicians and abortion [implications of court cases]. WOMEN'S RIGHTS LAW REPORTER 5:79-81, Winter-Spring, 1979.

Physicians and surgeons—damages—parents of an unplanned child, in suit for wrongful conception may recover damages for medical expenses, pain and suffering, loss of consortium, and costs of rearing the child to maturity. NORTH DAKOTA LAW REVIEW 54:619-626, 1978.

Physiological and psychological effects of vitamins E and B6 on women taking oral contraceptives, by W. V. Applegate, et al. INTERNATIONAL JOURNAL FOR VITAMIN AND NUTRITION RESEARCH 49(1):43-50, 1979.

The pill and amenorrhoea, by M. Katz. SOUTH AFRICAN MEDICAL JOURNAL 54(12):465, September 16, 1978.

The pill and the breast, by A. Gregl, et al. MEDIZINISCHE WELT 30(4):120-123, January 26, 1979.

The pill and circulatory disease, by V. Beral, et al. AMERICAN HEART JOURNAL 97(2):263-264, February, 1979.

The pill and endocrine diseases, by I. Werner-Zodrow, et al. GYNAEKOLOGISCHE RUNDSCHAU 18(3-4):246-252, 1978.

Pill and heart attacks: exaggerated? SCIENCE NEWS 115:247, April 14, 1979.

The pill and mortality from cardiovascular disease: another look, by C. Tietze. FAMILY PLANNING PERSPECTIVES 11(2): 80, March-April, 1979.

—: another outlook [United States] , by C. Tietze. INTERNA-TIONAL FAMILY PLANNING PERSPECTIVES 5:8-12, March, 1979.

The pill and other drugs, by E. S. Johnson. TRANSACTIONS OF THE MEDICAL SOCIETY OF LONDON 92-93:131-134, 1975-1977.

Pill: a cleaner bill of health. MACLEANS' 91:53, October 9, 1978.

The 'pill,' disease of civilization? [news] , by R. Veylon. NOU-VELLE PRESSE MEDICALE 7(44):4064+, December 9, 1978.

A pill for abortion. THE ECONOMIST 272:53, August 25, 1979.

The pill in Bangladesh, by T. Dejanikus. OFF OUR BACKS 9:12, May, 1979.

Pill linked to slight blood pressure rise; minor side effects greater among underweight women [news] . FAMILY PLANNING PERSPECTIVES 10(5):300-301, September-October, 1978.

The pill: a perspective for assessing risks and benefits, by F. S. Jaffe. NEW ENGLAND JOURNAL OF MEDICINE 297: 612-614, September 17, 1977.

Pill raises blood pressure slightly; side effects vary with weight. FAMILY PLANNING PERSPECTIVES 10:300-301, September-October, 1978.

Pitchford acquitted of criminal abortion. NOW 11(11):11, October, 1978.

Pitfalls in contraception, by B. W. Simcock. AUSTRALIAN FAMILY PHYSICIAN 7(10):1243-1251, October, 1978.

Pituitary adenoma and oral contraceptives: a case-control study, by C. B. Coulam, et al. FERTILITY AND STERILITY 31(1):25-28, January, 1979.

Placental histopathology of midtrimester termination, by A. Babaknia, et al. OBSTETRICS AND GYNECOLOGY 53(5):583-586, May, 1979.

Placental lesions in habitually aborting cats, by C. R. Huxtable, et al. VETERINARY PATHOLOGY 16(3):283-289, May, 1979.

Planned childbirth, by S. Maehara. KANGO 30(12):18-24, December, 1978.

Planned fertility and fertility socialization in Kwangtung province, by P. P. T. Ng. CHINA QUARTERLY (78):351-359, June, 1979.

Planned parenthood fights back. NOW 11(8):12, July, 1978.

Planned parenthood: a port in the storm (problem pregnancy a lonely experience), by R. K. Rein. NEW JERSEY MONTHLY 3:49, July, 1979.

Planning families or checking population? by T. Lukk. AFRICA REPORT 23:35-38, November, 1978.

Planning for sex, marriage, contraception, and pregnancy, by A. L. Graber, et al. DIABETES CARE 1(3):202-203, May-June, 1978.

Plasma and urine levels produced by an oral dose of ampicillin 0.5 G administered to women taking oral contraceptives, by A. Philipson. ACTA OBSTETRICIA ET GYNECOLOGICA SCANDINAVICA 58(1):69-71, 1979.

Plasma bradykininogen levels before and after ovulation: studies in women and guinea pigs, with observations on oral contraceptives and menopause, by C. Smith, et al. AMERICAN JOURNAL OF OBSTETRICS AND GYNECOLOGY 133(8): 868-876, April 15, 1979.

Plasma levels of adrenocorticotropin and cortisol in women receiving oral contraceptive steroid treatment, by B. R. Carr, et al. JOURNAL OF CLINICAL ENDOCRINOLOGY AND METABOLISM 49(3):346-349, September, 1979.

Plasminogen activator levels in plasma and urine during exercise and oral contraceptive use, by A. M. Hedlin, et al. THROMBOSIS AND HAEMOSTASIS 39(3):743-750, June 30, 1978.

Platelet aggregation during various phases of the menstrual cycle and after therapy with ovulation inhibitors, by E. E. Ohnhaus, et al. SCHWEIZERISCHE MEDIZINISCHE WOCHENSCHRIFT 108(41):1580-1581, October 14, 1978.

A plea for the condom, especially for teenagers, by Y. M. Felman. JAMA 241(23):2517-2518, June 8, 1979.

A plea to all vasectomists [letter], by W. K. Yeates. BRITISH MEDICAL JOURNAL 1(6155):55, January 6, 1979.

Political will and family planning: the implications of India's emergency experience [under the former Prime minister Indira Gandhi, during 1975 and 1976], by D. R. Gwatkin. POPULATION AND DEVELOPMENT REVIEW 5:29-59, March, 1979.

The politics of the Burger court toward women, by L. F. Goldstein. POLICY STUDIES JOURNAL 7:213-218, Winter, 1978.

Politics of Latin American: family-planning policy, by J. L. Weaver. JOURNAL OF DEVELOPING AREAS 12:415-437, July, 1978.

Politics: want to make an issue of it? THE ECONOMIST 269:44-45, November 25, 1978.

Pope John Paul I and birth control, by K. Withers. AMERICA 140:233-234, March 24, 1979.

Population and poverty, by M. Wolfson. OECD OBSERVER (95):17-22, November, 1978.

Population control: the next steps; education, an "ideal contraceptive," and a new world economic order, by R. M. Salas, et al. ATLAS 26:20-22, September, 1979.

Population outpaces food supply, by P. Niesewant. GUARDIAN p. 13, December 31, 1979.

Population policy and public goods, by F. Miller, et al. PHILOSOPHY AND PUBLIC AFFAIRS 8:148-174, Winter, 1979.

The population policy of China, by Y. C. Yu. POPULATION STUDIES 33:125-142, March, 1979.

Position statement on abortion. AMERICAN JOURNAL OF PSYCHOLOGY 136:272, February, 1979.

Possibility of sterilizing eyedrops by a bacterial filtration method, by A. A. Danilenko, et al. FARMATSIIA 27(5):50-52, September-October, 1978.

Possible harzards of oral contraceptive use, by W. B. Kannel. CIRCULATION 60(3):490-491, September, 1979.

A possible new treatment for twin pregnancy in the mare, by R. R. Pascoe. EQUINE VETERINARY JOURNAL 11(1): 64-65, January, 1979.

Possible ovulatory deficiency after tubal ligation, by G. S. Berger, et al. AMERICAN JOURNAL OF OBSTETRICS AND GYNECOLOGY 132(6):699-700, November 15, 1978.

Post-abortion babies alive, kicking. NEW TIMES 10(2):24, January 23, 1978.

Postabortion intrauterine device, by C. Morales Lepe, et al.

GINECOLOGIA Y OBSTETRICIA DE MEXICO 43(260): 429-432, June, 1978.

Post-abortion septicemia. Human equivalent of the Shwartzman-Sanarelli phenomenon, by A. Larcan, et al. SEMAINE DES HOPITAUX DE PARIS 54(17-20):585-594, June, 1978.

Post-coital antifertility activity of Annona squamosa and Ipomoea fistulosa, by A. Mishra, et al. PLANTA MEDICA 35(3):283-285, March, 1979.

Postcoital contraception, by M. Beckmann, et al. MEDIZINISCHE WELT 29(40):1576-1578, October 6, 1978.

Postcoital contraception in primates. II. Examination of STS 153 and STS 287 as interceptives in the baboon (Papio hamadryas), by A. Komor, et al. ZENTRALBLATT FUR GYNAEKOLOGIE 100(22):1454-1458, 1978.

Postcoital copper IUD found to be effective in preventing pregnancy. FAMILY PLANNING PERSPECTIVES 11:195, May-June, 1979.

Postconceptional prostaglandin therapy, by M. Sas. ACTA BIOLOGICA ET MEDICA GERMANICA 37(5-6):931-935, 1976.

Postpartum amenorrhea: hormones versus nutrition, by D. B. Jelliffe, et al. BIRTH AND THE FAMILY JOURNAL 6: 49-50, Spring, 1979.

Post-partum contraception, by H. Ruf, et al. JOURNAL DE GYNECOLOGIE, OBSTETRIQUE ET BIOLOGIE DE LA REPRODUCTION 7(3 pt 2):590-595, April, 1978.

Post-partum sterilization, by M. Kubica, et al. CESKOSLOVEN-SKA GYNEKOLOGIE 43(9):713-714, November, 1978.

Post-partum sterilisation—an anaesthetic hazard? by A. L. Rennie, et al. ANAESTHESIA 34(3):267-269, March, 1979.

Post-pill amenorrhea and menarche, by J. M. Wenderlein. FORT-

SCHRITTE DER MEDIZIN 96(44):2243-2248, November 28, 1978.

Power of fetal politics; anti-abortion groups, by R. M. Williams. SATURDAY REVIEW 6:12-15, June 9, 1979.

Practical problems in contraceptive counseling, by M. Vienonen. DUODECIN 95(2):55-62, 1979.

Precautions for use of ethylene oxide, by D. K. McLeod. AORN JOURNAL 29:340-343, February, 1979.

The predicament [abortion], by M. Gordon. NEW YORK REVIEW OF BOOKS 25:37-39, July 20, 1978.

Preemptive genocide, by D. Sibeko. AFRICA REPORT 23:36-37, November, 1978.

Pregnancies of Irish residents terminated in England and Wales in 1976, by D. Walsh. IRISH MEDICAL JOURNAL 71(9): 279-280, June 30, 1978.

Pregnancy and abortion counseling, by American Academy of Pediatrics. Committee on Adolescence. PEDIATRICS 63(6):920-921, June, 1979.

Pregnancy and abortion [medical benefits]. OFFICE 88:76+, September, 1978.

Pregnancy and labor complications in women who have had a threatened abortion and who have preserved the pregnancy till labor, by N. G. Kosheleva. AKUSHERSTVO I GINE-KOLOGIIA (4):17-19, April, 1979.

Pregnancy complications following legally induced abortion with special reference to abortion technique, by E. Obel. ACTA OBSTETRICIA ET GYNECOLOGIA SCANDINAVICA 58(2):147-152, 1979.

Pregnancy counselling: two views, by M. Scott, et al. HEALTH AND SOCIAL SERVICE JOURNAL 88:766-767, July 7, 1978.

157

Pregnancy disability bill cleared after compromise on abortion, by L. B. Weiss. CONGRESSIONAL QUARTERLY WEEK-LY REPORT 36(42):3073-3074, October 21, 1978.

The pregnancy occuring during oral contraception or intra uterine device (i.u.d.), by A. Brémond, et al. JOURNAL DE GYNECOLOGIE, OBSTETRIQUES, ET BIOLOGIE DE LA REPRODUCTION 7(3 pt 2):581-589, April, 1978.

Pregnancy, oral contraceptives and multiple sclerosis, by S. Poser, et al. ACTA NEUROLOGICA SCANDINAVICA 59(2-3):108-118, March, 1979.

Pregnancy-specific beta-1-glycoprotein and chorionic gonado-tropin levels after first-trimester abortions, by M. Mandelin, et al. OBSTETRICS AND GYNECOLOGY 52(3):314-317, September, 1978.

Pregnancy termination in the control of the tibial hemimelia syndrome in Galloway cattle, by D. L. Pollock, et al. VETERINARY RECORD 104(12):258-260, March 24, 1979.

Preliminary study of the behavior of urinary polyamines in non-pregnant conditions, in pregnant women and in abortive pathology of the 1st trimester, by M. D'Anna. MINERVA GINECOLOGIA 31(5):327-335, May, 1979.

Premarital coitus and the southern black: a comparative view, by H. T. Christensen, et al. JOURNAL OF MARRIAGE AND THE FAMILY 40(4):721-731, November, 1978.

Premarital contraceptive use: a test of two models, by J. Delamater, et al. JOURNAL OF MARRIAGE AND THE FAMILY 40:235-247, May, 1978.

Premarital contraceptives usage among male and female adoles-cents, by J. P. Hornick, et al. FAMILY COORDINATOR 28(2):181-190, April, 1979.

Premarital sex: no, teen contraception: yes. FAMILY PLAN-NING PERSPECTIVES 10:301-302, September-October,

1978.

Premarital sexual attitudes and behavior, by J. P. Hornick. SO-
CIOLOGICAL QUARTERLY 19:534-544, Autumn, 1978.

Prenatal diagnosis after abortus imminens—further progress of
pregnancy and peculiarity of amniotic cell cultivation, by
K. G. Wurster, et al. GEBURTSHILFE UND FRAUENHEIL-
KUNDE 39(3):222-227, March, 1979.

Prenatal diagnosis, selective abortion, and the ethics of withholding treatment from the defective newborn, by J. Fletcher.
BIRTH DEFECTS 15(2):239-254, 1979.

Preoperative cervical dilation with 15(S)15-methyl PGF2alpha
methyl ester pessaries, by T. K. Chatterjee, et al. INTER-
NATIONAL JOURNAL OF GYNAECOLOGY AND OB-
STETRICS 15(5):423-427, 1978.

Prescribing and family planning [letter], by N. Chisholm.
BRITISH MEDICAL JOURNAL 2(6145):1167-1168,
October 21, 1978.

Prescribing—is a second opinion required? [letter], by N. Chisholm. BRITISH MEDICAL JOURNAL 1(6158):272-273,
January 27, 1979.

The present and future of immunologic approaches to contraception, by G. P. Talwar. INTERNATIONAL JOURNAL
OF GYNAECOLOGY AND OBSTETRICS 15(5):410-414,
1978.

Prevalence of Mycoplasma hominis in patients with gynecologic
diseases and abortion in the 2nd—3rd month of pregnancy,
by M. W. Zalman, et al. VIROLOGIE 29(4):293-297,
October-December, 1978.

Preventing malignant-cell transfer during endoscopic brush cytology, by M. R. Keighley, et al. LANCET 1(8111):298-
299, February 10, 1979.

Preventing unwanted adolescent pregnancy: a cognitive-be-

havioral approach, by S. P. Schinke, et al. AMERICAN
JOURNAL OF ORTHOPSYCHOLOGY 49:81-88, January,
1979.

Preventing unwanted pregnancies, by K. Nowosad. PIELEG-
NIARKA I POLOZNA (12):5-7, 1978.

Preventive measures for reducing infection in the dental office,
by B. Raptes. STOMATOLOGIA 35(5):267-274, September-October, 1978.

Primary carcinoma of the Fallopian tube: a surprise finding in a
postpartum tubal ligation, by A. J. Starr, et al. AMERICAN
JOURNAL OF OBSTETRICS AND GYNECOLOGY 132(3):
344-345, October 1, 1978.

The primary health care team. The Ron Society of Primary
Health Care Nursing, by M. Chapple. NURSING MIRROR
AND MIDWIVES' JOURNAL 147:xix+, October 5, 1978.

Primary liver neoplasms due to estroprogestational agents: 1st
results of a registry opened in France [letter] , by G. Rauber,
et al. NOUVELLE PRESSE MEDICALE 8(23):1945, May
26, 1979.

Primary malignant liver tumors: association with oral contraceptives, by J. Vana, et al. NEW YORK STATE JOURNAL
OF MEDICINE 79(3):321-325, March, 1979.

Priming with intracervically administered prostaglandin F2 alpha
before abortion, by H. Gstöttner, et al. ZENTRALBLATT
FUR GYNAEKOLOGIE 101(6):404-408, 1979.

Principle complications and contraindications of the use of oral
contraceptives, by P. Mutti, et al. MINERVA GINECOLO-
GIA 31(5):363-375, May, 1979.

Prior induced abortion experience among clinic patients in Australia, by G. Davis, et al. JOURNAL OF BIOSOCIAL SCI-
ENCE 11(1):77-83, January, 1979.

Pro & anti-choice dialogue: cooptation or cooperation, by

M. Rylance, et al. OFF OUR BACKS 9:4-5+, March, 1979.

Probation with a flair: a look at some out-of-the ordinary conditions, by H. J. Jaffe, et al. FEDERAL PROBATION QUARTERLY 43(1):25-36, March, 1979.

The problem of abortion and negative and positive duty, by J. L. Smith. JOURNAL OF MEDICAL PHILOSOPHY 3(3):245-252, September, 1978.

The problem of abortion and negative and positive duty: a reply to James LeRoy Smith, by P. Foot. JOURNAL OF MEDICAL PHILOSOPHY 3(3):253-255, September, 1978.

Problem of abortion on demand and the tasks of gynecologic consultation in its control, by I. Dimitrov. AKUSHERSTVO I GINEKOLOGIIA 17(6):456-460, 1978.

The problem of hypertension and ovulation inhibitors, by I. Weise, et al. ZEITSCHRIFT FUR DIE GESAMTE INNERE MEDIZIN 34(11):320-322, June 1, 1979.

Problem of oral surgical interventions during pregnancy, menstruation and under the intake of hormonal contraceptives, by E. Stech. STOMATOLOGIE DER DDR 29(4):298-303, April, 1979.

Problem-solving skills, locus of control, and the contraceptive effectiveness of young women, by B. Steinlauf. CHILD DEVELOPMENT 50:268-271, March, 1979.

A problem to be solved not in the uterus but in the human mind..., by T. Vittachi. GUARDIAN p. 17, August 28, 1979.

Problems of interrupted pregnancy among working women, by G. Marinova. AKUSHERSTVO I GINEKOLOGIIA 17(6): 412-417, 1978.

Problems of teaching sex education—a survey of Ontario secondary schools, by E. S. Herold, et al. FAMILY COORDINATOR 28(2):199-203, April, 1979.

161

Pro-choice candidates face tough races, by J. Clarke. NOW 11(10):7, September, 1978.

Pro-choice is pro-life, by J. Blockwick. ENGAGE/SOCIAL ACTION 11:41-46, December, 1979.

Progestagen and contraceptive activity of a 16alpha-methylene derivative of progesterone, by G. V. Nikitina. PROBLEMY ENDOKRINOLOGII I GORMONOTERAPII 25(1):68-71, January-February, 1979.

The progesterone releasing I.U.D. Its indictions in function of the menstrual disorders, by P. Bourgoin. JOURNAL OF GYNECOLOGIE, OBSTETRIQUE ET BIOLOGIE DE LA REPRODUCTION 7(8):1447-1451, December, 1978.

Prognostic value of ultrasonic study in threatened abortion, by M. Mantoni, et al. UGESKRIFT FOR LAEGER 140(46): 2851-2855, November 13, 1978.

Program consultation by a clinical specialist, by R. L. Anders. JOURNAL OF NURSING ADMINISTRATION 8:34-38, November, 1978.

A program of IUD insertions by paraprofessionals and physicians in the Philippines, by R. Ramos, et al. INTERNATIONAL JOURNAL OF GYNAECOLOGY AND OBSTETRICS 16(4):321-323, 1978-1979.

A project report follow-up of trained nurse-midwives, by R. Weinstein. JOURNAL OF NURSE-MIDWIFERY 23:36-39 Spring-Summer, 1978.

Projected extramarital sexual involvement in unmarried college students, by L. H. Buckstel, et al. JOURNAL OF MARRIAGE AND THE FAMILY 40(2):337-340, May, 1978.

Pro-life groups gain momentum, by L. Johnson. CATHOLIC DIGEST 4:48, March, 1978.

Pro-life moves ahead, by C. Collins. SIGNS 58:24, February, 1979.

Pro-life vs. pro-choice, by M. Bourgoin. NATIONAL CATHOLIC REPORTER 15:18-19, July 27, 1979.

Pro-lifers score sweeping victory in California's abortion-funding battle. OUR SUNDAY VISITOR 68:1, June 24, 1979.

Pro-lifers: ultimate victory is at hand, by R. McMunn. OUR SUNDAY VISITOR 67:1, February 4, 1979.

A promising new low-dose "pill". NURSES DRUG ALERT 3:46-47, April, 1979.

Pronatalism and fertility: the case of the military, by C. S. Stokes, et al. SOCIAL BIOLOGY 25:259-271, Winter, 1978.

Prophylactic medication to prevent miscarrige in pregnant women with a history of sterility, by K. Philipp, et al. WIENER MEDIZINISCHE WOCHENSCHRIFT 90(18):670-672, September 29, 1978.

Prospects and programs for fertility reduction: what? where? by B. Berelson. POPULATION AND DEVELOPMENT REVIEW 4:579-616, December, 1978.

Prostaglandins E2 and F2a in induction of labor, induced abortion and molar abortion: 70 case histories, by F. Laffargue, et al. JOURNAL DE GYNECOLOGIE, OBSTETRIQUE ET BIOLOGIE DE LA REPRODUCTION 7(3):503-513, 1978.

Prostaglandins: physiology, biochemistry, pharmacology and clinical applications, by T. M. Elattar. JOURNAL OF ORAL PATHOLOGY 7(5):253-282, October, 1978.

Providing holistic patient care as a sex educator, by B. Henshaw. NURSING 9(6):78-80, June, 1979.

Proximity as a factor in the selection of health care providers: emergency room visits compared to obstetric admissions and abortions, by K. J. Roghmann, et al. SOCIAL SCIENCE AND MEDICINE 13D(1):61-69, March, 1979.

Psychiatric aspects of infertility, by H. E. Walker. UROLOGIC CLINICS OF NORTH AMERICA 5(3):581-588, October, 1978.

Psychiatric aspects of sterilization, by I. C. Bernstein. JOURNAL OF REPRODUCTIVE MEDICINE 22(2).97-100, February, 1979.

Psychiatric aspects of therapeutic abortion, by G. Van Niekerk. SOUTH AFRICAN MEDICAL JOURNAL 55(11):421-424, March 17, 1979.

The psychiatrist in a family planning center, by G. Maruani, et al. ANNALES MEDICO-PSYCHOLOGIQUES 136(6-8):879-891, June-October, 1978.

Psychiatry and sexuality (preliminary reports), by P. A. Gloor. SCHWEIZER ARCHIV FUER NEUROLOGIE, NEURO-CHIRURGIE UND PSYCHIATRIE 122(1):87-89, 1978.

Psychologic effects of vasectomy in voluntarily childless men, by R. A. Brown, et al. UROLOGY 14(1):55-58, July, 1979.

Psychological adjustment to first-trimester abortion, by J. R. Muhr. DISSERTATION ABSTRACTS INTERNATIONAL 39(8-B):4045-4046, February, 1979.

Psychological dimensions of effective and ineffective contraceptive use in adolescent girls, by J. S. Spain. DISSERTATION ABSTRACTS INTERNATIONAL 38(7-B):3373-3374, January, 1978.

The psychological effects of hysterectomy, by S. Meikle. CANADIAN PSYCHOLOGICAL REVIEW 18:128-141, April, 1977.

Psychological reaction to abortion, by S. Cherazi. JOURNAL OF THE AMERICAN MEDICAL WOMEN'S ASSOCIATION 34:287-288, July, 1979.

A psychosexual study of abortion—seeking behaviour, by M. Vachher, et al. MEDICAL JOURNAL OF MALASIA 33(1):

50-56, September, 1978.

Psycho-social correlates of regular contraceptive use in young unmarried women, by E. M. Smith. DISSERTATION ABSTRACTS INTERNATIONAL 39(3-A):1845, September, 1978.

Public policies in conflict: land reform and family planning in Costa Rica [conference paper], by M. A. Seligson. COMPARATIVE POLITICS 12:49-62, October, 1979.

Pure crystalline estradiol pellet implantation for contraception, by R. H. Asch, et al. INTERNATIONAL JOURNAL OF FERTILITY 23(2):100-105, 1978.

Q-banding of chromosomes in human spontaneous abortions, by D. H. Carr, et al. CANADIAN JOURNAL OF GENETICS AND CYTOLOGY 20(3):415-425, September, 1978.

Quantitative enhancement of dinitrochlorobenzene responsivity in women receiving oral contraceptives, by T. H. Rea. ARCHIVES OF DERMATOLOGY 115(3):361-362, March, 1979.

Questions about the diaphragm; pills and weight gain, by P. Sarrel, et al. REDBOOK 152:43+, January, 1979.

Rabbi, archbishop urge talks to reconcile views on abortion, school aid, by C. Savitsky, Jr. OUR SUNDAY VISITOR 67:2, March 4, 1979.

Radiographic appearance of laparoscopic tubal ring, by M. L. McJumkin, et al. AJR INFORMATION 132(2):297-298, February, 1979.

A radioimmunoassay for norethindrone (NET): measurement of serum NET concentrations following ingestion of NET-containing oral contraceptive steroids, by F. Z. Stanczyk, et al. CONTRACEPTION 18(6):615-633, December, 1978.

Radioimmunoassay of a new progestagen, ORG 2969, and its metabolite, by L. Viinikka. JOURNAL OF STEROID BIO-

CHEMISTRY 9(10):979-982, 1978.

Randomized comparison of clinical performance of two copper-releasing IUDs, Nova-T and Copper-T-200, in Denmark, Finland and Sweden, by T. Luukkainen, et al. CONTRACEPTION 19(1):1-10, 1979.

A randomized double-blind trial of two low dose combined oral contraceptives, by W. Bounds, et al. BRITISH JOURNAL OF OBSTETRICS AND GYNAECOLOGY 86(4):325-329, April, 1979.

A randomized prospective study of the use-effectiveness of two methods of natural family planning: an interim report, by M. E. Wade, et al. AMERICAN JOURNAL OF OBSTETRICS AND GYNECOLOGY 134(6):628-631, July 15, 1979.

Rapid sterilization of suture materials, by N. I. Kameneva. MEDITSINSKAIA SESTRA 38(1):40-41, January, 1979.

A rare obstetric contraindication to the use of vaginal prostaglandins for fetal demise, by S. J. Waszak. JOURNAL OF REPRODUCTIVE MEDICINE 22(4):204-206, April, 1979.

Rate of "R" (increasing use of condoms). MOTHER JONES 3:11, June, 1978.

Rated "R". MOTHER JONES 3(5):11, June, 1978.

Reaction of vaginal tissue of rabbits to inserted sponges made of various materials, by M. Chvapil, et al. JOURNAL OF BIOMEDICAL MATERIALS RESEARCH 13(1):1-13, January, 1979.

Reanastomosis of fallopian tubes [letter], by V. Gomel. FERTILITY AND STERILITY 30(4):483-484, October, 1978.

A re-appraisal of contraception: benefits v. risks. HEALTH VISITOR 52(4):157, April, 1979.

Reappraisal of the predictive value of the beta-human chorionic gonadotropin assay in an infertile population, by S. Belisle, et al. FERTILITY AND STERILITY 31(5):492-495, May, 1979.

Reasonable surgical treatment for tumors of the liver associated with the use of oral contraceptives, by P. W. Catalano, et al. SURGERY, GYNECOLOGY, AND OBSTETRICS 148(5): 759-763, May, 1979.

Reasons for nonuse of contraception by sexually active women aged 15-19, by M. Zelnik, et al. FAMILY PLANNING PER-SPECTIVES 11:289-296, September-October, 1979.

Recanalisation of vas after vasectomy. Evaluation of various techniques in dogs, by O. P. Taneja, et al. BRITISH JOUR-NAL OF UROLOGY 50(5):342-347, August, 1978.

Recent advances in the pharmacologic regulation of fertility in men, by B. N. Barwin. CANADIAN MEDICAL ASSOCIA-TION JOURNAL 119(7):757-759, October 7, 1978.

Recent developments in woman's rights: a symposium. The moral interest in abortion funding: a comment on Beal, Maher and Poelker. D. J. Horan, Roe v. Wade and Doe v. Bolton: revised in 1976 and 1977—reviewed?, revived?; revested?; reversed or revoked? by F. Susman. ST. LOUIS UNIVERSITY LAW JOURNAL 22:566-595, 1979.

Recent work on the history of sexuality, by R. P. Neuman. JOURNAL OF SOCIAL HISTORY 11(3):419-425, Spring, 1978.

Recommendations arising out of the findings by the RCGP oral contraception study on the mortality risks of oral contra-ceptive users. From the Royal College of General Practi-tioners and the Royal College of Obstetricians mad Gynae-cologists. JOURNAL OF THE ROYAL COLLEGE OF GEN-ERAL PRACTITIONERS 27(184):700, November, 1977.

Recommendations for hygiene in dental practice. Prepared by the Commission on Dental Practice. INTERNATIONAL DENTAL JOURNAL 29(1):72-79, March, 1979.

Reconstructive tubal surgery after surgical sterilization, by J. Anselmo. REVISTA CHILENA DE OBSTETRICIA Y GINECOLOGIA 42(4):256-260, 1977.

The record of family planning programs, by R. Freedman, et al. STUDIES IN FAMILY PLANNING 7(1):40, January, 1976.

Recovery of spores from impregnated filter paper [letter] , by D. I. Annear, et al. JOURNAL OF CLINICAL PATHOLOGY 32(1):93, January, 1979.

Reduce operator exposure and environmental levels of ethylene oxide, by T. M. Samuels, et al. HOSPITAL TOPICS pp. 48-54, September-October, 1979.

Reduces process cycle time for pouches and trays, keeps energy usage at minimum [food sterilizer] . FOOD PROCESS 40: 87+, July, 1979.

Reducing the morbidity of vacuum aspiration abortion, by M. S. Burnhill, et al. INTERNATIONAL JOURNAL OF GYNAE-COLOGY AND OBSTETRICS 16(3):204-209, 1978-1979.

Re-evaluation of the current method of disinfection—on disinfection of the hands by a supersonic washing device, by S. Taki, et al. KANGO KENKYU 11(4):275-281, Autumn, 1978.

Regeneration of the fallopian tubes following sterilization, by K. Semm, et al. GEBURTSHILFE UND FRAUENHEIL-KUNDE 39(1):14-19, January, 1979.

Relation between endometritis post abortum and oestrogen levels in the plasma, by G. Reck, et al. GEBURTSHILFE UND FRAUENHEILKUNDE 39(3):239-242, March, 1979.

Relation between toxoplasmosis and fetal losses, by U. A. gomes, et al. BOLETIN DE LA OFICINA SANITARIA PARAMERICANA 85(4):315-324, October, 1978.

Relation of steroids to liver oncogenesis, by W. M. Christopher-son, et al. JOURNAL OF TOXICOLOGY AND ENVIRON-

MENTAL HEALTH 5(2-3):207-230, March-May, 1979.

Relationship between contraceptive sex role stereotyping and attitudes toward contraception among males, by S. A. Weinstein, et al. JOURNAL OF SEX RESEARCH 15:235-242, August, 1979.

The relationship between first sexual intercourse and ways of handling contraception among college students, by R. H. Needle. JOURNAL OF THE AMERICAN COLLEGE HEALTH ASSOCIATION 24(2):106-111, December, 1975.

Relationship between nurse counseling and sexual adjustment after hysterectomy, by J. C. Krueger, et al. NURSING RESEARCH 28:145-150, May-June, 1979.

The relationship between previous elective abortions and postpartum depressive reactions, by N. E. Devore. JOGN 8:237-240, July-August, 1979.

Relationship between spontaneous abortion and presence of antibody to Toxoplasma gondii, by A. M. Johnson, et al. MEDICAL JOURNAL OF AUSTRALIA 1(12):579-580, June 16, 1979.

Relationship between uterotrophic and interceptive activities of steroidal estrogens, by M. Oettel, et al. ENDOKRINOLOGIE 72(1):25-35, April, 1978.

The relationship of age to nurses' attitudes toward abortion, by J. M. Berger. JOGN 8:231-233, July-August, 1979.

The relationship of creativity variables to sex role types for males and females, by C. H. Crawford. DISSERTATION ABSTRACTS INTERNATIONAL 39(3-A):1431-1433, September, 1978.

Reliability and reversibility of female sterilisation. BRITISH MEDICAL JOURNAL 2(6154):1734-1745, December 23-30, 1978.

Religion & contraception, by B. Delatiner. McCALLS 106:70,

October, 1978.

Religious freedom and the American community, by L. Pfeffer. JUDICATURE 28:137-146, Spring, 1979.

Remember your rubbers (condoms of the past). PLAYBOY 26:162+, February, 1979.

Renal artery thrombosis in a young woman taking oral contraceptives, by S. M. Golbus, et al. ANNALS OF INTERNAL MEDICINE 90(6):939-940, June, 1979.

A renewed focus on contraception, by P. Gupte. POPULI 5(3):45, 1978.

Repeated abortions increase risk of miscarriage, premature births and low-birth-weight babies. FAMILY PLANNING PERSPECTIVES 11(1):39-40, January-February, 1979.

Repeated abortions, sterility and sytemic dysimmunopathy, by B. Plouvier, et al. ANNALS DE MEDECINE INTERNE 130(1):39-44, 1979.

Report of the Committee on Operation of the Abortion Law, 1977 [Canada], introduction by J. Haliburton. ATLANTIS 4:205-210, Spring, 1979.

Report on a computer based evaluation of 1,800 cases of abortion, by P. Richter, et al. ZENTRALBLATT FUR GYNAEKOLOGIE 101(4):254-260, 1979.

Reproduction, ethics, and public policy: the federal sterilization regulations, by R. P. Petchesky. HASTINGS CENTER REPORT 9:29-41, October, 1979.

Reproduction in American history [review article], by M. P. Ryan. JOURNAL OF INTERDISCIPLINARY HISTORY 10:319-332, Autumn, 1979.

Reproductive and contraceptive knowledge among undergraduate university students, by D. S. Godbole, et al. JOURNAL OF FAMILY WELFARE 24:27-31, December, 1977.

Reproductive freedom issues in legal services practice, by S. Law. CLEARING HOUSE REVIEW 12:289-403, November, 1978.

Reproductive mortality [from contraceptives as well as pregnancy or abortion], by V. Beral. BRITISH MEDICAL JOURNAL 6191:632-634, September 15, 1979.

Requests for abortion and outcomes of pregnancy in Jerusalem, Israel, by P. E. Slater, et al. JOURNAL OF REPRODUCTIVE MEDICINE 21(4):279-282, October, 1978.

Research in family planning, symposium. WORLD HEALTH pp. 2-37, August, 1978.

Research on male 'pill' intensifies, by T. Schultz. NEW YORK TIMES pp. C-1, August 7, 1979.

Research pitfalls. THE ECONOMIST 266:26, January 21, 1978.

Response of low income women and abortion facilities to restriction of public funds for abortion: a study of a large metropolitan area, by G. L. Rubin, et al. AMERICAN JOURNAL OF PUBLIC HEALTH 69(9):948-950, September, 1979.

Restricting Medicaid funds for abortions: projections of excess mortality for women of childbearing age, by D. B. Petitti, et al. AMERICAN JOURNAL OF PUBLIC HEALTH 67: 860-862, September, 1977; Discussion, 68:270-272+, March, 1978+.

Restriction of federal funds for abortion: 18 months later, by J. Gold, et al. AMERICAN JOURNAL OF PUBLIC HEALTH 69(9):929-930, September, 1979.

Restrictions on women's rights to abortion: informed consent, spousal consent, and recordkeeping provisions, by B. Karg. WOMEN'S RIGHTS LAW REPORTER 5:35-51, Fall, 1978.

Restrictions violate privacy rights. NOW 11(10):2, September, 1978.

Restrictive funding policies adopted by most states. SPOKES-
WOMAN 8(12):5, June, 1978.

Results of clinical genealogical studies of married couples with
habitual abortion, by M. F. Iankova, et al. AKUSHERSTVO
I GINEKOLOGIIA (4):5-8, April, 1979.

Retained fetus in the sow, by M. J. Meredith. VETERINARY
RECORD 103(3):53-54, July 15, 1978.

Return of Mr. Hyde. SEVEN DAYS 2(11):5, July, 1978.

The reverse effect of sexual steroids on the serum-lysozyme, by
G. Klinger, et al. ZENTRALBLATT FUR GYNAEKOLO-
GIE 101(8):502-505, 1979.

Reversibility as a consideration in laparoscopic sterilization, by
R. Palmer. JOURNAL OF REPRODUCTIVE MEDICINE
21(1):57-58, July, 1978.

The reversibility of sterilisation, by S. Whitehead. NURSING
TIMES 75(25):1048-1049, June 21, 1979.

—, by R. M. L. Winston. IPPF MEDICAL BULLETIN 12(6):
1, December, 1978.

Reversible changes in the eye after long term use of oral contraceptive agents, by T. Pasanku, et al. MEDICINSKI PREG-
LED 31(11-12):493-496, 1978.

Reversible sterilization, by A. Ingelman-Sundberg, et al. INTER-
NATIONAL JOURNAL OF FERTILITY 23(2):156-157,
1978.

—, by G. Largey. SOCIETY 14(5):57-59, July-August, 1977.

Reversible sterilization: socio-ethical considerations, by G.
Largey. SOCIAL BIOLOGY 25(2):135-144, Summer, 1978.

Reversible sterilization technique shows promise [news]. JAMA
242(1):16, July 6 1979.

A review of the birth control pill and its relationship to thrombophlebitis, by M. E. Julsrud. JOURNAL OF THE AMERICAN PODIATRY ASSOCIATION 69(6):376-382, June, 1979.

A review of standards of infant hygiene in the home, by A. Gatherer. NURSING TIMES 74:1684-1685, October 12, 1978.

Rheumatoid arthritis and oral contraception [letter] , by H. Berry. LANCET 1(8068):829, April 15, 1978.

Rheumatoid arthritis: pill users half as likely to develop the disease [news] . FAMILY PLANNING PERSPECTIVES 10(4):239-240, July-August, 1978.

Right rewrites our rights, by T. Dejanikus. OFF OUR BACKS 8(5):11, May, 1978.

"Right" to an abortion, the scope of fourteenth amendment "personhood," and the Supreme Court's birth requirement, by J. D. Gorby. SOUTHERN ILLINOIS UNIVERSITY LAW JOURNAL 1979:1-36, March, 1979.

Right to life lobbyist quits over ERA. NOW 11(11):3, October, 1978.

Right to procreate: the dilemma of overpopulation and the United States judiciary, by J. Bolner, et al. LOYOLA LAW REVIEW 25:235-262, Spring, 1979.

Rights are not enough; prospects for a new approach to the morality of abortion, by P. Rossi. LINACRE QUARTERLY 46:109-117, May, 1979.

Rights Commission may be barred from considering abortion. SPOKESWOMAN 9(4):4, October, 1978.

Ripening of the cervix by intracervical application of PGE2-gel before termination of pregnancy with dilatation and evacuation, by L. Wingerup, et al. ACTA OBSTETRICIA ET GYNECOLOGICA SCANDINAVICA (84):15-18, 1979.

Rise in female-initiated sexual activity at ovulation and its suppression by oral contraceptives, by D. B. Adams, et al. NEW ENGLAND JOURNAL OF MEDICINE 299(21):1145-1150, November 23, 1978.

Rising cost of birth control pills, by D. Clayton. FINANCIAL POST 72:16, December 30, 1978.

Risk factors in endometrial carcinoma with special reference to the use of estrogens, by T. Salmi. ACTA OBSTETRICIA ET GYNECOLOGICA SCANDINAVICA (86):1-119, 1979.

Risk of adverse effects of contraception, by U. Larsson-Cohn. LAKARTIDNINGEN 75(41):3670-3672, October 11, 1978.

Risk of cancer caused by the pill? [news] . MEDIZINISCHE KLINIK 73(43):4, October 27, 1978.

Risk of myocardial infarction in oral-contraceptive users [letter] , by H. Jick. LANCET 1(8127):1187, June 2, 1979.

Risk of vascular disease in women. Smoking, oral contraceptives, noncontraceptive estrogens, and other factors, by P. B. Petitti, et al. JAMA 242(11):1150-1154, September 14, 1979.

Risking jail for a backstreet job: trials postponed, the ordeal continues for women accused of abortion, by J. Flint. NEW STATESMAN p. 763, November 16, 1979.

Risks and benefits of culdoscopic female sterilization, by M. F. McCann, et al. INTERNATIONAL JOURNAL OF GYNAECOLOGY AND OBSTETRICS 16(3):242-247, 1978-1979.

The risks of oral contraception, by J. McEwan. BRITISH JOURNAL OF HOSPITAL MEDICINE 21(2):144+, February, 1979.

Risks to the offspring from parental occupational exposures, by J. F. Haas, et al. JOURNAL OF OCCUPATIONAL MEDICINE 21:607-613, September, 1979.

Risky abortions: Chicago clinics. TIME 112:52, November 27,

1978.

Role experiences of young women: a longitudinal test of the
role hiatus hypothesis, by G. D. Spitze. JOURNAL OF
MARRIAGE AND THE FAMILY 40(3):471-479, August,
1978.

The role of chromosomes in the aetiology of human abortion,
by G. M. Kotzé, et al. SOUTH AFRICAN MEDICAL JOUR-
NAL 54(14):562-566, September 30, 1978.

Role of combined oral contraceptives in the pathogenesis of
urodynamic disorders of the upper urinary tracts, by T. D.
Datuashvili, et al. AKUSHERSTVO I GINEKOLOGIIA
(2):13-15, 1979.

The role of family planning in recent rapid fertility declines in
developing countries, by J. W. Brackett, et al. STUDIES
IN FAMILY PLANNING 9(12):314-323, December, 1978.

Role of listeriosis in the etiology of spontaneous and habitual
abortions, by T. Despodova, et al. AKUSHERSTVO I
GINEKOLOGIIA 17(6):396-402, 1978.

The role of medical factors in the failure to achieve desired
family size, by C. M. Young. JOURNAL OF BIOSOCIAL
SCIENCE 11(2):159-171, April, 1979.

The role of methylergonovine maleate in augmenting extra-
amniotic saline for midtrimester abortion, by M. R. Narvekar,
et al. INTERNATIONAL JOURNAL OF GYNAECOLOGY
AND OBSTETRICS 15(6):545-547, 1978.

The role of oestrogen test in threatened abortion, by R. Rizvi,
et al. INDIAN JOURNAL OF PATHOLOGY AND MICRO-
BIOLOGY 21(2):165-170, April, 1978.

Role of oral contraception in congenital malformations of offspring, by M. B. Bracken, et al. INTERNATIONAL JOUR-
NAL OF EPIDEMIOLOGY 7(4):309-317, December, 1978.

Role of oral contraceptive agents in the pathogenesis of liver

175

tumors, by E. D. Nissen, et al. JOURNAL OF TOXICOLO-
GY AND ENVIRONMENTAL HEALTH 5(2-3):231-254,
March-May, 1979.

The role of personality and family relationship factors in adolescent unwed pregnancy, by L. D. Inman. DISSERTATION
ABSTRACTS INTERNATIONAL 38(6-B):2864, December,
1977.

Romania's 1966 anti-abortion decree: the demographic experience of the first decade, by B. Berelson. POPULATION
STUDIES 33:209-222, July, 1979.

Romantic love and sexual expression, by M. L. Wilkinson. THE
FAMILY COORDINATOR 27(1):141-148, April, 1978.

Routines for prescription of contraceptives (estrogen + gestagen),
by B. I. Nesheim, et al. TIDSSKRIFT FOR DEN NORSKE
LAEGEFORENING 99(3):180-181, February 28, 1979.

Rupture of the uterus following treatment with 16-16-dimethyl
E 2 prostaglandin vagitories, by F. Jerve, et al. PROSTA-
GLANDINS 17(1):121-123, January, 1979.

Rural and urban family planning services in the United States,
by A. Torres. FAMILY PLANNING PERSPECTIVES
11:109-114, March-April, 1979.

Safe and effective use of ethylene oxide, by L. Rendell-Baker,
et al. MEDICAL INSTRUMENTATION 13(2):106, March-
April, 1979.

Safe? Effective? Experts disagree on status of birth control
today, by M. Carpenter. SCIENCE DIGEST 84:73-76,
November, 1978.

Safe package deal. FAMILY HEALTH 10:14, September, 1978.

Safes, sheaths, stockstoppers and why print is the only way, by
J. Fisher. MARKETING 83:14-15, February 27, 1978.

Safety last. OFF OUR BACKS 8(1):16, January, 1978.

Safety of intrauterine devices, by J. Guillebaud. STUDIES IN FAMILY PLANNING 10:174-176, May, 1979.

The safety of a steam sterilization process using Thermalog-S indicators in the field of pharmaceutics, by G. Franchi, et al. BOLLETTINO CHIMICO FARMACEUTICO 117(10):620-626, October, 1978.

Safety to laparoscopy. LANCET 1(8068):807, April 15, 1978.

The saga of positive cultures—ETO sterilization, by M. S. Fox. HOSPITAL TOPICS 57:18-20+, May-June, 1979.

The St. Paul fire-bombing: new wave of terrorism against abortion? by G. Lichtenstein. MS MAGAZINE 7:58-60+, November, 1978.

Saline abortions. . .to the membership. . .responsibility of RNs who assist in the performance of abortions, by D. Smith. CALIFORNIA NURSE 74:20-21, March-April, 1979.

Salpingography in infertile women following abortion or pelvic surgery, by S. Roopnarinesingh, et al. WEST INDIAN MEDICAL JOURNAL 27(4):201-204, December, 1978.

Sanctions for performing illegal abortions, by S. Ulitskii. SOVIET LAW AND GOVERNMENT 17(1):40-43, 1978.

Scarce resources and civil liberties, by J. Shattuck. CENTER MAGAZINE 11:18-19, January, 1978.

Scarlet A; M. Pitchford prosecuted for self-abortion. TIME 112:22, September 11, 1978.

Schmid still struggles to place contraceptive ads, by M. Christopher. ADVERTISING AGE 49:2+, May 22, 1978.

School achievement: risk factor in teenage pregnancies? by H. Hansen, et al. AMERICAN JOURNAL OF PUBLIC HEALTH 68:753-759, August, 1978.

Schoolchildren and contraception. Knowledge, attitudes and behavior, by L. Bernsted, et al. UGESKRIFT FOR LAEGER 141(6):397-399, February 5, 1979.

Sciatic nerve injury in a patient undergoing laparoscopy, by F. D. Loffer, et al. JOURNAL OF REPRODUCTIVE MEDICINE 21(6):371-372, December, 1978.

Screening of Indian plants for antifertility activity, by S. K. Garg, et al. INDIAN JOURNAL OF EXPERIMENTAL BIOLOGY 16(10):1077-1079, October, 1978.

Search for the ideal contraceptive speeds up. DRUG TOPICS 123:26, January 5, 1979.

Seasons of birth and marriage in two Chinese localities, by B. Pasternak. HUMAN ECOLOGY 6(3):299, September, 1978.

Second trimester abortion with 5% intraamniotic saline—a pilot study, by A. K. Ghosh, et al. INTERNATIONAL JOURNAL OF GYNAECOLOGY AND OBSTETRICS 15(5):436-439, 1978.

Secondary effects of hormonal contraception on the breast, by J. Bonte. GYNAEKOLOGISCHE RUNDSCHAU 18(3-4): 220-245, 1978.

The select committee reports. . .the select committee on population, U. S. House of Representatives, by R. Lincoln. FAMILY PLANNING PERSPECTIVES 11:101-104, March-April, 1979.

The self concept of pregnant adolescent girls, by C. E. Zongker. ADOLESCENCE 12(48):477-488, Winter, 1977.

Self-esteem, locus of control, and adolescent contraception, by E. S. Herold, et al. JOURNAL OF PSYCHOLOGY 101(first half):83-88, January, 1979.

Self-reliance in research, by N. Dusitsin, et al. WORLD HEALTH pp. 34-37, August, 1978.

Senate passage: family planning, crib death funds authorized, by

L. B. Weiss. CONGRESSIONAL QUARTERLY WEEKLY REPORT 36:2063-2065, August 5, 1978.

Senate passes education-department bill, by E. K. Coughlin, et al. CHRONICLE OF HIGHER EDUCATION 17:17, October 10, 1978.

Senate retreats from position on abortion, by H. H. Donnelly. CONGRESSIONAL QUARTERLY WEEKLY REPORT 37(30):1531-1533, June 28, 1979.

Senate votes on abortion. CONGRESSIONAL QUARTERLY WEEKLY REPORT 37:1459, July 21, 1979.

Septic abortion and acute renal failure in a patient with an intrauterine contraceptive device, by C. M. Wiles, et al. INTERNATIONAL JOURNAL OF GYNAECOLOGY AND OBSTETRICS 15(5):464-465, 1978.

Sequential analysis of spontaneous abortion. II. Collaborative study data show that gravidity determines a very substantial rise in risk, by A. F. Naylor, et al. FERTILITY AND STERILITY 31(3):282-286, March, 1979.

Sequential changes in the human renin-angiotensin system following therapeutic termination of pregnancy, by F. B. Pipkin, et al. BRITISH JOURNAL OF OBSTETRICS AND GYNAECOLOGY 86(4):285-289, April, 1979.

Serious liver diseases in women on hormonal contraceptives, by M. Brodanová, et al. CASOPIS LEKARU CESKYCH 118(1) 22-27, January 5, 1979.

Serotonin metabolism disorders and their relationship to inability to complete pregnancy in women with rheumatism, by I. M. Mellina. PEDIATRIIA AKUSHERSTVO I GINEKOLOGIIA (4):43-45, July-August, 1978.

Serum level and 24hr. excretion pattern of potassium following the intake of combined oral contraceptives, by S. Kamyab, et al. ACTA MEDICA IRANICA 21(2):87-94, 1978.

Serum prolactin levels in short-term and long-term use of inert plastic and copper intrauterine devices, by M. Wenof, et al. CONTRACEPTION 19(1):21-28, 1979.

Serum relaxin levels in prostaglandin E2 induced abortions, by J. Quagliarello, et al. PROSTAGLANDINS 16(6):1003-1006, December, 1978.

Services, policies and costs in U.S. abortion facilities, by B. L. Lindheim. FAMILY PLANNING PERSPECTIVES 11:283-289, September-October, 1979.

Seven-nation WHO study finds future pregnancies not endangered by 1st trimester legal abortion [news]. FAMILY PLANNING PERSPECTIVES 10(4):238-239, July-August, 1978.

Severe liver diseases in women using hormonal contraception, by M. Brodanová, et al. CESKOSLOVENSKA GASTROEN-TEROLOGIE A VYZIVA 32(8):515-516, December, 1978.

Sex and adaptation to the environment, by D. Ferembach. LA RECHERCHE 9(85):14-19, January, 1978.

Sex and cancer prevention, by C. SerVaas. SATURDAY EVENING POST 251(2):86, March, 1979.

Sex and confinement, by A. Neier. CIVIL LIBERTIES REVIEW 5:6-16, July-August, 1978.

Sex and family planning in Denmark and in Danish communes, by T. H. Shey. INTERNATIONAL JOURNAL OF SOCIOLOGY OF THE FAMILY 7(1):15-24, January-June, 1977.

Sex and Jewish teenagers, by A. S. Maller. JEWISH DIGEST 23:60-64, June, 1978.

Sex and the single punk. MOTHER JONES 3(9):8, November, 1978.

Sex differences in adolescent family communication and media use about occupations and family planning, by P. V. Miller.

DISSERTATION ABSTRACTS INTERNATIONAL 38(6-A): 3123, December, 1977.

Sex education for teenagers, by J. H. Ford. WESTERN JOURNAL OF MEDICINE 130(3):273-276, March, 1979.

Sex films, by R. T. Francoeur. SOCIETY 14(5):33-37, July-August, 1977.

Sex guilt and contraceptive use, by M. L. Upchurch. JOURNAL OF SEX EDUCATION AND THERAPY 4:27-31, Spring-Summer, 1978.

Sex hormone binding globulin capacity as an index of oestrogenicity or androgenicity in women on oral contraceptive steroids, by M. N. El Makhzangy, et al. CLINICAL ENDOCRINOLOGY 10(1):39-45, January, 1979.

Sex-role attitudes and the anticipated timing of the initial stages of family formation among Catholic university students, by J. W. Wicks, et al. JOURNAL OF MARRIAGE AND THE FAMILY 40(3):505-514, August, 1978.

Sex role attitudes and contraceptive practices among never-married university students, by M. Hedin-Pourghasemi. DISSERTATION ABSTRACTS INTERNATIONAL 38(10-A): 6344-6345, April, 1978.

Sex-role identification and success, by C. Katz, et al. CONTEMPORARY PSYCHOANALYSIS 12(2):251-257, April, 1976.

Sex role perceptions and the abortion decision, by R. H. Rosen, et al. JOURNAL OF SEX RESEARCH 14:231-245, November, 1978.

Sex steroids and thyroid function tests: the role of estrogen and progestogen, by J. Miyamoto. INTERNATIONAL JOURNAL OF GYNAECOLOGY AND OBSTETRICS 16(1):28-33, 1978.

Sexology in West Germany, by B. Meyenburg, et al. THE JOUR-

NAL OF SEX RESEARCH 13(3):197-209, August, 1977.

Sexual attitude and sexual behavior among college students, by M. C. McBride, et al. JOURNAL OF COLLEGE STUDENT PERSONNEL 18:183-187, May, 1977.

Sexual attitudes among British and Japanese students, by S. Iwawaki, et al. JOURNAL OF PSYCHOLOGY 98:289-298, March, 1978.

The sexual attitudes of aggressive sexual offenders, by K. Howells, et al. THE BRITISH JOURNAL OF CRIMINOLOGY 18(2):170-174, April, 1978.

Sexual behavior in adolescence, by J. R. Hopkins. JOURNAL OF SOCIAL ISSUES 33(2):67-85, 1977.

Sexual behaviour and contraceptive practice of undergraduates at Oxford University, by P. Anderson, et al. JOURNAL OF BIOSOCIAL SCIENCE 10(3):277-286, July, 1978.

Sexual contraceptive attitudes and behaviour of high school and college females, by E. S. Herold, et al. CANADIAN JOURNAL OF PUBLIC HEALTH 69(4):311-314, July-August, 1978.

Sexual correlates of homosexual experience: an exploratory study of college women, by E. Goode, et al. THE JOURNAL OF SEX RESEARCH 13(1):12-21, February, 1977.

Sexual enhancement groups for dysfunctional women: an evaluation, by S. R. Leiblum, et al. JOURNAL OF SEX AND MARITAL THERAPY 3(2):139-152, Summer, 1977.

Sexual permissiveness: evidence for a theory, by J. Kelley. JOURNAL OF MARRIAGE AND THE FAMILY 40(3): 455-468, August, 1978.

Sexual preference, sex role appropriateness, and restriction of social access, by J. Millham, et al. JOURNAL OF HOMO-SEXUALITY 2(4):343-357, Summer, 1977.

Sexual profile of women requesting laparoscopical sterilization, by M. Samsula, et al. CESKOSLOVENSKA GYNEKOLO-GIE 44(4):253-256, May, 1979.

Sexuality and birth control decisions among Lebanese couples, by M. Chamie. SIGNS 3(1):294-312, Autumn, 1977.

Sexuality—the mature of childbearing years and the effect of gynecologic surgery, by J. D. Chapman. JAOA 78(7):509-514, March, 1979.

Sexuality of youth: attempt at forming a theory, by C. J. Straver. SOZIOLOGENKORRESPONDENZ 4:121-150, May, 1977.

Shifting of menstruation in female athletes, by J. Artner. FORT-SCHRITTE DER MEDIZIN 97(19):901-906, May 17, 1979.

Should the mentally handicapped be sterilized? by D. Robillard. CANADIAN MEDICAL ASSOCIATION JOURNAL 120(6): 756-757, March 17, 1979.

Shoulder-hand syndrome after laparoscopic sterilisation, by L. C. Low, et al. BRITISH MEDICAL JOURNAL 2(6144):1059-1060, October 14, 1978.

The significance of social conditions for choice of termination of pregnancy. A comparative sociomedical study of 104 patients with more than one termination and 427 patients in whom pregnancy was terminated for the first time, by F. Møller-Larsen, et al. UGESKRIFT FOR LAEGER 141(27): 1866-1869, July 2, 1979.

The significance of social factors in choice of legal abortion. A social-medical study of 531 women applying for abortion and 285 pregnant control patients, by M. Wohlert, et al. UGESKRIFT FOR LAEGER 140(30):1835-1841, July 24, 1978.

Silicone band sterilization with radiographic and laparoscopic evaluation, by P. Beck, et al. OBSTETRICS AND GYNE-COLOGY 53(6):698-702, June, 1979.

Silicone band technique for laparoscopic tubal sterilization in the gravid and nongravid patient, by P. Beck, et al. OBSTETRICS AND GYNECOLOGY 53(5):653-656, May, 1979.

A simple solution to five of the major problems of the microsurgical reversal of sterilization, by J. J. Hoffman. FERTILITY AND STERILITY 30(4):480-481, October, 1978.

Simultaneity in the birth rate equation: the effects of education, labor force participation, income and health, by D. J. Conger, et al. ECONOMETRICA 46:631-641, May, 1978.

The sin of birth control: gone but not forgotten, by J. Breig. US CATHOLIC 44:6-12, January, 1979.

Sixth session: the women's movement; presentation, by L. Chanin; Discussion, by Z. Falk, et al. CONGRESSIONAL MONITOR 45:34-38, March-April, 1978.

The small, healthy family project, by H. Suyono, et al. STUDIES IN FAMILY PLANNING 9(7):201-202, July, 1978.

Smoking: a risk factor for spontaneous abortion, by J. Kline, et al. NEW ENGLAND JOURNAL OF MEDICINE 297:793-796, October 13, 1977.

Sniff a day keeps pregnancy away, LRH analog nasal spray. SCIENCE NEWS 116:133, August 25, 1979.

Soapbox: abortion—a thought before choosing v. Muchanic. NEW JERSEY MONTHLY 2:41, April, 1978.

The social context of rape: sexual scripts and motivation, by S. Jackson. WOMEN'S STUDIES INTERNATIONAL QUARTERLY 1(1):27-38, 1978.

Social worker's role in teenage abortions, by L. P. Cain. SOCIAL WORK 24:52-56, January, 1979.

Socialization factors in contraceptive attitudes: role of affective responses, parental attitudes, and sexual experience, by K. Kelley. JOURNAL OF SEX RESEARCH 15:6-20, February, 1979.

Some consequences of premarital heterosexual cohabitation for marriage, by D. E. Olday. DISSERTATION ABSTRACTS INTERNATIONAL 38(9-A):5745-5746, March, 1978.

Some factors related to men's stated willingness to use a male contraceptive pill, by H. G. Gough. JOURNAL OF SEX RESEARCH 15:27-37, February, 1979.

Some questions about double effect, by G. C. Graber. ETHICS IN SCIENCE AND MEDICINE 6(1):65-84, 1979.

Sort of dampens your spirits: suit against Dr. C. H. Pierce for sterilizing welfare patients, by S. Derks. NATION 227:675-676, December 16, 1978.

Sources of sex bias in evaluations of performance, by J. C Froess. DISSERTATION ABSTRACTS INTERNATIONAL 38(12-B):6148, June, 1978.

Sources of sex information and premarital sexual behavior, by G. B. Spanier. JOURNAL OF SEX RESEARCH 13:73-88, May, 1977.

Spain legalizes contraception, by M. Jones. POPULI 5(4):3, 1978.

Special guide to contraception: what's new, what's right for you? by L. Cherry. GLAMOUR 77:287-290, August, 1979.

Specific prophylaxis of enzootic chlamydial ovine abortion, by G. Sorodoc, et al. VIROLOGIE 30(2):131-134, April-June, 1979.

Spell back phoned-in Rxs. DRUG TOPICS 122:79, November 7, 1978.

Spermatozoa repellent as a contraceptive, by W. W. Tso, et al. CONTRACEPTION 19(3):207-212, March, 1979.

Spiritual abortion, by Sydney. COMMUNITIES 31:2, March,

1978.

Split decision on abortions; regulating teenage abortion; Supreme Court decision, by S. Begley, et al. NEWSWEEK 94:63-64, July 16, 1974.

Spontaneous abortion after midtrimester amniocentesis, by I. J. Park, et al. OBSTETRICS AND GYNECOLOGY 53(2):190-194, February, 1979.

Spontaneous abortions in sibship of children with congenital malformation or malignant disease, by A. Spira, et al. EURO-PEAN JOURNAL OF OBSTETRICS, GYNECOLOGY AND REPRODUCTIVE BIOLOGY 9(2):89-96, 1979.

Spontaneous dislocation of the sterno-clavicular joint, by B. Sadr, et al. ACTA ORTHOPAEDICA SCANDINAVICA 50(3):269-274, June, 1979.

Spontaneous rupture of a liver adenoma following many years' ingestion of an oral contraceptive, by H. Pollak. MMW 121(3):93-94, January 19, 1979.

Staff face danger in the operating theatre, by S. Light. NURS-ING MIRROR AND MIDWIVE'S JOURNAL 148(2):20-22, January 11, 1979.

Staff for family policy and education services needlessly limited, by E. Tuomainen. SAIRAANHOITAJA 55(4):19-20, February 20, 1979.

Stage set for annual abortion funding battle, by H. H. Donnelly. CONGRESSIONAL QUARTERLY WEEKLY REPORT 37:1089, June 2, 1979.

Standard treatment of dysmenorrhea with special reference to treatment with spasmolytics and hormones, by M. Olser. ACTA OBSTETRICIA ET GYNECOLOGICA SCANDINA-VICA 87:69-72, 1979.

Standards of social welfare in pregnancy and with voluntary pregnancy interruption. PROFESSIONI INFERMIERISTICHE

31(3):133-140, July-September, 1978.

State abortion funds ordered resumed, by M. M. Smith. NOW 11(7):11, June, 1978.

State of health and the subsequent development of infants born of women who have had a threatened abortion, by N. G. Kosheleva. AKUSHERSTVO I GINEKOLOGIIA (4):3-5, April, 1979.

States & medicaid. OFF OUR BACKS 8(1):12, January, 1978.

States' right to dictate abortion procedure disputed, by D. B. Moskowitz. MEDICAL WORLD NEWS 19:99-100, October 16, 1978.

Statistical survey of gynecological laparoscopy/pelviscopy in Germany till 1977, by K. Semm. ENDOSCOPY 11(2):101-106, May, 1979.

Status and developmental trends of immunologic contraceptive technics, by H. Donat. ZENTRALBLATT FUR GYNAE-KOLOGIE 101(7):433-441, 1979.

Status and problems of contraception in the world and in Belgium in 1978, by U. Gaspard, et al. REVUE MEDICALE DE LIEGE 34(6):203-208, March 15, 1979.

Status of research in the field of developing modern methods of birth rate regulation (based on data of the WHO enlarged program on human reproduction in 1977), by L. S. Persianinov, et al. AKUSHERSTVO I GINEKOLOGIIA (2):3-5, 1979.

Status of women and fertility in India, by J. C. Bhatia. JOURNAL OF FAMILY WELFARE 25:20-32, March, 1979.

Step right up! by J. Severn. WEEKLY 2(49):8, March 1, 1978.

Sterile days for drug firms as women shy from the pill, by D. Clayton. FINANCIAL POST 72:1+, December 30, 1978.

Sterile fluids—recent developments, by W. Woodside. NAT NEWS 16(5):10+, May, 1979.

Sterilisation des arrieres mentaux, by D. J. Roy. RELATIONS 39:35, February, 1979.

Sterility in oxygen humidifiers, by T. P. Meehan. RESPIRA-TORY TECHNOLOGY 14:14-15+, Summer, 1978.

Sterilization, by G. H. Holtzhausen. SOUTH AFRICAN MEDICAL JOURNAL 54(5):182, July 29, 1978.

Sterilization and contraceptive services in Catholic hospitals, by J. M. O'Lane. AMERICAN JOURNAL OF GYNAECOLOGY AND OBSTETRICS 133(4):355-357, February 15, 1979.

Sterilization and its importance, by C. Trifan. VIATA MEDICALA 26(5):111-114, May, 1978.

Sterilization and laparoscopy. SOUTH AFRICAN MEDICAL JOURNAL 54(7):260-261, August 12, 1978.

Sterilization and pill top U.S. birth control methods. SPOKES-WOMAN 9(5):6, November, 1978.

Sterilization and sterile preparations in pharmacy. XI. Aseptic procedures, by A. Burelová, et al. CESKOSLOVENSKA FARMACIE 27(9):412-418, November, 1978.

Sterilization as a contraceptive method, by S. Ivanov, et al. AKUSHERSTVO I GINEKOLOGIIA 17(5):366-370, 1978.

— [letter], by N. S. Louw. SOUTH AFRICAN MEDICAL JOURNAL 54(14):555, September 30, 1978.

Sterilization: a conference and a report, by B. Dillingham. AMERICAN INDIAN JOURNAL 4(1):13-16, January, 1978.

Sterilization in 1977, by S. C. Christensen, et al. UGESKRIFT FOR LAEGER 141(4):260, January 22, 1979.

Sterilization in Panama: in Panama, one-third of women who want no more children have been sterilized; sterilization now prevents almost one unwanted birth per woman over her reproductive career, by C. F. Westoff, et al. INTERNATIONAL FAMILY PLANNING PERSPECTIVES 5:111-117, September, 1979.

Sterilization in the Unied States, by C. F. Westoff, et al. FAMILY PLANNING PERSPECTIVES 11(3):147, May-June, 1979.

Sterilization—judge who granted petition to sterilize a "somewhat retarded" minor held immune from liability because he had not acted in "clear absence of all jurisdiction," despite the lack of a specific statute granting jurisdiction and despite procedural errors. JOURNAL OF FAMILY LAW 17:611-616, May, 1979.

Sterilization of a non-scrotal mammal (Suncus murinus L.) by intratesticular injection of cadmium chloride, by S. K. Singh, et al. ACTA EUROPAEA FERTILITATIS 9(1):65-70, March, 1978.

Sterilization of the woman, by E. V. van Hall. NEDERLANDS TIJDSCHRIFT VOOR GENEESKUNDE 122(52):2052-2055, December 30, 1978.

Sterilization of women through a minilaparotomy, by M. Rabøl, et al. DANISH MEDICAL BULLETIN 25(4):177-178, August, 1978.

Sterilization of young women [letter], by D. K. Quinlan. SOUTH AFRICAN MEDICAL JOURNAL 54(17):688, October 21, 1978.

Sterilization regulation: government efforts to guarantee informed consent. SANTA CLARA LAW REVIEW 18:981-996, Fall, 1978.

Sterilization reversal for women. STOREFRONT 6(3):4, August, 1978.

A sterilization technique [letter] , by W. D. Marais. SOUTH AFRICAN MEDICAL JOURNAL 54(20):809, November 11, 1978.

Sterilization technqiues, by J. Kagan. McCALLS 106:69, October, 1978.

Steroid contraception and the risk of neoplasia. SOUTH AFRICAN MEDICAL JOURNAL 54(19):763-764, November 4, 1978.

Stitch in time, by E. Austen. TEXAS MONTHLY 7(6):146, June, 1979.

Stop sterilization abuse, by B. Ehrenreich. HERESIES 6:45, 1978.

Stopcock contamination, by G. E. Dryden, et al. ANESTHESIA AND ANALGESIA 58(2):141-142, March-April, 1979.

Strong attacks against abortion put Italian Church on hot seat, by C. Savitsky, Jr. OUR SUNDAY VISITOR 67:3, February 4, 1979.

Student nurses view an abortion client: attitude and context effects, by E. H. Fischer. JOURNAL OF POPULATION 2(1):33-46, 1979.

Studies in family planning. The MCH/FP approach: report from Bohol, the Philippines. MATERNAL AND CHILD HEALTH/FAMILY PLANNING 10(6-7):   , June-July, 1979.

Studies in mice on the mutagenicity of two contraceptive drugs, by M. E. Wallace, et al. JOURNAL OF MEDICAL GENETICS 16(3):206-209, June, 1979.

Studies on liver function under the influence of oral contraceptives, by E. Brügmann, et al. INTERNATIONAL JOURNAL OF GYNAECOLOGY AND OBSTETRICS 16(5):394-397, March-April, 1979.

Studies on the maternal immune response to placental antigens: absence of a blocking factor from the blood of abortion-prone women, by W. H. Stimson, et al. BRITISH JOURNAL OF OBSTETRICS AND GYNAECOLOGY 86(1):41-45, January, 1979.

Studies show smoking raises pill risk. FDA CONSUMER 12:3, November, 1978.

Study: abortion may raise risk in future pregnancy. MEDICAL WORLD NEWS 19:12, September 4, 1978.

Study by W.H.O. Task Force on sequelae of abortion. LANCET 1(8108):142-145, January 20, 1979.

Study confirms accentuated heart attack risk among pill users who are also heavy smokers. FAMILY PLANNING PERSPECTIVES 11:196-197, May-June, 1979.

Study of the activity of antithrombin—III in latent cholestasis (a clinico-pharmacological study of the relationship between antithrombin-III activity and steroid cholestasis), by T. Horváth, et al. ACTA MEDICA ACADEMIAE SCIENTIARUM HUNGARICAE 35(2):105-113, 1978.

Study of attitudes of women attending an immunization clinic towards fertility regulations and fertility regulating methods, by M. Karkal, et al. JOURNAL OF FAMILY WELFARE 24:17-25, June, 1978.

A study of fetal pathology in saline induced abortion, by A. V. Kher, et al. INDIAN JOURNAL OF PATHOLOGY AND MICROBIOLOGY 21(3):189-192, July, 1978.

A study of placental pathology in mid trimester therapeutic abortions induced by hypertonic saline and prostaglandin, by M. Khardekar, et al. INDIAN JOURNAL OF PATHOLOGY AND MICROBIOLOGY 21(2):141-145, April, 1978.

Study of sterilization equipment offered for dental practice, by L. Grün. DEUTSCHE ZAHNAERZTLICHE ZEITSCHRIFT 34(1):59-63, January, 1979.

Study of women seeking abortion, by K. Sidenius. SOCIAL SCI-
ENCE AND MEDICINE 12(5A):423-424, September, 1978.

A study on experiences and causes of artificial abortion of gynecology patients in Seoul National University Hospital, by
S. N. Park. KOREAN CENTRAL JOURNAL OF MEDICINE
33(6):657-661, 1977.

Stump v. Sparkman (98 Sup Ct 1099): the doctrine of judicial
impunity, by L. M. Rosenberg. VIRGINIA LAW REVIEW
64:833-858, October, 1978.

Styles of sexual expression in women: clinical implications of
multivariate analyses, by E. F. Hoon, et al. ARCHIVES OF
SEXUAL BEHAVIOR 7(2):105-116, March, 1978.

Subjective expected utility and the prediction of birth-planning
decisions, by L. R. Beach, et al. ORGANIZATIONAL BE-
HAVIOR AND HUMAN PERFORMANCE 24:18-28, August, 1979.

Subjective sexual experience in college women, by R. E. Clifford.
ARCHIVES OF SEXUAL BEHAVIOR 7:183-197, May,
1978.

Substantive and metholological issues in replication research:
Reiss' proposition one of the theory of premarital sexual
permissiveness as a case in point, by R. Walsh, et al. INTER-
NATIONAL JOURNAL OF SOCIOLOGY OF THE FAMI-
LY 6(2):211-223, 1976.

Suction termination of pregnancy under local anesthesia [letter] ,
by J. Guiilebaud. BRITISH MEDICAL JOURNAL 1(6171):
1148, April 28, 1979.

Sudden collapse and death of women obtaining abortions in-
duced with prostaglandin F2alpha, by W. Cates, Jr., et al.
AMERICAN JOURNAL OF OBSTETRICS AND GYNE-
COLOGY 133(4):398-400, February 15, 1979.

Summing up, by M. Sanger. HUMANIST 38:62, July, 1978.

Suppression of uterine activity by prostaglandin synthetase inhibitors, by M. O. Pulkkinen. ACTA OBSTETRICIA ET GYNECOLOGICA SCANDINAVICA 87:39-43, 1979.

Supraventricular arrhythmia caused by ovulation inhibitors? [letter], by C. Lauritzen. DEUTSCH MEDIZINISCHE WOCHENSCHRIFT 104(17):613, April 27, 1979.

Supreme Court Report: abortion, by R. L. Young. AMERICAN BAR ASSOCIATION JOURNAL 64:1912, December, 1978.

—: Pennsylvania's abortion law is unconstitutionally 'ambiguous', by R. L. Young. AMERICAN BAR ASSOCIATION JOURNAL 65:448+, March, 1979.

Supreme Court upholds right of mature minor to obtain abortion without parental consent. FAMILY PLANNING PERSPECTIVES 11:252-253, July-August, 1979.

The Supreme Court's abortion decisions and public opinion in the United States, by J. Blake. POPULATION AND DEVELOPMENT REVIEW pp. 45-62, 1977.

Surfacing: Margaret Atwood's nymph complaining, by E. J. Hinz, et al. CONTEMPORARY LITERATURE 20:221-236, Spring, 1979.

Surgical contraception: a key to normalization and prevention, by M. S. Bass. MENTAL RETARDATION 16:399-404, December, 1978.

Surgical female sterilisation: it's all done with tubes and clips, by A. Bennett. NURSING MIRROR AND WIDWIVE'S JOURNAL 148:42-44, March 8, 1979.

Surgical sterilisation in a New Town practice by A. F. Wright. HEALTH BULLETIN 36(5):229-234, September, 1978.

Surgical sterilization of women. Personal experience with Pomeroy's method, by P. Guccione. MINERVA GINECOLOGIA 31(1-2):61-65, January-February, 1979.

Surveillance of women taking oral contraceptives by determination of antithrombin III [letter], by M. O. Benoit, et al. NOUVELLE PRESSE MEDICALE 8(7):528-529, February 10, 1979.

Survey of abortion providers in Seoul, Korea, by S. B. Hong, et al. STUDIES IN FAMILY PLANNING 10:161-163, May, 1979.

Survey of adolescent sexuality and life values, New York City, by S. Ross. EDUCATIONAL DIGEST 44:44-47, May, 1979.

Survey of congressional voting records. SPOKESWOMAN 9(3): 3, September, 1978.

Survey of contraceptive services available to college students, by B. E. Pruitt. RESEARCH QUARTERLY 48:489-491, May, 1977.

Survey of primary liver tumors and oral contraceptive use, by J. Vana, et al. JOURNAL OF TOXICOLOGY AND ENVIRON-MENTAL HEALTH 5(2-3):255-273, March-May, 1979.

A survey of systems in use for disposal/disinfection of bedpans and associated equipment, by C. M. Hawkins. NURSING TIMES 75(36):suppl 13-15, September 6, 1979.

A survey of tubal ectopic pregnancy, with particular reference to cases following sterilization, by S. M. Walton. AUSTRALIAN AND NEW ZEALAND JOURNAL OF OBSTETRICS AND GYNAECOLOGY 18(4):266-267, November, 1978.

Survey on knowledge and interest on family planning, by Y. Sakamoto, et al. JOSANPU ZASSHI 33(3):3-6, March, 1979.

Swedish contraceptive uses brain hormone. BRAIN/MIND 3(17):3, July 17, 1978.

Symmetrical anteroposterior projections of the sternoclavicular joints with motion studies, by M. S. Abel. RADIOLOGY 132(3):757-759, September, 1979.

Symposium on bioethical issues in nursing. Human values in determining the fate of persons with mental retardation, by M. L. de Leon Siantz. NURSING CLINICS OF NORTH AMERICA 14:57-67, March, 1979.

Symposium on contraceptive technology, by L. Mastroianni, Jr. FEDERATION PROCEEDINGS 37:2664-2665, November, 1978.

Symposium on nutrition. Nutrition during pregnancy, lactation, and oral contraception, by B. Worthington. NURSING CLINICS OF NORTH AMERICA 14:269-283, June, 1979.

Synthetic progestins: in vitro potency on human endometrium and specific binding to cytosol receptor, by S. S. Shapiro, et al. AMERICAN JOURNAL OF OBSTETRICS AND GYNECOLOGY 132(5):549-554, 1978.

A synthetic steroid (R2323) as a once-a-week oral contraceptive, by S. S. David, et al. FERTILITY AND STERILITY 31(3): 278-281, March, 1979.

Systemic lupus erythematosus, repeated abortions and thrombocytopenia, by M. H. Pritchard, et al. ANNALS OF THE RHEUMATIC DISEASES 37(5):476-478, 1978.

Taking control: a contraception guide, by S. Gregg. ESSENCE 10:46-48+, May, 1979.

Taking precautions, by B. Trench. NEW STATESMAN 97:2-3, January 5, 1979.

Tale of tape unwinds in Springfield, Mass. NATIONAL UNDERWRITER LIFE AND HEALTH INSURANCE EDITION 83: 4-5, January 20, 1979.

Tapestry: going to the barricades, by C. Perozino. AMERICAN ATHEIST

Tasks of family and maternal counseling. ORVOSI HETILAP 120(6):341, February 11, 1979.

Tax-paid abortions, by R. McMunn. OUR SUNDAY VISITOR 67:1, January 14, 1979.

Teaching family relations to dating couples versus non-couples: who learns better? by A. W. Avery, et al. FAMILY CO-ORDINATOR 28(1):41-45, January, 1979.

Teaching successful use of the diaphragm, by L. L. Gorline. AMERICAN JOURNAL OF NURSING 79:1732-1735, October, 1979.

A technical aid for vasovasostomy, by F. J. Leary, et al. UROLOGY 13(3):256, March, 1979.

Technical problems and early complications of laparoscopic sterilization done on a day-case basis, by E. J. Coetzee, et al. SOUTH AFRICAN MEDICAL JOURNAL 54(27):1132-1134, December 30, 1978.

Teenage abortion goes back to court, by L. Sharf. MAJORITY REPORT 8:1, September 30-October 13, 1978.

Teenage birth control. SOCIETY 16:3, March, 1979.

Teenage sexual behaviour: perceptive and behavioural outcomes associated with receipt of family planning services, by C. A. Akpom, et al. JOURNAL OF BIOSOCIAL SCIENCE 11(1): 85-92, January, 1979.

The teen-ager's abortion decision: included are a summary of the decision: an excerpt from the dissenting opinion and reaction to the decision. ORIGINS 9:134-143, August 2, 1979.

Teenagers and pregnancy: the law in 1979 [the right of teen-agers to consent for their own birth control and other reproductive health care; United States], by E. W. Paul, et al. FAMILY PLANNING PERSPECTIVES 11:297-302, September-October, 1979.

Teenagers, birth control and the nurse, by C. Sklar. CANADIAN NURSE 74:14-16, November, 1978.

Ten-year overview; symposium commemorating issuance of Humanae vitae. NATIONAL REVIEW 30:1530, December 8, 1978.

10-year survey of 485 sterilisations. Part I—Sterilisation or hysterectomy? by R. G. Whitelaw. BRITISH MEDICAL JOURNAL 1(6155):32-33, January 6, 1979.

—. Part II: patients' views on their sterilization, by R. G. Whitelaw. BRITISH MEDICAL JOURNAL 1(6155):34-35, January 6, 1979.

Termination of pregnancy [letter], by W. Thomson. MEDICAL JOURNAL OF AUSTRALIA 2(8):387+, October 7, 1978.

Termination of pregnancy during the second and third trimester with Sulproston (SH B 286 AD), by M. Cornely. MEDIZINISCHE KLINIK 73(37):1281-1287, September 15, 1978.

Termination of pregnancy following ultrasonic diagnosis of anencephaly, by Z. Weintraub, et al. HAREFUAH 94(12): 422-424, June 15, 1978.

Termination of second trimester pregnancy with intraamniotic administration of 16-phenoxy-omega-tetranor-PgE2-methylsulfonamide (SHB 286) alone and combined with oxytocin and calcium gluconate, by A. S. van den Bergh, et al. CONTRACEPTION 18(6):635-639, December, 1978.

Termination of second trimester pregnancy with intra-muscular administration of 16 phenoxy-omega-17,18,19,20 tetranor PGE2 methylsulfonylamide, by S. M. Karim, et al. PROSTAGLANDINS 15(6):1063-1068, June, 1978.

A test and reformulation of reference group and role correlates of premarital sexual permissiveness theory, by R. W. Libby, et al. JOURNAL OF MARRIAGE AND THE FAMILY 40(1):79-92, February, 1978.

Test bed, by J. Langdon. GUARDIAN p. 17, February 17, 1979.

A test of knowledge of contraceptive methods: pharmacists and pharmacy students, by M. Smith, et al. AMERICAN JOURNAL OF PHARMACEUTICAL EDUCATION 43(1):19-21, February, 1979.

Thanks for Humanae Vitae, by P. Spencer. HOMILETIC AND PASTORAL REVIEW 79:25-29+, March, 1979.

Theory of rapid fertility decline in homogeneous populations, by R. D. Retherford. STUDIES IN FAMILY PLANNING 10: 61, February, 1979.

Therapeutic abortion and psychiatric disturbance in Canadian women, by E. R. Greenglass. CANADIAN PSYCHIATRIC ASSOCIATION JOURNAL 21(7):453-460, November, 1976.

Therapeutic abortion on psychiatric grounds. Part I. A local study, by S. J. Drower, et al. SOUTH AFRICAN MEDICAL JOURNAL 54(15):604-608, October 7, 1978.

—. Part II. The continuing debate, by S. J. Drower, et al. SOUTH AFRICAN MEDICAL JOURNAL 54(16):643-647, October 14, 1978.

'Therapeutic abortion' payments restored. SEVEN DAYS 2(1): 4, January, 1978.

Therapeutic and prophylactic care in abortion in women with genital infantilism, by N. K. Moskvitina, et al. AKUSHER-STVO I GINEKOLOGIIA (4):12-14, April, 1979.

Therapeutics basis of threatened abortions, by J. L. Viala. JOURNAL DE GYNECOLOGIE, OBSTETRIQUE ET BIOLOGIE DE LA REPRODUCTION 7(3 pt 2):678-682, April, 1978.

Therapy with oral contraceptive steroids and antibiotics, by M. L. Orme, et al. JOURNAL OF ANTIMICROBIOL CHEMO-THERAPY 5(2):124-126, March, 1979.

There just wasn't room in our lives for another baby, by L. B. Francke. FAMILY CIRCLE 91:54+, March 27, 1978.

Thermal injury to the bowel as a complication of laparoscopic sterilization, by R. F. Maudsley, et al. CANADIAN JOURNAL OF SURGERY 22(3):232-234, May, 1979.

They hammered at abortion to unclutter debate, by C. Anthony. OUR SUNDAY VISITOR 68:6, October 28, 1979.

Thinking about abortion, by G. Kuykendali. CROSS CURRENTS 27:403-416, Winter, 1977-1978.

Thirty abortions for 100 births, by Bishop G. Duchene. LA DOCUMENTATION CATHOLIQUE 76:91-92, January 21, 1979.

This ad really works, by E. J. Wood. MARKETING 83:16, January 23, 1978.

Thousands try male "pill" in China, by W. Sullivan. NEW YORK TIMES p. C1, September 25, 1979.

Thousands will march for life, will media bury story again? by C. Anthony. OUR SUNDAY VISITOR 67:1, January 21, 1979.

Threatened abortion: patient characteristics, treatment results and consequences for the child, by U. H. Eggimann, et al. SCHWEIZERISCHE MEDIZINISCHE WOCHENSCHRIFT 109(8):288-292, February 24, 1979.

3 further cases of icterus after taking estroprogestational agents and troleandomycin [letter], by J. Descotes, et al. NOUVELLE PRESSE MEDICALE 8(14):1182-1183, March 24, 1979.

Thromboembolic accidents in patients on oral contraceptive treatment, by L. Pedrini, et al. ANGIOLOGIA 31(2):51-56, March-April, 1979.

Thrombosis [letter], by M. D. Birnbaum. OBSTETRICS AND GYNECOLOGY 53(6):768, June, 1979.

Thrombotic thrombocytopoenic purpura during oral contraceptive treatment [letter] , by S. Vesconi, et al. THROMBOSIS AND HAEMOSTASIS 40(3):563-564, February 15, 1979.

Throwing out baby with the legislation? by S. Kingman. HEALTH AND SOCIAL SERVICE JOURNAL 89:962-963, August 3, 1979.

Timing of female sterilisation, by J. M. Emens, et al. BRITISH MEDICAL JOURNAL 2(6145):1126, October 21, 1978.

Tip of the anti-abortion iceberg, by A. Jones. AMERICAN ATHEIST 21(7):37, July, 1979.

To have—or not to have—another child: family planning attitudes, intentions, and behavior, by D. Vinokur-Kaplan. JOURNAL OF APPLIED SOCIAL PSYCHOLOGY 8(1): 29-46, January-March, 1978.

To test or not to test? It's a pregnant question [anti-pregnancy vaccines] , by G. Bicker. MACLEANS 91:42, December 18, 1978.

Torts—cause of action on behalf of parents for the negligent sterilization of mother resulting in the birth of an unwanted child held sufficiently supported by case law to warrant denial of motion for summary judgment and to allow claimant-parents to prove all items of damage, including the anticipated cost of rearing the child, less any benefit conferred by the birth. DRAKE LAW REVIEW 28:503-512, 1978-1979.

Torts—cause of action recognized for wrongful pregnancy—measure of damages to be applied. WAYNE LAW REVIEW 25: 961-974, March, 1979.

Torts—judicial immunity—absolute immunity reaffirmed in Stump v. Sparkman (98 Sup Ct 1099). KANSAS LAW REVIEW 27:518-528, Spring, 1979.

Torts—judicial immunity—state court judge has absolute immunity in § 1983 action. WASHINGTON UNIVERSITY LAW QUARTERLY 1979:288-293, Winter, 1979.

Torts—judicial immunity: a sword for the malicious or a shield for the conscientious? UNIVERSITY OF BALTIMORE LAW REVIEW 8:141-163, Fall, 1978.

Toward an assessment of the social role of rural midwives and its implication for the family planning program: an Iranian case study, by W. O. Beeman, et al. HUMAN ORGANIZATION 37:295-300, Fall, 1978.

Toward greater reproductive freedom: Wiconsin's new family planning act. WISCONSIN LAW REVIEW 1979:509-536, 1979.

Towards an understanding of the American abortion rate, by C. Francome, et al. JOURNAL OF BIOSOCIAL SCIENCE 11:303-314, July, 1979.

Toxic liver diseases after hormonal contraception, by C. W. Schmidt, et al. ZEITSCHRIFT FUR AERZTLICHE FORT- BILDUNG 72(22):1097-1099, November 15, 1978.

Toxico-septic abortion—a major medical emergency, by M. Enachescu. VIATA MEDICALA 27(4):83-84, April, 1979.

Tragedy that did not have to happen; M. E. Pitchford's abortion trial, by E. P. Frank. GOOD HOUSEKEEPING 118:78+, June, 1979.

Training physicians of developing nations in female surgical con- traception, by V. Benchakan, et al. INTERNATIONAL JOURNAL OF GYNAECOLOGY AND OBSTETRICS 15(5):459-461, 1978.

Transcervical extraamniotic Rivanol instillations as a method of avoiding complications in pregnancy interruption, by R. Barthel, et al. FORTSCHRITTE DER MEDIZIN 96(35): 1767-1770, September 21, 1978.

The transition from natural to controlled fertility in Taiwan: a cross-sectional analysis of demand and supply factors, by S. J. Jejeebhoy. STUDIES IN FAMILY PLANNING 9(8): 206, August, 1978.

Transition may open up new ground, by T. N. Krishnan. GUAR-DIAN p. 18, August 28, 1979.

Transitory hypoadrenalism due to long-term treatment with anti-ovulatory compounds, by S. Leiba, et al. ISRAEL JOUR-NAL OF MEDICAL SCIENCES 15(5):434-437, May, 1979.

Transplantation immunity reactions in women during physiologi-cal and pathological pregnancies, by V. I. Govallo, et al. AKUSHERSTVO I GINEKOLOGIIA (3):33-36, March, 1979.

Treatment of feline misalliances [letter], by T. J. Gruffydd-Jones. VETERINARY RECORDS 103(22):498, November 25, 1978.

Treatment of imminent abortion, by S. Saarikoski. DUODECIM 95(4):198-203, 1979.

Treatment of possibilities of early stages of venous insufficiency caused by oral contraceptives, by S. Kalinski, et al. MEDI-ZINISCHE KLINIK 30(31-32):1169-1172, August 10, 1979.

Treatment with a single vaginal suppository containing 15-methyl PGF2 alpha methyl ester at expected time of men-struation, by K. Kinoshita, et al. PROSTAGLANDINS 17(3):469-481, March, 1979.

Trends in attitudes toward abortion: 1972-1976, by L. M. Tedrow, et al. PUBLIC OPINION QUARTERLY 43:181-189, Summer, 1979.

Trials start for nasal-spray contraceptive [for women or men]. MEDICAL WORLD NEWS 19:58, August 21, 1978.

Triploidy in human abortions, by A. Ornoy, et al. TERATOLO-GY 18(3):315-320, December, 1978.

True confession of one one-issue voter, by G. Rees, 3d, et al. NATIONAL REVIEW 31:669-672+, May 25, 1979; Dis-cussion, 31:808-809, June 22, 1979.

Trying to put the clock back, by P. Ferris. OBSERVER p. 34, November 4, 1979.

Tryptophan and tyrosine availability and oral contraceptives [letter], by S. E. Møller. LANCET 2(8140):472, September 1, 1979.

Tubal and uterine secretions; the possibilities for contraceptive attack, by R. J. Aitken. JOURNAL OF REPRODUCTION AND FERTILITY 55(1):247-254, January, 1979.

Tubal ligation by colptomy incision, by C. F. Whitaker, Jr. AMERICAN JOURNAL OF OBSTETRICS AND GYNE-COLOGY 134(8):885-888, August 15, 1979.

Tubal microsurgery—a review, by P. Paterson. AUSTRALIAN AND NEW ZEALAND JOURNAL OF OBSTETRICS AND GYNAECOLOGY 18(3):182-184, August, 1978.

Tubal pregnancy subsequent to transperitoneal migration of spermatozoa, by K. G. Metz, et al. OBSTETRICAL AND GYNECOLOGICAL SURVEY 34(7):554-560, July, 1979.

Tubal reanastomosis using absorbable stent, by A.H. Ansari. INTERNATIONAL JOURNAL OF FERTILITY 23(4):242-243, 1978.

Tubal repermeabilisation after sterilisation. Techniques and results, by R. Henrion, et al. NOUVELLE PRESSE MEDI-CALE 8(13):1091-1094, March 17, 1979.

Tubal sterilization, by E. Golob. WIENER MEDIZINISCHE WOCHENSHRIFT 91(4):130-133, February 16, 1979.

Tubal sterilization and ovarian perfusion: selective arteriography in vivo and in vitro, by R. Manzanilla-Sevilla, et al. INTER-NATIONAL JOURNAL OF GYNECOLOGY AND OBSTE-TRICS 16(2):137-143, 1978-1979.

Tubal sterilization with the tupla-clip per laparoscopiam, by J. Babenerd, et al. MEDIZINISCHE KLINIK 74(20):769-773, May 18, 1979.

25 years on the pill, by E. Shorter. WEEKEND MAGAZINE 29: 14-16, August 18, 1979.

Twin pregnancy complicated by the death of 1 of the fetuses, by M. Geneja, et al. WIADOMOSCI LEKARSKIE 31(17):1241-1243, September 1, 1978.

2 countries, 2 approaches to controlling populations, by J. Thomas. NEW YORK TIMES p. 16E, September 2, 1979.

Two million ever-married women are IUD users; Lippes Loop most popular, followed by Copper 7. FAMILY PLANNING PERSPECTIVES 11:119-120, March-April, 1979.

Two steps back. THE ECONOMIST 273:30-31, October 27, 1979.

2000 protest against Califano, by G. Blair. VILLAGE VOICE 22:22, November 21, 1977.

A typology of intimate relationships, by C. J. Sager. JOURNAL OF SEX AND MARITAL THERAPY 3(2):83-112, Summer, 1977.

UK women plot suts in US over pill ills, by J. H. Miller. BUSINESS INSURANCE 13:4, May 28, 1979.

U.S. abortion battle. STOREFRONT 6(3):1, August, 1978.

US being urged to change stand on a birth drug. CHEMICAL MARKETING REPORTER 214:4+, August 14, 1978.

U.S. bishops' conferences file suit on abortion benefits. ORIGINS 9:97+, July 5, 1979.

U.S. report: violence marks intensity of abortion debate, by B. Scott. PERCEPTION 3:43, September-October 1979.

U.S. Supreme Court has agreed. SPOKESWOMAN 8(10):5, April, 1978.

Uchida tubal sterilization failure: a report of four cases, by

T. J. Benedetti, et al. AMERICAN JOURNAL OF OBSTE-
TRICS AND GYNECOLOGY 132(1):116-117, September 1,
1978.

An ultimate compromise? by M. Bain. OBSERVER p. 54, October 21, 1979.

Ultra-flash sterilization of fluid food by friction, by C. Alais, et
al. ANNALES DE LA NUTRITION ET DE L'ALIMENTA-
TION 32(2-3):511-521, 1978.

Ultrasonic assessment of uterine emptying in first-trimester abortions induced by intravaginal 15-methyl prostaglandin F2
alpha methyl ester, by T. P. Dutt, et al. AMERICAN JOUR-
NAL OF OBSTETRICS AND GYNECOLOGY 133(5):484-
488, March 1, 1979.

Ultrasonic diagnosis of retroperitoneal hematoma following
therapeutic abortion, by W. C. Buss. MEDICAL ULTRA-
SOUND 3(1):33-34, 1979.

Ultrasonic visualization of a dilated cervix during pregnancy,
by D. A. Sarti, et al. RADIOLOGY 130(2):417-420, February, 1979.

Ultrasound observations in multiple gestation with first trimester
bleeding: the blighted twin, by H. J. Finberg, et al. RADI-
OLOGY 132(1):137-142, July, 1979.

Unborn again; Catholic Church, by R. Shrum. NEW TIMES
12:16, January 8, 1979.

The unborn child, by W. Preston. LINACRE QUARTERLY
46:50-54, February, 1979.

Unconscious factors in provoked abortions, by J. Aray. ALTER-
JORNAL DE ESTUDOS PSICODINAMICOS 3(1):50-60,
January-April, 1973.

Underlying family-size preferences and reproductive behavior, by
L. C. Coombs. STUDIES IN FAMILY PLANNING 10(1):
25-36, January, 1979.

Undiagnosed Wilson's disease as cause of unexplained miscarriage [letter], by J. G. Klee. LANCET 2(8139).423, August 25, 1979.

Unliberated. THE ECONOMIST 272:53, July 28, 1979.

Unmet needs. PEOPLE 5(3):25, 1978.

Unnatural birth control. EAST WEST 8(8):20, August, 1978.

Untangling structural and normative aspects of the minority status-fertility hypothesis, by D. E. Lopez, et al. AMERICAN JOURNAL OF SOCIOLOGY 83:1491-1497, May, 1978.

An unusual side-effect of the pill [letter], by A. Barmania. SOUTH AFRICAN MEDICAL JOURNAL 54(5):181, July 29, 1978.

Update: abortion fight threatens pregnant workers coalition. SPOKESWOMAN 8(11):3, May, 1978.

Update: house holds hearings on Depo Provera ban. SPOKESWOMAN 9(4):6, October, 1978.

Update: Hyde battle. SPOKESWOMAN 9(1):7, July, 1978.

Upjohn, Carnation vie for dog pill market, by M. Moskowitz. THE INSIDERS CHRONICLE 3:7, August 10, 1978.

Up-yours-john. OFF OUR BACKS 8(5):4, May, 1978.

Urihesive: a new aid in the management of urinary incontinence in male paraplegic patients, by J. de Leval, et al. PARAPLEGIA 16(3):299-302, November, 1978.

Use and abuse of the minipill in adolescence, by A. Maranzana. MINERVA MEDICA 69(46):3180-3182, September 30, 1978.

Use and acceptance of the 'paper pill.' A novel approach to oral contraception, by R. R. Damm, et al. CONTRACEPTION

19(3):273-281, March, 1979.

Use of the bicoagulation technic in irreversible contraception, by O. Havemann, et al. ZENTRALBLATT FUR GYNAE-KOLOGIE 101(2):100-106, 1979.

Use of contraceptive methods by the mentally retarded, by N. Riendeain-Wallace. MENTAL RETARDATION 26(3):59-61, July, 1976.

The use of a contraceptive vaginal ring governed by the pattern of individual uterine bleeding, by J. Toivonen, et al. CON-TRACEPTION 19(4):401-409, April, 1979.

The use of human chorionic gonadotropin in recurrent abortion, by S. W. Sandler, et al. SOUTH AFRICAN MEDICAL JOURNAL 55(21):832-835, May 19, 1979.

Use of the immunodiffusion test for trophoblastic beta 1-globulin in abortion, by L. V. Abramova, et al. AKUSHERSTVO I GINEKOLOGIIA (4):10-12, April, 1979.

Use of intra- an extra-amniotic prostaglandins for the termination of pregnancies—report of multicentric trial in India, by S. Tejuja, et al. CONTRACEPTION 18(6):641-652, December, 1978.

Use of intramuscular 15(S)-15-methyl prostaglandin F2alpha in failed abortions, by S. L. Corson, et al. AMERICAN JOURNAL OF OBSTETRICS AND GYNECOLOGY 133(2):145-148, January 15, 1979.

Use of morphogram in the prognosis of miscarriage, by L. V. Timoshenko, et al. VOPROSY OKHRANY MATERINSTVA I DETSTVA 23(11):81, November, 1978.

The use of prostaglandins in the abortion of a dead fetus, by D. Mladencvić, et al. SRPSKI ARHIV ZA CELOKUPNO LEKARSTVO 105(10):839-846, October, 1977.

Use of prostaglandins in gynecology and obstetrics and outlook on the second generation of prostaglandins, by N. Wiqvist.

GYNAEKOLOGISCHE RUNDSCHAU 18(suppl 1):1-8, 1978.

Use of a radioreceptor test for HCG in women practicing contraception, by S. M. Shahani, et al. CONTRACEPTION 18(5): 543-550, November, 1978.

The use of simulation games in teaching family sociology, by M. W. Osmond. FAMILY COORDINATOR 28(2):205-216, April, 1979.

The use of ultrasound in threatened abortion, by G. B. Duff. NEW ZEALAND MEDICAL JOURNAL 88(624):398-400, November 22, 1978.

Usefulness of alpha fetoprotein determination in risk pregnancies, by L. Wiśniewski, et al. GINEKOLOGIA POLSKA 50(1):37-40, January, 1979.

The user perspective [based on address], by G. Zeidenstein. PEOPLE 6:31-33, November 4, 1979.

Using the pill can affect the gingiva and periodontium, by S. Bonner. DENTAL STUDENT 56(4):54-60+, January, 1978.

Uterine artery ligation for postabortal hemorrhage, by J. H. Mullins, Jr., et al. OBSTETRICS AND GYNECOLOGY 54(3): 383-384, September, 1979.

Uterine contractility and plasma levels of steroid hormones after intravaginal treatment of pregnant Japanese monkeys (Macaca fuscata fuscata) with 16,16-dimethyl-trns-delta2-prostaglandin E-1 methyl ester, by K. Oshima, et al. JOURNAL OF REPRODUCTION AND FERTILITY 55(2):353-358, March, 1979.

Uterine rupture after intra-amniotic injection of prostaglandin E2 [letter], by S. Emery, et al. BRITISH MEDICAL JOURNAL 2(6181):51, July 7, 1979.

Uterine rupture with the use of vaginal prostaglandin E2 suppositories, by R. Z. Sandler, et al. AMERICAN JOURNAL OF

OBSTETRICS AND GYNECOLOGY 134(3):348-349, June 1, 1979.

Uterotubal implantation and obstetric outcome after previous sterilization [proceedings] , by E. P. Peterson, et al. INTERNATIONAL JOURNAL OF FERTILITY 23(4):254, 1978.

Utilization of paramedical personal in family planning services in rural areas: an experimental study, by R. Rivera Damm, et al. SPM 20(2):177-194, March-April, 1978.

VK0-4 portable steam sterilizer, by A. S. Viatkin. MEDITSINSKAIA TEKHNIKA (1):60, January-February, 1979.

Vaccine link with sow abortions, by I. C. Ross. VETERINARY RECORDS 104:83, January 27, 1979.

Vaginal hysterectomy for elective sterilization, by W. C. Daniell, et al. MILITARY MEDICINE 143(12):864-865, December, 1978.

Vaginal hysterectomy in a community hospital: study of 491 cases, by B. A. Harris. NEW YORK STATE JOURNAL OF MEDICINE 76:1304-1307, August, 1976.

Vaginal lesion: etiology—a malfitting diaphragm? by M. V. Widhalm. JOURNAL OF NURSE-MIDWIFERY 24:39-40, September-October, 1979.

Vaginal progesterone for contraception, by A. Victor, et al. FERTILITY AND STERILITY 30(6):631-635, December, 1978.

Value of the cornified cells in urocytograms of threatening abortion, by D. J. Chiarasini, et al. ARCHIVES D'ANATOMIE ET DE CYTOLOGIE PATHOLOGIQUE 26(2):102-105, 1978.

The value of determinations of human chorionic gonatrophin, humn placental lactogen, progesterone and oestriol in women with threatened abortion, by I. Gerhard, et al. GEBURTSHILFE UND FRAUENHEILKUNDE 38(10):785-799,

October, 1978.

The value of echography in cases of threatened abortion in the first trimester of pregnancy, by B. Leroy. JOURNAL DE GYNECOLOGIE, OBSTETRIQUE ET DE BIOLOGIE DE LA REPRODUCTION 7(3 pt 2):665-672, April, 1978.

The value of the gingival cytogram for the evaluation of hormonal contraceptives, by G. Klinger, et al. STOMATOLOGIE DER DDR 29(1):11-15, January, 1979.

The value of irreversible contraception, by O. Havemann, et al. ZENTRALBLATT FUR GYNAEKOLOGIE 101(2):107-113, 1979.

Variations in serum protein fractions following a continuous long term intake of eugynon and lyndiol by Iranian women, by S. Kamyab, et al. JOURNAL OF STEROID BIOCHEMISTRY 9(8):811-812, August, 1978.

Vasectomy. AMERICAN JOURNAL OF NURSING 79:447+, March, 1979.

—. [letter], by E. R. Owen. MEDICAL JOURNAL OF AUSTRALIA 1(5):184, March 10, 1978.

Vasectomy and its microsurgical reversal, by S. J. Silber. UROLOGIC CLINICS OF NORTH AMERICA 5(3):573-584, October, 1978.

Vasectomy news. STOREFRONT 5(6):4, February, 1978.

Vasectomy: operative procedures and sterility tests not standardized. FAMILY PLANNING PERSPECTIVES 11:122-125, March-April, 1979.

Vasectomy reversal, by R. D. Amelar, et al. JOURNAL OF UROLOGY 121(5):547-550, May, 1979.

Vasovasostomy, by S. S. Schmidt. UROLOGIC CLINICS OF NORTH AMERICA 5(3):585-592, October, 1978.

Vasovasostomy and vas occlusion: preliminary observations using artificial devices in guinea pigs, by K. L. Mohr, et al. FERTILITY AND STERILITY 30(6):696-701, December, 1978.

Vasovasostomy: evaluation of success, by R. Wicklund, et al. UROLOGY 13(5):532-534, May, 1979.

Venereal disease: college students' knowledge and attitudes, by I. Arafat, et al. THE JOURNAL OF SEX RESEARCH 13(3): 223-230, August, 1977.

Verdict on Akron abortion ordinance brings mixed victory for pro-life forces, by J. McKenna. OUR SUNDAY VISITOR 68:1, September 9, 1979.

Vermont chapters march for abortion rights. NOW 11(2):11, February, 1978.

Vertical sterilizer for the separate chemical treatment of long needles, by F. A. Astrakhantsev, et al. MEDITZINSKAYA SESTRA 37(7):49-50, July, 1978.

'Viability' revisits the court in Colautti v. Franklin, by D. V. Horan. HOSPITAL PROGRESS 60(2):18-21+, February, 1979.

Viable alternative, by L. Forgan. GUARDIAN p. 9, June 26, 1979.

Viet church stifling told, by M. Winiarski. NATIONAL CATHOLIC REPORTER 14:1+, February 3, 1978.

Views on abortion, by N. Breitsprecher. CHRISTIAN CENTURY 95:961-963, October 11, 1978.

Violable rights of Italian women, by J. Walston. NEW STATESMAN 96:427, October 6, 1978.

Violence erupts against pro-choice facilities. NOW 11(5&6):5, April, 1978.

Visit with a practicing midwife: Ms. Suzuki Suzuki who is active as a public health nurse at the town office of Tsukui-machi, Kanagawa Pref.—a promoter of regional health care and family planning, by M. Fujiwaza. JOSANPU ZASSHI 32(7):450-453, July, 1978.

Vitamin A and oral contraceptives [letter], by J. Bohner. DEUTSCH MEDIZINISCHE WOCHENSCHRIFT 104(13): 480, March 30, 1979.

Vitamin A transporting plasma proteins and female sex hormones, by A. Vahlquist, et al. AMERICAN JOURNAL OF CLINICAL NUTRITION 32(7):1433-1438, July, 1979.

The vitamin B6 requirement in oral contraceptive users. I. Assessment by pyridoxal level and transferase activity in erythrocytes, by T. R. Bossé, et al. AMERICAN JOURNAL OF CLINICAL NUTRITION 32(5):1015-1023, May, 1979.

—. II. Assessment by tryptophan metabolites, vitamin B6, and pyridoxic acid levels in urine, by E. A. Donald, et al. AMERICAN JOURNAL OF CLINICAL NUTRITION 32(5):1024-1032, May, 1979.

Voluntary agencies in transition: changing patterns of relationships in countries with governmental family planning programs, by S. M. Keeny. JOURNAL OF VOLUNTARY ACTION RESEARCH 291):16-23, January, 1973.

Voluntary sterilization: USA and China, by J. Presl. CESKOSLOVENSKA GYNEKOLOGIE 43(8):626, September, 1978.

Voluntary sterilization: world's leading contraceptive method, by C. P. Green. POPULATION REPORT (2):1, March, 1978.

WHO study finds natural family planning to be 'relatively ineffective' even with careful teaching. FAMILY PLANNING PERSPECTIVES 11(1):40-41, January-February, 1979.

Waddill strangled infant, says witness in murder trial of California abortionist, by K. Granville. OUR SUNDAY VISITOR 67: 2, April 1, 1979.

Wages of sin? THE ECONOMIST 265:36, December 10, 1977.

War of the roses: real abortion fight is not in the legislature or the courts—it's in our hospitals, by R. K. Rein. NEW JERSEY MONTHLY 3:45+, July, 1979.

Warning for women! by I. Honorof. ACRES USA 8(5):34, May, 1978.

Washington knows? by P. Ramsey. THEOLOGY TODAY 35: 428-437, January, 1979.

Washington Post reported recently. SPOKESWOMAN 9(2):8, August, 1978.

Water intoxication after oxytocin-induced midtrimester abortion, by J. Jensen, et al. NEW ZEALAND MEDICAL JOURNAL 89(634):300-302, April 25, 1979.

We quit, bishop tells United Way; Planned Parenthood won't play in Peoria. OUR SUNDAY VISITOR 68:1, August 12, 1979.

Weekend poll: abortion. WEEKEND MAGAZINE 29:3, June 23, 1979.

What abortion counselors want from their clients, by C. Joffe. SOCIAL PROBLEMS 26:112-121, October, 1978.

What the antiabortion folks don't want you to know. MS MAGAZINE 7:91-94, May, 1979.

What every women should know. . .about "The Pill" and other forms of contraception, by J. P. Sauvage, et al. DIABETES FORECAST 32:14, January-February, 1979.

What I thought during my abortion, by K. G. Levine. MADEMOISELLE 85(5):110, May, 1979.

What is to be done with the XYY feuts? BRITISH MEDICAL
JOURNAL 1(6177):1519-1520, June 9, 1979.

What now: tactics. OFF OUR BACKS 8(1):13, January, 1978.

What oral contraceptives do to migrane headache. NURSES
DRUG ALERT 3:13-14, February, 1979.

What should we do about future people? by T. Grovier. AMERI-
CAN PHILOSOPHICAL QUARTERLY 16:105-113, April,
1979.

What's new in the law: abortions. . .denying Medicaid funds, by
A. Ashman. AMERICAN BAR ASSOCIATION JOURNAL
65:116-117, January, 1979.

When the pill causes a rise in blood pressure, by R. J. Weir.
DRUGS 16(6):522-527, December, 1978.

Where are the deaths? FAMILY PLANNING PERSPECTIVES
11(2):78+, March-April, 1979.

Where population planning makes a dent: Indonesia's growth
rate is 1.9%—and going down, by J. W. McCulla. AGENDA
2:2-5, March, 1979.

Which contraceptive to choose at age 40? INFIRMIERE FRAN-
CAISE (199):21-25, November, 1978.

White House adviser Midge Costanza. SPOKESWOMAN 8(11):
4, May, 1978.

Who can have a Medicaid abortion? SPOKESWOMAN 8(7&8):
5, January, 1978.

Who fills in natural contraceptive gap? NEW SCIENTIST 79:
622, August 31, 1978.

Why abortion sit-ins? by D. Gaetano. COLUMBIA 59:18-23,
May, 1979.

Why aren't more pill-using Blacks hypertensive? MEDICAL

WORLD NEWS 20:50-52, February 5, 1979.

Why family planning is failing, by M. A. Qadeer. SOCIAL
POLICY 6(3):19-23, November-December, 1975.

Why infertility services should be provided by family planning
agencies, by R. S. Atlas, et al. JOURNAL OF NURSE MID-
WIFERY 24:33-35, July-August, 1979.

Why it is right for family planning nurses to prescribe the pill, by
S. Thompson. NURSING MIRROR AND MIDWIVES'
JOURNAL 147(16):9, October 19, 1978.

Why research into contraception faces a barren future, by P.
Chorlton. GUARDIAN p. 2, December 31, 1979.

Why we need a human life amendment, by Sen. J. Helms.
CATHOLIC DIGEST 4:24+, June, 1978.

Why women drop out of a medical termination of pregnancy
clinic, by N. N. Wig, et al. JOURNAL OF FAMILY WEL-
FARE 25:34-40, September, 1978.

Wink from the bench: the federal courts and abortion, by B. J.
Uddo. TULANE LAW REVIEW 53:398-464, February,
1979.

Women, wife, mother: coping with miscarriage, by M. Newton.
FAMILY HEALTH 10:12+, October, 1978.

Woman's body, woman's right: a social history of birth control
in America, by L. Gordon. SIGNS 4(1):170, 1978.

Women claim Cyanamid forced sterilization. CHEMICAL AND
ENGINEERING NEWS 57:6, January 8, 1979.

Women-power in Korea; Mother's Clubs, by J. C. Abcede.
WORLD HEALTH pp. 16-19, January, 1979.

Women to appeal decision on forced sterilization suit. NOW
11(10):9, September, 1978.

Women who obtain repeat abortions: a study based on record linkage [Hawaii, 1970-76], by P. G. Steinhoff, et al. FAMILY PLANNING PERSPECTIVES 11:30-31+, January-February, 1979.

Women's rights, by A. Smelser. OUR SUNDAY VISITOR 67:15, January 21, 1979.

Women's work and fertility. An inquiry in Quebec in 1971, by E. LaPierre-Adamcyk. POPULATION 33:609-632, May-June, 1978.

Work conditions for the midwife assigned to group "K" by N. Gozdek, et al. PIELEGNIARKA I POLOZNA (3):18-19, 1979.

Working class birth control in Wilhelmine Germany, by R. P. Newman. COMPARATIVE STUDIES IN SOCIETY AND HISTORY 20:408-428, July, 1978.

Workshop on Reversal of Sterilization. HARPERS' BAZAAR 1977.

World leaders declaration on population. STUDIES IN FAMILY PLANNING 9(7):180-181, July, 1978.

World-wide spread of voluntary sterilization [news]. MEDIZINISCHE WELT 30(5):20, February 2, 1979.

Worst law ever: ten years of legalized abortion, by A. De Valk. CHELSEA JOURNAL 5:111-119, May-June, 1979.

Wrong cure, by L. Adamson. GUARDIAN p. 9, August 21, 1979.

Wrong sex can mean death by abortion for unborn child. OUR SUNDAY VISITOR 68:3, September 23, 1979.

Wrongful conception as a cause of action and damages recoverable. MODERN LAW REVIEW 44:589-599, Summer, 1979.

Wrongful conception: a new kind of medical malpractice? by H. H. Clark, Jr. FAMILY LAW QUARTERLY 12:259-274, Winter, 1979.

Wrongful conception: who pays for bringing up baby? FORDHAM LAW REVIEW 47:418-436, December, 1978.

A year of deliveries at the Adjamé maternity hospital in Abidjan (Ivory Coast), by M. C. Reinhardt, et al. HELVETICA PAEDIATRICA ACTA (41):7-20, December, 1978.

You and the law: teenagers, birth control and the nurse, by C. Sklar. CANADIAN NURSE 74(10):14-16, November, 1978.

Zbaraz v. Quern (596 F 2d 196): abortion and medicaid: the public funding dilemma. JOHN MARSHALL JOURNAL OF PRACTICE AND PROCEDURE 12:609-636, Spring, 1979.

PERIODICAL LITERATURE

SUBJECT INDEX

ACLU
ACLU harasses pro-lifers (ACLU suggests that the pro-life movement is part of a papal plot), by N. Thimmesch. CATHOLIC DIGEST 4:49, May, 1978.

ACLU's holy war. NATIONAL REVIEW 31:74+, January 19, 1979.

American Civil Liberties Union. SPOKESWOMAN 8(11):3, May, 1978.

AID
AID investment of $1 billion in family planning/population is resulting in sharp birthrate declines. FAMILY PLAN-NING PERSPECTIVES 11(1):45-46, January-February, 1979.

ABORTION (GENERAL)
Abortion. MOTHER JONES 3(1):14, January, 1978.

—. NEW SOCIETY 40(75):118-119, 1977.

—, by S. R. Isbister. QUEEN'S QUARTERLY 86:127-133, Spring, 1979.

Abortion [letter], by J. F. Cattanach. MEDICAL JOURNAL OF AUSTRALIA 1(5):182, March 10, 1979.

—, by K. Hume. MEDICAL JOURNAL OF AUSTRALIA

1(8):343, April 21, 1979.

—, by F. Long. MEDICAL JOURNAL OF AUSTRALIA 1(12):572, June 16, 1979.

Abortion [review essay], by B. Hayler. SIGNS 5:307-323, Winter, 1979.

Abortion: alive issue. THE ECONOMIST 271:23, May 5, 1979.

Abortion and the abuse of the English language, by H. B. Gow. MADEMOISELLE 85:38-39, July, 1979.

Abortion and the arms race: the same sickness, by J. Mc-Gowan. NATIONAL CATHOLIC REPORTER 14:11, April 7, 1978.

Abortion and an attempt at dialogue, by J. Loesch. AMERI-CA 140:234-236, March 24, 1979.

Abortion anniversary, by C. Rice. AMERICA 140:65, February 3, 1979.

Abortion battle heats up, by R. S. Bingham. U. S. A. TO-DAY 108:38-41, November, 1979.

Abortion—controversy we can't seem to solve, by E. R. Dobell. REDBOOK 153(2):42, June, 1979.

Abortion: a dyadic perspective, by A. Rothstein. AMERI-CAN JOURNAL OF ORTHOPSYCHIATRY 47(1):111-118, 1977.

Abortion harassment, by M. Stucky. McCALLS 106:52, March, 1979.

Abortion: here we go again [Britain]. THE ECONOMIST 272:25, July 14, 1979.

Abortion—in brief. SPOKESWOMAN 9(6):6, December, 1978.

Abortion: is detente ahead? by A. Baron. POLITICS TO-DAY 6:7, January, 1979.

Abortion: listening to the middle, by E. A. Langerak. HAST-INGS CENTER REPORT 9:24-28, October, 1979.

Abortion: major wrong or basic right, by R. Gordis. MID-STREAM 24(3):44-49, 1978.

Abortion: public opinion pendulum swings back, by D. F. Phillips. HOSPITALS 52(22):83-84+, November 16, 1978.

Abortion: reward for conscientious contraceptive use, by E. R. Allgeier, et al. JOURNAL OF SEX RESEARCH 15:64-75, February, 1979.

Abortion update. OFF OUR BACKS 8(4):13, April, 1978.

—, by J. E. Rodgers. MADEMOISELLE 85(2):64, February, 1979.

Abortions, by W. Goodman. NEW LEADER 61:11-12, November 6, 1978.

Ambivalence of abortion, by L. B. Frank. SAN FRANCISCO REVIEW OF BOOKS 4(2):20, June, 1978.

American letter: hunting season in American, by A. Brass. BRITISH JOURNAL OF HOSPITAL MEDICINE 29(1): 86, July, 1978.

Another abortion decision coming up, by G. Reed, et al. ORIGINS 8:510-512, January 25, 1979.

Arrivals and departures: new patents (fertility prediction), by

E. Schlossberg. QUEST 2:106, January-February, 1978.

Aspects on ripening of the cervix and induction of labor by intracervical application of PGE2 in viscous gel, by U. Ulmsten. ACTA OBSTETRICIA ET GYNECOLOGICA SCANDINAVICA (84):5-9, 1979.

Assistance to the dying or protection of life? by A. C. Gokstad. SYKEPLEIEN 65(20):1290-1292, December 5, 1978.

Birth (and nonbirth) news. NEW AGE 4(4):15, September, 1978.

Birth interval study in a culturally stable urban population, by S. O. Ayangade. INTERNATIONAL JOURNAL OF GYNAECOLOGY AND OBSTETRICS 15(6):497-500, 1978.

The Bohol project and its impact, by N. E. Williamson. STUDIES IN FAMILY PLANNING 10(6-7):195, June-July, 1979.

Bourgeois abortion, by D. Vree. NATIONAL REVIEW 30: 1351, October 27, 1978.

A brief and better abortion. EMERGENCY MEDICINE 11: 200+, October 15, 1979.

Choice candidates. SEVEN DAYS 2(16):14, October 27, 1978.

The circumstances surrounding pregnancy of a group of young coloured mothers, by P. J. Van Regenmortel. HUMANITAS 4(2):203-206, 1977.

Closer links between IPPF and WHO. IPPF MEDICAL BULLETIN 12:2-3, October, 1978.

Concepts in emergency childbirth, by D. A. Zschoche. CRITICAL CARE UPDATE! 6:32-35, October, 1979.

Coping with pregnancy resolution among never-married women, by M. B. Bracken, et al. AMERICAN JOURNAL OF ORTHOPSYCHIATRY 48:320-334, April, 1978.

Corrective surgery of obstructive azoospermia, by H. Y. Lee. ARCHIVES OF ANDROLOGY 1(1):115-121, 1978.

The couple to couple league, by J. Kippley. LIGUORIAN 67:17-21, January, 1979.

Crowding and human reproduction, by D. R. Johnson, et al. THE MILBANK MEMORIAL FUND QUARTERLY 54(3):321-337, Summer, 1976.

DOD: life abortion ban, kin limits. AIR FORCE TIMES 39:29, July 2, 1979.

Dare men "play God?" by S. J. Spiro. JEWISH SPECTATOR 43:13-16, Fall, 1978.

Depo provera for third world women? OFF OUR BACKS 8(10):5, November, 1978.

Despite data gathered. SPOKESWOMAN 9(3):4, September, 1978.

Development of a dual-form abortion scale, by J. K. Bowers, et al. JOURNAL OF SEX RESEARCH 15:158-165, May, 1979.

Diary of my decision: why I had an abortion, by J. Maynard. REDBOOK 153:62+, September, 1979.

A difficult problem [editorial], by L. Valvanne. KATILO-LEHTI 83(10):349-350, October, 1978.

Do-it-yourself abortions. NEW SCIENTIST 78:733, June 15, 1978.

Does liberal abortion improve perinatal outcome? by A. G. Philip. JOURNAL OF PERINATAL MEDICINE 6(4): 197-205, 1978.

The effect of tobacco and alcohol on pregnancy course and child development, by K. Knörr. BULLETIN DER SCHWEIZERISCHEN AKADEMIE DER MEDIZINI-SCHER WISSENSCHAFTEN 35(1-3):137-146, March, 1979.

Effectiveness of abortion as birth control, by S. J. Williams, et al. SOCIAL BIOLOGY 22(1):23-33, Spring, 1975.

An estimate of the effect of abortions on the stillbirth rate, by R. J. Gandy. JOURNAL OF BIOSOCIAL SCIENCE 11(2):173-178, April, 1979.

An evaluation of cytogenetic analysis as a primary tool in the assessment of recurrent pregnancy wastage, by M. T. Mennuti, et al. OBSTETRICS AND GYNECOLOGY 52(3):308-313, September, 1978.

Experience with midtrimester abortion, by I. R. Pahl, et al. OBSTETRICS AND GYNECOLOGY 53(5):387-391, May, 1979.

The facts of life. CONGRESSIONAL MONTHLY 46:13, April, 1979.

Fetal diagnosis and abortion [30 min.], by R. L. Shinn. THESIS THEOLOGICAL CASSETTES 10(1). February, 1979.

Final weapon in war on native peoples, by A. Carmen. WIN MAGAZINE 14(43):4, December 28, 1978.

From here to 2000: a look at the population problem, by
J. F. Kantner. JOHNS HOPKINS MEDICAL JOURNAL
144(1):18-24, January, 1979.

Goose-stepping against abortion. . .and some tripping attempts. OFF OUR BACKS 8(3):13, March, 1978.

Greening of the future: population control (motherwort,
zoapatle plants used as c.), by N. Vietmeyer. QUEST 3:
32, September, 1979.

A hardening of the heart on abortion, by T. Kelly. ORIGINS
8:509-510, January 25, 1979.

Health aspect, by Tager, et al. NEW AGE 4(3):56, August,
1978.

Health problems of anaesthetists and their families [letter] ,
by J. Nunn, et al. BRITISH MEDICAL JOURNAL
1(6170):1079, April 21, 1979.

A hidden twin-pregnancy, by J. W. Bijlsma, et al. TROPI-
CAL DOCTOR 9(1):41, January, 1979.

Hotline to health, by C. Fredericks. PREVENTION 30(6):
42, June, 1978.

How images function, by N. Morton. QUEST 3(2):54-59,
Fall.

Humanae Vitae—ten years afterwards; towards a more human
civilization, by L. Moreira Neves. L'OSSERVATORE
ROMANO 3(564):10-11, January 15, 1979.

I would like to have a word with you, by S. Aberg. KATILO-
LEHTI 83(10):351-354, October, 1978.

In necessity and sorrow, by M. Denes. SPOKESWOMAN
8(12):16, June, 1978.

In the states. OFF OUR BACKS 8(10):17, November, 1978.

Increasing anti-choice activity. SPOKESWOMAN 9(6):7, December, 1978.

Indomethacin increases abortifacient effect of PGE2 in man, by J. Piotrowski, et al. PROSTAGLANDINS 17(3):451-459, March, 1979.

Inquiry on abortion views of J. T. Noonan, Jr., by B. J. Uddo. AMERICA 141:14-15, July 7, 1979.

Interruption of pregnancy. TIJDSCHRIFT VOR ZIEKEN-VERPLEGING 31(25):1185-1186, December 12, 1978.

It's reigning again, by W. Stevens. OFF OUR BACKS 8(4): 6, April, 1978.

It's time for a change? by P. Morris. NURSING MIRROR AND MIDWIVES' JOURNAL 148(19):5, May 10, 1979.

Karyotype studies in abortion, by J. Markowska, et al. GINEKOLOGIA POLSKA 49(5):395-400, May, 1978.

Legal abortion: are American black women healthier because of it? by W. Cates, Jr. PHYLON 38(3):267-281, September, 1977.

Legal abortion. A prospective study by the Sociomedical Department of the University Clinic for Obstetrics and Gynecology of Basel, by M. Mall-Haefeli, et al. FORTSCHRITTE DER MEDIZIN 97(12):531-532+, March 29, 1979.

Live children and abortion of p mothers [letter], by R. Sanger, et al. TRANSFUSION 19(2):222-224, March-April, 1979.

Menstrual extraction: politics by Laura Punnett. QUEST 4(3):48-60, 1978.

Menstrual extraction: procedures by Lorraine Rothman. QUEST 4(3):44-48, 1978.

Menstrual regulation in Ibadan, Nigeria, by O. A. Ladipo, et al. INTERNATIONAL JOURNAL OF GYNAECOLOGY AND OBSTETRICS 15(5):428-432, 1978.

Mind & body, by L. Africano. WORKING WOMEN 4:28-29, August, 1979.

No victory. NATIONAL NOW 11(11):6, October, 1978.

Of two minds about abortion, by A. Hacker. HARPERS' BAZAAR 259:16-18+, September, 1979.

On abortion, by A. Amendola. AMERICAN ATHEIST 21(10):10, October, 1979.

On second thought. OFF OUR BACKS 8(5):19, May, 1978.

Others don't see it that way. CRIME CONTROL DIGEST 13(2):8-9, January 15, 1979.

Our bodies, ourselves and them, by K. Whitehorn. OB-SERVER p. 43, July 15, 1979.

Our findings in patients examined before artificial abortion in 1973-1977, by M. Lisá, et al. CESKOSLOVENSKA DERMATOLOGIE 54(2):91-93, April, 1979.

Philippa Foot and the doctrine of double effect, by R. Weatherford. PERSONALIST 60:105-113, January, 1979.

A pill for abortion. THE ECONOMIST 272:53, August 25, 1979.

Placental histopathology of midtrimester termination, by A. Babaknia, et al. OBSTETRICS AND GYNECOLOGY 53(5):583, 586, May, 1979.

Post-abortion babies alive, kicking. NEW TIMES 10(2):24, January 23, 1978.

The predicament [abortion], by M. Gordon. NEW YORK REVIEW OF BOOKS 25:37-39, July 20, 1978.

Preemptive genocide, by D. Sibeko. AFRICA REPORT 23: 36-37, November, 1978.

Pro & anti-choice dialogue: cooptation or cooperation, by M. Rylance, et al. OFF OUR BACKS 9:4-5+, March, 1979.

The problem of abortion and negative and positive duty, by J. L. Smith. JOURNAL OF MEDICAL PHILOSOPHY 3(3):245-252, September, 1978.

—: a reply to James LeRoy Smith, by P. Foot. JOURNAL OF MEDICAL PHILOSOPHY 3(3):253-255, September, 1978.

A problem to be solved not in the uterus but in the human mind..., by T. Vittachi. GUARDIAN p. 17, August 28, 1979.

Rated "R". MOTHER JONES 3(5):11, June, 1978.

Restrictions on women's right to abortion: informed consent, spousal consent, and recordkeeping provisions, by B. Karg. WOMEN'S RIGHTS LAW REPORTER 5:35-51, Fall, 1978.

The role of chromosomes in the aetiology of human abortion, by G. M. Kotzé, et al. SOUTH AFRICAN MEDICAL JOURNAL 54(14):562-566, September 30, 1978.

The role of methylergonovine maleate in augmenting extra-amniotic saline for midtrimester abortion, by M. R. Narvekar, et al. INTERNATIONAL JOURNAL OF GYNAECOLOGY AND OBSTETRICS 15(6):545-547, 1978.

Sex role perceptions and the abortion decision, by R. H. Rosen, et al. JOURNAL OF SEX RESEARCH 14:231-245, November, 1978.

The significance of social conditions for choice of termination of pregnancy. A comparative sociomedical study of 104 patients with more than one termination and 427 patients in whom pregnancy was terminated for the first time, by F. Møoller-Larsen, et al. UGESKRIFT FUR LAEGER 141(27):1866-1869, July 2, 1979.

Soapbox: abortion—a thought before choosing, by V. Muchanic. NEW JERSEY MONTHLY 2:41, April, 1978.

Some questions about double effect, by G. C. Graber. ETHICS IN SCIENCE AND MEDICINE 6(1):65-84, 1979.

Status of research in the field of developing modern methods of birth rate regulation (based on data of the WHO enlarged program on human reproduction in 1977), by L. S. Persianinov, et al. AKUSHERSTVOI GINEKOLOGIIA (2):3-5, 1979.

Step right up! by J. Steven. WEEKLY 2(49):8, March 1, 1978.

Study by W.H.O. Task Force on sequelae of abortion. LANCET 1(8108):142-145, January 20, 1979.

Study of women seeking abortion, by K. Sidenius. SOCIAL SCIENCE AND MEDICINE 12(5A):423-424, September, 1978.

Tale of tape unwinds in Springfield, Mass. NATIONAL
UNDERWRITER LIFE AND HEALTH INSURANCE
EDITION 83:4-5, January 20, 1979.

Ten-year overview; symposium commemorating issuance of
Humanae Vitae. NATIONAL REVIEW 30:1530, December 8, 1978.

Termination of pregnancy [letter], by W. Thomson. MEDICAL
JOURNAL OF AUSTRALIA 2(8):387, October 7, 1978.

Termination of pregnancy during the second and third trimester with sulproston (SH B 286 AD), by M. Cornely.
MEDIZINISCHE KLINIK 73(37):1281-1287, September 15, 1978.

Thanks for Humanae Vitae, by P. Spencer. HOMILETIC
AND PASTORAL REVIEW 79:25-29+, March, 1979.

Thinking about abortion, by G. Kuykendall. CROSS CUR-
RENTS 27:403-416, Winter, 1977-1978.

Tip of the anti-abortion iceberg, by A. Jones. AMERICAN
ATHEIST 21(7):37, July, 1979.

Trying to put the clock back, by P. Ferris. OBSERVER
p. 34, November 4, 1979.

Twin pregnancy complicated by the death of 1 of the fetuses,
by M. Geneja, et al. WIADOMOSCI LEKARSKIE
31(17):1241-1243, September 1, 1978.

Two steps back. ECONOMIST 273:30-31, October 27, 1979.

An ultimate compromise? by M. Bain. OBSERVER p. 54,
October 21, 1979.

The unborn child, by W. Preston. LINACRE QUARTERLY
46:50-54, February, 1979.

Update: House holds hearings on Depo Provera ban. SPOKESWOMAN 9(4):6, October, 1978.

Up-yours-john. OFF OUR BACKS 8(5):4, May, 1978.

Use of the immunodiffusion test for trophoblastic beta 1-globulin in abortion, by L. V. Abramova, et al. AKU-SHERSTVO I GINEKOLOGIIA (4):10-12, April, 1979.

The user of perspective [based on address] , by G. Zeidenstein. PEOPLE 6:31-33, November 4, 1979.

Viable alternative, by L. Fogan. GUARDIAN p. 9, June 26, 1979.

Views on abortion, by N. Breitsprecher. CHRISTIAN CENTURY 95:961-963, October 11, 1978.

Wages of sin? THE ECONOMIST 265:36, December 10, 1977.

Warning for women! by I. Honorof. ACRES U.S.A. 8:5-34, May, 1978.

What is to be done with the XYY fetus? [editorial] . BRITISH MEDICAL JOURNAL 1(6177):1519-1520, June 9, 1979.

What now: tactics. OFF OUR BACKS 8(1):13, January, 1978.

Wrongful conception as a cause of action and damages recoverable. MODERN LAW REVIEW 44:589-599, Summer, 1979.

AFRICA
A year of deliveries at the Adjamé maternity hospital in Abidjan (Ivory Coast), by M. C. Reinhardt, et al. HELVETICA PAEDIATRICA ACTA (41):7-20, December, 1978.

ASIA
Developing Asia's countryside, by P. C. Stuart. NEW
LEADER 62:8-10, March 12, 1979.

AUSTRALIA
Abortion in the adolescent, by D. Lancaster. AUS-
TRALIAN FAMILY PHYSICIAN 7(spec. no.):25-
27, August, 1978.

Abortion in New South Wales—legal or illegal? by B.
Lucas. AUSTRALIAN LAW JOURNAL 52:327-
332, June, 1978.

Another pregnancy vaccine is developed in Australia.
SCIENCE FORUM 10:32, October, 1977.

Legalized abortion in South Australia: the first 7 years'
experience, by F. Yusuf, et al. JOURNAL OF BIO-
SOCIAL SCIENCE 11(2):179-192, April, 1979.

Prior induced abortion experience among clinic patients
in Australia, by G. Davis, et al. JOURNAL OF BIO-
SOCIAL SCIENCE 11(1).77-83, January, 1979.

CANADA
Birth control and abortion in Canada, 1870-1920, by A.
McLaren. CANADIAN HISTORICAL REVIEW 59:
319-340, September, 1978.

Getting a second opinion, role of father in estranged husband-wife case, by S. Kimber. MACLEANS 92:25,
September 3, 1979.

Income and childlessness in Canada: a further examination, by J. E. Wolowyna. SOCIAL BIOLOGY 24:
326-331, Winter, 1977.

Therapeutic abortion and psychiatric disturbance in
Canadian women, by E. R. Greenglass. CANADIAN

CANADA
PSYCHIATRIC ASSOCIATION JOURNAL 21(7): 453-460, November, 1976.

CHILE
Determinant factors in the illegal abortion trends in Chile, by T. Monreal. BOLETIN DE LA OFICINA SANITARIA PANAMERICANA 86(3):206-218, March, 1979.

CHINA
The population policy of China, by Y. C. Yu. POPULA-TION STUDIES 33:125-142, March, 1979.

COLOMBIA
Abortion decision making: some findings from Colombia, by C. Browner. STUDIES IN FAMILY PLANNING 10(3):96-106, March, 1979.

ETHIOPIA
Feasibility of the randomized response technique in rural Ethiopia, by L. P. Chow, et al. AMERICAN JOUR-NAL OF PUBLIC HEALTH 69:273-276, March, 1979.

FRANCE
Dix ans apres Humanae Vitae, by G. Martelet. NOU-VELLE REVUE THEOLOGIQUE 101:246-259, March-April, 1979.

The French bishops on abortion, by J. O'Leary. FUR-ROW 30:353-360, June, 1979.

Induced abortions in France in 1976, by C. Blayo. POPULATION 34:307-342, March-April, 1979.

Thirty abortions for 100 births, by G. Duchene. LA DOCUMENTATION CATHOLIQUE 76:91-92, January 21, 1979.

GREAT BRITAIN
>Abortion and the NHS [letter], by J. R. Ashton. BRIT-
>ISH MEDICAL JOURNAL 1(6164):689, March 10,
>1979.

>—, by W. Belton. BRITISH MEDICAL JOURNAL
>1(6160):415, February 10, 1979.

>—, by C. Brewer, et al. BRITISH MEDICAL JOURNAL
>1(6162):554-555, February 24, 1979.

>—, by D. Flint. BRITISH MEDICAL JOURNAL
>1(6162):555, February 24, 1979.

>—, by A. Noble. BRITISH MEDICAL JOURNAL
>1(6162):554, February 24, 1979.

>Abortion and the NHS: the first decade, by F. G. Fowkes,
>et al. BRITISH MEDICAL JOURNAL 1(6158(:217-
>219, January 27, 1979.

>—, by R. Greenham, et al. BRITISH MEDICAL JOUR-
>NAL 1(6161):492, February 17, 1979.

>Abortion: here we go again [Britain]. THE ECONO-
>MIST 272:25, July 14, 1979.

>Abortion: myths and facts [Great Britain]. LABOUR
>RESEARCH 68:197-198, September, 1979.

>Abortion: women's choice in practice, by L. Owen. OB-
>SERVER p. 39, May 6, 1979.

>Anti-abortion in England. OFF OUR BACKS 8(8):11,
>August, 1978.

>Comparison of central nervous system malformations in
>spontaneous absortions in Northern Ireland and
>south-east England, by J. C. MacHenry, et al. BRIT-

GREAT BRITAIN
ISH MEDICAL JOURNAL 1(6175):1395-1397,
May 26, 1979.

England: women's right to choose, by J. Rosiello. OFF
OUR BACKS 8(3):3, March, 1978.

Here we go again. THE ECONOMIST 272:25, July 14,
1979.

Pregnancies of Irish residents terminated in England and
Wales in 1976, by D. Walsh. IRISH MEDICAL
JOURNAL 71(9):279-280, June 30, 1978.

HUNGARY
Econometric model of pronatalist and abortion policies,
by S. P. Coelen, et al. JOURNAL OF POLITICAL
ECONOMY 86:1077-1101, December, 1978.

INDIA
Evaluation of 496 menstrual regulation and abortion
patients in Calcutta, by D. Lilaram, et al. INTER-
NATIONAL JOURNAL OF GYNECOLOGY AND
OBSTETRICS 15(6):503-506, 1978.

Health care system—related factors affecting population
control, by D. N. Kakar. NURSING JOURNAL OF
INDIA 70:157-159, June, 1979.

Indiana abortion clinic sues pro-life picketers, seeks
$700,000 in damages, by C. Anthony. OUR SUN-
DAY VISITOR 67:1, January 28, 1979.

Letter from Calcutta, by J. Sarkar. FAR EASTERN
ECONOMIC REVIEW 103:90, March 30, 1979.

Overall achievements in the training of physicians in
medical termination of pregnancy in India, by M. D.
Sharma. JOURNAL OF FAMILY WELFARE 25:3-

INDIA
12, December, 1978.

Use of intra- and extra-amniotic prostaglandins for the termination of pregnancies—report of multicentric trial in India, by S. Tejuja, et al. CONTRACEPTION 18(6):641-652, December, 1978.

IRAN
Consultant report: incomplete abortions treated at Jahanshah Seleh Hospital in Tehran, Iran from May 14, 1973 to April 30, 1974, by Y. Bejhatnia. ACTA MEDICA IRANICA 21(1):53-67, 1978.

IRELAND
Comparison of central nervous sytem malformations in spontaneous absortions in Northern Ireland and south-east England, by J. C. MacHenry, et al. BRITISH MEDICAL JOURNAL 1(6175):1395-1397, May 26, 1979.

Difficult birth. THE ECONOMIST 270:28+, January 6, 1979.

Ireland: difficult birth. THE ECONOMIST 270:28+, January 6, 1979.

ISRAEL
Abortion in Israel: social demand and political responses, by Y. Yisai. POLICY STUDIES JOURNAL 7:270-290, Winter, 1978.

Israel's abortion controversy, by R. G. Weisbord. CONGRESSIONAL MONITOR 46:11-13, April, 1979.

Requests for abortion and outcomes of pregnancy in Jerusalem, Israel, by P. E. Slater, et al. JOURNAL OF REPRODUCTIVE MEDICINE 21(4):279-282, October, 1978.

ITALY
Abortion law in Italy, by F. Havránek. CESKOSLOVEN-SKA GYNEKOLOGIE 44(3):223, April, 1979.

Church v state, continued. THE ECONOMIST 270:42, January 13, 1979.

La communaute chretienne et l'accueil de la vie humaine naissante; instruction pastorale du Conseil permanent de la Conference episcopale italienne. LA DOCU-MENTATION CATHOLIQUE 76:262-271, March 18, 1979.

Italy: abortion meeting. OFF OUR BACKS 8(4):7, April, 1978.

Italy: abortionist-rapist resisted, by Noon, et al. OFF OUR BACKS 8(4):7, April, 1978.

Italy: church v state continued. THE ECONOMIST 270:42, January 13, 1979.

Italy resists abortion. OFF OUR BACKS 8(10):6, November, 1978.

Strong attacks against abortion put Italian Church on hot seat, by C. Savitsky, Jr. OUR SUNDAY VISITOR 67:3, February 4, 1979.

JAPAN
Demographic transition in Japan, 1920-1960 [summary of doctoral dissertation with reply by L. P. Cain], by C. Mosk. JOURNAL OF ECONOMIC HISTORY 38: 285-286+, March, 1978.

Increased induced abortion rate in 1966, an aspect of a Japanese folk superstition, by K. Kaku. ANNALS OF HUMAN BIOLOGY 2(2):111-115, April, 1975.

JAPAN
Induced abortion and contraceptive method choice among urban Japanese marrieds, by S. J. Coleman. DISSERTATION ABSTRACTS INTERNATIONAL 39(4-A):2381-2382, October, 1978.

KOREA
A study on experiences and causes of artificial abortion of gynecology patients in Seoul National University Hospital, by S. N. Park. KOREAN CENTRAL JOURNAL OF MEDICINE 33(6):657-661, 1977.

Survey of abortion providers in Seoul, Korea, by S. B. Hong, et al. STUDIES IN FAMILY PLANNING 10:161-163, May, 1979.

MEXICO
Population policy and public goods, by F. Miller, et al. PHILOSOPHY AND PUBLIC AFFAIRS 8:148-174, Winter, 1979.

NEW ZEALAND
Abortion in New Zealand public hospitals: a twenty-five year review, by R. A. Brown, et al. NEW ZEALAND PSYCHOLOGIST 6(2):124-133, November, 1977.

Abortion: some observations on the contraceptive practice of women referred for psychiatric assessment in Dunedin, by D. J. Lord. NEW ZEALAND MEDICAL JOURNAL 88(626):487-489, December 27, 1978.

Confusion about New Zealand abortion [letter], by W. Savage. BRITISH MEDICAL JOURNAL 2(6133): 356, July 29, 1978.

PAKISTAN
Education, income, and fertility in Pakistan, by M. A. Khan, et al. ECONOMIC DEVELOPMENT AND CULTURAL CHANGE 27:519-547, April, 1979.

THE PHILIPPINES
Abortion choices in the Philippines, by M. Gallen. JOUR-
NAL OF BIOSOCIAL SCIENCE 11:281-288, July,
1979.

SOUTH AFRICA
The Abortion and Sterilization Act in 1975—experience
of the Johannesburg Hospital Pregnancy Advisory
Clinic, by B. Bloch, et al. SOUTH AFRICAN MEDI-
CAL JOURNAL 53(21):861-864, May 27, 1978.

An analysis of the first 200 legal abortions at the Johannesburg General Hospital, by T. Kopenhager, et al.
SOUTH AFRICAN MEDICAL JOURNAL 53(21):
858-860, May 27, 1978.

SPAIN
Legal in Spain. OFF OUR BACKS 8(2):8, February,
1978.

Risking jail for a backstreet job: trials postponed, the ordeal continues for women accused of abortion, by J.
Flint. NEW STATESMAN p. 763, November 16,
1979.

SUDAN
Epidemiological analysis and reproductive characteristics
of incomplete abortion patients in Khartoum, the
Sudan, by H. Rushwan. JOURNAL OF BIOSOCIAL
SCIENCE 11(1):67-75, January, 1979.

SWEDEN
Occupational and environmental risks in and around a
smelter in northern Sweden. V. Spontaneous abortion among female employees and decreased birth
weight in their offspring, by S. Nordström, et al.
HEREDITAS 90(2):291-296, 1979.

THAILAND
Abortion in rural Thailand: a survey of practitioners, by
T. Narkavonnakit. STUDIES IN FAMILY PLAN-
NING 10:223-229, August-September, 1979.

TRINIDAD
Abortion attitudes in Trinidad, by S. Roopnarinesingh.
WEST INDIAN MEDICAL JOURNAL 27(3):147-
151, September, 1978.

UNITED STATES
Abortions in America [letter], by S. Shea. NEW ENG-
LAND JOURNAL OF MEDICINE 299(17):960-961,
October 26, 1978.

Abortions in America: the effects of restrictive funding,
by L. R. Berger. NEW ENGLAND JOURNAL OF
MEDICINE 298:1474-1477, June 29, 1978.

American shock tactics, by C. Doyle. OBSERVER p.39,
May 6, 1979.

Another storm brewing over abortion. U.S. NEWS AND
WORLD REPORT 85:65, July 24, 1978.

Class conflict over abortion, by P. Skerry. PUBLIC
INTEREST (52):69-84, Summer, 1978.

Family planning and abortion policy in the United States,
by K. H. Gould. SOCIAL SERVICE REVIEW 53:
452-463, September, 1979.

Reproduction in American history [review article], by
M. P. Ryan. JOURNAL OF INTERDISCIPLINARY
HISTORY 10:319-332, Autumn, 1979.

U.S. bishops' conferences file suit on abortion benefits.
ORIGINS 9:97+, July 5, 1979.

UNITED STATES
  CALIFORNIA
    California doctor charged with homicide: trial ex-
      poses consequences of abortion on demand (Dr.
      Waddill Jr. charged with strangling live aborted
      baby), by D. Duggan. HUMAN EVENTS 39:10+,
      March 10, 1979.

  HAWAII
    Completeness and accuracy of reporting induced abor-
      tions performed in Hawaii's hospitals, 1970-74,
      by C. S. Chung, et al. PUBLIC HEALTH RE-
      PORTS 94:454-458, September-October, 1979.

  ILLINOIS
    Full story of Chicago abortion scandal untold, pro-
      life leaders say, by C. Anthony. OUR SUNDAY
      VISITOR 67:1, November 26, 1978.

  NEW YORK
    New York State report: prevention is key to teen
      pregnancy reduction. FAMILY PLANNING
      PERSPECTIVES 10:293-294, September-Octo-
      ber, 1978.

  OHIO
    Akron gets restrictive abortion measure, by J. Petosa.
      NATIONAL CATHOLIC REPORTER 14:20,
      March 10, 1978.

    Akron, Ohio abortion ordinance outrageous, by M.
      M. Smith. NATIONAL NOW 11(5&6):5, April,
      1978.

    Akron ordinance challenged. OFF OUR BACKS
      8(10):5, November, 1978.

    Akron's pro-life experiment (provisions of a pro-life
      ordinance), by N. Thimmesch. CATHOLIC DI-

UNITED STATES
OHIO
GEST 4:23, June, 1978.

Anti-abortion forces seek Akron's consent law as exploding myths, by J. Petosa. NATIONAL CATHOLIC REPORTER 14:32, March 17, 1978.

Cleveland abortion clinic firebombed. WIN MAGAZINE 14(9):24, March 9, 1978.

Cleveland clinic bombed, by D. Holland. NATIONAL CATHOLIC REPORTER 14:2, March 3, 1978.

Newspaper's about-face on abortion astounds, delights Ohio right-to-lifers, by J. McKenna. OUR SUNDAY VISITOR 67:3, February 18, 1979.

OREGON
Liberalized abortion in Oregon: effects on fertility, prematurity, fetal death, and infant death, by J. D. Quick. AMERICAN JOURNAL OF PUBLIC HEALTH 68:1003-1008, October, 1978.

PENNSYLVANIA
Court drives home final nail in coffin of unborn with Pennsylvania decision, by R. McMunn. OUR SUNDAY VISITOR 67:2, January 21, 1979.

TEXAS
Determinants of genocide fear in a rural Texas community: a research note, by W. C. Farrell, Jr., et al. AMERICAN JOURNAL OF PUBLIC HEALTH 69:605-607, June, 1979.

ABORTION: ATTITUDES
Abortion and opinion, by C. Francome. NEW SOCIETY

p. 678, March 22, 1979.

Abortion and the status of women [letter] , by W. Blair.
INQUIRY 9(1):28, February, 1979.

Abortion applicants: characteristics distinguishing dropouts
remaining pregnant and those having abortion, by M. E.
Swigar, et al. AMERICAN JOURNAL OF PUBLIC
HEALTH 67(2):142-146, 1977.

Abortion attitude of nurses: a cognitive dissonance perspective, by P. J. Estok. IMAGE 10(3):70-74, October, 1978.

Abortion attitudes among university students in India, by
P. D. Bardis. INTERNATIONAL JOURNAL OF SO-
CIOLOGY OF THE FAMILY 6(2):163-178, 1976.

Abortion attitudes in Trinidad, by S. Roopnarinesingh.
WEST INDIAN MEDICAL JOURNAL 27(3):147-151,
September, 1978.

Abortion: a changing morality and policy? by R. A. McCormick.
HOSPITAL PROGRESS 60(2):36-44, February, 1979.

Abortion in teenagers, by M. S. Hanson. CLINICAL OBSTE-
TRICS AND GYNECOLOGY 21(4):1175-1190, December, 1978.

Abortion: a social-psychological perspective, by N. E. Adler.
JOURNAL OF SOCIAL ISSUES 35(1):100-119, 1979.

Abortion work: strains, coping strategies, policy implications,
by C. Joffe. SOCIAL WORK 24:485-490, November, 1979.

Adolescent mourning reactions to infant and fetal loss, by N.
H. Horowitz. SOCIAL CASEWORK 59:551-559, November, 1978.

Attitude toward abortion and attitude-relevant overt behavior, by E. H. Fischer, et al. SOCIAL FORCES 57: 585-599, December, 1978.

Attitudes of adolescent males toward abortion, contraception, and sexuality, by E. Vadies, et al. SOCIAL WORK HEALTH CARE 3(2):169-174, Winter, 1971.

Attitudes toward abortion and prenatal diagnosis of fetal abnormalities: implications for educational programs, by R. R. Sell, et al. SOCIAL BIOLOGY 25:288-301, Winter, 1978.

Attitudes toward abortion have changed little since '75 [United States]. GALLUP OPINION INDEX pp. 20-24, May, 1979.

Attitudes toward and knowledge of abortion, by S. Snegroff. JOURNAL OF SEX EDUCATION AND THERAPY 4:22-26, Spring-Summer, 1978.

Changing views of abortion, by T. C. Wagenaar, et al. HUMAN BEHAVIOR 7:58, March, 1978.

Child's reaction to mother's abortion: case report, by J. O. Cavenar, Jr., et al. MILITARY MEDICINE 144(6):412-413, June, 1979.

Church attendance and attitudes toward abortion: differentials in liberal and conservative churches, by H. R. Ebaugh, et al. JOURNAL FOR THE SCIENTIFIC STUDY OF RELIGION 17(4):407-413, December, 1978.

The class conflice over abortion, by P. Skerry. THE PUBLIC INTEREST 52:69-84, Summer, 1978.

Consultation: when abortion is demanded, by W. Greve, et al. PSYCHOTHERAPIE UND MEDIZINISCHE PSYCHOLOGIE 27(2):58-63, March, 1977.

Dare man "play God?" by S. J. Spiro. JEWISH SPECTATOR

43:13-16, Fall, 1978.

The effects of familial support systems on Black mothers'
childrearing attitudes and behaviors, and on their children's competence, by C. A. Trufant. DISSERTATION
ABSTRACTS INTERNATIONAL 39(1-B) 450-451,
July, 1978.

Feminism, socialism and abortion, by C. Roberts, et al.
WOMEN'S STUDIES INTERNATIONAL QUARTERLY
1(1):3-14, 1978.

Home remedy aggrevates abortion woes [dangers and inef-
fectiveness of pennyroyal oil]. MEDICAL WORLD
NEWS 20:72, May 14, 1979.

Husbands of abortion applicants: a comparison with husbands of women who complete their pregnancies, by F.
Lieh-Mak, et al. SOCIAL PSYCHIATRY 14(2):59-64,
1979.

I had an abortion, by M. Grayson. COSMOPOLITAN 184:
106+, March, 1978.

Invasion of the fetus-snatchers [national abortion summit
meeting, Feb. 15, 1979, Washington, D.C.], by N. Borman. MAJORITY REPORT 8:1+, January 1, 1979+.

Investigation of the abortion decision process, by P. C.
Shaw, et al. PSYCHOLOGY 16:11-20, Summer, 1979.

Is zero preferred? American attitudes toward childlessness
in the 1970's, by J. Blake. JOURNAL OF MARRIAGE
AND THE FAMILY 41:245-258, May, 1979.

A legal and psychological study of pro and anti-abortion
groups, by E. M. Silverstein. DISSERTATION AB-
STRACTS INTERNATIONAL 38(12-B):6174, June,
1978.

Objective versus subjective responses to abortion, by J. M. Robbins. JOURNAL OF CONSULTING AND CLINICAL PSYCHOLOGY 47:994-995, October, 1979.

Observations on abortion, by H. Wallot. UNION MEDICALE DU CANADA 108(3):301-302, March, 1979.

Permissible scope of parental involvement in the abortion decision of an unmarried minor. GEORGE MASON UNIVERSITY LAW REVIEW 2:235-263, Winter, 1978.

Personal and moral concepts: a study of women's reasoning and decision-making about abortion, by J. G. Smetana. DISSERTATION ABSTRACTS INTERNATIONAL 39(7-B):3595-3596, January, 1979.

Perspectives on the abortion decision. NEW MEXICO LAW REVIEW 9:175-186, Winter, 1978-1979.

The relationship of age to nurses' attitudes toward abortion, by J. M. Berber. JOGN 8:231-233, July-August, 1979.

Student nurses view an abortion client: attitude and context effects, by E. H. Fischer. JOURNAL OF POPULATION 2(1):33-46, 1979.

Trends in attitudes toward abortion: 1972-1976, by L. M. Tedrow, et al. PUBLIC OPINION QUARTERLY 43: 181-189, Summer, 1979.

Unconscious factors in provoked abortions, by J. Aray. ALTER-JORNAL DE ESTUDOS PSICODINAMICOS 3(1):50-60, January-April, 1973.

What I thought during my abortion, by K. G. Levine. MADEMOISELLE 85(5):110, May, 1979.

ABORTION: COMPLICATIONS
Abortion and maternal health: an American perspective, by

L. Keith, et al. INTERNATIONAL SURGERY 63(5): 31-35, July-August, 1978.

Abortions don't hurt later pregnancies. SPOKESWOMAN 8(10):4, April, 1978.

Abortions performed before the sixteenth week of pregnancy. SPOKESWOMAN 8(11):4, May, 1978.

Administration of 15-(S)-15-methyl prostaglandins F2 alpha in intrauterine fetal death, missed abortion and hydatidiform mole, by P. Husslein, et al. WINER KLINISCHE WOCHENSCHRIFT 91(13):458-460, June 22, 1979.

Aftermath of abortion. Anniversary depression and abdominal pain, by J. O. Cavenar, Jr., et al. MENNINGER CLINIC. BULLETIN 42(5):433-438, 1978.

Anatomic and chromosomal anomalies in 944 induced abortuses, by T. Kajii, et al. HUMAN GENETICS 43(3): 247-258, September 19, 1978.

Arachidonic acid in amniotic fluid after extra-amniotic instillation of rivanol for midtrimester abortion, by A. Olund, et al. PROSTAGLANDINS 16(6):989-994, December, 1978.

Artificial interruption of the early stages of pregnancy (regulation, menstruation, mini-interruption), by F. Havránek. CESKOSLOVENSKA GYNEKOLOGIE 44(5):374-378, June, 1979.

Behavior of satellite associations of acrocentric chromosomes in women with a history of obstetric-genetic abnormalities, by A. Midro, et al. GINEKOLOGIA POLSKA 50(3):251-257, March, 1979.

Breakage of falope-ring applicator forcepts prongs [letter], by T. H. Goh. BRITISH MEDICAL JOURNAL 1(6171):

247

1148-1149, April 28, 1979.

A case of intraligamentous tumor of the late post abortion, by K. Tshibangu, et al. JOURNAL DE GYNECOLOGIE, OBSTETRIQUE ET BIOLOGIE DE LA REPRODUCTION 7(1):73-76, 1978.

Case of premature labor with unusual course, by E. Jaworski. WIADOMOSCI LEKARSKIE 31(23):1705-1707, December 1, 1978.

Central nervous system defects in early human abortuses, by J. E. Bell. DEVELOPMENTAL MEDICINE AND CHILD NEUROLOGY 21(3):231-332, June, 1979.

Chest pain, shock, arrhythmias and death in a young woman [clinical conference]. AMERICAN JOURNAL OF MEDICINE 66(5):853-861, May, 1979.

Clinical and exfoliative-cytology studies made prior and subsequent to the action of antiovulatory agents upon oral and vaginal mucous membranes, by H. Ehrke, et al. ZAHNNAERZTLICHE MUNDEN UND KIEFERHEILKUNDE MIT ZENTRALBLATT 67(1):5-9, 1979.

Clinical studies on the connection between preceding abruption placentae and abortus and subsequent complications during the afterbirth phase, by R. Voigt, et al. ZEITXCHRIFT FUR GEBURTSCHILFE UND PERINATOLOGIE 182(4):302-306, August, 1978.

Complications of abortion performed with plastic suction curet: intrauterine loss of the curet tip, by T. W. McElin, et al. AMERICAN JOURNAL OF OBSTETRICS AND GYNECOLOGY 132(3):343-344, October 1, 1978.

Contraindications in the interruption of pregnancy, by P. Drobnjak. JUGOSLAVENSKA GINEKOLOGIJA I OPSTETRICIJA 17(5-6):349-350, 1977.

248

Description of post-abortion sepsis with a fatal result in the noval 'Seobe' by Miloś Crnjanski, by B. Berić, et al. SRPSKI ARHIV ZA CELOKUPNO LEKARSTVO 105(10):917-923, October, 1977.

The disappearance of HCG and return of pituitary function after abortion, by P. Lähteenmäki. CLINICAL ENDOCRINOLOGY 9(2):101-112, August, 1978.

Does abortion affect later pregnancies? by D. Maine. FAMILY PLANNING PERSPECTIVES 11:98-101, March-April, 1979.

Down's syndrome in Nigeria: pregnancy wastage in mothers of Down's syndrome, by R. A. Boroffice. NIGERIAN MEDICAL JOURNAL 9(1):89-92, January, 1979.

Drug-induced pulmonary disease, by E. C. Rosenow. JOURNAL OF PRACTICAL NURSING 29:23-26+, January, 1979.

Early ultrastructural changes in the rat testis after ductuli efferentes ligation, by E. Anton. FERTILITY AND STERILITY 31(2):187-194, February, 1979.

The effect of indomethacin on the instillation-abortion interval in rivanol-induced mid-trimester abortion, by A. Olund. ACTA OBSTETRICIA ET GINECOLOGICA SCANDINAVICA 58(1):121-122, 1979.

Effect of medical termination of pregnancy on haemoglobin status, by K. Prema, et al. INDIAN JOURNAL OF MEDICAL RESEARCH 69:605-608, April, 1979.

Effect of past abortions and the sequence of gestations on the course of the next pregnancy and labor as well as the state-at-delivery, maturity, dystrophia and mortality rate of the newborn infants, by R. Osuch-Jaczewska, et al. GINEKOLOGIA POLSKA 50(2):127-133, February, 1979.

The effect of termination of pregnancy on maturity of subsequent pregnancy, by G. J. Ratten, et al. MEDICAL JOURNAL OF AUSTRALIA 1(11):479-480, June 2, 1979.

The effects of longacting paracervical block anesthesia on the abortifacient efficacy of intra-amniotic PGF2alpha and hypertonic saline, by M. I. Ragab, et al. ACTA OBSTETRICIA ET GYNECOLOGICA SCANDINAVICA 57(4): 327-331, 1978.

Examination of the hypophysis-thyroid system feedback in recent pregnancy and following its interruption, by W. Hartwig, et al. GINEKOLOGIA POLSKA 50(5):431-436, May, 1979.

Experience with the conservative treatment of intrauterine adhesions in women suffering from abortion, by N. M. Pobedinskii, et al. AKUSHERSTVO I GINEKOLOGIIA (4):20-21, April, 1979.

Fetus papyraceus causing dystocia: inability to detect blighted twin antenatally, by P. C. Leppert, et al. OBSTETRICS AND GYNECOLOGY 54(3):381-383, September, 1979.

Gonadotropic activity of the immunoglobulins from placental, abortion and donor blood, by L. V. Minakova, et al. ZHURNAL MIKROBIOLOGII, EPIDEMIOLOGII I IMMUNOBIOLOGII (3):66-71, March, 1979.

Gonorrhea, candidiasis and vaginal trichomoniasis in patients requesting legal abortion, by O. C. Evjen, et al. TIDSSKRIFT FOR DEN NORSKE LAEGEFORENING 99(9-10):470-471, March 30, 1979.

H-1 and X14 parvovirus antibodies in women with abortions or still-births, by S. Guglielmino, et al. ACTA VIROLOGICA 22(5):426-428, September, 1978.

HLA-A,B compatibility in parents of offspring with neural-tube defects or couples experiencing involuntary fetal wastage, by B. Schacter, et al. LANCET 1(8120):796-799, April 14, 1979.

Hemophilus influenza septicemia and midtrimester abortion, by E. Ogden, et al. JOURNAL OF REPRODUCTIVE MEDICINE 22(2):106-108, February, 1979.

Hepatic changes caused by contraceptive steroids, by M. Uribe, et al. REVISTA DE GASTROENTEROLOGIA DE MEXICO 42(3):139-147, September-December, 1977.

'Incessant ovulation' and ovarian cancer, by J. T. Casagrande, et al. LANCET 2(8135):170-173, July 28, 1979.

Intravascular spill of hyperosmolar urea durinr induced midtrimester abortion, by B. M. Kovasznay, et al. OBSTETRICS AND GYNECOLOGY 53(1):127-130, January, 1979.

Is interruption of pregnancy indicated in osteo-articular tuberculosis? by C. Kopác, et al. ACTA CHIRURGIAE ORTHOPAEDICAE ET TRAUMATOLOGIAE CECHOSLOVACA 46(1):11-14, February, 1979.

Legal abortion—ambulatory or in hospital? A prospective analysis of the frequency of complications during ambulatory care or during hospital stay, by P. Saksø, et al. UGESKRIFT FOR LAEGER 140(44):2712-2714, October 30, 1978.

Management of obstetric and gynecologic infections resulting from trauma, by W. J. Ledger. BULLETIN OF THE NEW YORK ACADEMY OF MEDICINE 55(2):241-247, February, 1979.

May spina bifida result from an X-linked defect in a selective abortion mechanism? by J. Burn, et al. JOURNAL OF MEDICAL GENETICS 16(3):210-214, June, 1979.

Medical contraindications in professional interruption of pregnancy, by N. Bregun-Dragić, et al. JUGOSLAVEN-SKA GINEKOLOGIJA I OBSTETRICIJA 17(5-6):341-347, 1977.

Medical termination of pregnancy: public opinion in an urban population, by S. X. Charles, et al. INTERNATION-AL JOURNAL OF GYNAECOLOGY AND OBSTE-TRICS 16(5):408-411, March-April, 1979.

Morbidity in nursing infants depending on pregnancy pathology and previous abortions in the mothers, by A. V. Filyk. PEDIATRIJA, AKUSHERSTVO I GINEKOLOL-OGIJA (6):24-25, November-December, 1978.

Pain of first-trimester abortion: its quantification and relations with other variables, by G. M. Smith, et al. AMERI-CAN JOURNAL OF OBSTETRICS AND GYNECOLO-GY 133(5):489-498, March 1, 1979.

Parkinsonism after traumatic childbirth, by R. P. Murphy. JOURNAL OF NEUROLOGY, NEUROSURGERY AND PSYCHIATRY 42(4):384-385, April, 1979.

Pathological and embryological studies on abortion cases related to the Seveso accident, by H. Rehder, et al. SCHWEIZERISCHE MEDIZINISCHE WOCHEN-SCHRIFT 108(42):1617-1625, October 21, 1978.

Post-abortion septicemia. Human equivalent of the Shwartz-man-Sanarelli phenomenon, by A. Larcan, et al. SE-MAINE DES HOPITAUX DE PARIS 54(17-20):585-594, June, 1978.

Postpartum amenorrhea: hormones versus nutrition, by D. B. Jelliffe, et al. BIRTH AND THE FAMILY JOURNAL

6:49-50, Spring, 1979.

Pregnancy-specific beta-1-glycoprotein and chorionic gonadotropin levels after first-trimeter abortions, by M. Mandelin, et al. OBSTETRICS AND GYNECOLOGY 52(3):
314-317, September, 1978.

Prenatal diagnosis after abortus imminens—further progress
of pregnancy and peculiarity of amniotic cell cultivation,
by K. G. Wurster, et al. GEBURTSHILFE UND FRAUEN-
HEILKUNDE 39(3):222-227, March, 1979.

Prevalence of mycoplasma hominis in patients with gynecologic diseases and abortion in the 2nd—3rd month of pregnancy, by M. W. Zalman, et al. VIROLOGIE 29(4):293-
297, October-December, 1978.

Preventing malignant-cell transfer during endoscopic brush
cytology, by M. R. Keighley, et al. LANCET 1(8111):
298-299, February 10, 1979.

Primary carcinoma of the Fallopian tube: a surprise finding
in a postpartum tubal ligation, by A. J. Starr, et al.
AMERICAN JOURNAL OF OBSTETRICS AND GYNE-
COLOGY 132(3):344-345, October 1, 1978.

Psychological adjustment to first-trimester abortion, by J. R.
Muhr. DISSERTATION ABSTRACTS INTERNATION-
AL 39(8-B):4045-4056, February, 1979.

Psychological reaction to abortion, by S. Cherazi. JOUR-
NAL OF THE AMERICAN MEDICAL WOMEN'S AS-
SOCIATION 34:287-288, July, 1979.

Reducing the morbidity of vacuum aspiration abortion, by
M. S. Burnhill, et al. INTERNATIONAL JOURNAL OF
GYNAECOLOGY AND OBSTETRICS 16(3):204-209,
1978-1979.

Relation between endometritis post abortum and oestrogen levels in the plasma, by G. Reck, et al. GEBURTSHILFE UND FRAUENHEILKUNDE 39(3):239-242, March, 1979.

Relation between toxoplasmosis and fetal losses, by U. A. Gomes, et al. BOLETIN DE LA OFICINA SANITARIA PARAMERICANA 85(4):315-324, October, 1978.

Relation of steroids to liver oncogenesis, by W. M. Christopherson, et al. JOURNAL OF TOXICOLOGY AND ENVIRONMENTAL HEALTH 5(2-3):207-230, March-May, 1979.

The relationship between previous elective abortions and postpartum depressive reactions, by N. E. Devore. JOGN 8:237-240, July-August, 1979.

Risk abortions: Chicago clinics. TIME 112:52, November 27, 1978.

Salpingography in infertile women following abortion or pelvic surgery, by S. Roopnarinesingh, et al. WEST INDIAN MEDICAL JOURNAL 27(4):201-204, December, 1978.

Serotonin metabolism disorders and their relationship to inability to complete pregnancy in women with rheumatism, by I. M. Mellina. PEDIATRIIA AKUSHERSTVO I GINEKOLOGIIA (4):43-45, July-August, 1978.

Seven-nation WHO study finds future pregnancies not endangered by 1st trimester legal abortion [news]. FAMILY PLANNING PERSPECTIVES 10(4):238-239, July-August, 1978.

Studies on the maternal immune response to placental antigents: absence of a blocking factor from the blood of abortion-prone women, by W. H. Stimson, et al. BRITISH JOURNAL OF OBSTETRICS AND GYNAECOLOGY

86(1):41-45, January, 1979.

Study: abortion may raise risk in future pregnancy. MEDI-CAL WORLD NEWS 19:12, September 4, 1978.

Termination of pregnancy following ultrasonic diagnosis of anencephaly, by Z. Weintraub, et al. HAREFUAH 94(12):422-424, June 15, 1978.

Transcervical extraamniotic rivanol instillation as a method of avoiding complications in pregnancy interruption, by R. Barthel, et al. FORTSCHRITTE DER MEDIZIN 96(35):1767-1770, September 21, 1978.

Triploidy in human abortions, by A. Ornoy, et al. TERA-TOLOGY 18(3):315-320, December, 1978.

Uterine artery ligation for postabortal hemorrhage, by J. H. Mullins, Jr., et al. OBSTETRICS AND GYNECOLOGY 54(3):383-384, September, 1979.

ABORTION: DEVELOPING COUNTRIES
Developing Asia's countryside, by P. C. Stuart. NEW LEAD-ER 62:8-10, March 12, 1979.

ABORTION: ECONOMICS
Affirmative abortion fundng proposals to be introduced, by M. M. Smith. NATIONAL NOW 11(2):4, February, 1978.

Budgeting against abortion. SEVEN DAYS 2(12):5, August, 1978.

Congress aborts medicaid. OFF OUR BACKS 8(1):13, January, 1978.

Congress ends abortion funds deadlock. SPOKESWOMAN 8(7&8):5, January, 1978.

Denial of state medicaid funds for abortions not 'medically necessary' does not violate the equal protection clause: Maher v. Roe, by C. K. Barber. HOWARD LAW JOURNAL 21(3):937-954), 1978.

Does the cash register ring louder than freedom for rights of women? by F. Franzonia. OUR SUNDAY VISITOR 68:1, July 22, 1979+.

The economical and political consequences of generative behaviour, by W. Maier. GEBURTSHILFE UND FRAUEN-HEILKUNDE 39(5):410-412, May, 1979.

Equal access to legal abortion [letter], by W. Pick. NEW ENGLAND JOURNAL OF MEDICINE 301(6):335, August 9, 1979.

Government funding, abortions, and the public forum, by W. C. Canby, Jr. ARIZONA STATE LAW JOURNAL 1979:11-21, 1979.

HEW funds abortions, promiscuity, by C. Marshner. CONSERVATIVE DIGEST 5:28+, January, 1979.

The health impact of restricting public funds for abortion. October 10, 1977-June 10, 1978, by W. Cates, Jr., et al. AMERICAN JOURNAL OF PUBLIC HEALTH 69(9): 945-947, September, 1979.

Indiana abortion clinic sues pro-life picketers, seeks $700,000 in damages, by C. Anthony. OUR SUNDAY VISITOR 67:1, January 28, 1979.

Limiting public funds for abortions: state response to Congressional action. SUFFOLK UNIVERSITY LAW REVIEW 13:923-959, Summer, 1979.

Nonprotective abortions OK o'seas if paid ahead, by R. Sanders. AIR FORCE TIMES 39:6, January 29, 1979.

Packwood and his pro-abortion backers (Gloria Steinem writes fundraising letter to help Sen. Robert Packwood battle his anti-abortion opponent forgetting that no such opponent now exists), by J. D. Lofton, Jr. HUMAN EVENTS 39:9+, July 28

Population and poverty, by M. Wolfson. OECD OBSERVER (95):17-22, November, 1978.

Pregnancy and abortion [medical benefits]. OFFICE 88: 76+, September, 1978.

Pregnancy disability bill cleared after compromise on abortion, by L. B. Weiss. CONGRESSIONAL QUARTERLY WEEKLY REPORT 36(42):3073-3074, October 21, 1978.

Problems of interrupted pregnancy among working women, by G. Marinova. AKUSHERSTVO I GINEKOLOGIIA 17(6):412-417, 1978.

Response of low income women and abortion facilities to restriction of public funds for abortion: a study of a large metropolitan area, by G. L. Rubin, et al. AMERICAN JOURNAL OF PUBLIC HEALTH 69(9):948-950, September, 1979.

Restricting medicaid funds for abortions: projections of excess mortality for women of childbearing age, by D. B. Petitti, et al. AMERICAN JOURNAL OF PUBLIC HEALTH 67:860-862, September, 1977; Discussion 68:270-272+, March, 1978+.

Restrictions of federal funds bor abortion: 18 months later, by J. Gold, et al. AMERICAN JOURNAL OF PUBLIC HEALTH 69(9):929-930, September, 1979.

Restrictive funding policies adopted by most states. SPOKESWOMAN 8(12):5, June, 1978.

Services, policies and costs in U.S. abortion facilities, by B. L. Lindheim. FAMILY PLANNING PERSPECTIVES 11: 283-289, September-October, 1979.

Stage set for annual abortion funding battle, by H. H. Donnelly. CONGRESSIONAL QUARTERLY WEEKLY REPORT 37:1089, June 2, 1979.

Standards of social welfare in pregnancy and with voluntary pregnancy interruption. PROFESSIONI INFERMIERISTICHE 31(3):133-140, July-September, 1978.

States & medicaid. OFF OUR BACKS 8(1):12, January, 1978.

Tax-paid abortions, by R. McMunn. OUR SUNDAY VISITOR 67:1, January 14, 1979.

'Therapeutic abortion' payments restored. SEVEN DAYS 2(1):4, January, 1978.

What's new in the law: abortions. . .denying Medicaid funds, by A. Ashman. AMERICAN BAR ASSOCIATION JOURNAL 65:116-117, January, 1979.

Who can have a medicaid abortion? SPOKESWOMAN 8(7&8):5, January, 1978.

Wrongful conception: who pays for bringing up baby? FORDHAM LAW REVIEW 47:418-436, December, 1978.

Zbaraz v. Quern (596 F 2d 196): abortion and medicaid: the public funding dilemma. JOHN MARSHALL JOURNAL OF PRACTICE AND PROCEDURE 12:609-636, Spring, 1979.

ABORTION: EDUCATION
Attitudes toward abortion and prenatal diagnosis of fetal

abnormalities: implications for educational programs, by R. R. Sell, et al. SOCIAL BIOLOGY 25:288-301, Winter, 1978.

New poll funds majority support for abortion, sex education. SPOKESWOMAN 9(1):9, July, 1978.

Recent developments in woman's rights: a symposium. The moral interest in abortion funding: a comment on Beal, Maher and Poelker. D. J. Horan; Roe v. Wade and Doe v. Bolton: revised in 1976 and 1977—reviewed?, revived?, revested?, reversed or revoked? by F. Susman. ST. LOUIS UNIVERSITY LAW JOURNAL 22:566-595, 1979.

State abortion funds ordered resumed, by M. M. Smith. NATIONAL NOW 11(7):11, June, 1978.

ABORTION: FAILED
Antimicrobial therapy in incomplete abortion [letter], by G. White. SOUTH AFRICAN MEDICAL JOURNAL 55(14):533, March 31, 1979.

Use of intramuscular (15(S)-15-methyl prostaglandin F1alpha in failed abortions, by S. L. Corson, et al. AMERICAN JOURNAL OF OBSTETRICS AND GYNECOLOGY 133(2):145-148, January 15, 1979.

ABORTION: HABITUAL
Adrenocorticotropic and steroid secretion in hirsute pregnant women with habitual abortion, by T. Despodova, et al. AKUSHERSTVO I GINEKOLOGIIA 17(6):417-423, 1978.

Characteristics of the action of oxidizing drugs in women with habitual abortion, by T. M. Shul'zhenko. PEDIA-TRIYA, AKUSHERSTVO I GINEKOLOHIYA (3):46-47, May-June, 1979.

Effect of treatment of habitual and spontaneous abortion

using gestanon on birth weight, by S. Andjelković. SRPSKI ARHIV ZA CELOKUPNO LEKARSTVO 106(1):53-55, 1978.

An habitual aborter's self-concept during the course of a successful pregnancy, by Y. Chao. MATERNAL-CHILD NURSING JOURNAL 6(3):165-175, Fall, 1977.

Habitual abortion. Analytic study of 57 cases, by F. Elizondo Elizondo, et al. GINECOLOGIA Y OBSTETRICIA DE MEXICO 43(259):311-316, May, 1978.

Placental lesions in habitually aborting cats, by C. R. Huxtable, et al. VETERINARY PATHOLOGY 16(3):283-289, May, 1979.

Results of clinical genealogical studies of married couples wtih habitual abortion, by M. F. Iankova, et al. AKUSHERSTVO I GINEKOLOGIIA (4):5-8, April, 1979.

Role of listeriosis in the etiology of spontaneous and habitual abortions, by T. Despodova, et al. AKUSHERSTVO I GINEKOLOGIIA 17(6):396-402, 1978.

ABORTION: HISTORY
Abortion: back to 1966? by M. Simms. NEW HUMANIST 95:95-96, Autumn, 1979.

Abortion: historical and biblical perspectives, by J. A. Rasmussen. CONCORDIA THEOLOGIAL QUARTERLY 43:19-25, January, 1979.

Abortion in America: the origins and evolution of national policy, 1800-1900 by James C. Mohr, a review by E. Farrell. FRONTIERS 3(3):65-67, Fall, 1978.

Demographic transition in Japan, 1920-1960 [summary of doctoral dissertation with reply by L. P. Cain], by C. Mosk. JOURNAL OF ECONOMIC HISTORY 38:285-

286+, March, 1978.

Emergence of countercyclical U.S. fertility, by W. P. Butz, et al. AMERICAN ECONOMIC REVIEW 69:318-328, June, 1979.

History of abortion: technology, morality, and law, by J. W. Dellapenna. UNIVERSITY OF PITTSBURGH LAW REVIEW 40:359-428, Spring, 1979.

Neural-tube defects: importance of a history of abortion in aetiology, by D. R. Evans. BRITISH MEDICAL JOURNAL 1(6169):975-976, April 14, 1979.

Reproduction in American history [review article] , by M. P. Ryan. JOURNAL OF INTERDISCIPLINARY HISTORY 10:319-332, Autumn, 1979.

ABORTION: ILLEGAL
Determinant factors in the illegal abortion trends in Chile, by T. Monreal. BOLETIN DE LA OFICINA SANITARIA PANAMERICANA 86(3):206-218, March, 1979.

Fatal air embolism during an attempt at criminal abortion, by M. Srch. CESKOLOVENSKA GYNEKOLOGIE 43(8): 615-618, September, 1978.

Sanctions for performing illegal abortions, by S. Ulitskii. SOVIET LAW AND GOVERNMENT 17(1):40-43, 1978.

ABORTION: INCOMPLETE
Curettage because of incomplete abortion in a 15-year-old girl, by W. Weissauer. ANAESTHESIOLOGISCHE UND INTENSIVMEDIZINISCHE PRAXIS 16:27-28, February, 1979.

Incidence of aerobic and anaerobic infection in patients with incomplete abortion, by D. E. Kowen, et al. SOUTH

AFRICAN MEDICAL JOURNAL 55(4):129-132, January 27, 1979.

ABORTION: INDUCED

Completeness and accuracy of reporting induced abortions performed in Hawaii's hospitals, 1970-74, by C. S. Chung, et al. PUBLIC HEALTH REPORTS 94:454-458, September-October, 1979.

Determination of selected coagulation parameters in induced abortion by means of 15-methyl-PGF2 alpha, by R. During, et al. FOLIA HAEMATOLOGICA 106(1):72-79, 1979.

Dispute over some herbicides rages in wake of Agent Orange, by P. Gunby. JAMA 241(14):1443-1444, April 6, 1979.

Endocervical heterotopia by fetal implants during induced abortion [letter], by M. Trojani, et al. NOUVELLE PRESSE MEDICALE 8(7):521, February 10, 1979.

Estimation of births averted due to induced abortions, by K. B. Pathak, et al. JOURNAL OF BIOSOCIAL SCIENCE 10:361-366, October, 1978.

Experiences with early induced abortion, the so-called 'overtime treatment' [letter]. NEDERLANDS TIJDSCHRIFT VOOR GENEESKUNDE 123(2):57-58, January 13, 1979.

Extraamniotic induction of abortion with a new prostaglandin E-2 derivative, by U. Gethmann, et al. FORTSCHRITTE DER MEDIZIN 96(35):1771-1773, September 21, 1978.

Gestation, birth-weight, and spontaneous abortion in pregnancy after induced abortion. Report of collaborative study by W.H.O. Task Force on sequelae of abortion. LANCET 1(8108):142-145, January 20, 1979.

Hematological studies in induction abortion by extra-amniotic administration of sulproston, by R. C. Briel, et al. ARCHIV FUR GYNAEKOLOGIE 226(4):297-302, 1978.

Hormone level changes caused by abortion induced with prostaglandin F2 alpha in pregnancy interruption during the 1st trimester, by J. Sárdi, et al. ORVOSI HETILAP 120(24):1429-1431, June 17, 1979.

Increased induced abortion rate in 1966, an aspect of a Japanese folk superstition, by K. Kaku. ANNALS OF HUMAN BIOLOGY 2(2):111-115, April, 1975.

Induced abortion, by J. V. Larsen. SOUTH AFRICAN MEDICAL JOURNAL 53(21):853-857, May 27, 1978.

Induced abortion after the 12th week of pregnancy. I., by P. E. Treffers, et al. NEDERLANDS TIJDSCHRIFT VOOR GENEESKUNDE 123(26):1103-1110, June 30, 1979.

Induced abortion and congenital malformations in offspring of subsequent pregnancies, by M. B. Bracken, et al. AMERICAN JOURNAL FO EPIDEMIOLOGY 109(4): 425-432, April, 1979.

Induced abortion. Report of a WHO scientific group. WHO TECHNICAL REPORT SERIES (623):1-65, 1978.

Induction of abortion with prostaglandins, by U. Haller. GYNAEKOLOGISCHE RUNDSCHAU 18(Suppl 1):9-15, 1978.

--, by F. Jerve. TIDSSKRIFT VOOR LAEGEFORENUNG 98(29):1433-1434, October 20, 1978.

Induction of mid-term abortion by trichosanthin in laboratory animals, by M. C. Chang, et al. CONTRACEPTION 19(2):175-184, February, 1979.

Induction of second trimester abortion: comparison between vaginal 15-methyl-PGF2alpha methyl ester and intra-amniotic PGF2alpha, by M. Mandelin, et al. PROSTA-GLANDINS 16(6):995-1001, December, 1978.

Investigations of hormones during early abortion induced by prostaglandin F2alpha and 15(S)-methyl-PGF2alpha, by B. Seifert, et al. ACTA BIOLOGICA ET MEDICA GERMANICA 37(5-6):955-957, 1976.

Laminaria use in midtrimester abortions induced by intra-amniotic prostaglandin F2alpha with urea and intra-venous oxytocin, by J. H. Strauss, et al. AMERICAN JOURNAL OF OBSTETRICS AND GYNECOLOGY 134(3):260-264, June 1, 1979.

Patient recall of induced abortion, by P. E. Slater, et al. EUROPEAN JOURNAL OF OBSTETRICS, GYNE-COLOGY AND REPRODUCTIVE BIOLOGY 8(4): 185-186, 1978.

Prostaglandins E2 and F2a in induction of labor, induced abortion and molar abortion: 70 case histories, by F. Laffargue, et al. JOURNAL DE GYNECOLOGIE, OB-STETRIQUE ET BIOLOGIE DE LA REPRODUCTION 7(3):503-513, 1978.

Serum relaxin levels in prostaglandin E2 induced abortions, by J. Quagliarello, et al. PROSTAGLANDINS 16(6): 1003-1006, December, 1978.

A study of fetal pathology in saline induced abortion, by A. V. Kher, et al. INDIAN JOURNAL OF PATHOLOGY AND MICROBIOLOGY 21(3):189-192, July, 1978.

Sudden collapse and death of women obtaining abortions induced with prostaglandin F2alpha, by W. Cates, Jr., et al. AMERICAN JOURNAL OF OBSTETRICS AND GYNECOLOGY 133(4):398-400, February 15, 1979.

Ultrasonic assessment of uterine emptying in first-trimester abortions induced by intravaginal 15-methyl prostaglandin F2 alpha methyl ester, by T. P. Dutt, et al. AMERICAN JOURNAL OF OBSTETRICS AND GYNECOLOGY 133(5):484-488, March 1, 1979.

Water intoxication after oxytocin-induced midtrimester abortion, by I. Jensen, et al. NEW ZEALAND MEDICAL JOURNAL 89(634):300-302, April 25, 1979.

ABORTION: INDUCED: COMPLICATIONS
Association of extrauterine fetal death with failure of prostaglandin E2 suppositories, by J. W. Orr, Jr., et al. OBSTETRICS AND GYNECOLOGY 53(3 Suppl):56S-58S, March, 1979.

Complications from legally-induced abortion, a review by D. A. Grimes, et al. OBSTETRICAL AND GYNECOLOGICAL SURVEY 34(3):177-191, March, 1979.

Consequences of induced abortion [letter], by J. Craft, et al. LANCET 1(8113):437, February 24, 1979.

Effects of anesthesia [letter]. SCIENCE 203(4382):705, February 23, 1979.

Effects of cyclic AMP altering drugs on endotoxin-induced termination of pregnancy, by R. Shaw, Jr., et al. RESEARCH COMMUNICATIONS IN CHEMICAL PATHOLOGY AND PHARMACOLOGY 24(1):49-56, April, 1979.

Experience with early induced abortion, the socalled 'menstrual extraction' method, by P. Voskuijl, et al. NEDERLANDS TIJDSCHRIFT VOOR GENEESKUNDE 122(41): 1551-1554, October 14, 1978.

Induced abortion and psychotherapy, by R. Mester. PSYCHOTHERAPY AND PSYCHOSOMATICS 30(2):98-

104, 1978.

Induced abortion as a risk factor for perinatal complications, a review by M. B. Bracken. YALE JOURNAL OF BIOLOGY AND MEDICINE 51(5):539-548, September-October, 1978.

Induced abortions in France in 1976, by C. Blayo. POPULATION 34:307-342, March-April, 1979.

Obstetrical complications in induced abortions, by M. Renkielska. GINEKOLOGIA POLSKA 49(5):389-393, May, 1978.

Pregnancy complications following legally induced abortion with special reference to abortion technique, by E. Obel. ACTA OBSTETRICIA ET GYNECOLOGIA SCANDINAVICA 58(2):147-152, 1979.

Prenatal diagnosis, selective abortion, and the ethics of withholding treatment from the defective newborn, by J. Fletcher. BIRTH DEFECTS 15(2):239-254, 1979.

ABORTION: JOURNALISM
Abortion and the press, by M. Kenny. SPECTATOR p. 13, July 28, 1979.

ABORTION: LAWS AND LEGISLATION
Abortion aquittal. OFF OUR BACKS 8(9):10, October, 1978.

Abortion case hinges on parents' rights, Catholic league tells Supreme Court. OUR SUNDAY VISITOR 67:1, April 1, 1979.

Abortion—a clarification, by T. G. A. Bowles, et al. NEW LAW JOURNAL 129:944-946, September 27, 1979.

Abortion control act struck down, Supreme Court/fetal

viability. ORIGINS 8:497+, January 25, 1979.

Abortion decisions—how will the United States Supreme Court define "necessary"? by M. A. Duffy. WOMEN LAWYERS JOURNAL 64:3-16+, Winter, 1978.

Abortion for 'wrong' fetal sex: an ethical-legal dilemma [news], by J. Elliott, JAMA 242(14):1455-1456, October 5, 1979.

Abortion funding cases: a comment on the Supreme Court's role in American government, by M. J. Perry. GEORGE-TOWN LAW JOURNAL 66:1191-1245, June, 1978.

Abortion funding conflict in temporary truce. OUR SUN-DAY VISITOR 68:2, November 4, 1979.

Abortion funding cut-offs: the human cost, by M. M. Smith. NATIONAL NOW 11(5&6):10, April, 1978.

Abortion: how early, how late, and how legal, by V. Tunkel. BRITISH MEDICAL JOURNAL 6184:253-256, July 28, 1979.

Abortion in America: the origins and evolution of national policy, 1800-1900 by James C. Mohr, a r. by E. Farrell. FRONTIERS 3(3):65-67, Fall, 1978.

Abortion in the courts: a laywoman's historical guide to the new disaster area, by K. B. Glen. FEMINIST STUDIES 4(1):1-26, February, 1978.

Abortion law and problems experienced by operating nursing staff, by H. Twelftree. AUSTRALASIAN NURSES JOURNAL 8(4):3-5, December, 1978.

Abortion, medicaid, and the constitution. NEW YORK UNIVERSITY LAW REVIEW 54:120-160, April, 1979.

Abortion—parental consent—equal protection—due process—
U.S. Court of Appeals (7th Cir.). JUVENILE LAW DI-
GEST 11(3):84-88, March, 1979.

Abortion, poverty and the equal protection of the laws, by
G. J. Simson. GEORGIA LAW REVIEW 13:505-514,
Winter, 1979.

Abortion: a public health and social policy perspective, by
B. M. Sneiderman. NEW YORK UNIVERSITY REVIEW
OF LAW AND SOCIAL CHANGE 7:187-213, Spring,
1978.

Abortion restrictions approved by Congress, by M. M. Smith.
NATIONAL NOW 11(1):5, January, 1978.

Abortion—termination of parental rights—physician-patient—
right to privacy—U.S. Court of Appeals (8th Circ.).
JUVENILE LAW DIGEST 11(2):44-46, February, 1979.

Abortions in America: the effects of restrictive funding, by
L. R. Berger. NEW ENGLAND JOURNAL OF MEDI-
CINE 298:1474-1477, June 29, 1978.

Abortions—juveniles—parental or judicial consent. CRIMI-
NAL LAW REPORTER: SUPREME COURT PROCEED-
INGS 24(22):4221-4223, March 7, 1979.

Affirm government aid of abortions for indigents. AMERI-
CAN BAR ASSOCIATION JOURNAL 64:1336, September, 1978.

An analysis of Bellotti v. Baird, by D. V. Horan. HOSPITAL
PROGRESS 60(8):18-20, August, 1979.

Atheist news: Bill Baird wins a big one. AMERICAN ATHE-
IST 21(7):6, July, 1979.

Baird v. Bellotti (450 F Supp 997): abortion—the minor's

right to decide. UNIVERSITY OF MIAMI LAW RE-
VIEW 33:705-722, March, 1979.

Barnyard sex, morality and birth control week [reprint
Catholic Register] , by Father Raby. CATHOLIC TRUS-
TEE 17(2):20-21, March, 1977.

Battle lines drawn again in Congress on federal financing.
SPOKESWOMAN 9(2):6, August, 1978.

Battle over funding for abortion resumes, by J. M. Clarke.
NATIONAL NOW 11(8):2, July, 1978.

Beal (97 Sup Ct 2366), Maher (97 Sup Ct 2376) and Poelker
(97 Sup Ct 2391): the end of an era? JOURNAL OF
FAMILY LAW 17:49-92, November, 1978.

Board practice before and after the new abortion act of June
13, 1975. A comparison of boards in Oslo during 1971/
1972, and 1975 and 1976, by O. M. Sejersted, et al. TID-
SSKRIFT FOR DEN NORSKE LAEGEFORENING
98(29):1428-1432, October 20, 1978.

Borderline cases in law and medicine, by G. Sorgo. ZEIT-
SCHRIFT FUER RECHTSMEDIZIN 82(3):175-178,
December 20, 1978.

Brief reports decline of Down's syndrome after abortion re-
form in New York State, by H. Hansen. AMERICAN
JOURNAL OF MENTAL DEFICIENCY 83(2):185-188,
September, 1978.

Byrn and Roe: the threshold question and juridical review,
by P. J. Riga. CATHOLIC LAWYER 23:309-331, Autumn, 1978.

Calls for constitutional conventions [United States] , by M.
Leepson. EDITORIAL RESEARCH REPORTS pp. 187-
204, March 16, 1979.

Can the birth of an unwanted child be grounds for a damage claim against a 3d party? Review of the facts, by H. Roesch. MEDIZINISCHE KLINIK 74(20):782-787, May 18, 1979.

Capitol Hill update. SPOKESWOMAN 9(3):3, September, 1978.

Carter defense appointments angers pro-life groups (appoints Dr. John H. Moxley as Asst. Sec. of Defense for Health Affairs; he discriminated against anti-abortion doctors at UCSD medical school). HUMAN EVENTS 39:3, July 21,

Carter launches new campaign to aid pregnant adolescents. JUVENILE JUSTICE DIGEST 7(14):6, July 27, 1979.

Catholics' lawsuit suspends forced abortion payments. BUSINESS INSURANCE 13:1+, July 23, 1979.

Choice rights and abortion: the begetting choice right and state obstacles to choice in light of artificial womb technology. SOUTHERN CALIFORNIA LAW REVIEW 51: 877-921, July, 1978.

Civil liability arising from 'wrongful birth' following an unsuccessful sterilization operation, by G. B. Robertson. AMERICAN JOURNAL OF LAW AND MEDICINE 4(2):131-156, Summer, 1978.

Colautti v. Franklin (99 Sup Ct 675): the Court questions the use of "viability" in abortion statutes. WESTERN STATE UNIVERSITY LAW REVIEW 6:311-323, Spring, 1979.

Community determinants of U.S. legal abortion rates, by J. A. Borders, et al. FAMILY PLANNING PERSPECTIVES 11:227-233, July-August, 1979.

Congress aborts medicaid. OFF OUR BACKS 8(1):13, January, 1978.

Congress acts on other anti-abortion measures. SPOKESWO-MAN 9(4):5, October, 1978.

Congress bows to anti-choice pressure. SPOKESWOMAN 9(5):8, November, 1978.

Congress ends abortion funds deadlock. SPOKESWOMAN 8(7&8):5, January, 1978.

Constitutional Convention advances, by J. M. Clark. NATIONAL NOW 11(7):11, June, 1978.

Constitutional law—civil rights—section 1983—requirement of state action in discrimination suit against medical doctor. WISCONSIN LAW REVIEW 1978:583-605, 1978.

Constitutional law: a constitutional analysis of the new Oklahoma abortion stature. OKLAHOMA LAW REVIEW 32:138-144, Winter, 1979.

Constitutional law—denial of state medicaid funds for abortions not 'medically necessary' does not violate the equal protection clause. HOWARD LAW JOURNAL 21:937-954, 1978.

The Court, the Congress and the President: turning back the clock on the pregnant poor, by R. Lincoln, et al. FAMILY PLANNING PERSPECTIVES 9(5):207-214, September-October, 1977.

Court drives home final nail in coffin of unborn with Pennsylvania decision, by R. McMunn. OUR SUNDAY VISITOR 67:2, January 21, 1979.

Court kills law calling late abortions murder. MEDICAL WORLD NEWS 20:85-86, February 5, 1979.

Court labors over Roe v. Wade and gives birth to new standard. MERCER LAW REVIEW 30:761-768, Spring,
1979.

The Court's dissenters; abortion control law, by B. White, et
al. ORIGINS 8:506-509, January 25, 1979.

Courts: judicial immunity—courts of general jurisdiction.
WASHBURN LAW JOURNAL 18:158-165, Fall, 1978.

Decline of Down's syndrome after abortion reform in New
York state, by H. Hansen. AMERICAN JOURNAL OF
MENTAL DEFICIENCY 83:185-188, Spring, 1978.

Decoding the election game plan of the new right; Life
Amendment Political Action Committee, Inc., by L. C.
Wohl. MS MAGAZINE 8:57-59+, August, 1979.

Denial of state medicaid funds for abortions not 'medically
necessary' does not violate the equal protection clause:
Maher v. Roe, by C. K. Barber. HOWARD LAW JOUR-
NAL 21(3):937-954, 1978.

Determinants of abortion policy in the developed nations,
by M. J. Field. POLICY STUDIES JOURNAL 7:771-
781, Summer, 1979.

Developments in criminal law and penal systems: Norway
1977-78, by J. Andenaes, et al. THE CRIMINAL LAW
REVIEW pp. 447-451, July, 1979.

Did the Supreme Court impose its morality on us? by H.
Gow. LIGUORIAN 67:35-38, January, 1979.

Does the First amendment bar the Hyde amendment? symposium of "McRae v. Califano" [a class-action lawsuit
in which the plaintiffs contend that legislation prohibiting medicaid payment for most abortions violates the establishment and free exercise of religion clauses of the

First amendment] . CHRISTIANITY AND CRISIS 39:
34-43, March 5, 1979.

An ecological analysis of the impact of the Supreme Court's
1973 abortion decision, by J. M. Richards. JOURNAL
OF APPLIED SOCIAL PSYCHOLOGY 8(1):15-28,
January-March, 1978.

The economical and political consequences of generative behaviour, by W. Maier. GEBURTSHILFE UND FRAUEN-
HEIKUNDE 39(5):410-412, May, 1979.

Ecumenical war over abortion; McRae v. Califano lawsuit on
the medicaid issue. TIME 113:62-63, January 29, 1979.

FDA acts on Depo-Provera. SPOKESWOMAN 8(11):6, May,
1978.

FDA says it is concerned. SPOKESWOMAN 9(2):8, August,
1978.

Fanatical abortion fight. TIME 114:26-27, July 9, 1979.

Finally resolving abortion issue, Congress votes money for
colleges: 1979 appropriations, by A. C. Roark. CHRONI-
CLE OF HIGHER EDUCATION 17:17, October 16,
1978.

"Forced pregnancy" group holds convention. NATIONAL
NOW 11(9):12, August, 1978.

Frieman v. Ashcroft, 443 F Supp 1390. JOURNAL OF
FAMILY LAW 17:153-157, November, 1978.

HEW gets Hyde amendment: right will cause 100,000 medical abortions this year, by J. D. Lofton, Jr. CATHOLIC
DIGEST 4:48, May, 1978.

HEW makes mockery of Hyde amendment (allows loose

interpretation of rules by which medicaid would fund abortions). HUMAN EVENTS 38:5, February 11, 1978.

HEW sets rules for implementing Hyde ban. SPOKESWO-MAN 8(9):6, March, 1978.

Husband denied a say in abortion decision, by I. M. Kennedy. MODERN LAW REVIEW 42:324-331, May, 1979.

Hyde amendment battle starting all over again. SPOKES-WOMAN 8(12):6, June, 1978.

The Hyde amendment: a tradition, by M. Bourgoin. NATIONAL CATHOLIC REPORTER 15:18, July 27, 1979.

In the courts. SPOKESWOMAN 9(2):6, August, 1978.

The Infant Life (Preservation) Act after fifty years, by M. Simms. NEW HUMANIST 95:11-13, June, 1979.

Interruption of pregnancy: the predicament indication and legal points of view, by J. Römer. FORTSCHRITTE DER MEDIZIN 96(35):1774-1776, September 21, 1978.

Investigation of a wrongful death; case of R. Jimenez, by E. Frankfort, et al. MS MAGAZINE 7:66-67+, January, 1979.

John Corrie's abortion bill [Great Britain], by T. Woodcraft. LABOUR MONTHLY 61:419-423, September, 1979.

Judge dismisses anti-abortion demonstrators' claims. NATIONAL NOW 11(7):10, June, 1978.

Judges—immunities—judicial act and jurisdiction broadly defined. MARQUETTE LAW REVIEW 62:112-123, Fall, 1978.

Judicial immunity or imperial judiciary. UNIVERSITY OF MISSOURI-KANSAS CITY LAW REVIEW 47:81-94, Fall, 1978.

Judicial immunity: an unqualified sanction of tyranny from the beach. UNIVERSITY OF FLORIDA LAW REVIEW 30:810-819, Summer, 1978.

Jury: charges not proved, by P. Moore. NATIONAL CATHOLIC REPORTER 15:5, February 2, 1979.

KNXT policymakers assigned news team to create "expose" that would inhibit abortions. MEDIA REPORT TO WOMEN 7:6, November 1, 1979.

Law number 194 of 22 May 1978. Regulations for social protection of maternity and on voluntary interruption of pregnancy. Practical observations for complying with the law, by V. S. Pesce. MINERVA GINECOLOGIA 31(1-2):1-7, January-February, 1979.

Lawsuits, protests follow EPA suspension of 2,4,5-T. FOREST INDUSTRIES 106(5):80, May, 1979.

A legal and psychological study of pro and anti-abortion groups, by E. M. Silverstein. DISSERTATION ABSTRACTS INTERNATIONAL 38(12-B):6174, June, 1978.

Legal briefs; questions and answers, by E. Elliot, et al. WORKING WOMEN 4:16, March, 1979.

Legal in Spain. OFF OUR BACKS 8(2):8, February, 1978.

The legal position of the physician with reference to abortion, by W. Becker. MEDIZINISCHE KLINIK 73(37): 1292-1297, September 15, 1978.

Legally speaking: when it comes to consent, empty gestures

won't do, by W. A. Regan. RN 42(1):25-26, January, 1979.

Legislation to watch—and work for—in the 95th Congress [abortion, childcare, family planning, health, home-makers, welfare, Congressional staffing, work] , by S. Tenenbaum, et al. MS MAGAZINE 5:99-102, February, 1977.

Limiting public funds for abortions: state response to Congressional action. SUFFOLK UNIVERSITY LAW RE-VIEW 13:923-959, Summer, 1979.

MacRae case: theology and the constitution, by A. Neier. NATION 227:721+, December 30, 1978; Discussion, 228:34, January 20, 1979.

Media agendas and human rights: the Supreme Court decision on abortion, by J. C. Pollock, et al. JOURNALISM QUARTERLY 55(3):544-548+, Fall, 1978.

Medicaid abortion rules tightened. OFF OUR BACKS 8(8): 12, August, 1978.

National board zeros in on reproductive rights. NATIONAL NOW 11(1):5, January, 1978.

Necessity and the case of Dr. Morgentaler [Morgentaler v. Regina (1975) 53 D L R (3d) 161] , by L. H. Leigh. CRIMINAL LAW REVIEW 1978:151-158, March, 1978.

Necessity as a defense to a charge of criminal trespass in an abrotion clinic. UNIVERSITY OF CINCINNATI LAW REVIEW 48:501-516, 1979.

New federal abortion regulations, by M. M. Smith. NATION-AL NOW 11(5&6):5, April, 1978.

New government rules may snuff out national scandal, Indian

doctor hopes, by F. Franzonia. OUR SUNDAY VISI-
TOR 68:3, June 24, 1979.

Nun on trial for her baby's death: will Sister Maureen's
tragedy shake the church? by C. Breslin. MS MAGA-
ZINE 5:68-71, March, 1977.

On trial for abortion. SEVEN DAYS 2(14):6, September
29, 1978.

Opening debates range from abortions to estates. AMERI-
CAN BAR ASSOCIATION JOURNAL 64:1652, November, 1978.

Packwood and his pro-abortion backers (Gloria Steinem
writes fundraising letter to help Sen. Robert Packwood
battle his anti-abortion opponent forgetting that no such
opponent now exists), by J. D. Lofton, Jr. HUMAN
EVENTS 39:9+, July 28,

Parents, children, and the supreme court, by G. J. Annas.
HASTINGS CENTER REPORT 9:21-23, October,
1979.

Paton v. British Pregnancy Advisory Serv. Trustees [1978]
3 W L R 687. LAW QUARTERLY REVIEW 95:332-
335, July, 1979.

Paul and Judy Brown vow they'll change the constitution to
stamp out abortion, by C. Crawford. PEOPLE 11(3):
28, January 22, 1979.

Pitchford acquitted of criminal abortion. NATIONAL NOW
11(11):11, October, 1978.

The politics of the Burger court toward women, by L. F.
Goldstein. POLICY STUDIES JOURNAL 7:213-218,
Winter, 1978.

Position statement on abortion. AMERICAN JOURNAL OF PSYCHOLOGY 136:272, February, 1979.

Probation with a flair: a look at some out-of-the ordinary conditions, by H. J. Jaff. FEDERAL PROBATION QUARTERLY 43(1):25-35, March, 1979.

Recent developments in woman's rights: a symposium. The moral interest in abortion funding: a comment on Beal, Maher and Poelker, D. J. Horan; Roe v. Wade and Doe v. Bolton: revised in 1976 and 1977—reviewed?; revived?; revested?; reversed or revoked? by F. Susman. ST. LOUIS UNIVERSITY LAW JOURNAL 22:566-595, 1979.

Report of the Committee on Operation of the Abortion Law, 1977 [Canada]. Introduction, by J. Haliburton. ATLANTIS 4:205-210, Spring, 1979.

Reproductive freedom issues in legal services practice, by S. Law. CLEARINGHOUSE REVIEW 12:389-403, November, 1978.

Restrictions violate privacy rights. NATIONAL NOW 11(10):2, September, 1978.

Return of Mr. Hyde. SEVEN DAYS 2(11):5, July, 1978.

Right rewrites our rights, by T. Dejanikus. OFF OUR BACKS 8(5):11, May, 1978.

"Right" to an abortion, the scope of fourteenth amendment "personhood," and the Supreme Court's birth requirement, by J. D. Gorby. SOUTHERN ILLINOIS UNIVERSITY LAW JOURNAL 1979:1-36, March, 1936.

Right to life lobbyist quits over ERA. NATIONAL NOW 11(11):3, October, 1978.

Rights are not enough; prospects for a new approach to the

morality of abortion, by P. Rossi. LINACRE QUARTER-
LY 46:109-117, May, 1979.

Rights Commission may be barred from considering abortion.
SPOKESWOMAN 9(4):4, October, 1978.

Scarlet A; M. Pitchford prosecuted for self-abortion. TIME
112:22, September 11, 1978.

The Select Committee reports. . .The Select Committee on
Population, U.S. House of Representatives, by R. Lincoln. FAMILY PLANNING PERSPECTIVES 11:101-
104, March-April, 1979.

Senate passes education-department bill, by E. K. Coughlin,
et al. CHRONICLE OF HIGHER EDUCATION 17:17,
October 10, 1978.

Senate retreats from position on abortion, by H. H. Donnelly. CONGRESSIONAL QUARTERLY WEEKLY RE-
PORT 37(30):1531-1533, June 28, 1979.

Senate votes on abortion. CONGRESSIONAL QUARTER-
LY WEEKLY REPORT 37:1459, July 21, 1979.

States' right to dictate abortion procedure disputed, by D.
B. Moskowitz. MEDICAL WORLD NEWS 19:99-100,
October 16, 1978.

Stump v. Sparkman (98 Sup Ct 1099): the doctrine of judicial impunity, by I. M. Rosenberg. VIRGINIA LAW RE-
VIEW 64:833-858, October, 1978.

Supreme Court report: abortion, by R. L. Young. AMERI-
CAN BAR ASSOCIATION JOURNAL 64:1912, December, 1978.

Supreme Court upholds right of mature minor to obtain
abortion without parental consent. FAMILY PLAN-

NING PERSPECTIVES 11:252-253, July-August, 1979.

Survey of Congressional voting records. SPOKESWOMAN 9(3):3, September, 1978.

Teenage abortion goes back to court, by L. Sharf. MA-JORITY REPORT 8:1, September 30-October 13, 1978.

They hammered at abortion to unclutter debate, by C. Anthony. OUR SUNDAY VISITOR 68:6, October 28, 1979.

Throwing out baby with the legislation? by S. Kingman. HEALTH SOCIAL SERVICE JOURNAL 89:962-963, August 3, 1979.

Torts—cause of action recognized for wrongful pregnancy—measure of damages to be applied. WAYNE LAW RE-VIEW 25:961-974, March, 1979.

Torts—judicial immunity—absolute immunity reaffirmed in Stump v. Sparkman (98 Sup Ct 1099). KANSAS LAW REVIEW 27:518-528, Spring, 1979.

Torts—judicial immunity—state court judge has absolute immunity in § 1983 action. WASHINGTON UNIVERSITY LAW QUARTERLY 1979:288-293, Winter, 1973.

Torts—judicial immunity: a sword for the malicious or a shield for the conscientious? UNIVERSITY OF BALTI-MORE LAW REVIEW 8:141-163, Fall, 1978.

Tragedy that did not have to happen, M. E. Pitchford's abortion trial, by E. P. Frank. GOOD HOUSEKEEPING 188:78+, June, 1979.

True confession of one one-issue voter, by R. Rees, 3d, et al. NATIONAL REVIEW 31:669-672+, May 25, 1979; Discussion, 31:808-809, June 22, 1979.

2000 protest against Califano, by G. Blair. VILLAGE VOICE 22:22, November 21, 1977.

Update: abortion fight threatens pregnant workers coalition. SPOKESWOMAN 8(11):3, May, 1978.

Update: Hyde battle. SPOKESWOMAN 9(1):7, July, 1978.

'Viability' revisits the Court in Colautti v. Franklin, by D. V. Horan. HOSPITAL PROGRESS 60(2):18-21+, February, 1979.

Violence erupts against pro-choice facilities. NATIONAL NOW 11:5&6):5, April, 1978.

War of the roses: real abortion fight is not in the legislature or the courts—it's in our hospitals, by R. K. Rein. NEW JERSEY MONTHLY 3:45+, July, 1979.

Washington knows? by P. Ramsey. THEOLOGY TODAY 35:428-437, January, 1979.

Weekend poll: abortion. WEEKEND MAGAZINE 29:3, June 23, 1979.

What the antiabortion folks don't want you to know. MS MAGAZINE 7:91-94, May, 1979.

What's new in the law: abortions. . .denying medicaid funds, by A. Ashman. AMERICAN BAR ASSOCIATION JOURNAL 65:116-117, January, 1979.

White House adviser Midge Costanza. SPOKESWOMAN 8(11):4, May, 1978.

Why abortion sit-ins? by D. Gaetano. COLUMBIA 59:18-23, May, 1979.

Why we need a human life amendment, by Sen. J. Helms. CATHOLIC DIGEST 4:24+, June, 1978.

Wink from the bench: the federal courts and abortion, by B. J. Uddo. TULANE LAW REVIEW 53:998-464, February, 1979.

Worst law ever: ten years of legalized abortion, by A. De Valk. CHELSEA JOURNAL 5:111-119, May-June, 1979.

Zharaz v. Quern (596 F 2d 196): abortion and medicaid: the public funding dilemma. JOHN MARSHALL JOURNAL OF PRACTICE AND PROCEDURE 12:609-636, Spring, 1979.

CANADA
Abortion in New South Wales—legal or illegal? by B. Lucas. AUSTRALIAN LAW JOURNAL 52:327-332, June, 1978.

Canada's abortion law: an obstacle to safer management of Canadian women, by C. A. D. Ringrose. LEGAL MEDICAL QUARTERLY 2(2):97-99, 1978.

FRANCE
No going back. THE ECONOMIST 273:44+, October 13, 1979.

GERMANY
Abortion law reform in the German Federal Republic, by K. C. Horton. INTERNATIONAL AND COMPARATIVE LAW QUARTERLY 28:288-296, April, 1979.

GREAT BRITAIN
The Abortion (Amendment) Bill. NEW HUMANIST 95:61-72, August, 1979.

GREAT BRITAIN
Alive issue. THE ECONOMIST 271:23, May 5, 1979.

ISRAEL
Abortion and judicial review of statutes, by E. Livneh.
ISRAEL LAW REVIEW 12(1):15-31, 1977.

ITALY
Abortion law in Italy, by F. Havránek. CESKOSLOVEN-
SKA GYNEKOLOGIE 44(3):223, April, 1979.

Despite Church opposition, Italy adopts new law providing free abortion for a variety of indications [news].
FAMILY PLANNING PERSPECTIVES 10(4):241-
243, July-August, 1978.

Italy: the best abortion law in the world, by J. Spivak.
WALL STREET JOURNAL 193:22, February 28,
1979.

Italy's abortion law [letter], by G. Neri, et al. LANCET
(8095):895-896, October 21, 1978.

Violable rights of Italian women, by J. Walston. NEW
STATESMAN 96:427, October 6, 1978.

NEW ZEALAND
Abortion and the crimes amendment act 1977, by D.
Kember. NEW ZEALAND LAW JOURNAL 1978:
109-117, April 4, 1978.

Initial consequences of the 1977 New Zealand abortion
law, by W. A. Facer, et al. NEW ZEALAND NURS-
ING FORUM 6(2):9-12, December, 1978+.

PORTUGAL
Unliberated. THE ECONOMIST 272:53, July 28, 1979.

RUMANIA
Romania's 1966 anti-abortion decree: the demographic experience of the first decade, by B. Berelson. POPULATION STUDIES 33:209-222, July, 1979.

UNITED STATES
Abortion and government policy [argues that the exclusion of abortion services under programs of medical and social aid to the poor is discriminatory], by D. Callahan. FAMILY PLANNING PERSPECTIVES 11:275-279, September-October, 1979.

Abortion and the law. OUR SUNDAY VISITOR 67:9-11, January 21, 1979.

Abortion—the Illinois abortion act of 1975 was declared unconstitutional in part for the reason that some sections were void and unenforceable because they conflicted with rights guaranteed by the due process clause. JOURNAL OF FAMILY LAW 17:797-805, August, 1979.

CA 7 strikes down provisions of two Illinois abortion statutes. THE CRIMINAL LAW REPORTER: COURT DECISIONS AND PROCEEDINGS 25(13): 2284-2285, June 27, 1979.

Depo: the debate continues, by D. Maine. FAMILY PLANNING PERSPECTIVES 10:342-345, November-December, 1978.

Illinois abortion parental consent act of 1977: a far cry from permissible consultation. JOHN MARSHALL JOURNAL OF PRACTICE AND PROCEDURE 12:135-164, Fall, 1978.

Kentucky law makes abortion more painful. NEW TIMES 11(7):15, October 2, 1978.

UNITED STATES
Kentucky woman indicted for criminal abortion, manslaughter. NATIONAL NOW 11(9):12, August, 1978.

Louisiana adopts strict abortion law. NATIONAL NOW 11(10):9, September, 1978.

Louisiana Legislature has just enacted. SPOKESWOMAN 9(3):3, September, 1978.

Massachusetts NOW commemorates right to choose decision, by M. A. Hart. NATIONAL NOW 11(3):13, March, 1978.

New Jersey update: Trojan war (Young Drug Products Company), by R. K. Rein. NEW JERSEY MONTHLY 3:40+, August, 1979.

New murder trial begins for California abortionist Waddill, by L. Welborn. OUR SUNDAY VISITOR 67:1, March 4, 1979.

Oklahoma legislators. SPOKESWOMAN 8(10):8, April, 1978.

Opinion of the United States Supreme Court: abortion. CRIMINAL LAW REPORTER: TEXT SECTION 24(14):3043-3051, January 10, 1979.

Oregonians to battle anti-choice initiative. NATIONAL NOW 11(10):9, September, 1978.

Pennsylvania abortion law ruled unconstitutional. IACP LAW ENFORCEMENT LEGAL REVIEW 83:3, May, 1979.

Right to procreate: the dilemma of overpopulation and the United States judiciary, by J. Bolner, et al.

UNITED STATES
LOYOLA LAW REVIEW 25:235-262, Spring, 1979.

Supreme Court Report: Pennsylvania's abortion law is unconstitutionally 'ambiguous', by R. L. Young. AMERICAN BAR ASSOCIATION JOURNAL 65: 448+, Marcy, 1979.

The Supreme Court's abortion decisions and public opinion in the United States, by J. Blake. POPULATION AND DEVELOPMENT REVIEW pp. 45-62, 1977.

U.S. abortion battle. STOREFRONT 6(3):1, August, 1978.

U.S. report: violence marks intensity of abortion debate, by B. Scott. PERCEPTION 3:43, September-October, 1979.

U.S. Supreme Court has agreed. SPOKESWOMAN 8(10):5, April, 1978.

Vermont chapters march for abortion rights. NATIONAL NOW 11(2):11, February, 1978.

Waddill strangled infant, says witness in murder trial of California abortionist, by K. Granville. OUR SUNDAY VISITOR 67:2, April 1, 1979.

ABORTION: MISSED
Administration of 15-(S)-15-methyl prostaglandins F2 alpha in intrauterine fetal death, missed abortion and bydatidiform mole, by P. Husslein, et al. WIENER KLINISCHE WOCHENSCHRIFT 91(13):458-460, June 22, 1979.

Influence on haemostasis exercised by prostaglandin F2alpha in missed abortion, by R. C. Briel, et al. BEGURTSHILFE UND FRAUENHEILKUNDE 38(10):862-867, October, 1978.

Pathomorphological and histochemical characteristics of the
fetus and placenta in missed abortion and labor, by M. M.
Kliherman. PEDIATRIIA AKUSHERSTVO I GINE-
KOLOGIIA (6):51-54, November-December, 1978.

ABORTION: MORTALITY AND MORTALITY STATISTICS
Abortion and maternal health: an American perspective, by
L. Keith, et al. INTERNATIONAL SURGERY 63(5):
31-35, July-August, 1978.

Abortion and mortality study. Twenty-year study in New
York State exclusive of New York City, by R. A. McLean,
et al. NEW YORK STATE JOURNAL OF MEDICINE
79(1):49-52, January, 1979.

Assessment of surveillance and vital statistics data for moni-
toring abortion mortality, United States, 1972-1975, by
W. Cates, Jr., et al. AMERICAN JOURNAL OF EPI-
DEMOLOGY 108(3):200-206, September, 1978.

Fertility and child mortality over the life cycle: aggregate
and individual evidence, by T. P. Schultz. AMERICAN
ECONOMIC REVIEW 68:208-215, May, 1978.

Fertility desires and child mortality experience among
Guatemalan women, by A. R. Pebley, et al. STUDIES
IN FAMILY PLANNING 10(4):129-136, April, 1979.

Maternal mortality study: abortion and mortality study:
twenty-year study in New York State exclusive of New
York City, by R. McLean, et al. NEW YORK STATE
JOURNAL OF MEDICINE 79:49-52, January, 1979.

—: teenage pregnancy and maternal mortality in New York
State, by R. McLean, et al. NEW YORK STATE JOUR-
NAL OF MEDICINE 79:226-230, February, 1979.

Mortality from abortion: the NHS record [letter], by C.
Brewer, et al. BRITISH MEDICAL JOURNAL 2(6136):

562, August 19, 1978.

Reproductive mortality [from contraceptives as well as pregnancy or abortion] , by V. Beral. BRITISH MEDICAL JOURNAL 6191:632-634, September 15, 1978.

ABORTION: OUTPATIENT TREATMENT
Ambigulatory legal abortion, by J. Philip. UGESKRIFT FOR LAEGER 140(44):2727, October 30, 1978.

Assessment of the promotion component in the postpartum/postabortion program, by J. M. Arredondo, et al. SPM 20(4):401-412, July-August, 1978.

An evaluation of cytogenetic analysis as a primary tool in the assessment of recurrent pregnancy wastage, by M. T. Mennuti, et al. OBSTETRICS AND GYNECOLOGY 52(3):308-313, September, 1978.

Proximity as a factor in the selection of health care providers: emergency room visits compared to obstetric admissions and abortions, by K. J. Roghmann, et al. SOCIAL SCIENCE AND MEDICINE 13D91):61-69, March, 1979.

ABORTION: REPEATED
Chromosome analysis in cases with repeated spontaneous abortions, by R. L Neu, et al. OBSTETRICS AND GYNECOLOGY 53(3):373-375, March, 1979.

Early repeated abortions and karyotypes. A cytogenic study of 80 consecutive couples, by G. Pescia, et al. JOURNAL DE GYNECOLOGIE, OBSTETRIQUE ET BIOLOGIE DE LA REPRODUCTION 8(1):35-38, January-February, 1979.

Frequency of endocrine disorders in repeated spontaneous abortion, by A. M. D. Serban. REVUE ROUMAINE DE MEDICINE. SERIE ENDOCRINOLOGIE 16(1):55-60,

1978.

Listeria monocytogenes' isolation from a urine specimen of a subject with repeated abortions, by V. M. Nicolosi, et al. ANNALI SCLAVO 20(5):692-695, September-October, 1978.

The mathematics of repeat abortion: explaining the increase, by C. Tietze, et al. STUDIES IN FAMILY PLANNING 9(12):294-299, December, 1978.

Repeated abortions increase risk of miscarriage, premature births and low-birth-weight babies. FAMILY PLANNING PERSPECTIVES 11(1):39-40, January-February, 1979.

Repeated abortions, sterility and systemic dysimmunopathy, by B. Plouvier, et al. ANNALES DE MEDECINE INTERNE 130(1):39-44, 1979.

Systemic lupus erythematosus, repeated abortions and thrombocytopenia, by M. H. Pritchard, et al. ANNALS OF THE RHEUMATIC DISEASES 37(5):476-478, 1978.

Women who obtain repeat abortions: a study based on record linkage [Hawaii, 1970-76], by P. G. Steinhoff, et al. FAMILY PLANNING PERSPECTIVES 11:30-31+, January-February, 1979.

ABORTION: SEPTIC
Hemodialysis in the treatment of acute renal insufficiency in septic abortions, by G. I. Salashnyi, et al. KLINICHESKAYA MEDITZINA 56(8):83-86, August, 1978.

Septic abortion and acute renal failure in a patient with an intrauterine contraceptive device, by C. M. Wiles, et al. INTERNATIONAL JOURNAL OF GYNAECOLOGY AND OBSTETRICS 15(5):464-465, 1978.

Toxico-septic abortion—a major medical emergency, by M. Enachescu. VIATA MEDICALA 27(4):83-84, April, 1979.

ABORTION: SPONTANEOUS

Chromosome analysis in cases with repeated spontaneous abortions, by R. L. Neu, et al. OBSTETRICS AND GYNECOLOGY 53(3):373-375, 1979.

Effect of treatment of habitual and spontaneous abortion using Gestanon on birth weight, by S. Andjelković. SRPSKI ARHIV ZA CELOKUPNO LEKARSTVO 106(1):53-55, 1978.

Febrile spontaneous abortion and the IUD, by R. J. Kim-Farley, et al. CONTRACEPTION 18(6):561-570, December, 1978.

Maternal origin of a trisomy 7 in a spontaneous abortus, by J. del Mazo, et al. OBSTETRICS AND GYNECOLOGY 53(suppl 3):18S-20S, March, 1979.

Measurement of plasma human chorionic gondatropin (hCG) and beta-hCG activities in the late luteal phase: evidence of the occurrence of spontaneous menstrual abortions in infertile women, by M. Chartier, et al. FERTILITY AND STERILITY 31(2):134-137, February, 1979.

Mosaic autosomal trisomy in cultures from spontaneous abortions, by D. Warburton, et al. AMERICAN JOURNAL OF HUMAN GENETICS 30(6):609-617, November, 1978.

Natural prevention of genetic defects; spontaneous abortion or miscarriage in Down's syndrome. SCIENCE NEWS 114:379, November 25, 1978.

Occupational and renvironmental risks in and around a

smelter in northern Sweden. V. Spontaneous abortion among female employees and decreased birth weight in their offspring, by S. Nordström, et al. HEREDITAS 90(2):291-296, 1979.

Origin of trisomies in human spontaneous abortions, by T. Hassold, et al. HUMAN GENETICS 46(3):285-294, February 15, 1979.

Pathomorphological studies of spontaneous and experimental abortions in cows and guinea pigs, by S. Savova-Burdarova, et al. VETERINARNO-MEDITSINSKI NAUKI 15(5):59-68, 1978.

Q-banding of chromosomes in human spontaneous abortions, by D. H. Carr, et al. CANADIAN JOURNAL OF GENETICS AND CYTOLOGY 20(3):415-425, September, 1978.

Relationship between spontaneous abortion and presence of antibody to toxoplasma gondii, by A. M. Johnson, et al. MEDICAL JOURNAL OF AUSTRALIA 1(12):579-580, June 16, 1979.

Role of listeriosis in the etiology of spontaneous and habitual abortions, by T. Despodova, et al. AKUSHERSTVO I GINEKOLOGIIA 17(6):396-402, 1978.

Sequential analysis of spontaneous abortion. II. Collaborative study data show that gravidity determines a very substantial rise in risk, by A. F. Naylor, et al. FERTILITY AND STERILITY 31(3):282-286, March, 1979.

Spontaneous abortion after midtrimester amniocentesis, by I. J. Park, et al. OBSTETRICS AND GYNECOLOGY 53(2):190-194, February, 1979.

Spontaneous abortions in sibship of children with congenital malformation or malignant disease, by A. Spira, et al.

EUROPEAN JOURNAL OF OBSTETRICS, GYNE-
COLOGY AND REPRODUCTIVE BIOLOGY 9(2):89-
96, 1979.

ABORTION: SPONTANEOUS COMPLICATIONS
Cigarette smoking during pregnancy and the occurrence of
spontaneous abortion and congenital abnormality, by D.
U. Himmelberger, et al. AMERICAN JOURNAL OF
EPIDEMIOLOGY 108(6):470-479, December, 1978.

Comparison of central nervous system malformations in
spontaneous absortions in Northern Ireland and south-
east England, by J. C. MacHenry, et al. BRITISH MEDI-
CAL JOURNAL 1(6175):1395-1397, May 26, 1979.

Cytogenetic and histologic analyses of spontaneous abortions, by M. Geisler, et al. HUMAN GENETICS 45(3):
239-251, December 29, 1978.

Cytogenetic investigation in 413 couples with spontaneous
abortions, by C. Turleau, et al. EUROPEAN JOURNAL
OF OBSTETRICS, GYNECOLOGY AND REPRODUC-
TIVE BIOLOGY 9(2):65-74, 1979.

5-hydroxytryptamine (seroterin), copper and ceruloplasmin
plasma concentrations in spontaneous abortion, by B. A.
Bassiouni, et al. EUROPEAN JOURNAL OF OBSTE-
TRICS, GYNECOLOGY AND REPRODUCTIVE BI-
OLOGY 9(2):81-88, 1979.

Frequency of endocrine disorders in repeated spontaneous
abortion, by A. M. D. Serban. REVUE ROUMAINE DE
MEDECINE. SERIE ENDOCRINOLOGIE 16(1):55-60,
1978.

Gestation, birth-weight, and spontaneous abortion in pregnancy after induced abortion, by WHO Task Force on
Sequelae of Abortion. LANCET 1(8108):142-145,
1979.

292

The importance of cytogenetic investigation of the couples
with multiple sponteanous abortions and malformed offsprings, by D. Duca, et al. ENDOCRINOLOGIE 17(1):
17-22, January-March, 1979.

Incidence of spontaneous abortion with and without previous
use of contraceptive agents based on morphological studies, by G. Dallenbach-Hellweg. GYNAEKOLOGISHE
RUNDSCHAU 18(3-4):213-219, 1978.

Smoking: a risk factor for spontaneous abortion, by J. Kline,
et al. NEW ENGLAND JOURNAL OF MEDICINE 297:
793-796, October 13, 1977.

ABORTION: STATISTICS
New abortion statistics published. SPOKESWOMAN 9(5):9,
November, 1978.

Report on a computer based evaluation of 1,800 cases of
abortion, by P. Richter, et al. ZENTRALBLATT FUR
GYNAEKOLOGIE 101(4):254-260, 1979.

The significance of social factors in choice of legal abortion.
A social-medical study of 531 women applying for abortion and 285 pregnant control patients, by M. Wohlert,
et al. UGESKRIFT FOR LAEGER 140(30):1835-1841,
July 24, 1978.

Thirty abortions for 100 births, by G. Duchene. LA DOCU-
MENTATION CATHOLIQUE 76:91-92, January 21,
1979.

Towards an understanding of the American abortion rate, by
C. Francome, et al. JOURNAL OF BIOSOCIAL SCI-
ENCE 11:303-314, July, 1979.

ABORTION: TECHNIQUES
Acceptability of a nonsurgical method to terminate very
early pregnancy in comparison to vacuum aspiration, by

A. S. Rosén, et al. CONTRACEPTION 19(2):107-117, February, 1979.

Alpha-fetoprotein concentration in maternal serum and abortion via VA and PGF2alpha, by H. A. Sande, et al. INTERNATIONAL JOURNAL OF GYNAECOLOGY AND OBSTETRICS 15(5):419-422, 1978.

A comparative study of the tubal ring applied via minilaparotomy and laparoscopy in postabortion cases, by R. V. Bhatt, et al. INTERNATIONAL JOURNAL OF GYNAECOLOGY AND OBSTETRICS 16(2):162-166, 1978-1979.

Comparison of extra-amniotic instillation of rivanol and PGF2alpha either separately or in combination followed by oxytocin for second trimester abortion, by A. Olund, et al. ACTA OBSTETRICIA ET GYNECOLOGICA SCANDINAVICA 57(4):333-336, 1978.

Cruel and unusual tactics, by G. Lichtenstein. THE VILLAGE VOICE 24(17):1+, April 30, 1979.

The development of instruments to measure attitudes toward abortion and knowledge of abortion, by S. Snegroff. JOURNAL OF SCHOOL HEALTH 46(5):273-277, May, 1976.

'The earlier the safer' applies to all abortions [interview], by W. Cates, Jr. FAMILY PLANNING PERSPECTIVES 10(4):243, July-August, 1978.

Evaluation of a balloon dilator before second-trimester abortion by vacuum curettage, by P. G. Stubblefield, et al. AMERICAN JOURNAL OF OBSTETRICS AND GYNECOLOGY 135(2):199-201, September 15, 1979.

First trimester abortion by vacuum aspiration: interphysician variability, by E. R. Miller, et al. INTERNATIONAL

JOURNAL OF GYNAECOLOGY AND OBSTETRICS 16(2):144-149, 1978-1979.

The impact of midtrimester abortion techniques on patients and staff, by N. B. Kaltreider, et al. AMERICAN JOURNAL OF OBSTETRICS AND GYNECOLOGY 135(2): 235-238, September 15, 1979.

Legal abortion of advanced pregnancy—methods, by M. Bujalić. SRPSKI ARHIV ZA CELOKUPNO LEKARSTVO 105(9):737-741, September, 1977.

Menstrual regulation as a method for early termination of pregnancy, by M. Mandelin, et al. ACTA OBSTETRICIA ET GYNECOLOGICA SCANDINAVICA 58(2):169-173, 1979.

Midtrimester abortion procedures [letter], by W. Cates, Jr., et al. AMERICAN JOURNAL OF OBSTETRICS AND GYNECOLOGY 133(8):934-937, April 15, 1979.

A pill for abortion. THE ECONOMIST 272:53, August 25, 1979.

Pregnancy complications following legally induced abortion with special reference to abortion technique, by E. Obel. ACTA OBSTETRICIA ET GYNECOLOGIA SCANDINAVICA 58(2):147-152, 1979.

Preoperative cervical dilatation with 15(S)15-methyl PGF2-alpha methyl ester pessaries, by T. K. Chatterjee, et al. INTERNATIONAL JOURNAL OF GYNAECOLOGY AND OBSTETRICS 15(5):423-427, 1978.

Priming with intracervically administered prostaglandin F2 alpha before abortion, by H. Gstöttner, et al. ZENTRALBLATT FUR GYNAEKOLOGIE 101(6):404-408, 1979.

ABORTION: TECHNIQUES

Suction termination of pregnancy under local anesthesia
[letter], by J. Buiilebaud. BRITISH MEDICAL JOUR-
NAL 1(6171):1148, April 28, 1979.

ABORTION: THERAPEUTIC
Contraceptive practice before and after therapeutic abortion.
II. Use-effectiveness of oral contraceptives and intra-
uterine devices, by P. Fylling, et al. FERTILITY AND
STERILITY 32(1):24-27, July, 1979.

Diagnostic/therapeutic preabortion interview, by P. D. Boekelheide. JOURNAL OF AMERICAN COLLEGE
HEALTH ASSOCIATION 27:157-160, December, 1978.

An ecological analysis of urban therapeutic abortion rates, by
E. M. Nett. SOCIAL BIOLOGY 25(3):235-242, Fall,
1978.

Gestational age at termination of pregnancy on medical indications [letter], by P. E. Polani, et al. LANCET
2(8139):410, August 25, 1979.

Medical consideration on timing of laparoscopic sterilization
in first trimester therapeutic abortion patients, by H. M.
Kwak, et al. YONSEI MEDICAL JOURNAL 19(2):105-
110, 1978.

Psychiatric aspects of therapeutic abortion, by G. Van Niekerk. SOUTH AFRICAN MEDICAL JOURNAL 55(11):
421-424, March 17, 1979.

Sequential changes in the human renin-angiotensin system
following therapeutic termination of pregnancy, by F. B.
Pipkin, et al. BRITISH JOURNAL OF OBSTETRICS
AND GYNAECOLOGY 86(4):285-289, April, 1979.

A study of placental pathology in mid trimester therapeutic
abortions induced by hypertonic saline and prostaglandin, by M. Khardekar, et al. INDIAN JOURNAL OF PA-

296

THOLOGY AND MICROBIOLOGY 21(2):141-145, April, 1978.

Therapeutic abortion and psychiatric disturbance in Canadian women, by E. R. Greenglass. CANADIAN PSYCHIATRIC ASSOCIATION JOURNAL 21(7):453-460, November, 1976.

Therapeutic abortion on psychiatric grounds. Part I. A local study, by S. J. Drower, et al. SOUTH AFRICAN MEDICAL JOURNAL 54(15):604-608, October 7, 1978.

—. Part II. The continuing debate, by S. J. Drower, et al. SOUTH AFRICAN MEDICAL JOURNAL 54(16):643-647, October 14, 1978.

'Therapeutic abortion' payments restored. SEVEN DAYS 2(1):4, January, 1978.

Treatment of imminent abortion, by S. Saarikoski. DUODECIM 95(4):198-203, 1979.

Ultrasonic diagnosis of retroperitoneal hematoma following therapeutic abortion, by W. C. Buss. MEDICAL ULTRASOUND 3(1):33-34, 1979.

ABORTION: THERAPEUTIC: COMPLICATIONS
Changes in peripheral hormone levels after therapeutic abortion, by D. M. Saunders, et al. EUROPEAN JOURNAL OF OBSTETRICS, GYNECOLOGY AND REPRODUCTIVE BIOLOGY 8(1):1-4, 1978.

Occurrence of gonococcal perihepatitis after therapeutic abortion [letter], by D. Portnoy, et al. CANADIAN MEDICAL ASSOCIATION JOURNAL 120(4):408, February 17, 1979.

Therapeutic and prophylactic care in abortion in women with genital infantilism, by N. K. Moskvitina, et al. AKU-

SHERSTVO I GINEKOLOGIIA (4):12-14, April, 1979.

ABORTION: THERAPEUTIC: OUTPATIENT TREATMENT
Desire for therapeutic abortion in the dependents of foreign
workers. Outpatients psychiatric evaluation, by H. von
der Mühlen. GEBURTSHILFE UND FRAUENHEIL-
KUNDE 38(10):858-861, October, 1978.

ABORTION: THREATENED
Alpha-fetoprotein: a marker for threatened abortion, by H.
A. Sande, et al. INTERNATIONAL JOURNAL OF
GYNAECOLOGY AND OBSTETRICS 16(4):293-295,
1978-1979.

Management in threatened abortions, by P. Magnin. JOUR-
NAL DE GYNECOLOGIE, OBSTETRIQUE ET BI-
OLOGIE DE LA REPRODUCTION 7(3 pt 2):663-664,
April, 1978.

Management of threatened abortion in the first trimester,
by P. Magnin. JOURNAL DE GYNECOLOGIE, OBSTE-
TRIQUE ET BIOLOGIE DE LA REPRODUCTION
7(3 pt 2):683-685, April, 1978.

Outcome of pregnancy for the fetus and the condition of
newborn infant after threatened abortion, by N. G.
Kosheleva. VOPROSY OKHRANY MATERINSTVA I
DETSTVA 23(12):51-53, December, 1978.

Pregnancy and labor complications in women who have had a
threatened abortion and who have preserved the pregnancy till labor, by N. G. Kosheleva. AKUSHERSTVO I
GINEKOLOGIIA (4):17-19, April, 1979.

Prognostic value of ultrasonic study in threatened abortion,
by M. Mantoni, et al. UGESKRIFT FOR LAEGER
140(46):2851-2855, November 13, 1978.

The role of oestrogen test in threatened abortion, by R. Rizvi,

et al. INDIAN JOURNAL OF PATHOLOGY AND
MICROBIOLOGY 21(2):165-170, April, 1978.

State of health and the subsequent development of infants
born of women who have had a threatened abortion, by
N. G. Kosheleva. AKUSHERSTVO I GINEKOLOGIIA
(4):3-5, April, 1979.

Therapeutics basis of threatened abortions, by J. L. Viala.
JOURNAL DE GYNECOLOGIE, OBSTETRIQUE ET
BIOLOGIE DE LA REPRODUCTION 7(3 pt 2):678-
682, April, 1978.

Threatened abortion: patient characteristics, treatment results and consequences for the child, by U. H. Eggimann,
et al. SCHWEIZERISCHE MEDIZINISCHE WOCHEN-
SCHRIFT 109(8):288-292, February 24, 1979.

The use of ultrasound in threatened abortion, by G. B. Duff.
NEW ZEALAND MEDICAL JOURNAL 88(624):398-
400, November 22, 1978.

Value of the cornified cells in urocytograms of threatening
abortion, by D. J. Chiarasini, et al. ARCHIVES D'AN-
ATOMIE ET DE CYTOLOGIE PATHOLOGIQUE
26(2):102-105, 1978.

The value of determinations of human chorionic gonatrophin, human placental lactogen, progesterone and oestriol
in women with threatened abortion, by I. Gerhard, et al.
BEGURTSHILFE UND FRAUENHEILKUNDE 38(10):
785-799, October, 1978.

The value of echography in cases of threatened abortion in
the first trimester of pregnancy, by B. Leroy. JOUR-
NAL OF GYNECOLOGIE, OBSTETRIQUE ET DE
BIOLOGIE DE LA REPRODUCTION 7(3 pt 2):665-
672, April, 1978.

ABORTION AND ACUPUNCTURE
Acupuncture anesthesia in obstetrical surgery and nursing during delivery, by M. Isozaki, et al. JOSANPU ZASSHI 33(2):94-97, February, 1979.

ABORTION AND ADOLESCENTS
Adolescent mourning reactions to infant and fetal loss, by N. H. Horowitz. SOCIAL CASEWORK 59(9):551-559, 1978.

ABORTION AND COLLEGE STUDENTS
Abortion attitudes among university students in India, by P. D. Bardis. INTERNATIONAL JOURNAL OF SOCI-OLOGY OF THE FAMILY 6(2):163-178, 1976.

Becoming close: intimate relations among college students, by G. Margolis. JOURNAL OF THE AMERICAN COLLEGE HEALTH ASSOCIATION 27(3):153-156, December, 1978.

Finally resolving abortion issue, Congress votes money for colleges: 1979 appropriations, by A. C. Roark. CHRONICLE OF HIGHER EDUCATION 17:17, October 16, 1978.

ABORTION AND HORMONES
Administration of 15-(S)-15-methyl prostaglandins F2 alpha in intrauterine fetal death, missed abortion and hydatidi-form mole, by P. Husslein, et al. WIENER KLINISCHE WOCHENSCHRIFT 91(13):458-460, June 22,1979.

The antifertility action of alpha-chlorohydrin: enzyme inhibition by alpha-chlorohydrin phosphate, by P. M. Mashford, et al. EXPERIENTIA 34(10):1267-1268, October 15, 1978.

Application of prostaglandins in obstetrics and gynecology, by F. J. Brunnberg. ACTA BIOLOGICA ET MEDICA GERMANICA 37(5-6):917-921, 1976.

Arachidonic acid in amniotic fluid after extra-amniotic instil-lation of rivanol for midtrimester abortion, by A. Olund, et al. PROSTAGLANDINS 16(6):989-994, 1978.

The augmentary effect of intramuscular prostaglandins on ethacridine lactate, by V. B. Raote, et al. JOURNAL OF POST-
GRADUATE MEDICINE 25(1):30-32, January, 1979.

Birth control news: once-a-month pill; prostaglandin pill, by
M. Jeffery. HARPER'S BAZAAR 111:24+, August, 1978.

Clinical uses of prostaglandins in human reproduction, by P.
Bajaja. NURSING JOURNAL OF INDIA 69(9):197-
199, September, 1978.

The comparative efficacy and safety of intraamniotic prostaglandins F2 alpha and hypertonic saline for second-trimester abortion. A review and critique, by D. A. Grimes,
et al. JOURNAL OF REPRODUCTIVE MEDICINE
22(5):248-254, May, 1979.

Comparative studies on the termination of intact and disturbed pregnancies by intramuscular application of
15(s)-15-methyl-prostaglandin F2alpha, by H. Schridde,
et al. GEBURTSHILFE UND FRAUENHEILKUNDE
38(10):845-848, October, 1978.

A direct evidence for the involvement of prostaglandin F2a in
the first step of estrone-induced blastocyst implantation
in the spayed rat, by M. Oettel, et al. STEROIDS 3(1):
1-8, 1979.

Effect of intra-scrotal implants of prostaglandin E2 or F2a on
blood steroids in the adult male rats, by S. K. Sakena, et
al. INTERNATIONAL JOURNAL OF ANDROLOGY
1(2):180-187, 1978.

The effects and side-effects of the intra-cervical application
of prostaglandin F-2 alpha during early pregnancy, by S.
Sievers, et al. GEBURTSHILFE UND FRAUENHEIL-
KUNDE 38(10):800-804, October, 1978.

Efficacy and acceptability of intravenously administered sulprostone, a tissue-selective prostaglandin-E2 derivative,
for induction of first-trimester abortion, by B. Schuessler,
et al. CONTRACEPTION 19(1):29-38, January, 1979.

Extraamniotic induction of abortion with a new prostaglandin E-2 derivative, by U. Gethmann, et al. FORT-
SCHRITTE DER MEDIZIN 96(35):1771-1773, September 21, 1978.

Extra-amniotic prostaglandin for mid-trimester abortion.
MEDICAL WORLD NEWS 19:32+, December 11, 1978.

(15S)-15 methyl prostaglandin F2 alpha levels in amniotic
fluid and blood in second trimester abortions, by L.
Weinstein, et al. SOUTHERN MEDICAL JOURNAL
72(9):1159-1160, September, 1979.

Functional luteolysis in the pseudopregnant rat: effects of
prostaglandin F2a and 16-aryloxy prostaglandin F2a in
vitro, by A. K. Hall, et al. JOURNAL OF ENDOCRIN-
OLOGY 81(1):157-166, 1979.

Hormonal considerations in early normal pregnancy and
blighted ovum syndrome, by M. O. Schweditsch, et al.
FERTILITY AND STERILITY 31(3):252-257, March,
1979.

The hormonal levels in case of abortion during the first
trimester, by M. Chartier. JOURNAL DE GYNECOLO-
GIE, OBSTETRIQUE ET BIOLOGIE DE LA REPRO-
DUCTION 7(3 pt 2):673-676, April, 1978.

The hormonal treatment of paraphiliacs with depo-provera,
by M. K. Spodak, et al. CRIMINAL JUSTICE AND
BEHAVIOR 5(4):304-314, December, 1978.

Hormone level changes caused by abortion induced with
prostaglandin F2 alpha in pregnancy interruption during

the 1st trimester, by J. Sárdi, et al. ORVOSI HETILAP 120(24):1429-1431, June 17, 1979.

Immunological control of fertility: measurement of affinity of antibodies to human chorionic gonadotrophin, by Y. M. Thanavala, et al. CLINICAL AND EXPERIMENTAL IMMUNOLOGY 33(3):403-409, September, 1978.

Induction of abortion with prostaglandins, by F. Jerve. TIDSSKRIFT VOOR LAEGEFORENUNG 98(29) 1433-1434, October 20, 1978.

Influence on haemostasis exercised by prostaglandin F2alpha in missed abortion, by R. C. Briel, et al. GEBURT-SHILFE UND FRAUENHEILKUNDE 38(10):862-867, October, 1978.

Interruption of early first trimester pregnancy by single vaginal administration of 15-methyl-pgf2 alpha-methyl ester, by K. Gréen, et al. CONTRACEPTION 18(6): 551-560, December, 1978.

Interruption of the second and third trimester of a normal and missed pregnancy by extraamnial prostaglandin E administration combined with oxytocin infusion, by F. Havránek, et al. CESKOSLOVENSKA GYNEKOLOGIE 44(3):179-182, April, 1979.

Intra-amniotic prostaglandin F2alpha termination of mid-trimester abortion, by J. M. Luwuliza-Kirunda. EAST AFRICAN MEDICAL JOURNAL 56(1):10-14, January, 1979.

Intramuscular 16-phenoxy PGE2 ester for pregnancy termi-nation, by M. Toppozada, et al. PROSTAGLANDINS 17(3):461-467, March, 1979.

Intranasal gonadotropin-releasing hormone agonist as a con-traceptive agent, by C. Bergquist, et al. LANCET

2(8136):215-217, August 4, 1979.

Investigation of prostaglandins for abortion, by N. H. Lauersen. ACTA OBSTETRICA ET GYNECOLOGIA SCANDINAVICA (81):1-36, 1979.

Investigations of hormones during early abortion induced by prostaglandin F2alpha and 15(S)-methyl-PGF2alpha, by Seifert, et al. ACTA BIOLOGICA ET MEDICA GERMANICA 37(5-6):955-957, 1976.

Laminaria use in midtrimester abortions induec by intra-amniotic prostaglandin F2a with urea and intravenous oxytocin, by J. H. Strauss, et al. AMERICAN JOURNAL OF OBSTETRICS AND GYNECOLOGY 134(3): 260-264, 1979.

Limitations of a single extra-amniotic injection of prostaglandins in viscous gel to induce midtrimester abortion, by I. Craft, et al. GYNECOLOGIC AND OBSTETRIC INVESTIGATION 9(5):256-261, 1978.

Lysozyme in amniotic fluid during rivanol-induced second trimester abortion, by A. Olund. PROSTAGLANDINS 17(1):149-154, January, 1979.

A maternal death associated with prostaglandin E2, by S. P. Patterson, et al. OBSTETRICS AND GYNECOLOGY 54(1):123-124, July, 1979.

Maternal death caused by prostaglandin abortion. NURSES DRUG ALERT 3:94-95, August, 1979.

The mechanism of prostaglandin action on the pregnant human uterus, by A. I. Dxapo, et al. PROSTAGLANDINS 17(2):283-299, February, 1979.

Mid trimester abortion by single dose of betamethasone, by R. Baveja, et al. INDIAN JOURNAL OF MEDICAL RE-

SEARCH 69:83-87, January, 1979.

Midtrimester abortion utilizing intraamniotic prostaglandin F2alpha, laminaria and oxytocin, by A. J. Horowitz. JOURNAL OF REPRODUCTIVE MEDICINE 21(4): 236-240, October, 1978.

Midgrimester abortion with prostaglandin and hypertonic saline—a comparative study, by R. V. Bhatt, et al. IN-TERNATIONAL JOURNAL OF GYNAECOLOGY AND OBSTETRICS 16(3):254-258, 1978-1979.

A new gel for intracervical application of prostaglandin E2, by U. Ulmsten, et al. ACTA OBSTETRICIA ET GYNE-COLOGICA SCANDINAVICA (84):19-21, 1979.

New prostaglandin E2 analogue for pregnancy termination [letter] , by M. Bygdeman, et al. LANCET 1(8126): 1136, May 26, 1979.

On the mechanism of action of 15-methyl-PGF2 alpha as an abortifacient, by K. Gréen, et al. PROSTAGLANDINS 17(2):277-282, February, 1979.

Outpatient termination of pregnancy via intramural single-shot application of the prostaglandin derivative sh b 286 (sulproston), by H. Wiechell. BEGURTSHILFE UND FRAUENHEILKUNDE 39(5):401-403, May, 1979.

The pharmacological activity of a new prostaglandin ana-logue, 13-dehydro-a-ethyl prostaglandin F2a, by H. Shu, et al. ACTA ZOOLOGICA SINICA 24(4):314-321, 1978.

Postconceptional prostaglandin therapy, by M. Sas. ACTA BIOLOGICA ET MEDICA GERMANICA 37(5-6):931-935, 1976.

Radioimmunoassay of a new progestagen, ORG 2969, and its

metabolite, by L. Viinikka. JOURNAL OF STEROID BIOCHEMISTRY 9(10):979-982, 1978.

Reappraisal of the predictive value of the beta-human chorionic gonadotropin assay in an infertile population, by S. Belisle, et al. FERTILITY AND STERILITY 31(5): 492-495, May, 1979.

Relationship between ulterotrophic and interceptive activities of steroidal estrogens, by M. Oettel, et al. ENDOKRIN-OLOGIE 72(1):25-35, April, 1978.

Rupture of the uterus following treatment with 16-16-dimethyl E 2 prostaglandin vagitories, by F. Jerve, et al. PROSTAGLANDINS 17(1):121-123, January, 1979.

Serum relaxin levels in prostaglandin E2 induced abortion, by J. Quagliarello, et al. PROSTAGLANDINS 16(6):1003-1006, 1978.

Sex steroids and thyroid function tests: the role of estrogen and progestogen, by J. Miyamoto. INTERNATIONAL JOURNAL OF GYNAECOLOGY AND OBSTETRICS 16(1):28-33, 1978.

Standard treatment of dysmenorrhea with special reference to treatment with spasmolytics and hormones, by M. Osler. ACTA OBSTETRICIA ET GYNECOLOGICA SCANDINAVICA 87:69-72, 1979.

A study of placental pathology in mid trimester therapeutic abortions induced by hypertonic saline and prostaglandin, by M. Khardekar, et al. INDIAN JOURNAL OF PATHOLOGY AND MICROBIOLOGY 21(2):141-145, April, 1978.

Sudden collapse and death of women obtaining abortions induced with prostaglandin F2alpha, by W. Cates, Jr., et al. AMERICAN JOURNAL OF OBSTETRICS AND GYNE-

COLOGY 133(4):398-400, February 15, 1979.

Suppression of uterine activity by prostaglandin synthetase inhibitors, by M. O. Pulkkinen. ACTA OBSTETRICIA ET GYNECOLOGICA SCANDINAVICA 87:39-43, 1979.

Termination of second trimester pregnancy with intra-amniotic administration of 16-phenoxy-omega-tetranor-PgE2-methylsulfonamide (SHB 286) alone and combined with oxytocin and calcium gluconate, by A. S. van den Bergh, et al. CONTRACEPTION 18(6):635-639, December, 1978.

Termination of second trimester pregnancy with intra-muscular administration of 16 phenoxy-omega-17,18,19,20 tetranor PGE2 methylsulfonylamide, by S. M. Karim, et al. PROSTAGLANDINS 15(6):1063-1068, June, 1978.

Ultrasonic assessment of uterine emptying in first-trimester abortions induced by intravaginal 15-methyl prostaglandin F2 alpha methyl ester, by T. P. Dutt, et al. AMERICAN JOURNAL OF OBSTETRICS AND GYNECOLOGY 133(5):484-488, March 1, 1979.

The use of human chorionic gonadotropin in recurrent abortion, by S. W. Sandler, et al. SOUTH AFRICAN MEDICAL JOURNAL 55(21):832-835, May 19, 1979.

Use of intra- and extra-amniotic prostaglandins for the termination of pregnancies—report of multicentric trial in India, by S. Tejuja, et al. CONTRACEPTION 18(6): 641-652, December, 1978.

Use of intramuscular 15(S)-15-methyl prostaglandin F2alpha in failed abortions, by S. L. Corson, et al. AMERICAN JOURNAL OF OBSTETRICS AND GYNECOLOGY 133(2):145-148, January 15, 1979.

The use of prostaglandins in the abortion of a dead fetus, by D. Mladencvić, et al. SRPSKI ARHIV ZA CELOKUPNO LEKARSTVO 105(10):839-846, October, 1977.

Use of prostaglandins in gynecology and obstetrics and outlook on the second generation of prostaglandins, by N. Eiqvist. GYNAEKOLOGISCHE RUNDSCHAU 18(supp 1):1-8, 1978.

Uterine contractility and plasma levels of steroid hormones after intravaginal treatment of pregnant Japanese monkeys (Macaca fuscata fuscata) with 16,16-dimethyl-trans-delta2-prostaglandin E-1 methyl ester, by K. Oshima, et al. JOURNAL OF REPRODUCTION AND FERTILITY 55(2):353-358, March, 1979.

Uterine rupture after intra-amniotic injection of prostaglandin E2 [letter], by S. Emery, et al. BRITISH MEDICAL JOURNAL 2(6181):51, July 7, 1979.

ABORTION AND HOSPITALS
Abortions in clinics as safe as in hospitals [news]. FAMILY PLANNING PERSPECTIVES 10(5):298, September-October, 1978.

Class action brought against hospital to allow abortions, by W. A. Regan. HOSPITAL PROGRESS 59(10):34+, October, 1978.

Clinical experience with a single silastic implant-D containing norethindrone acetate in a Bombay hospital, by A. Mandlekar, et al. INDIAN JOURNAL OF MEDICAL RESEARCH 68:437-443, September, 1978.

Hospital counseling in Khartoum: a study of factors affecting contraceptive acceptance after abortion, by H. E. Rushwan, et al. INTERNATIONAL JOURNAL OF GYNAECOLOGY AND OBSTETRICS 15(5):440-443, 1978.

Physical sensations during stressful hospital procedures: a
preliminary study of saline abortion patients, by K. Aby-
Nielsen. JOGN 8(2):105-106, March-April, 1979.

Staff face danger in the operating theatre, by S. Light.
NURSING MIRROR AND MIDWIVE'S JOURNAL
148(2):20-22, January 11, 1979.

Staff for family policy and education services needlessly
limited, by E. Tuomainen. SAIRAANHOITAJA 55(4):
19-20, February 20, 1979.

War of the roses: real abortion fight is not in the legislature
or the courts—it's in our hospitals, by R. K. Rein. NEW
JERSEY MONTHLY 3:45+, July, 1979.

A year of deliveries at the Adjamé maternity hospital in
Abidjan (Ivory Coast), by M. C. Reinhardt, et al. HEL-
VETICA PAEDIATRICA ACTA (41):7-20, December,
1978.

ABORTION AND JOURNALISM
Despite media attack; pro-lifers march on (inability of media
to cover anti-abortion advocates honestly), by C. Kincaid.
NEW GUARD 19:10+, Spring, 1979.

Media agendas and human rights: the Supreme court decision
on abortion, by J. C. Pollock, et al. JOURNALISM
QUARTERLY 55:544-548+, Autumn, 1978.

Ms Magazine: some old fashioned anti-Catholicism, by M.
Schwartz. OUR SUNDAY VISITOR 68:3, July 29,
1979.

Newspaper's about-face on abortion astounds, delights Ohio
right-to-lifers, by J. McKenna. OUR SUNDAY VISITOR
67:3, February 18, 1979.

An open letter to Walter Cronkite (attack Walter Cronkite

for his smear of Catholich Church on abortion issue),
by W. F. Gavin. HUMAN EVENTS 38:16+, March 11,
1978.

Surfacing: Margaret Atwood's Nymph complaining, by E. J.
Hinz, et al. CONTEMPORARY LITERATURE 20:221-
236, Spring, 1978.

Thousands will march for life, will media bury story again?
by C. Anthony. OUR SUNDAY VISITOR 67:1, Janu-
ary 21, 1979.

Washington Post reported recently. SPOKESWOMAN 9(2):
8, August, 1978.

ABORTION AND MALES
Men and abortion, by P. Marchand. CHATELAINE 51(63):
168+, November, 1978.

ABORTION AND THE MILITARY
DOD: life abortion ban, kin limits. AIR FORCE TIMES 39:
29, July 2, 1979.

Fit for duty: pregnancy. Adaptation, by A. L. Brekken. AIR
FORCE TIMES 40:34, October 8, 1979.

Frontlines: no abortions for soldiers (DOD hoped for defeat
of recent anti-abortion legislation). MOTHER JONES
4:8, January, 1979.

ABORTION AND NURSES
Abortion attitude of nurses: a cognitive dissonance perspective, by P. J. Estok. IMAGE 10(3) 70-74, October,
1978.

Abortion law and problems experienced by operating nursing
staff, by H. Twelftree. AUSTRALASIAN NURSES
JOURNAL 8:3-4+, December, 1978.

Community nursing: roll down your stockings, by M. Tepper. NURSING MIRROR AND MIDWIVE'S JOURNAL 148(9):46, March 1, 1979.

Dreams and verbal reactions of nursing students to abortion, by A. Hurwitz, et al. CURRENT PRACTICE IN OB-STETRIC AND GYNECOLOGIC NURSING 2:232-237, 1978.

High-risk pregnancy screening techniques: a nursing overview, by F. Diamond. JOGN 7(6):15-20, November-December, 1978.

Patients' evaluations of gynecologic services provided by nurse practitioners, by J. M. Wagener, et al. JOURNAL OF THE AMERICAN COLLEGE HEALTH ASSOCIA-TION 27:98-100, October, 1978.

Precautions for use of ethylene oxide, by D. K. McLeod. AORN JOURNAL 29:340-343, February, 1979.

The primary health care team. The Ron Society of Primary Health Care Nursing. Part 4, by M. Chapple. NURSING MIRROR AND MIDWIVE'S JOURNAL 147:xix+, October 5, 1978.

Program consultation by a clinical specialist, by R. L. Anders. JOURNAL OF NURSING ADMINISTRATION 8:34-38, November, 1978.

A project report follow-up of trained nurse-midwives, by R. Weinstein. JOURNAL OF NURSE-MIDWIFERY 23:36-39, Spring-Summer, 1978.

The relationship of age to nurses' attitudes toward abortion, by J. M. Berger. JOGN 8:231-233, July-August, 1979.

Saline abortions. . .to the membership. . .responsibility of RNs who assist in the performance of abortions, by D.

Smith. CALIFORNIA NURSE 74:20-21, March-April, 1979.

Student nurses view an abortion client: attitude and context effects, by E. H. Fischer. JOURNAL OF POPULATION 2(1):33-46, 1979.

Women-power in Korea; Mother's Clubs, by J. C. Abcede. WORLD HEALTH pp. 16-19, January, 1979.

Work conditions for the midwife assigned to group "K", by N. Gozdek, et al. PIELEGNIARKA I POLOZNA (3):18-19, 1979.

ABORTION AND PHYSICIANS
Abortionist strangles baby (Dr. Wm. B. Wadill on trial for allegedly strangling baby after aborting it), by L. Jeffries. CATHOLIC DIGEST 4:16+, June, 1978.

Ask a psychiatrist, by G. E. Robinson. CHATELAINE 52: 16, July, 1979.

California doctor charged with homicide: trial exposes consequences of abortion on demand (Dr. Wadill Jr. charged with strangling live aborted baby), by D. Duggan. HUMAN EVENTS 39:10+, March 10, 1979.

A certain point of view: 'abortion, ethics and the physician', by S. Aberg. KATILOLEHTI 83(10):355-360, October, 1978.

Change in the classic gynecologic surgery: review of 3,300 pelviscopies in 1971-1976, by K. Semm. INTERNATIONAL JOURNAL OF FERTILITY 24(1):13-20, 1979.

Constitutional law—civil rights—section 1983—requirement of state action in discrimination suit against medical doctor. WISCONSIN LAW REVIEW 1978:583-605, 1978.

Counseling, consulting, and consent: abortion and the doctor-patient relationship, by M. A. Wood, et al. BRIGHAM YOUNG UNIVERSITY LAW REVIEW 1978: 783-845, 1978.

Doctors and the Islamic penal code [letter] , by R. J. Brereton. LANCET 1(8117):672, March 24, 1979.

The legal position of the physician with reference to abortion, by W. Becker. MEDIZINISCHE KLINIK 73(37): 1292-1297, September 15, 1978.

MD's prosecution for abortion blocked [news] , by L. V. Jowers. LEGAL ASPECTS OF MEDICAL PRACTICE 6(9):29, September, 1978.

Office gynecology. Part II, by J. V. Kelly. ARIZONA MEDICINE 35(11):730-731, November, 1978.

Office termination of pregnancy by 'menstrual aspiration', by R. W. Hale, et al. AMERICAN JOURNAL OF OBSTETRICS AND GYNECOLOGY 134(2):213-218, May 15, 1979.

One culprit in unwanted pregnancies: the patients' doctor, by S. J. Barr. MEDICAL WORLD NEWS 20:108, February 5, 1979.

Physician behavior as a determinant of utilization patterns: the case of abortion, by C. A. Nathanson, et al. AMERICAN JOURNAL OF PUBLIC HEALTH 68:1104-1114, November, 1978.

Physicians and abortion [implications of court cases] . WOMEN'S RIGHT LAW REPORTER 5:79-81, Winter-Spring, 1979.

Physicians and surgeons—damages—parents of an unplanned child, in suit for wrongful conception may recover

313

damages for medical expenses, pain and suffering, loss of consortium, and costs of rearing the child to maturity. NORTH DAKOTA LAW REVIEW 54:619-626, 1978.

Problem of abortion on demand and the tasks of gynecologic consultation in its control, by I. Dimitrov. AKUSHER-STVO I GINEKOLOGIIA 17(6):456-460, 1978.

Waddill strangled infant, says witness in murder trial of California abortionist, by K. Granville. OUR SUNDAY VISITOR 67:2, April 1, 1979.

ABORTION AND POLITICS
Abortion, religion and political life. COMMONWEAL 106:35-38, February 2, 1979.

Calls for constitutional conventions [United States], by M. Leepson. EDITORIAL RESEARCH REPORTS pp. 187-204, March 16, 1979.

Capitol Hill update. SPOKESWOMAN 9(3):3, September, 1978.

Carter defense appointments angers pro-life groups (appoints Dr. John H. Moxley as Asst. Sec. of Defense for Health Affairs; he discriminated against anti-abortion doctors at UCSD medical school). HUMAN EVENTS 39:3, July 21,

Carter launches new campaign to aid pregnant adolescents. JUVENILE JUSTICE DIGEST 7(14):6, July 27, 1979.

Coming election [editorial], by A. DeValk. CHELSEA JOURNAL 5:51, March-April, 1979.

Congress acts on other anti-abortion measures. SPOKESWO-MAN 9(4):5, October, 1978.

Congress bows to anti-choice pressure. SPOKESWOMAN

9(5):8, November, 1978.

Congress ends abortion funds deadlock. SPOKESWOMAN 8(7&8):5, January, 1978.

Constitutional Convention advances, by J. M. Clark. NA-TIONAL NOW 11(7):11, June, 1978.

The Court, the Congress and the President: turning back the clock on the pregnant poor, by R. Lincoln, et al. FAMI-LY PLANNING PERSPECTIVES 9(5):207-214, September-October, 1977.

Decoding the election game plan of the new right: Life Amendment Political Action Committee, Inc., by L. C. Wohl. MS MAGAZINE 8:57-59+, August, 1979.

Does the first amendment bar the Hyde amendment [symposium on "McRae vs Califano"], by J. P. Wogaman, et al. CHRISTIANITY AND CRISIS 39:35-43, March 5, 1979.

"Fathers united" fights abortion (group in favor of father's rights in deciding on abortion), by J. Beck. CATHOLIC DIGEST 4:45, January, 1978.

The fetus as parasite and mushroom; Judith Jarvis Thompson's defense of abortion, by G. Meilaender. LINACRE QUARTERLY 46:126-135, May, 1979.

Legislation to watch—and work for—in the 95th Congress [abortion, childcare, family planning, health, homemakers, welfare, congressional staffing, work], by S. Tenenbaum, et al. MS MAGAZINE 5:99-102, February, 1977.

Mad at Jimmy. CHRISTIANITY TODAY 23:64, October 20, 1978.

Manufacture of by-election news. NEW STATESMAN 95: 515, April 21, 1978.

Meanwhile, back on the hill, by A. Brewer. POLITICKS 1:9, March 28, 1978.

New poll finds majority support for abortion, sex education. SPOKESWOMAN 9(1):9, July, 1978.

Paul and Judy Brown vow they'll change the constitution to stamp out abortion, by C. Crawford. PEOPLE 11(3): 28, January 22, 1979.

The politics of the Burger court toward women, by L. F. Goldstein. POLICY STUDIES JOURNAL 7:213-218, Winter, 1978.

Politics: want to make an issue of it? THE ECONOMIST 269:44-45, November 25, 1978.

Power of fetal politics; anti-abortion groups, by R. M. Williams. SATURADY REVIEW 6:12-15, June 9, 1979.

Pro-choice candidates face tough races, by J. Clarke. NATIONAL NOW 11(10):7, September, 1978.

Pro-choice is pro-life, by J. Blockwick. ENGAGE/SOCIAL ACTION 11:41-46, December, 1979.

Pro-life groups gain momentum, by L. Johnson. CATHOLIC DIGEST 4:48, March, 1978.

Pro-life moves ahead, by C. Collins. SIGNS 58:24, February, 1979.

Pro-life vs. pro-choice, by M. Bourgoin. NATIONAL CATHOLIC REPORTER 15:18-19, July 27, 1979.

Pro-lifers score sweeping victory in California's abortion-funding battle. OUR SUNDAY VISITOR 68:1, June 24, 1979.

Pro-lifers ultimate victory is at hand, by R. McMunn. OUR SUNDAY VISITOR 67:1, February 4, 1979.

The Select Committee Reports, by R. Lincoln. FAMILY PLANNING PERSPECTIVES 11(2):101-104, March-April, 1979.

True confession of one one-issue voter, by G. Rees, 3d, et al. NATIONAL REVIEW 31:669-672+, May 25, 1979; Discussion, 31:808-809, June 22, 1979.

2000 protest against Califano, by G. Blair. VILLAGE VOICE 22:22, November 21, 1977.

U.S. Supreme Court has agreed. SPOKESWOMAN 8(10): 5, April, 1978.

ABORTION AND RAPE
I was a rape victim. . .communication breakdown. NURSING MIRROR AND MIDWIVE'S JOURNAL 147:21, November 9, 1978.

Italy: abortionist-rapist resisted, by Noon, et al. OFF OUR BACKS 8(4):7, April, 1978.

Lord Hale, witches, and rape, by G. Geis. BRITISH JOURNAL OF LAW AND SOCIETY 5:26-44, Summer, 1978.

ABORTION AND RELIGION
ACLU harasses pro-lifers (ACLU suggests tha the pro-life movement is part of a papal plot), by N. Thimmesch. CATHOLIC DIGEST 4:49, May, 1978.

ACLU's holy war. NATIONAL REVIEW 31:74+, January 19, 1979.

Abortion alternative and the patient's right to know. WASH-
INGTON UNIVERSITY LAW QUARTERLY 1978:167-
210, Winter, 1978.

Abortion and the Church, by E. Bryce. OUR SUNDAY
VISITOR 67:12-14, January 21, 1979.

Abortion and the duty to preserve life, by J. R. Connery.
THEOLOGICAL STUDIES 40:318-333, June, 1979.

Abortion and the law. OUR SUNDAY VISITOR 67:9-11,
January 21, 1979.

Abortion and the "Right-to-Life": facts, fallacies, and fraud—
II. Psychometric studies, by J. W. Prescott, et al. HU-
MANIST 38:36-43, November-December, 1978.

—: a rejoinder, by L. Robinson. CANADIAN FORUM 59:
20-22, April, 1979.

Abortion case hinges on parents' rights, Catholic league tells
Supreme Court. OUR SUNDAY VISITOR 67:1, April
1, 1979.

Abortion clinics targets of "right-to-life" violence. SPOKES-
WOMAN 8(10):5, April, 1978.

Abortion debate: a call for civility, by J. C. Evans. CHRIS-
TIAN CENTURY 96:300-301, March 21, 1979.

Abortion, ethics, and biology, by J. Wind. PERSPECTIVES
IN BIOLOGY AND MEDICINE 21(4):492-504, 1978.

Abortion fight: crusade of many faces, by M. Winiarski.
NATIONAL CATHOLIC REPORTER 14:5+, March 3,
1978.

Abortion flap puts archdiocese on spot, N.Y. Times fans
flames, priest charges, by F. Franzonia. OUR SUNDAY

VISITOR 68:1, June 3, 1979.

Abortion for 'wrong' fetal sex: an ethical-legal dilemma [news], by J. Elliott. JAMA 242(14):1455-1456, October 5, 1979.

Abortion: historical and biblical perspectives, by J. A. Rasmussen. CONCORDIA THEOLOGICAL QUARTERLY 43:19-25, January, 1979.

Abortion: is it murder? by W. F. Sayers. CATHOLIC DIGEST 4:18+, June, 1978.

Abortion: is it right or is it murder?, by D. L. Stein, et al. CHATELAINE 51:22, August, 1978.

Abortion: the issue none wanted, so Catholics took it on, by M. Winiarski. NATIONAL CATHOLIC REPORTER 14: 1+, February 24, 1978.

Abortion: its social and ethical issues: an invitation to responsibility and moral discourse, by B. C. Bangert. FOUNDATIONS 22:198-217, July, 1979.

Abortion, property rights, and the right to life, by L. H. O'Driscoll. PERSONALIST 58:99-114, April, 1977; Reply, by W. J. Boehmer, 60:325-335, July, 1979.

Abortion, religion and political life. COMMONWEAL 106: 35-38, February 2, 1979.

Abortion: review of Mennonite literature, 1970-1977, by G. Brenneman. MENNONITE QUARTERLY REVIEW 53:160-172, April, 1979.

Abortionist strangles baby (Dr. Wm. B. Wadill on trial for allegedly strangling baby after aborting it), by L. Jeffries. CATHOLIC DIGEST 4:16+, June, 1978.

L'accueil de l'enfant a naitre; déclaration du Conseil perma-
nent de l'Episocapat français aux catholiques de France.
LA DOCUMENTATION CATHOLIQUE 76:442-443,
May 6, 1979.

Akron gets restrictive abortion measure, by J. Petosa. NA-
TIONAL CATHOLIC REPORTER 14:20, March 10,
1978.

Akron, Ohio abortion ordinance outrageous, by M. M. Smith.
NATIONAL NOW 11(5&6):5, April, 1978.

Akron ordinance challenged [anti-abortion ordinance], by
T. Dejanikus. OFF OUR BACKS 8:5+, November,
1978.

Akron's pro-life experiment (provisions of a pro-life ordinance), by N. Thimmesch. CATHOLIC DIGEST 4:23,
June, 1978.

Allocution de. . .aux foyers des Equipes Notre-Dame, by R.
Etchegaray. LA DOCUMENTATION CATHOLIQUE
76:271-273, March 18, 1979.

Anti-abortion forces seek Akron's consent law as exploding
myths, by J. Petosa. NATIONAL CATHOLIC REPORT-
ER 14:32, March 17, 1978.

Anti-abortion tactics subtle, blatant, by M. Winiarski. NA-
TIONAL CATHOLIC REPORTER 14:15, March 10,
1978.

The baby—or the auto? by T. Blackburn. NATIONAL
CATHOLIC REPORTER 16:2, November 2, 1979.

Babykillers' retort stops dialogue dead, by M. Winiarski.
NATIONAL CATHOLIC REPORTER 15:3+, February
2, 1979.

Bishops gird for court clash over bill forcing employers to pay for abortions. OUR SUNDAY VISITOR 68:3, July 29, 1979.

Bishops, right to life hand-in-glove in N.Y., by M. Winiarski. NATIONAL CATHOLIC REPORTER 14:1+, January 27, 1978.

Byrn and Roe: the threshold question and juridical review, by P. J. Riga. CATHOLIC LAWYER 23:309-331, Autumn, 1978.

A call to responsible ecumenical debate on abortion and homosexuality, by National Council of Churches. ENGAGE/SOCIAL ACTION 7:41-44, October, 1979.

Catholic Church hits the hustings, by R. Shrum. NEW TIMES 12(1):16, January 8, 1979.

Catholic left: can it live with feminism? by K. Lindsey. SEVEN DAYS 2(16):23, October 27, 1978.

Catholicism and family planning attitudes in Brazil, by A. H. Gelbard. DISSERTATION ABSTRACTS INTERNATIONAL 39(9-A):5743, March, 1979.

Catholics aren't the only pro-lifers, by M. Novak. CATHOLIC DIGEST 4:26, June, 1978.

Catholics' lawsuit suspends forced abortion payments. BUSINESS INSURANCE 13:1+, July 23, 1979.

A certain point of view: 'abortion, ethics and the physicial', by S. Aberg. KATILOLEHTI 83(10):355-360, October, 1978.

Childfree marriage—a theological view, by D. Doherty. CHICAGO STUDIES 18:137-145, Summer, 1979.

The Christian community and the welcoming of unborn human life; pastoral instruction of the Permanent Council of the Italian episcopal Conference. OSSERVATORE ROMANO 11(572):6-9, March 11, 1979.

Church and state, by E. Doerr. HUMANIST 39:62, March, 1979.

Church attendance and attitudes toward abortion: differentials in liberal and conservative churches, by H. R. F. Ebaugh, et al. JOURNAL FOR THE SCIENTIFIC STUDY OF RELIGION 17:407-413, December, 1978.

Church funding of anti-abortion lobby investigated. WIN MAGAZINE 14(26):17, July 20, 1978.

Church v state, continued. THE ECONOMIST 270:42, January 13, 1979.

Clergy oppose abortion foes. NEW TIMES 11(11):26, November 27, 1978.

Cleveland clinic bombed, by D. Holland. NATIONAL CATHOLIC REPORTER 14:2, March 3, 1978.

Clinical observations, by S. L. Varnado. NATIONAL CATHOLIC REPORTER 14:9, April 28, 1978.

Les cliniques d'avortement: s'impliquer pour éduquer, by G. Durand. RELATIONS 38:308-311, November, 1978.

La communauté chrétienne et l'accueil de la vie humaine raissante; instruction pastorale du Conseil permanent de la Conférence épiscopale italienne. LA DOCUMENTATION CATHOLIQUE 76:262-271, March 18, 1979.

Defense tries to prove that baby never lived outside mother's womb, by K. Granville. OUR SUNDAY VISITOR 67:2, April 22, 1979.

The definition of death; interview by D. Duggan, by M. DeMere. OUR SUNDAY VISITOR 67:6-7, January 28, 1979.

Despite Church opposition, Italy adopts new law providing free abortion for a variety of indications [news] . FAMILY PLANNING PERSPECTIVES 10(4):241-243, July-August, 1978.

Differential impact of religious preference and church attendance on attitudes toward abortion, by W. A. Mc Intosh, et al. REVIEW OF RELIGIOUS RESEARCH 20:195-213, Spring, 1979.

Do Catholics have constitutional rights? Hyde Amendment challenge. COMMONWEAL 105:771-773, December 8, 1978.

Does the cash register ring louder than freedom for rights of women? by F. Franzonia. OUR SUNDAY VISITOR 68: 1, July 22, 1979+

Ecumenical war over abortion. TIME 113:62-63, January 29, 1979.

The embryo and the soul, by J. Cooper. MIDSTREAM 25:78-79, January, 1979.

The end of "Catholic" fertility, by E. F. Jones, et al. DEMOGRAPHY 16:209-218, May, 1979.

Ethical issues in genetic intervention, by C. C. Sammons. SOCIAL WORK 23:237-242, May, 1978.

Ethics and amniocentesis for fetal sex identification, by J. C. Fletcher. NEW ENGLAND JOURNAL OF MEDICINE 301(10):550-553, September 6, 1979.

Faith and Order's call to ecumenical debate, by R. J. Neuhaus.

CHRISTIAN CENTURY 96:205-206, February 28, 1979.

"Fathers united" fights abortion (group in favor of father's rights in deciding on abortion), by J. Beck. CATHOLIC DIGEST 4:45, January, 1978.

Fetal transplants could resolve abortion conflict, by R. McClory. NATIONAL CATHOLIC REPORTER 16:1+, October 26, 1979.

Fetus display upsets abortion leaders' talk, by M. Winiarski. NATIONAL CATHOLIC REPORTER 15:5, February 23, 1979.

The French bishops on abortion, by J. O'Leary. FURROW 30:353-360, June, 1979.

Full story of Chicago abortion scandal untold, pro-life leaders say, by C. Anthony. OUR SUNDAY VISITOR 67:1, November 26, 1978.

Furor in New York; for archdiocese, contract may dull abortion dilemma's horns, by F. Franzonia. OUR SUNDAY VISITOR 68:1, August 5, 1979.

Going to the barricades, by C. Perozino. AMERICAN ATHEIST 21(10):14, October, 1979.

Guidelines for ecumenical debate on abortion and homosexuality; Faith and Order Commission of the National Council of Churches. ORIGINS 8:517-519, February 1, 1979.

HEW gets Hyde amendment; right will cause 100,000 medical abortions this year, by J. D. Lofton, Jr. CATHOLIC DIGEST 4:48, May, 1978.

The hate campaign against Catholics (Catholics accused of

wanting to take away the right of decision in abortion), by M. J. Sobian. CATHOLIC DIGEST 4:27, June, 1978.

Health concerns, by J. Scheidler. OUR SUNDAY VISITOR 67:6-8, January 21, 1979.

Heil Mary! [note] . MOTHER JONES 3(9):9, November, 1978.

How dare they do this; by B. Baird. AMERICAN ATHEIST 21(5):24, May, 1979.

How many girls do parents drive to abortion, by M. Finley. OUR SUNDAY VISITOR 68:5, November 4, 1979.

The Hyde amendment; a tradition, by M. Bourgoin. NATIONAL CATHOLIC REPORTER 15:18, July 27, 1979.

Importance of being Sr Marie Augusta; a footnote by another hand, by R. G. Hoyt. CHRISTIANITY AND CRISIS 39:122-125, May 14, 1979.

Indian woman's sterilization suite starts, by P. Moore. NATIONAL CATHOLIC REPORTER 15:1+, January 19, 1979.

Indiana abortion clinic sues pro-life picketers, seeks $700,000 in damages, by C. Anthony. OUR SUNDAY VISITOR 67:1, January 28, 1979.

Is abortion a religious issue? [letter] , by G. M. Atkinson. INQUIRY 9(1):4+, February, 1979.

Is abortion a religious issue? (1) Religious, moral, and sociological issues: some basic distinctions, by B. Brody. THE HASTINGS CENTRE REPORT 8(4):12-17, August, 1978.

—? (2) Enacting religious beliefs in a pluralistic society, by F. S. Jafe. THE HASTINGS CENTRE REPORT 8(4): 12-17, August, 1978.

—? (3) The irrelevance of religion in the abortion debate, by L. Newton. THE HASTINGS CENTRE REPORT 8(4): 12-17, August, 1978.

Italy: church v state continued. THE ECONOMIST 270:42, January 13, 1979.

Jury: charges not proved, by P. Moore. NATIONAL CATHOLIC REPORTER 15:5, February 2, 1979.

Lost cause, by E. Johnson. WEEKEND MAGAZINE 29:18-20, June 23, 1979.

Major dailies blind to pro-life clout, by R. Shaw. OUR SUNDAY VISITOR 67:3, February 18, 1979.

Maze of conflicting testimony faces jurors in murder trial of abortionist, by K. Granville. OUR SUNDAY VISITOR 68:2, May 13, 1979.

Measuring tragedy; review article, with reply "Abortion and the 'right to life:' a rejoinder", by L. Robinson, et al. CANADIAN FORUM 58:34-37+, April, 1978+.

Ms Magazine: some old fashioned anti-Catholicism, by M. Schwartz. OUR SUNDAY VISITOR 68:3, July 29, 1979.

A new conscience of the pro-life movement, by M. Weinberger. CONSERVATIVE DIGEST 5:18+, December, 1979.

New government rules may snuff out national scandal, Indian doctor hopes, by F. Franzonia. OUR SUNDAY VISITOR 68:3, June 24, 1979.

Newspaper's about-face on abortion astounds, delights Ohio right-to-lifers, by J. McKenna. OUR SUNDAY VISITOR 67:3, February 18, 1979.

Nun on trial for her baby's death: will Sister Maureen's tragedy shake the church? by C. Breslin. MS MAGAZINE 5: 68-71, March, 1977.

Of many things; National Council of Churches' call for ecumenical debate, by J. O'Hare. AMERICA 140:inside cover, February 3, 1979.

An open letter to Walter Cronkite (attack Walter Cronkite for his smear of Catholic Church on abortion issue), by W. F. Gavin. HUMAN EVENTS 38:16+, March 11, 1978.

Rabbi, archbishop urge talks to reconcile views on abortion, school aid, by C. Savitsky, Jr. OUR SUNDAY VISITOR 67:2, March 4, 1979.

Religious freedom and the American community, by L. Pfeffer. JUDICATURE 28:137-146, Spring, 1979.

Rights are not enough, prospects for a new approach to the morality of abortion, by P. Rossi. LINACRE QUARTERLY 46:109-117, May, 1979.

The St. Paul fire-bombing: new wave of terrorism against abortion? by G. Lichtenstein. MS MAGAZINE 7:58-60+, November, 1978.

Spiritual abortion, by Sydney. COMMUNITIES 31:2, March, 1978.

Strong attacks against abortion put Italian Church on hot seat, by C. Savitsky, Jr. OUR SUNDAY VISITOR 67:3, February 4, 1979.

Summing up, by M. Sanger. THE HUMANIST 38:62, July, 1978.

Tax-paid abortions, by R. McMunn. OUR SUNDAY VISITOR 67:1, January 14, 1979.

They hammered at abortion to unclutter debate, by C. Anthony. OUR SUNDAY VISITOR 68:6, October 28, 1979.

Thousands will march for life, will media bury story again? by C. Anthony. OUR SUNDAY VISITOR 67:1, January 21, 1979.

U.S. bishops' conferences file suit on abortion benefits. ORIGINS 9:97+, July 5, 1979.

Unborn again; Catholic Church, by R. Shrum. NEW TIMES 12:16, January 8, 1979.

Verdict on Akron abortion ordinance brings mixed victory for pro-life forces, by J. McKenna. OUR SUNDAY VISITOR 68:1, September 9, 1979.

Viet church stifling told, by M. Winiarski. NATIONAL CATHOLIC REPORTER 14:1+, February 3, 1978.

Violence erupts against pro-choice facilities. NATIONAL NOW 11(5&6):5, April, 1978.

We quit, bishop tells United Ways; planned parenthood won't play in Peoria. OUR SUNDAY VISITOR 68:1, August 12, 1979.

What should we do about future people? by T. Grovier. AMERICAN PHILOSOPHICAL QUARTERLY 16:105-113, April, 1979.

Women's rights, by A. Smelser. OUR SUNDAY VISITOR 67:15, January 21, 1979.

Wrong sex can mean death by abortion for unborn child.

OUR SUNDAY VISITOR 68:3, September 23, 1979.

ABORTION AND YOUTH

Abortion in the adolescent, by D. Lancaster. AUSTRALIAN FAMILY PHYSICIAN 7(Spec No):25-27, August, 1978.

Abortions—juveniles—parental or judicial consent. CRIMINAL LAW REPORTER: SUPREME COURT PROCEEDINGS 24(22):4221-4223, March 7, 1979.

The circumstances surrounding pregnancy of a group of young coloured mothers, by P. J. Van Regenmortel. HUMANITAS 4(2):203-206, 1977.

Follow-up of 50 adolescent girls 2 years after abortion, by H. Cvejic, et al. CANADIAN MEDICAL ASSOCIATION JOURNAL 116(1):44-46, 1977.

Many teenagers and their parents talk together about contraception and decisions on abortion [news] . FAMILY PLANNING PERSPECTIVES 10(5):298-300, September-October, 1978.

Many teens and parents talk about contraception and abortion. FAMILY PLANNING PERSPECTIVES 10:298-299, September-October, 1978.

Social worker's role in teenage abortions [based on conference paper] , by L. P. Cain. SOCIAL WORK 24:52-56, January, 1979.

Split decision on abortions; regulating teenage abortion; Supreme Court decision, by S. Begley, et al. NEWSWEEK 94:63-64, July 16, 1979.

Spontaneous abortions in sibship of children with congenital malformation or malignant disease, by A. Spira, et al. EUROPEAN JOURNAL OF OBSTETRICS, GYNECOLOGY AND REPRODUCTIVE BIOLOGY 9(2):89-

ABORTION AND YOUTH

96, 1979.

Teenage abortion goes back to court, by L. Sharf. MAJORI-
TY REPORT 8:1, September 30-October 13, 1978.

The teen-ager's abortion decision; included are a summary of
the decision: an excerpt from the dissenting opinion and
reaction to the decision. ORIGINS 9:134-143, August
2, 1979.

ABORTION CLINICS
Abortion clinics found unsafe by reporters. EDITOR AND
PUBLISHER 111:15, December 16, 1978.

Abortion clinics rush to diversify: abortion clinics add sex
counseling, fertility help and simple surgery. BUSINESS
WEEK p. 68+, December 10, 1979.

Abortion clinics targets of "right-to-life" violence. SPOKES-
WOMAN 8(10):5, April, 1978.

Abortion clinics under siege, by Barton. PROGRESSIVE
43:27-29, March, 1979.

Abortions in clinics as safe as in hospitals. FAMILY PLAN-
NING PERSPECTIVES 10:298, September-October,
1978.

Experience of abortion; ed by D. D. Miller, by R. Petruso.
AMERICA 140:510-512, June 23, 1979.

Necessity as a defense to a charge of criminal trespass in an
abortion clinic. UNIVERSITY OF CINCINNATI LAW
REVIEW 48:501-516, 1979.

Why women drop out of a medical termination of pregnancy
clinic, by N. N. Wig, et al. JOURNAL OF FAMILY
WELFARE 25:34-40, September, 1978.

ABORTION COUNSELING
  Abortion counseling, by M. Kahn-Edrington. COUNSELING PSYCHOLOGIST 8(1):37-38, 1979.

  Abortion counseling in a general hospital, by B. A. Kaminsky, et al. HEALTH AND SOCIAL WORK 4:92-103, May, 1979.

  Counseling, consulting, and consent: abortion and the doctor-patient relationship, by M. A. Wood, et al. BRIGHAM YOUNG UNIVERSITY LAW REVIEW 1978:783-845, 1978.

  Efficacy of a group crisis-counseling program for men who accompany women seeking abortions, by R. H. Gordon. AMERICAN JOURNAL OF COMMUNITY PSYCHOLOGY 6(3):239-246, June, 1978.

  Evaluating abortion counselling, by R. J. Marcus. DIMENSIONS IN HEALTH SERVICE 56(8):16-18, August, 1978.

  Hospital counseling in Khartoum: a study of factors affecting contraceptive acceptance after abortion, by H. E. Rushwan, et al. INTERNATIONAL JOURNAL OF GYNAECOLOGY AND OBSTETRICS 15(5):440-443, 1978.

  Pregnancy and abortion counseling, by American Academy of Pediatrics. Committee on Adolescence. PEDIATRICS 63(6):920-921, June, 1979.

  What abortion counselors want from their clients, by C. Joffe. SOCIAL PROBLEMS 26:112-121, October, 1978.

ABORTION RESEARCH
  Antibodies to leptospira in the sera of aborted bovine fetuses, by W. A. Ellis, et al. VETERINARY RECORD 103:237-239, September 9, 1978.

Bovine abortion associated with mixed Movar 33/63 type herpesvirus and bovine viral diarrhea virus infection, by D. E. Reed, et al. CORNELL VETERINARIAN 69(1): 54-66, 1979.

Cloprostenol and pregnancy termination [letter] , by P. A. Boyd. VETERINARY RECORD 104(4):84, January 27, 1979.

Experimental production of corynebacterium pyogenes abortion in sheep, by P. B. Addo, et al. CORNELL VETERINARIAN 69:20-32, January, 1979.

Experiments on prevention of the endotoxin-abortifacient effect by radiodetoxified endotoxin pretreatment in rats, by T. Csordás, et al. GYNECOLOGIC AND OBSTETRIC INVESTIGATION 9(1):57-64, 1978.

The metabolic clearance rate and uterine metabolism and retention of progesterone and 20 a-hydroxypregn-4-en-3-one during the secretion of uteroglobin in ovariectomized, steroid-treated rabbits, by R. B. Billiar, et al. ENDOCRINOLOGY 103(3):990-996, 1978.

Pregnancy termination in the control of the tibial hemimelia syndrome in Galloway cattle, by D. L. Pollock, et al. VETERINARY RECORD 104(12):258-260, March 24, 1979.

Preliminary study of the behavior of urinary polyamines in non-pregnant conditions, in pregnant women and in abortive pathology of the 1st trimester, by M. D'Anna. MINERVA GINECOLOGIA 31(5):327-335, May, 1979.

A psychosexual study of abortion—seeking behaviour, by M. Vachher, et al. MEDICAL JOURNAL OF MALAYSIA 33(1):50-56, September, 1978.

Second trimester abortion with 5% intraamniotic saline—a

pilot study, by A. K. Ghosh, et al. INTERNATIONAL JOURNAL OF GYNAECOLOGY AND OBSTETRICS 15(5):436-439, 1978.

Uterine contractility and plasma levels of steroid hormones after intravaginal treatment of pregnant Japanese monkeys (Macaca fuscata fuscata) with 16,16-dimethyl-trans-delta2-prostaglandin E-1 methyl ester, by K. Oshima, et al. JOURNAL OF REPRODUCTION AND FERTILITY 55(2):353-358, March, 1979.

Vaccine link with sow abortions, by I. C. Ross. VETERINARY RECORDS 104:83, January 27, 1979.

ADOLESCENTS

Adolescent mourning reactions to infant and fetal loss, by N. H. Horowitz. SOCIAL CASEWORK 59:551-559, November, 1978.

Adolescent sexual behavior, by J. R. Faulkenberry, et al. HEALTH EDUCATION 10:5-7, May-June, 1979.

Adolescent sexuality: legal aspects, by L. Vick. AUSTRALIAN FAMILY PHYSICIAN 7(Spec No):12-15, August, 1978.

Adolescents and knowledge of population dynamics and family planning, by V. Gupta, et al. JOURNAL OF FAMILY WELFARE 25:33-40, March, 1979.

Adolescents' knowledge of childbearing, by J. Walter, et al. FAMILY COORDINATOR 28(2):163-171, April, 1979.

Antecedents of adolescent parenthood and consequences at age 30, by D. Russ-Eft, et al. FAMILY COORDINATOR 28(2):173-179, April, 1979.

The circumstances surrounding pregnancy of a group of young coloured mothers, by P. J. Van Regenmortel.

HUMANITAS 4(2):203-206, 1977.

Contraception in the adolescent. Alternative methods, by
G. Betheras. AUSTRALIAN FAMILY PHYSICIAN
7(Spec No):37-38, August, 1978.

—. Educational programmes, by K. Dunn. AUSTRALIAN
FAMILY PHYSICIAN 7(Spec No):21-24, August, 1978.

—. Introduction, by J. Leeton. AUSTRALIAN FAMILY
PHYSICIAN 7(Spec No):3-5, August, 1978.

—. Proceedings of a seminar held in Melbourne, March 10,
1978, by the Family Planning Association of Victoria.
AUSTRALIAN FAMILY PHYSICIAN 7(Spec No):3-
38, August, 1978.

—. Psychological aspects, by E. Koadlow. AUSTRALIAN
FAMILY PHYSICIAN 7(Spec No) 16-20, August, 1978.

—. Steps towards a situational ethic, by P. J. Hollingworth.
AUSTRALIAN FAMILY PHYSICIAN 7(Spec No):6-11,
August, 1978.

An exploration of factors affecting referral of adolescent girls
to a planned parenthood clinic, by S. E. Osterbusch.
DISSERTATION ABSTRACTS INTERNATIONAL
38(11-A):6943, May, 1978.

Fertility and possibilities of anticonception in adolescence,
by F. Havránek. CESKOSLOVENSKA GYNEKOLOGIE
44(4):304-308, May, 1979.

Follow-up of 50 adolescent girls 2 years after abortion, by
H. Cvejic, et al. CANADIAN MEDICAL ASSOCIATION
JOURNAL 116(1):44-46, 1977.

Gynecologic health problems: socially abused adolescent female, by M. J. Rothbard, et al. NEW YORK STATE

JOURNAL OF MEDICINE 76:1483-1484, September, 1976.

How many girls do parents drive to abortion, by M. Finley. OUR SUNDAY VISITOR 68:5, November 4, 1979.

Immediate postabortion intrauterine contraception in nulliparous adolescents, by J. A. Goldman, et al. ISRAEL JOURNAL OF MEDICAL SCIENCES 15(6):522-525, June, 1979.

Learning about the population problem: children's attitudes toward family planning in India, by S. Iyengar. YOUTH AND SOCIETY 10(3):275-295, March, 1979.

Legal aspects: the nurse and contraceptive practices among adolescents, by C. L. Sklar. INFIRMIERE CANADIENNE 21(1):16-19, January, 1978.

Male adolescent contraceptive utilization, by M. L. Finkel, et al. ADOLESCENCE 13(51):443-451, Fall, 1978.

Many teenagers and their parents talk together about contraception and decisions on abortion [news]. FAMILY PLANNING PERSPECTIVES 10(5):298-300, September-October, 1978.

Many teens and parents talk about contraception and abortion. FAMILY PLANNING PERSPECTIVES 10:298-299, September-October, 1978.

Middle-class Americans frown on premarital sex but think teens should be offered contraception. FAMILY PLANNING PERSPECTIVES 10(5):301-302, September-October, 1978.

Multivariate analysis of interstate variation in fertility of teenage girls, by E. A. Brann. AMERICAN JOURNAL OF PUBLIC HEALTH 69:661-666, July, 1979.

Myocardial infarction and other vascular diseases in young women. Role of estrogens and other factors, by H. Jick, et al. JAMA 240(23):2548-2552, December 1, 1978.

A new problem in adolescent gynecology, by M. J. Bulfin. SOUTHERN MEDICAL JOURNAL 72(8):967-968, August, 1979.

Oral contraception in the adolescent, by E. Weisberg. AUSTRALIAN FAMILY PHYSICIAN 7(Spec No):32-36, August, 1978.

A plea for the condom, especially for teenagers, by Y. M. Felman. JAMA 241(23):2517-2418, June 8, 1979.

Premarital contraceptives usage among male and female adolescents, by J. P. Hornick, et al. FAMILY COORDINATOR 28(2):181-190, April, 1979.

Premarital sex: no, teen contraception: yes. FAMILY PLANNING PERSPECTIVES 10:301-302, September-October, 1978.

Preventing unwanted adolescent pregnancy: a cognitive-behavioral approach, by S. P. Schinke, et al. AMERICAN JOURNAL OF ORTHOPSYCHOLOGY 49:81-88, January, 1979.

Psychological dimensions of effective and ineffective contraceptive use in adolescent girls, by J. S. Spain. DISSERTATION ABSTRACTS INTERNATIONAL 38(7-B): 3373-3374, January, 1978.

Reasons for nonuse of contraception by sexually active women aged 15-19, by M. Zelnik, et al. FAMILY PLANNING PERSPECTIVES 11:289-296, September-October, 1979.

The role of personality and family relationship factors in

adolescent unwed pregnancy, by L. D. Inman. DISSER-
TATION ABSTRACTS INTERNATIONAL 38(6-B):
2864, December, 1977.

School achievement: risk factor in teenage pregnancies? by
H. Hansen, et al. AMERICAN JOURNAL OF PUBLIC
HEALTH 68:753-759, August, 1978.

Schoolchildren and contraception. Knowledge, attitudes
and behavior, by L. Bernsted, et al. UGESKRIFT FOR
LAEGER 141(6):397-399, February 5, 1979.

The self concept of pregnant adolescent girls, by C. E. Zongker. ADOLESCENCE 12(48):477-488, Winter, 1977.

Self-esteem, locus of control, and adolescent contraception,
by E. S. Herold, et al. JOURNAL OF PSYCHOLOGY
101(First Half):83-88, January, 1979.

Sex and Jewish teenagers, by A. S. Maller. JEWISH DIGEST
23:60-64, June, 1978.

Sex differences in adolescent family communication and
media use about occupations and family planning, by
P. V. Miller. DISSERTATION ABSTRACTS INTER-
NATIONAL 38(6-A):3123, December, 1977.

Sex education for teenagers, by J. H. Ford. WESTERN
JOURNAL OF MEDICINE 130(3):273-276, March,
1979.

Sexual behavior in adolescence, by J. R. Hopkins. JOUR-
NAL OF SOCIAL ISSUES 33(2):67-85, 1977.

Sexuality of youth: attempt at forming a theory, by C. J.
Straver. SOZIOLOGENKORRESPONDENZ 4:121-150,
May, 1977.

Social worker's role in teenage abortions, by L. P. Cain.

SOCIAL WORK 24:52-56, January, 1979.

Split decision on abortions; regulating teenage abortion; Supreme Court decision, by S. Begley, et al. NEWSWEEK 94:63-64, July 16, 1979.

Survey of adolescent sexuality and life values; New York city, by S. Ross. EDUCATIONAL DIGEST 44:44-47, May, 1979.

Teenage abortion goes back to court, by L. Sharf. MAJORITY REPORT 8:1, September-October 13, 1978.

Teenage birth control. SOCIETY 16:3, March, 1979.

Teenage sexual behaviour: perceptive and behavioural outcomes associated with receipt of family planning services, by C. A. Akpom, et al. JOURNAL OF BIOSOCIAL SCIENCE 11(1):85-92, January, 1979.

The teen-ager's abortion decision: included are a summary of the decision: an excerpt from the dissenting opinion and reaction to the decision. ORIGINS 9:134-143, August 2, 1979.

Teenagers and pregnancy: the law in 1979 [the right of teenagers to consent for their own birth control and other reproductive health care, United States], by E. W. Paul, et al. FAMILY PLANNING PERSPECTIVES 11:297-302, September-October, 1979.

Teenagers, birth control and the nurse, by C. Sklar. CANADIAN NURSE 74:14-16, November, 1978.

Use and abuse of the minipill in adolescence, by A. Maranzana. MINERVA MEDICA 69(46):3180-3182, September 30, 1978.

Venereal diseases: college students' knowledge and attitudes,

by I. Arafat, et al. THE JOURNAL OF SEX RE-
SEARCH 13(3):223-230, 1977.

You and the law: teenagers, birth control and the nurse, by
C. Sklar. CANADIAN NURSE 74(10):14-16, Novem-
ber, 1978.

BIRTH CONTROL (GENERAL)
Alternatives to pregnancy prevention [letter] , by G. Hunt.
AMERICAN FAMILY PHYSICIAN 19(3):27, March,
1979.

Birth control update, by J. Engel. CHATELAINE 51:27-
29+, January, 1978-1980+.

Chemical inducers of ovulation: comparative results, by V.
Ruiz-Velasco, et al. INTERNATIONAL JOURNAL OF
FERTILITY 24(1):61-64, 1979.

Chemical synthesis and bioassay of anordrin and dinordrin I
and II, by P. Crabbé, et al. STEROIDS 33(1):85-96,
January, 1979.

Clinical trial of a new suction system for uterine curettage.
Preliminary report, by J. R. Ahued Ahued, et al. GINE-
COLOGIA Y OBSTETRICIA DE MEXICO 43(260):387-
391, June, 1978.

Clinically important drug interactions 1979, by F. E. Karch,
et al. NURSES DRUG ALERT 3:25-40, March, 1979.

Controlling the population explosion, by M. Potts. THE
CROWN AGENTS QUARTERLY REVIEW pp. 1-6,
Winter, 1978-1979.

Effectiveness of abortion as birth control, by S. J. Williams,
et al. SOCIAL BIOLOGY 22(1):23-33, Spring, 1975.

Electrosurgery in laparoscopy, by F. W. Harris. JOURNAL

OF REPRODUCTIVE MEDICINE 21(1):48-52, July, 1978.

Interval between pregnancies [editorial] . LANCET 2(8095): 879-880, October 21, 1978.

Keys to birth control still elude experts. CONSERVATION FOUNDATION LETTER p. 1, March, 1979.

The Muslim world [birth control and the status of women in several predominantly Muslim nations] . PEOPLE 6(4): 3-30, 1979.

Preventing unwanted pregnancies, by K. Nowosad. PIELEG-NIARKA I POLOZNA (12):5-7, 1978.

Subjective expected utility and the prediction of birth-planning decisions, by L. R. Beach, et al. ORGANIZA-TIONAL BEHAVIOR AND HUMAN PERFORMANCE 24:18-28, August, 1979.

Test bed, by J. Landgon. GUARDIAN p. 17, February 17, 1979.

Unnatural birth control. EAST WEST 8(8):20, August, 1978.

BANGLADESH
Population outpaces food supply, by P. Niesewand. GUARDIAN p. 13, December 31, 1979.

CANADA
The Alberta counsellor and medical care for minors, by L. Eberlein. ALBERTA COUNSELLOR 7(2):5-12, Summer, 1978.

Birth control and abortion in Canada, 1870-1920, by A. McLaren. CANADIAN HISTORICAL REVIEW 59: 319-340, September, 1978.

CHINA
>Birth pains. THE ECONOMIST 270:76, February 10, 1979.

>China's answer doesn't lie in the coil, by J. Gittings. GUARDIAN p. 16, April 23, 1979.

>Chinese birth controls penalise larger families, by J. Mathews. GUARDIAN p. 7, May 2, 1979.

>The Chinese experience [some of the ways in which China has established the small family norm, provided nationwide birth planning services, and measured the results] , by P. Chen. PEOPLE 6(2):17-20, 1979.

>Large families penalized in attempt to cut back births, by C. Douglas-Home. TIMES p. 5, December 8, 1979.

GERMANY
>Working class birth control in Wilhelmine Germany, by R. P. Neuman. COMPARATIVE STUDIES IN SOCIETY AND HISTORY 20:408-428, July, 1978.

GREAT BRITAIN
>Doctor knows best, by J. Chernaik. NEW SOCIETY pp. 779-780, June 28, 1979.

>Wrong cure, by L. Adamson. GUARDIAN p. 9, August 21, 1979.

HUNGARY
>Birth control in the eighteenth and nineteenth centuries in some Hungarian villages, by R. Andorka. LOCAL POPULATION STUDIES (22):38-43, Spring, 1979.

INDIA
>Antifertility effects of Embelia ribes Burm, by S. D. Kholkute, et al. INDIAN JOURNAL OF EXPERI-

INDIA
MENTAL BIOLOGY 16(10):1035-1037, October, 1978.

Birth control practices and levels of development in India, by P. P. Karan, et al. JOURNAL OF GE-OGRAPHY 77:229-237, November, 1978.

Experts still preach sterilization, by C. Douglas-Home. TIMES (London) p. 9, December 14, 1979.

Indian dilemma—coercive birth control or compulsory pregnancy, by T. Black, et al. CONTEMPORARY REVIEW 233:232-236, November, 1978.

IRAN
Variations in serum protein fractions following a continuous long term intake of eugynon and lyndiol by Iranian women, by S. Kamyab, et al. JOURNAL OF STEROID BIOCHEMISTRY 9(8):811-812, August, 1978.

IRELAND
All in the Irish family way, by A. McHardy. GUARDIAN p. 9, August 7, 1979.

Family planning: the Irish solution, by C. Walker. SPECTATOR p. 12, March 31, 1979.

JAPAN
Birth control with caution. THE ECONOMIST 272:31, August 25, 1979.

KENYA
Families question planning, by G. Mkangi. GUARDIAN p. 19, June 11, 1979.

LEBANON
Sexuality and birth control decisions among Lebanese

LEBANON
>couples, by M. Chamie. SIGNS 3(1):294-312, Autumn, 1971.

MALTA
>Fighting for the right to choose: the bishops' threat to Maltese women, by J. Condon. NEW STATESMAN p. 295, August 31, 1979.

MEXICO
>Mexico's birth-control effort catching on, by A. Riding. NEW YORK TIMES p. 2, April 29, 1979.

THE NETHERLANDS
>Models of contemporary Dutch family building, by G. Santow. POPULATION STUDIES 33:59-77, March, 1979.

TUNISIA
>Birth control in Tunisia. POPULATION 33:194-205, January-February, 1978.

UNITED STATES
>Woman's body, woman's right: a social history of birth control in America, by L. Gordon. SIGNS 4(1):170, 1978.

BIRTH CONTROL: ADVERTISING
>Condoms, by T. Thompson. MARKETING 84:6-7+, April 9, 1979.

BIRTH CONTROL: ATTITUDES
>Attitude of patients and health workers as a factor influencing the utilization of reproductive health services in connection with birth control, by B. Nalbanski. AKUSHERSTVO I GINEKOLOGIIA 18(3):214-218, 1979.

>Dealing in divorce: is birth control to blame? by R. T. Michael. HUMAN BEHAVIOR 7:37, November, 1978.

Fertility rights, by M. Potts. GUARDIAN p. 11, April 25, 1979.

BIRTH CONTROL: COMPLICATIONS
Bacteriology of the tubes in postpartum salpingoclasia, by R. Velasco Almeida, et al. GINECOLOGIA Y OBSTETRICIA DE MEXICO 44(266):473-478, December, 1978.

A dent in the shield, by A. Neustatter, et al. GUARDIAN p. 10, November 1, 1979.

Embryonal rhabdomyosarcoma. A case report, by A. A. Visser, et al. SOUTH AFRICAN MEDICAL JOURNAL 54(2):70-71, July 8, 1978.

Etiopathogenetic aspects and therapy of renal cortical necrosis. Report of a case, by G. Sorba, et al. MINERVA ANESTESIOLOGICA 45(1-2):55-66, January-February, 1979.

Features of liver damage caused by 17-alpha-alkyl-substituted anabolic steroids, by P. Lovisetto, et al. MINERVA MEDICA 70(11):769-790, March 3, 1979.

Intra-hepatic cholestasis after taking a triacetyloleandomycin-estroprogestational combination [letter], by S. Claudel, et al. NOUVELLE PRESSE MEDICALE 8(14):1182, March 24, 1979.

Liver resection for hepatic adenoma, by R. Weil, 3d, et al. ARCHIVES OF SURGERY 114(2):178-180, February, 1979.

The reverse effect of sexual steroids on the serum-lysozyme, by G. Klinger, et al. ZENTRALBLATT FUR GYNAEKOLOGIE 101(8):502-505, 1979.

Safe? Effective? Experts disagree on status of birth control today, by M. Carpenter. SCIENCE DIGEST 84:73-76, November, 1978.

Safe package deal. FAMILY HEALTH 10:14, September, 1978.

Safety last. OFF OUR BACKS 8(1):16, January, 1978.

US being urged to change stand on a birth drug. CHEMICAL MARKETING REPORTER 214:4+, August 14, 1978.

Variations in serum protein fractions following a continuous long term intake of eugynon and lyndiol by Iranian women, by S. Kamyab, et al. JOURNAL OF STEROID BIOCHEMISTRY 9(8):811-812, August, 1978.

Venereal disease: college students' knowledge and attitudes, by I. Arafat, et al. THE JOURNAL OF SEX RESEARCH 13(3):223-230, 1977.

BIRTH CONTROL: FAILURE
Failures following fimbriectomy: a further report, by K. G. Metz. FERTILITY AND STERILITY 30(3):269-273, September, 1978.

Postcoital contraception, by M. Beckmann, et al. MEDIZINISCHE WELT 29(40):1576-1578, October 6, 1978.

Postcoital contraception in primates. II. Examination of STS 153 and STS 287 as interceptives in the baboon (Papio hamadryas), by A. Komor, et al. ZENTRAL-BLATT FUR GYNAEKOLOGIE 100(22):1454-1458, 1978.

BIRTH CONTROL: HISTORY
Birth control in the eighteenth and nineteenth centuries in some Hungarian villages, by R. Andorka. LOCAL POPULATION STUDIES (22):38-43, Spring, 1979.

Contraception and its discontents: Sigmund Freud and birth control, by A. McLaren. JOURNAL OF SOCIAL HISTORY 12:513-529, Summer, 1979.

Parliament and birth control in the 1920s, by M. Simms. JOURNAL OF THE ROYAL COLLEGE OF GENERAL PRACTITIONERS 28(187):83-88, February, 1978.

BIRTH CONTROL: LAWS AND LEGISLATION
FDA revises birth pill warning. SPOKESWOMAN 8(9):7, March, 1978.

You and the law: teenagers, birth control and the nurse, by C. Sklar. CANADIAN NURSE 74(10):14-16, November, 1978.

BIRTH CONTROL: MALE
The antifertility actions of a-chlorohydrin in the male, by A. R. Jones. LIFE SCIENCES 23(16):1625-1646, 1978.

Cleaver: any man can. MOTHER JONES 3(3):10, April, 1978.

Condoms, by T. Thompson. MARKETING 84:6-7+, April 9, 1979.

BIRTH CONTROL: NATURAL
Avoid or achieve pregnancy naturally, by T. Guay. RAIN 4(9):6, July, 1978.

Co-operative method of natural birth control, by M. Nofziger. UNDERCURRENT 29:41, August, 1978.

Fertility awareness as a natural birth control, by C. Berry. MEDICAL SELF-CARE (4):24-29, 1978.

Mental birth control, by Jackson, et al. RAIN 5(3):14, December, 1978.

Natural birth control, by N. Dorr. WELL-BEING 35:18, August, 1978.

—, by L. LeMole. EAST WEST 8(6):6-58, June, 1978.

BIRTH CONTROL: PARENTERAL
Birth control by injection? from the sea: a possible revolution, by P. Lee. SCIENCE DIGEST 85:61, March, 1979.

BIRTH CONTROL: RESEARCH
Antifertility effects of the fruits of Piper longum in female rats, by S. D. Kholkute, et al. INDIAN JOURNAL OF EXPERIMENTAL BIOLOGY 17(3):289-290, March, 1979.

Antifertility effects of the steroid 5 alpha-stigmastane-3 beta, 5, 6 beta-triol 3-monobenzoate on mice, by A. Pakrashi, et al. CONTRACEPTION 19(2):145-150, February, 1979.

Electrophysiology of the rabbit oviduct following tubal microsurgery, by D. R. Archer, et al. FERTILITY AND STERILITY 31(4):423-427, April, 1979.

BIRTH CONTROL: TECHNIQUES
Current technics of birth control. CASOPIS LEKARU CESKYCH 118(13):415-416, March 30, 1979.

Dr. Ira Lubell's cautious crusade is working: sterilization becomes the no. 1 birth control technique, by P. Burstein. PEOPLE 10(24):71, December 11, 1978.

End-to-end tubal anastomosis using an absorbable stent, by A. H. Ansari. FERTILITY AND STERILITY 32(2): 197-201, August, 1979.

Falope ring application via culdoscopy, by S. M. Slim, et al. INTERNATIONAL JOURNAL OF GYNAECOLOGY AND OBSTETRICS 16(5):430-432, March-April, 1979.

Immunological procedure to regulate fertility, by V. C.
Stevens. BOLETIN DE LA OFICINA SANITARIA
PANAMERICANA 86(1):63-76, January, 1979.

Inhibition of ovulation in women by chronic treatment with
a stimulatoy LRH analogue–a new approach to birth
control, by S. J. Nillius, et al. CONTRACEPTION
17(6):537, June, 1978.

Permanent control of female fertility by surgical methods,
by A. de la Cruz Colorado, et al. GINECOLOGIA Y
OBSTETRICIA DE MEXICO 45(270):318-328, April,
1979.

Platelet aggregation during various phases of the menstrual
cycle and after therapy with ovulation inhibitors, by E.
E. Ohnhaus, et al. SCHWEIZERISCHE MEDIZINISCHE
WOCHENSCHRIFT 108(41):1580-1581, October 14,
1978.

Shifting of menstruation in female athletes, by J. Artner.
FORTSCHRITTE DER MEDIZIN 97(19):901-906,
May 17, 1979.

Sniff a day keeps pregnancy away, LRH analog nasal spray.
SCIENCE NEWS 116:133, August 25, 1979.

Supraventricular arrhythmia caused by ovulation inhibitors?
[letter], by C. Lauritzen. DEUTSCH MEDIZINISCHE
WOCHENSCHRIFT 104(17):613, April 27, 1979.

BIRTH CONTROL: UNDERDEVELOPED COUNTRIES
Transition may open up new ground, by T. N. Krishnan.
GUARDIAN p. 18, August 28, 1979.

BIRTH CONTROL AND HORMONES
Liver oncogenesis and steroids, by W. M. Christopherson, et
al. PROGRESS IN CLINICAL CANCER 7:153-163,
1978.

Pharmacological and clinical application of progestational hormone depot preparations, by J. Andor. GYNAE-KOLOGISCHE RUNDSCHAU 18(3-4):163-171, 1978.

Risk factors in endometrial carcinoma with special reference to the use of estrogens, by T. Salmi. ACTA OBSTETRI-CIA ET GYNECOLOGICA SCANDINAVICA (86):1-119, 1979.

3 further cases of icterus after taking estroprogestational agents and troleandomycin [letter], by J. Descotes, et al. NOUVELLE PRESSE MEDICALE 8(14):1182-1183, March 24, 1979.

BIRTH CONTROL AND HOSPITALS
The labs' search for safer birth control. BUSINESS WEEK 79(2581):40D, April 16, 1979.

BIRTH CONTROL AND MALES
Men and birth control, by K. Leishman. McCALLS 106:60, December, 1978.

BIRTH CONTROL AND THE MENTALLY RETARDED
Birth control denied to the mentally retarded, by M. S. Bass. THE HUMANIST 39:51-52, March, 1979.

Guide to birth control for trainable mentally retarded people, by J. D. Treubaft. MENTAL RETARDATION 26(3): 31-33, July, 1976.

BIRTH CONTROL AND NURSES
Teenagers, birth control and the nurse, by C. Sklar. CANAD-IAN NURSE 74:14-16, November, 1978.

BIRTH CONTROL AND THE PHYSICALLY HANDICAPPED
Guidelines to birth control counselling of the physically handicapped, by G. Szasz, et al. CANADIAN MEDICAL ASSOCIATION JOURNAL 120(11):1353-1368, June 9, 1979.

BIRTH CONTROL AND PHYSICIANS
Ask a doctor [teenagers], by W. Gifford-Jones. CHATE-
LAINE 52:10, September, 1979.

BIRTH CONTROL AND POLITICS
Bureaucracy minimizes birth control. OFF OUR BACKS
8(1):16, January, 1978.

Fay Wattleton has been appointed. NATIONAL NOW
11(3):2, March, 1978.

Pope John Paul I and birth control, by K. Withers. AMERI-
CA 140:233-234, March 24, 1979.

BIRTH CONTROL AND RELIGION
Fighting for the right to choose, by J. Condon. NEW
STATESMAN 98:295, August 31, 1979.

Pope John Paul I and birth control, by K. Withers. AMERI-
CA 140:233-234, March 24, 1979.

The sin of birth control: gone but not forgotten, by J. Breig.
U. S. CATHOLIC 44:6-12, January, 1979.

Tapestry: going to the barricades, by C. Perozino. AMERI-
CAN ATHEIST

BIRTH CONTROL AND YOUTH
Birth control for teenagers: diagram for disaster, by M.
Schwartz, et al. LINACRE QUARTERLY 46:71-81,
February, 1979.

The influence of others on teenagers' use of birth control, by
J. Cahn. DISSERTATION ABSTRACTS INTERNA-
TIONAL 39(3-B):1537, September, 1978.

Teenage birth control. SOCIETY 16:3, March, 1979.

Teenagers and pregnancy: the law in 1979 [the right of teen-

agers to consent for their own birth control and other reproductive health care; United States] , by E. W. Paul, et
al. FAMILY PLANNING PERSPECTIVES 11:297-302,
September-October, 1979.

Teenagers, birth control and the nurse, by C. Sklar. CANAD-
IAN NURSE 74:14-16, November, 1978.

You and the law: teenagers, birth control and the nurse, by C.
Sklar. CANADIAN NURSE 74(10):14-16, November, 1978.

BIRTH CONTROL COUNSELING
Guidelines to birth control counselling of the physically handi-
capped, by G. Szasz, et al. CANADIAN MEDICAL ASSO-
CIATION JOURNAL 120(11):1353-1368, June 9, 1979.

BIRTH CONTROL EDUCATION
Birth control guide. AMERICAN BABY 40:35-36+, November, 1978.

Birth control: how to choose what's best for you. McCALLS
106:65-67, October, 1978.

Practical problems in contraceptive counseling, by M. Vienonen. DUODECIM 95(2):55-62, 1979.

Pregnancy counselling: two views, by M. Scott, et al.
HEALTH AND SOCIAL SERVICE JOURNAL 88:766-
767, July 7, 1978.

Rising cost of birth control pills, by D. Clayton. FINAN-
CIAL POST 72:16, December 30, 1978.

CONTRACEPTION AND CONTRACEPTIVES
Antigenic cross-reactivity between human and marmoset
zonase pellucidae, potential target for immunocontraception, by C. A. Shivers, et al. JOURNAL OF MEDI-
CAL PRIMATOLOGY 7(4):242-248, 1978.

Contraception, by P. Senanayake. GUARDIAN p. 20, August 28, 1979.

—, by V. Lawrence. UNDERCURRENT 29:26, August, 1978.

Contraception after pregnancy, by E. J. Quilligan. JOURNAL OF REPRODUCTIVE MEDICINE 21(Suppl 5): 250-251, November, 1978.

Contraception at the crossroads, by C. Garcia. CONTEMPORARY OBSTETRICS AND GYNECOLOGY 13(1): 81, January, 1979.

Contraception before and after pregnancy, by P. Conquy. SOINS 24(2):3-6, January 20, 1979.

Contraception before pregnancy: evolution between 1972 and 1975 in the Rhone-Alpes region, by B. Blondel, et al. JOURNAL DE GYNECOLOGIE, OBSTETRIQUE ET BIOLOGIE DE LA REPRODUCTION 7(4):767-778, 1978.

The contraception consultant, by M. C. Smith, et al. AMERICAN PHARMACY 19(8):23-24, July, 1979.

Contraception: what's best for you, by M. Josephs. HARPER'S BAZAAR (3206):122B, January, 1979.

Contraceptive careers: toward a subjective approach to fertility regulating behaviour, by E. D. Boldt, et al. JOURNAL OF COMPARATIVE FAMILY STUDIES 8(3): 357-367, Fall, 1977.

A contraceptive device updated. NEWSWEEK 94:69, September 3, 1979.

Contraceptive evaluation, by H. Berendes. CONTRACEPTION 19(4):364-375, April, 1979.

The contraceptive habits of women applying for termination of pregnancy, by M. Wohlert, et al. UGESKRIFT FOR LAEGER 141(27):1863-1866, July 2, 1979.

Contraceptive PPIs called nearly useless. DRUG TOPICS 122:34, May 9, 1978.

Contraceptive practice after clinic discontinuation, by P. S. Cosgrove, et al. FAMILY PLANNING PERSPECTIVES 10(6):337-340, November-December, 1978.

Contraceptive practice before and after therapeutic abortion. II. Use-effectiveness of oral contraceptives and intrauterine devices, by P. Fylling, et al. FERTILITY AND STERILITY 32(1):24-27, July, 1979.

Current concepts in contraception: a discussion. JOURNAL OF REPRODUCTIVE MEDICINE 21(5 Suppl): 243-271, November, 1978.

Determination of fertility behavior in a non-contracepting population, by V. Jesudason. JOURNAL OF FAMILY WELFARE 24:3-13, March, 1978.

Development of a reversible vas deferens occlusive device. VI. Long-term evaluation of flexible prosthetic devices, by E. E. Brueschke, et al. FERTILITY AND STERILITY 31(5):575-586, May, 1979.

Diffusion of contraception through a tailoress—a study, by K. Mahadevan. JOURNAL OF FAMILY WELFARE 25:64-68, March, 1979.

Dr. Ira Lubell's cautious crusade is working: sterilization becomes the no. 1 birth control technique, by P. Burstein. PEOPLE 10(24):71, December 11, 1978.

Effect of the hippocampus on the luteinizing action of the adenohypophysis and contraceptive activity of mege-

stranol, by I. V. Tomilina. FARMAKOLOGIYA I
TOKSIKOLOGIYA 40(3):342-346, 1977.

Effect of the veneral diseases epidemic on the incidence of
ectopic pregnancy—implications for the evaluation of
contraceptives, by J. Urquhart. CONTRACEPTION
19(5):455-480, May, 1979.

An extended expectancy-value approach to contraceptive
alternatives, by J. B. Cohen, et al. JOURNAL OF POPU-
LATION 1(1):22-41, Spring, 1978.

Hormonal contraception today, by C. G. Nilsson. KATILO-
LEHTI 84(2):76-81, February, 1979.

Hot water as a tubal occluding agent, by T. S. Moulding, et
al. CONTRACEPTION 19(5):433-442, May, 1979.

In vivo evaluation of an effervescent intravaginal contraceptive insert by simulated coital activity, by W. H. Masters,
et al. FERTILITY AND STERILITY 32(2):161-165,
August, 1979.

A KAP study on MTP acceptors and their contraceptive practice, by M. Roy, et al. INDIAN JOURNAL OF PUBLIC
HEALTH 22(2):189-196, April-June, 1978.

Latest contraceptive gamble, by A. Connell. SEVEN DAYS
2(7):27, May 5, 1978.

Longitudinal predictive research: an approach to methodological problems in studying contraception, by B. Mindick,
et al. POPULATION 2(3):259, Fall, 1979.

The ovum, its milieu and possibilities for contraceptive at-
tack. Proceedings of a symposium of the Society for the
Study of Fertility and the World Health Organization,
Cambridge, July 1978. JOURNAL OF REPRODUC-
TION AND FERTILITY 55(1):221-275, January, 1979.

Pharmacology of the new steroid contraceptives, by V. V. Korkhov. AKUSHERSTVO I GINEKOLOGIIA (2):5-8, 1979.

Post-partum contraception, by H. Ruf, et al. JOURNAL DE GYNECOLOGIE, OBSTETRIQUE ET BIOLOGIE DE LA REPRODUCTION 7(3 Pt 2):590-595, April, 1978.

A re-appraisal of contraception: benefits v. risks. HEALTH VISITOR 52(4):157, April, 1979.

Routines for prescription of contraceptives (estrogen+gestagen), by B. I. Nesheim, et al. TIDSSKRIFT FOR DEN NORSKE LAEGEFORENING 99(3):180-181, February 28, 1979.

Special guide to contraception: what's new, what's right for you? by L. Cherry. GLAMOUR 77:287-290, April, 1979.

Steroid contraception and the risk of neoplasia [editorial]. SOUTH AFRICAN MEDICAL JOURNAL 54(19):763-764, November 4, 1978.

Surgical contraception: a key to normalization and prevention, by M. S. Bass. MENTAL RETARDATION 16: 399-404, December, 1978.

Taking control: a contraception guide, by S. Gregg. ESSENCE 10:46-48+, May, 1979.

Taking precautions, by B. Trench. NEW STATESMAN 97: 2-3, January 5, 1979.

Use of a radioreceptor test for HCG in women practicing contraception, by S. M. Shahani, et al. CONTRACEPTION 18(5):543-550, November, 1978.

The value of irreversible contraception, by O. Havemann,

et al. ZENTRALBLATT FUR GYNAEKOLOGIE 101(2):107-113, 1979.

What every woman should know. . .about "the pill" and other forms of contraception, by J. P Sauvage, et al. DIABETES FORECAST 32:14, January-February, 1979.

Which contraceptive to choose at age 40? INFIRMIERE FRANCAISE (199):21-25, November, 1978.

CONTRACEPTION AND CONTRACEPTIVES: COMPLICA-TIONS

Depot medroxyprogesterone acetate for contraception: a continuing controversy. INTERNATIONAL JOURNAL OF GYNAECOLOGY AND OBSTETRICS 16(5):433-441, March-April, 1979.

Effect of hormonal contraception on the fibrin-stabilizing factor (factor XIII), by M. Brandt, et al. ZENTRAL-BLATT FUR GYNAEKOLOGIE 100(17):1089-1092, 1978.

The effects of a once-a-week steroid contraceptive (R2323) on lipid and carbohydrate metabolism in women during three months of use, by W. N. Spellacy, et al. FER-TILITY AND STERILITY 30(3):289-292, September, 1978.

Evaluating acceptance strategies for timing of post-partum contraception, by R. G. Potter, et al. STUDIES IN FAMILY PLANNING 10(5):151, May, 1979.

Modern contraceptive substances, their use and complica-tions, by M. Kuprsanin. MEDICINSKI PREGLED 31(11-12):517-519, 1978.

Risk of adverse effects of contraception, by U. Larsson-Cohn. LAKARTIDNINGEN 75(41):3670-3672, October 11,

CONTRACEPTION AND CONTRACEPTIVES: COMPLICA-
TIONS

1978.

CONTRACEPTION AND CONTRACEPTIVES: LAWS
$5 million lawsuit over experimental contraceptive. OFF
OUR BACKS 8(11):7, December, 1978.

CONTRACEPTION AND CONTRACEPTIVES: RESEARCH
Action of oral contraceptive drugs on protein metabolism in
rats, by M. T. Khayyal, et al. JOURNAL OF THE
EGYPTIAN MEDICAL ASSOCIATION 60(7-8):633-
638, 1977.

Changes in laboratory tests after treatment with a new contraception agent, by L. F. Cervantes, et al. GINECO-
LOGIA Y OBSTETRICIA DE MEXICO 43(258):285-
297, April, 1978.

Chronic occlusion of the monkey fallopian tube with silicone
polymer, by R. H. Davis, et al. OBSTETRICS AND
GYNECOLOGY 53(4):527-529, April, 1979.

Clinical applications in the area of contraceptive development, by K. J. Ryan. ADVANCES IN EXPERIMENT-
AL MEDICINE AND BIOLOGY 112:737-742, 1979.

Clinical experience with implant contraception, by E. Coutinho. CONTRACEPTION 18(4):411, October, 1978.

Clinical experience wtih a low dose oral contraceptive con-
taining norethisterone and ethinyl oestradiol, by E. M.
Morigi, et al. CURRENT MEDICAL RESEARCH AND
OPINION 5(8):655-662, 1978.

Comparative electron microscopic studies on benign liver
tumors and jaundice associated with contraceptive drugs,
by M. Balázs. MORPHOLOGIAI ES IGAZSUGUGYI
ORVOSI SZEMLE 19(1):1-9, January, 1979.

Contraceptive acceptability research: its utility and limitations, by A. Keller. STUDIES IN FAMILY PLANNING 10:230-237, August-September, 1979.

Contraceptive development, by G. Bialy. CONTRACEP-TION 19(4):353-363, April, 1979.

Contraceptive device updated; cervical cap, by L. Seligmann. NEWSWEEK 94:69, September 3, 1979.

Contraceptive effects of intravaginal application of acrosin and hyaluronidase inhibitors in rabbit, by C. Joyce, et al. CONTRACEPTION 19(1):95-106, January, 1979.

Contraceptive effects of native plants in rats, by M. O. Guerra, et al. CONTRACEPTION 18(2):191-199, August, 1978.

Contraceptive properties of endotoxin in rabbits, by M. J. Harper, et al. FERTILITY AND STERILITY 31(4): 441-447, April, 1979.

Contraceptive research and population growth. FAMILY PLANNING PERSPECTIVES 10:294-297, September-October, 1978.

Contraceptive research funding: eroded by inflation, increasingly dependent upon government support. DRAPER FUND REPORT pp. 16-17, Summer, 1978.

Contraceptive technology: coming into its own? by L. Lohr. AMERICAN PHARMACY 18(10):42-45, September, 1978.

Contraceptive tetrapeptide in hamster embryos [letter], by H. A. Kent, Jr. FERTILITY AND STERILITY 31(5): 595, May, 1979.

Evaluation of polymer flock and metal alloy intra-tubal device in pigtail monkeys, by R. M. Richart, et al. CON-TRACEPTION 18(5):459-468, November, 1978.

$5 million lawsuit over experimental contraceptive. OFF OUR BACKS 8(11):7, December, 1978.

Improving contraceptive technology [eight articles] . DRAP-ER FUND REPORT pp. 3-30, Summer, 1978.

Interaction of local anesthesia and chronic treatment of con-traceptive medication in the rabbit, by P. Henry, et al. BULLETIN DE L'ACADAMIE DE CHIRURQU DEN-TAIRE 23(23):53-58, 1977-1978.

Mammary neoplasia in animals: pathologic aspects and the ef-fects of contraceptive steroids, by H. W. Casey, et al. RE-CENT RESULTS IN CANCER RESEARCH 66:129-160, 1979.

New frontiers of contraception, by D. R. Mishell, Jr. JOUR-NAL OF REPRODUCTIVE MEDICINE 21(4 Suppl): 254-256, November, 1978.

Reaction of vaginal tissue of rabbits to inserted sponges made of various materials, by M. Chavpil, et al. JOURNAL OF BIOMEDICAL MATERIALS RESEARCH 13(1):1-13, January, 1979.

Research pitfalls. THE ECONOMIST 266:26, January 21, 1978.

Search for the ideal contraceptive speeds up. DRUG TOPICS 123:26, January 5, 1979.

Studies in mice on the mutagenicity of two contraceptive drugs, by M. E. Wallace, et al. JOURNAL OF MEDICAL GENETICS 16(3):206-209, June, 1979.

Trials start for nasal-spray contraceptive [for women or men] . MEDICAL WORLD NEWS 19:58, August 21, 1978.

Why research into contraception faces a barren future, by

P. Chorlton. GUARDIAN p. 2, December 31, 1979.

CONTRACEPTION AND CONTRACEPTIVES: TECHNIQUES
Contraception using 3-monthly injections of depo-provera, by C. Revax, et al. GYNAEKOLOGISCHE RUND-SCHAU 18(3-4):183-192, 1978.

Status and developmental trends of immunologic contraceptive technics, by H. Donat. ZENTRALBLATT FUR GYNAEKOLOGIE 101(7):433-441, 1979.

CONTRACEPTIVE AGENTS
Anti-fertility effect of non-steroidal anti-inflammatory drugs, by R. Yegnanarayan, et al. JAPNESE JOURNAL OF PHARMACOLOGY 28(6):909-917, December, 1978.

Intranasal gonadotropin-releasing hormone agonist as a contraceptive agent, by C. Bergquist, et al. LANCET 2(8136):215-217, August 4, 1979.

CONTRACEPTIVE AGENTS: COMPLICATIONS
Abnormalities among offspring of oral and nonoral contraceptive users, by H. E. Ortiz-Pérez, et al. AMERICAN JOURNAL OF OBSTETRICS AND GYNECOLOGY 134(5): 512-517, July 1, 1979.

CONTRACEPTIVE CLINICS
Contraception at Port Elizabeth clinics [letter], by A. A. Gordon. SOUTH AFRICAN MEDICAL JOURNAL 54(11):424, September 9, 1978.

CONTRACEPTIVE COUNSELING
Counseling patients for contraception, by G. R. Huggins. CLINICAL OBSTETRICS AND GYNECOLOGY 22(2):509-520, June, 1979.

CONTRACEPTIVE METHODS
Contraception—a choice of methods, by W. E. Small. AMERICAN PHARMACY 19(8):16-22, July, 1979.

CONTRACEPTIVE METHODS

Contraceptive methods: risks and benefits, by M. P. Vessey.
BRITISH MEDICAL JOURNAL 2(6139):721-722, September 9, 1978.

Need new contraceptive method in next decade to make a major
impact on population growth. FAMILY PLANNING PER-
SPECTIVES 10(5):294-295, September-October, 1978.

CONTRACEPTIVE RISKS
Contraceptive risk taking among women entering a family
planning clinic, by E. E. Hall. DISSERTATION AB-
STRACTS INTERNATIONAL 38(10-B):5017, April,
1978.

Contraceptive risk-taking in white and black unwed females,
by H. Harari, et al. JOURNAL OF SEX RESEARCH
15:56-63, February, 1979.

CONTRACEPTIVES (GENERAL)
Contraceptive effectiveness warning issued; spermicide, encare oval. FDA CONSUMER 12:4, September, 1978.

Contraceptive efficacy of encare oval [letter], by B. A. Harris, Jr. FERTILITY AND STERILITY 31(5):595, May,
1979.

Contraceptives, by S. Koslow. LADIES HOME JOURNAL
96:82+, September, 1979.

Contraceptives: your questions answered, by D. Partie.
MADEMOISELLE 85:85-86+, August, 1979.

Effects of antiprogesterone on pregnancy: I. Midpregnancy,
by A. I. Csapo, et al. AMERICAN JOURNAL OF OB-
STETRICS AND GYNECOLOGY 133(2):176-183,
1979.

Evaluation of local contraceptives, by E. B. Connell. ZAH-
NAERZTLICHE MITTEILUNGEN 69(15):919, August

1, 1979.

Population control: the next steps; education, an "ideal contraceptive," and a new world economic order, by R. M. Salas, et al. ATLAS 26:20-22, September, 1979.

Post-coital antifertility activity of annona squamosa and ipomoea fistulosa, by A. Mishra, et al. PLANTA MEDICA 35(3):283-285, March, 1979.

Psycho-social correlates of regular contraceptive use in young unmarried women, by E. M. Smith. DISSERTATION ABSTRACTS INTERNATIONAL 39(3-A):1845, September, 1978.

Sex guilt and contraceptive use, by M. L. Upchurch. JOURNAL OF SEX EDUCATION AND THERAPY 4:27-31, Spring-Summer, 1978.

BANGLADESH
Contraceptive distribution in Bangladesh villages: the initial impact, by D. H. Huber, et al. STUDIES IN FAMILY PLANNING 10:246, August-September, 1979.

The pill in Bangladesh, by T. Dejanikus. OFF OUR BACKS 9:12, May, 1979.

CHINA
Chinese say their pill works for men. MEDICAL WORLD NEWS 20:13+, February 5, 1979.

From China: new pill for men, by D. Fortino. HARPER'S BAZAAR (3211):129, June, 1979.

Male pill; gossypol pill developed in China, by J. Seligmann, et al. NEWSWEEK 93:84, January 22, 1979.

Thousands try male "pill" in China, by W. Sullivan. NEW

CHINA
YORK TIMES p. C1, September 25, 1979.

EL SALVADOR
Contraceptive use and demographic trends in El Salvador, by L. Morris, et al. STUDIES IN FAMILY PLANNING 10(2):43, February, 1979.

FRANCE
Contraceptive practice in France in 1978, by H. Leridon. FAMILY PLANNING PERSPECTIVES 11(3):153, May-June, 1979.

Primary liver neoplasms due to estroprogestational agents: 1st results of a registry opened in France [letter], by G. Rauber, et al. NOUVELLE PRESSE MEDICALE 8(23):1945, May 26, 1979.

DENMARK
Randomized comparison of clinical performance of two copper-releasing IUDs, Nova-T and Copper-T-200, in Denmark, Finland and Sweden, by T. Luukkainen, et al. CONTRACEPTION 19(1):1-10, 1979.

FINLAND
Randomized comparison of clinical performance of two copper-releasing IUDs, Nova-T and Copper-T-200, in Denmark, Finland and Sweden, by T. Luukkainen, et al. CONTRACEPTION 19(1):1-10, 1979.

GREAT BRITAIN
Personality and the use of oral contraceptives in British university students, by R. Priestnall, et al. SOCIAL SCIENCE AND MEDICINE 12(5A):403-407, September, 1978.

UK women plot suits in US over pill ills, by J. H. Miller. BUSINESS INSURANCE 13:4, May 28, 1979.

INDIA
Contraceptive status in a community attached to a hospital in Delhi, by A. K. Madan, et al. JOURNAL OF FAMILY WELFARE 24:44-49, June, 1978.

JAPAN
Induced abortion and contraceptive method choice among urban Japanese marrieds, by S. J. Coleman. DISSERTATION ABSTRACTS INTERNATIONAL 39(4-A):2381-2382, October, 1978.

KENYA
The application of market research in contraceptive social marketing in a rural area of Kenya, by T. R. L. Black, et al. MARKET RESEARCH SOCIETY. JOURNAL 21:30-43, January, 1979.

NEW ZEALAND
Abortion: some observations on the contraceptive practice of women referred for psychiatric assessment in Dunedin, by D. J. Lord. NEW ZEALAND MEDICAL JOURNAL 88(626):487-489, December, 1978.

PAKISTAN
Past and current contraceptive use in Pakistan, by N. M. Shah. STUDIES IN FAMILY PLANNING 10(5): 164, May, 1979.

PARAGUAY
Contraceptive prevalence in Paraguay, by L. Morris, et al. STUDIES IN FAMILY PLANNING 9(10-11): 272-279, October-November, 1978.

THE PHILIPPINES
Continued use of contraception among Philippine family planning acceptors: a multivariate analysis, by J. F. Phillips. STUDIES IN FAMILY PLANNING 9(7): 182, July, 1978.

THE PHILIPPINES
A program of IUD insertions by paraprofessionals and physicians in the Philippines, by R. Ramos, et al. INTERNATIONAL JOURNAL OF GYNAECOLOGY AND OBSTETRICS 16(4):321-323, 1978-1979.

SPAIN
Spain legalizes contraception, by M. Jones. POPULI 5(4):3, 1978.

SWEDEN
Randomized comparison of clinical performance of two copper-releasing IUDs, Nova-T and Copper-T-200, in Denmark, Finland and Sweden, by T. Luukkainen, et al. CONTRACEPTION 19(1):1-10, 1979.

Swedish contraceptive uses brain hormone. BRAIN/MIND 3(17):3, July, 1979.

UNITED STATES
Contraceptive use in the United States, 1973-1976, by K. Ford. FAMILY PLANNING PERSPECTIVES 10(5):264, September-October, 1978.

Minors and medical contraceptive services in Connecticut, by D. W. Schneider. CONNECTICUT MEDICINE 42(8):523-527, August, 1978.

A National Fertility Survey [VI] : the contraceptive methods used by Belgian and American couples: an application of dependency analysis, by P. Guilmot. POPULATION ET FAMILLE 3(33):61-130, 1974.

Patterns of aggregate and individual changes in contraceptive practice. United States, 1965-1975, by C. F. Westoff, et al. VITAL HEALTH STATISTICS 3(17):iii-vi+, June, 1979.

Sterilization and pill top U.S. birth control methods.

UNITED STATES
SPOKESWOMAN 9(5):6, November, 1978.

Two-million ever-married women are IUD users: Lippes Loop most popular, followed by Copper-7. FAMILY PLANNING PERSPECTIVES 11:119-120, March-April, 1979.

UK women plot suits in US over pill ills, by J. H. Miller. BUSINESS INSURANCE 13:4, May 28, 1979.

CONTRACEPTIVES: ADVERTISING
Amore senza bambini gaining Italian favor, by E. Durie. ADVERTISING AGE 49:92, July 10, 1978.

The application of market research in contraceptive social marketing in a rural area of Kenya, by T. R. L. Black, et al. MARKET RESEARCH SOCIETY. JOURNAL 21: 30-43, January, 1979.

Community-based and commercial contraceptive distribution: an inventory and appraisal, by J. R. Foreit, et al. POPULATION REPORTS (19):1, March, 1978.

Condom ads aim at the youth market, by T. Thompson. MARKETING 83:18, November 27, 1978.

Datelene Europe [it was quite an innocent ad], by P. Wilson-Ferrill. MARKETING 83:15, October 30, 1978.

FDA criticizes contraceptives ads. PREVENTION 30:204, October, 1978.

Norwich intro spurs new posture in marketing of contraceptives, by G. Zern. PRODUCT MARKETING 6:1+, December, 1977.

P&G explores contraceptives, by L. Edwards. ADVERTISING AGE 49:3+, October 23, 1978.

P&G's contraceptive work could shake up market, by L. Edwards. ADVERTISING AGE 49:6, October 30, 1978.

Package primer; out of the closet and onto the shelf, by R. Glaxton. DRUG AND COSMETIC INDUSTRY 124: 76, February, 1979.

Schmid still struggles to place contraceptive ads, by M. Christopher. ADVERTISING AGE 49:2+, May 22, 1978.

This ad really works, by E. J. Wood. MARKETING 83:16, January 23, 1978.

CONTRACEPTIVES: ATTITUDES
American values and contraceptive acceptance, by J. R. Rzepka. JOURNAL OF RELIGION AND HEALTH 18:241-250, July, 1979.

Changes in sexual behavior among unmarried teenage women utilizing oral contraception, by P. A. Reichelt. JOURNAL OF POPULATION 1(1):57-68, Spring, 1978.

A comparison of the factors influencing husband and wife decisions about contraception, by H. M. Baum. DISSERTATION ABSTRACTS INTERNATIONAL 39(2-B): 671, August, 1978.

Holistic approach to contraception, by M. Kernis. COUNTRY WOMEN 27:52, December, 1977.

Relationship between contraceptive sex role stereotyping and attitudes toward contraception among males, by S. A. Weinstein, et al. JOURNAL OF SEX RESEARCH 15: 235-242, August, 1979.

A renewed focus on contraception, by B. Gupte. POPULI 5(3):45, 1978.

Socialization factors in contraceptive attitudes: role of affective responses, parental attitudes, and sexual experience, by K. Kelley. JOURNAL OF SEX RESEARCH 15:6-20, February, 1979.

CONTRACEPTIVES: BARRIER

Barrier contraception methods: the role of the pharmacist, by R. A. Hatcher. AMERICAN DRUGGIST 178:28+, August, 1979.

Barrier contraceptives: your questions answered, by D. Partie. MADEMOISELLE 85(8):85, August, 1979.

Barrier methods of contraception: they can be highly effective, by E. B. Connell. STUDIES IN FAMILY PLANNING 10(3):110-111, March, 1979.

Barrier methods: renewed interest, but more research needed, by D. Maine. FAMILY PLANNING PERSPECTIVES 11:237-240, July-August, 1979.

Contraceptive workload in general practice in the Trent Region, by D. W. Cammock, et al. JOURNAL OF THE ROYAL COLLEGE OF GENERAL PRACTICIONERS 27(183):610-613, October, 1977.

Contraceptives: the barrier methods are back, by T. Gorman. DRUG TOPICS 123:62-65, April 6, 1979.

Intelligent woman's guide to sex, diaphragm or pill, by J. Coburn. MADEMOISELLE 84:68, November, 1978.

Off the pill; new slant on the old diaphragm [smaller, uniform-size diaphragm] ; how to use the diaphragm, by V. Cava-Rizzuto. MAJORITY REPORT 8:8-9, September 30-October 13, 1978.

Questions about the diaphragm; pills and weight gain, by P. Sarrel, et al. REDBOOK 152:43+, January, 1979.

Teaching successful use of the diaphragm, by L. L. Gorline. AMERICAN JOURNAL OF NURSING 79:1732-1735, October, 1979.

Vaginal lesion: etiology—a malfitting diaphragm? by M. V. Widhalm. JOURNAL OF NURSE-MIDWIFERY 24:39-40, September-October, 1979.

CONTRACEPTIVES: COMPLICATIONS

Advantages and risks of different contraceptives, by B. Westerholm. LAKARTIDNINGEN 75(45):4123-4124, November 8, 1978.

Altered plasma lipid and lipoprotein levels associated with oral contraceptive and oestrogen use. Report from the Medications Working Group of the Lipid Research Clinics Program, by R. B. Wallace, et al. LANCET 2(8134):112-115, July 21, 1979.

Arcus senilis-like degeneration of the cornea following a probable lipid metabolic disorder due to the use of contraceptives, by N. Zolog. REVISTA DE: CHIRURGIE ONCOLOGIE RADIOLOGIE ORL OFTALMOLOGIE, STONATOLOGIE, OFTALMOLOGIA 23(1):69-72, January-March, 1979.

Artenal hypertension and oral contraceptives, by J. Lekieffre. ANNALES DE CARDIOLOGIE ET D'ANGEIOLOGIE 28(1):35-39, January-February, 1979.

Beneficial effects of contraceptive doses and large doses of medroxyprogesterone in the prevention and treatment of uterine hyperplasia, by J. Bonte. GYNAEKOLOGISCHE RUNDSCHAU 18(3-4):172-182, 1978.

Changes in the endometrium from the use of hormonal preparations and hormonal contraceptives, by G. Jellinek. ARKHIV PATOLOGII 40(11):36-45, 1978.

Chorea complicating oral contraceptive therapy. Case report and review of the literature, by W. A. Pulsinelli, et al. AMERICAN JOURNAL OF MEDICINE 65(3):557-559, September, 1978.

Complications of the new contraceptive preparations, by J. Clinch. IRISH MEDICAL JOURNAL 71(1):513-514, October 31, 1978.

Contraception in the cardiac patient, by R. Taurelle, et al. JOURNAL DE GYNECOLOGIE, OBSTETRIQUE ET BIOLOGIE DE LA REPRODUCTION 7(1):111-118, 1978.

Contraception in diabetic women, by G. Cathelineau. SE-MAINE DES HOPITAUX DE PARIS 54(45-46):1462-1464+, December, 1978.

Contraceptive-associated hepatic tumor, by K. T. Benedict, Jr., et al. AJR INFORMATION 132(3):452-454, March, 1979.

Contraceptive continuation in high-risk women, by M. D. Hoyos, et al. WEST INDIAN MEDICAL JOURNAL 27(4):196-200, December, 1978.

Contraceptive knowledge: antecedents and implications, by R. O. Hansson, et al. FAMILY COORDINATOR 28(1): 29-34, January, 1979.

Depo-provera and contraceptive risk: a case study of values in conflict, by C. Levine. HASTINGS CENTER REPORT 9:8-11, August, 1979.

Effect of copper intra-Fallopian tube device on the bio-chemical responses of rabbit Fallopian tube, by A. Kush-wah, et al. INDIAN JOURNAL OF EXPERIMENTAL BIOLOGY 16(8):928-929, August, 1978.

Effect of an estrogen-progestin contraceptive preparation on the enzymatic activity of the pentosephosphate carbohydrate metabolic pathway and nucleic acid metabolic indices, by V. V. Korukhov, et al. FARMAKOLOGIYA I TOKSIKOLOGIYA 41(5):604-608, September-October, 1978.

Effect of racemic and S(+) alpha-chlorohydrin-1-phosphate on glyceraldehyde-3-phosphate dehydrogenase in relation to its contraceptive action, by R. W. Fitzpatrick, et al. CONTRACEPTION 18(5):477-483, November, 1978.

Effect of salt consumption, psychological stress and contraceptives on the course of blood pressure in rats with hereditary spontaneous hypertension (SH rats), by A. Samizadeh, et al. VERHANDLUNGEN DER DEUTSCHEN GESELLSCHAFT FUR INNERE MEDIZIN (84):803-806, 1978.

Focal nodular hyperplasia of the liver and contraceptive steroids, by F. B. St. Omer, et al. ACTA HEPATOGASTROENTEROLOGICA 25(4):319-321, August, 1978.

Follow-up observation of the so-called normophasic method of hormonal contraception, by H. Fritzsche, et al. ZEITSCHRIFT FUR AERZTLICHE FORTBILDUNG 73(3): 113-114, February 1, 1979.

Hepatic neoplasms associated with contraceptive and anabolic steroids, by K. G. Ishak. RECENT RESULTS IN CANCER RESEARCH 66:73-128, 1979.

Influence of hormonal contraception on serum lipoproteins, by D. Pometta, et al. SCHWEIZERISCHE MEDIZINISCHE WOCHENSCHRIFT 108(50):2012-2015, December 16, 1978.

Inner ear disturbance following long-term usage of hormonal

contraceptives, by G. Okulicz. HNO 26(10):330-334, October, 1978.

Liver tumors as adverse effects of contraceptives, by H. Heiss-meyer, et al. VERHANDLUNGEN DER DEUTSCHEN GESELLSCHAFT FUR INNERE MEDIZIN (84):1612-1614, 1978.

Pitfalls in contraception, by B. W. Simcock. AUSTRALIAN FAMILY PHYSICIAN 7(10):1243-1251, October, 1978.

CONTRACEPTIVES: DEVELOPING COUNTRIES
The charge: gynocide; the accused: the U.S. government [distribution under aid programs of contraceptives and contraceptive devices to developing countries which have been banned in the United States], by B. Ehrenreich, et al. MOTHER JONES 4:26-31+, November, 1979.

Contraceptive distribution in Bangladesh villages: the initial impact, by D. H. Huber, et al. STUDIES IN FAMILY PLANNING 10:246, August-September, 1979.

CONTRACEPTIVES: FAILURE
Abortion: reward for conscientious contraceptive use, by E. R. Allgeier, et al. JOURNAL OF SEX RESEARCH 15: 64-75, February, 1979.

A longitudinal study of success versus failure in contraceptive planning, by S. Oskamp, et al. JOURNAL OF POPULATION 1(1):69-83, Spring, 1978.

Psychological dimensions of effective and ineffective contraceptive use in adolescent girls, by J. S. Spain. DISSERTATION ABSTRACTS INTERNATIONAL 38(7-B): 3373-3374, January, 1978.

CONTRACEPTIVES: FEMALE: COMPLICATIONS
Contraceptives for women in their forties? by G. A. Hauser. GYNAEKOLOGISCHE RUNDSHAU 18(3-4):193-212,

1978.

The problem of hypertension and ovulation inhibitors, by I. Weise, et al. ZEITSCHRIFT FUR DIE GESAMTE INNERE MEDIZIN 34(11):320-322, June 1, 1979.

CONTRACEPTIVES: FEMALE: IUD
Dalkon Shield: a "primer" in IUD liability, by J. M. Van Dyke. WESTERN STATE UNIVERSITY LAW REVIEW 6:1-52, Fall, 1978.

IUD information. CONGRESSIONAL QUARTERLY WEEKLY REPORT 35:922, May 14, 1977.

IUD questionnaire. SPOKESWOMAN 9(2):8, August, 1978.

IUDs and oral contraceptives. A follow-up study of 504 women, by A. Bergqvist, et al. LAKARTIDNINGEN 76(3): 125-128,

Intrauterine copper contraceptive. OFF OUR BACKS 8(10):5, November, 1978.

The nulliparous patient, the IUD, and subsequent fertility. BRITISH MEDICAL JOURNAL 6132:233, July 22, 1978.

Postabortion intrauterine device, by C. Morales Lepe, et al. GINECOLOGIA Y OBSTETRICIA DE MEXICO 43(260):429-432, June, 1978.

CONTRACEPTIVES: FEMALE: IUD: COMPLICATIONS
Abortifacient effect of intrauterine contraceptive devices? by P. J. Keller, et al. GYNECOLOGIC INVESTIGA-TION 9(4):219-221, 1978.

The causes, diagnosis and treatment of perforations of the uterus by intrauterine devices, by A. Treisser, et al. JOURNAL DE GYNECOLOGIE, OBSTETRIQUE ET

BIOLOGIE DE LA REPRODUCTION 7(4):837-848, 1978.

Complications with use of IUD and oral contraceptives among Navajo women, by J. C. Slocumb, et al. PUBLIC HEALTH REPORTS 94(3):243-247, June, 1979.

Copper intrauterine devices and the small intestine, by P. J. M. Watney. BRITISH MEDICAL JOURNAL 6132:255-256, July 22, 1978.

Development of an estriol-releasing intrauterine device, by R. W. Baker, et al. JOURNAL OF PHARMACEUTICAL STUDIES 68(1):20-26, 1979.

Febrile spontaneous abortion and the IUD, by R. J. Kim-Farley, et al. CONTRACEPTION 18(6):561-570, December, 1978.

Genital actinomycosis and intrauterine contraceptive devices. Cytopathologic diagnosis and clinical signifiance, by B. S. Bhagavan, et al. HUMAN PATHOLOGY 9(5):567-578, September, 1978.

Immediate postabortion intrauterine contraception in nulliparous adolescents, by J. A. Goldman, et al. ISRAEL JOURNAL OF MEDICAL SCIENCES 15(6):522-525, June, 1979.

Oral and intrauterine contraception: a 1978 risk assessment, by A. Rosenfield. AMERICAN JOURNAL OF OBSTETRICS AND GYNECOLOGY 132(1):92-106, September 1, 1978.

Patients treated for gynecologic cancer after use of oral contraceptives and IUD, by M. Szegvárie, et al. ORVOSI HETILAP 120(13):756-758, April 1, 1979.

The pregnancy occuring during oral contraception or intra

uterine device (i.u.d.), by A. Brémond, et al. JOURNAL DE GYNECOLOGIE, OBSTETRIQUES, ET BIOLOGIE DE LA REPRODUCTION 7(3 Pt 2):581-589, April, 1978.

The progesterone releasing I.U.D. Its indications in function of the menstrual disorders, by P. Bourgoin. JOURNAL DE GYNECOLOGIE, OBSTETRIQUE ET BIOLOGIE DE LA REPRODUCTION 7(8):1447-1451, December, 1978.

Randomized comparison of clinical performance of two copper-releasing IUDs, Nova-T and Copper-T-200, in Denmark, Finland and Sweden, by T. Luukkainen, et al. CONTRACEPTION 19(1):1-10, 1979.

Safety of intrauterine devices, by J. Guillebaud. STUDIES IN FAMILY PLANNING 10:174-176, May, 1979.

Septic abortion and acute renal failure in a patient with an intrauterine contraceptive device, by C. M. Wiles, et al. INTERNATIONAL JOURNAL OF GYNAECOLOGY AND OBSTETRICS 15(5):464-465, 1978.

Serum prolactin levels in short-term and long-term use of inert plastic and copper intrauterine devices, by M. Wenof, et al. CONTRACEPTION 19(1):21-28, 1979.

CONTRACEPTIVES: FEMALE: IUD: RESEARCH
Comparative IUD study: Lippes Loop D, Dalkon Shield and TCu-200, by M. Medel, et al. INTERNATIONAL JOURNAL OF GYNAECOLOGY AND OBSTETRICS 16(2): 157-161, 1978-1979.

IUDs—update on safety, effectiveness, and research. POPULATION REPORTS 7(3):1, May, 1979.

Morphologic studies on IUD-induced metrorrhagia: I. Endometrial changes and clinical correlations, by S. T. Shaw,

Jr., et al. CONTRACEPTION 19(1):47-62, 1979.

Reaction of vaginal tissue of rabbits to inserted sponges made of various materials, by M. Chvapil, et al. JOURNAL OF BIOMEDICAL MATERIALS RESEARCH 13(1):1-13, January, 1979.

CONTRACEPTIVES: FEMALE: IUD: TECHNIQUES
Actinomyces and the IUD. EMERGENCY MEDICINE 11: 48, August 15, 1979.

A collaborative study of the progesterone intrauterine device (Progestasert), by J. Newton, et al. CONTRACEPTION 19(6): , June, 1979.

Combined and national experience of postmenstrual IUD insertions of Nova-T and Copper-T in a randomized study, by T. Luukkainen, et al. CONTRACEPTION 19(1):11-20, 1979.

A program of IUD insertions by paraprofessionals and physicians in the Philippines, by R. Ramos, et al. INTERNATIONAL JOURNAL OF GYNAECOLOGY AND OBSTETRICS 16(4):321-323, 1978-1979.

CONTRACEPTIVES: FEMALE: IMPLANTED
Contraception with acting subdermal implants, by E. Coutinho, et al. CONTRACEPTION 18(4):315, October, 1978.

Contraception with the intrauterine pessary Progestasert, by K. W. Schweppe, et al. FORTSCHRITTE DU MEDIZIN 96(33):1685-1690, September 7, 1978.

CONTRACEPTIVES: FEMALE: IMPLANTED: COMPLICATIONS
Metabolic and endocrine studies in women using norethindrone acetate implant, by S. M. Shahani, et al. CONTRACEPTION 19(2):135-144, February, 1979.

Neoplasia and dysplasia of the cervix uteri and contraception: a possible protective effect of the diaphragm, by
N. H. Wright, et al. BRITISH JOURNAL OF CANCER
38(2):273-279, August, 1978.

Pure crystalline estradiol pellet implantation for contraception, by R. H. Asch, et al. INTERNATIONAL JOUR-
NAL OF FERTILITY 23(2):100-105, 1978.

CONTRACEPTIVES: FEMALE: ORAL
Former pill users: healthier babies? MEDICAL WORLD
NEWS 19:32, June 12, 1978.

IUDs and oral contraceptives. A follow-up study of 504 women, by A. Bergqvist, et al. LAKARTIDNINGEN
76(3):125-128,

In defense of the pill, by J. W. Goldzieher. GINECOLOGIA
Y OBSTETRICIA DE MEXICO 44(262):123-152,
August, 1978.

Intelligent woman's guide to sex: diaphragm or pill, by J.
Coburn. MADEMOISELLE 84:68, November, 1978.

Oral contraceptives and vitamins, by E. Heilmann. DEUTSCH
MEDIZINISCHE WOCHENSCHRIFT 104(4):144-146,
January 26, 1979.

Patient attitudes about two forms of printed oral contraceptive information, by M. Mazis, et al. MEDICAL CARE
16(12):1045-1054, December, 1978.

Physiological and psychological effects of vitamins E and B6
on women taking oral contraceptives, by W. V. Applegate, et al. INTERNATIONAL JOURNAL FOR VITA-
MIN AND NUTRITION RESEARCH 49(1):43-50,
1979.

Pill: a cleaner bill of health. MACLEAN'S 91:53, October 9,

1978.

A promising new low-dose "pill." NURSES DRUG ALERT
3:46-47, April, 1979.

Sex hormone binding globulin capacity as an index of oestrogenicity or androgenicity in women on oral contraceptive steroids, by M. N. El Makhzangy, et al. CLINICAL
ENDOCRINOLOGY 10(1):39-45, January, 1979.

Sterile days for drug firms as women shy from the pill, by
D. Clayton. FINANCIAL POST 72:1+, December 30,
1978.

Use and acceptance of the 'paper pill'. A novel approach to
oral contraception, by R. R. Damm, et al. CONTRA-
CEPTION 19(3):273-281, March, 1979.

CONTRACEPTIVES: FEMALE: ORAL: COMPLICATIONS
Acute intermittent porphyria on withdrawal of oral contra-
ceptives, by L. S. Gerlis. JOURNAL OF INTERNA-
TIONAL MEDICAL RESEARCH 6(4):255-256, 1978.

B-scan ultrasonography in the diagnosis of oral-contraceptive
related optic neuritis, by G. A. German. JOURNAL OF
AMERICAN OPTOMETRIC ASSOCIATION 50(2):243-
244, February, 1979.

Blessing and a curse: must she who lives by the pill also fear
dying by it? by J. Webb. MACLEAN'S 91:55-58+,
April 17, 1978.

Cardiovascular disease and oral contraceptives: a reappraisal
of vital statistics data, by M. A. Belsey, et al. FAMILY
PLANNING PERSPECTIVES 11(2):84-89, March-April,
1979.

Cardiovascular risks and oral contraceptives [editorial].
LANCET 1(8125):1063, May 19, 1979.

Case-control of oral contraceptive pills and endometrial cancer, by R. I. Horwitz, et al. ANNALES DE MEDECINE INTERNE 91(2):226-227, August, 1979.

Central retinal vascular occlusion associated with oral contraceptives, by G. C. Stowe, 3d, et al. AMERICAN JOURNAL OF OPTHALMOLOGY 86(6):798-801, December, 1978.

Cholestatic jaundice after administration of triacetyloleandomycin: interaction with oral contraceptives? 10 cases [letter], by J. P. Miguet, et al. NOUVELLE PRESSE MEDICALE 7(47):43-4, December 30, 1978.

Cholestatic jaundice in women taking triacetyloleandomycin and oral contraceptives simultaneously [letter], by D. Goldfain, et al. NOUVELLE PRESSE MEDICALE 8(13):1099, March 17, 1979.

Chromosome abnormalities in oral contraceptive breakthrough pregnancies [letter], by S. Harlap, et al. LANCET 1(8130):1342-1343, June 23, 1979.

Comparison of the sebaceous secretions of the skin of the forehead under the treatment with three oral contraceptives. Diane, Neogynon and Lyndiol, by D. Leis, et al. GEBURTSHILFE UND FRAUENHEILKUNDE 39(1): 54-57, January, 1979.

Complications with use of IUD and oral contraceptives among Navajo women, by J. C. Slocumb, et al. PUBLIC HEALTH REPORTS 94(3):243, May-June, 1979.

Cyclic use of combination oral contraceptives and the severity of endometriosis, by V. C. Buttram, Jr. FERTILITY AND STERILITY 31(3):347-348, March, 1979.

Disorders of the retinal vascular system in long-term use of oral contraceptives, by D. Fabiszewska-Górna, et al.

KLINIKA OCZNA 81(2):157-159, 1979.

Disposition of chlordiazepoxide: sex differences and effects of oral contraceptives, by R. K. Roberts, et al. CLINICAL PHARMACOLOGY AND THERAPEUTICS 25(6): 826-831, June, 1979.

Drug therapy today: what we know now about oral contraceptives, by M. J. Rodman. RN 42(9):133-146, September, 1979.

The effect of hormones on the periodontal condition—clinical studies on 300 female patients, by G. Klinger, et al. STOMATOLOGIE DER DDR 29(1):7-11, January, 1979.

Effect of oral contraceptive drugs on carbohydrate metabolism in alloxan diabetic rats, by M. T. Khayyal, et al. JOURNAL OF THE EGYPTIAN MEDICAL ASSOCIATION 60(7-8):625-632, 1977.

Effect of oral contraceptive steroids on vitamin A status of women and female rats, by M. S. Bamji, et al. WORLD REVIEW OF NUTRITION AND DIETETICS 31:135-140, 1978.

Effect of oral contraceptives on antithrombin III measurement [letter], by J. T. Brandt, et al. AMERICAN JOURNAL OF CLINICAL PATHOLOGY 71(3):360, March, 1979.

Effect of oral contraceptives on folate economy—a study in female rats, by N. Lakshmaiah, et al. HORMONE AND METABOLIC RESEARCH 11(1):64-67, January, 1979.

Effects of manufacturing oral contraceptives on blood clotting, by L. Poller, et al. BRITISH MEDICAL JOURNAL 1(6180):1761-1762, June 30, 1979.

Effects of a new oral progestagen on pituitary ovarian function, by L. Viinikka, et al. CONTRACEPTION 17(1): 19, January, 1978.

Effects of oral contraceptives and pregnancy on melanomas [letter], by A. B. Lerner, et al. NEW ENGLAND JOURNAL OF MEDICINE 301(1):47, July 5, 1979.

Effects of oral contraceptives of cancerogenesis of cervical epithelium, by H. J. Soost, et al. ARCHIV FUER GESCHWULSTFORSCHUNG 48(4):345-355, 1978.

Effects of oral contraceptives on laboratory test results. MEDICAL LETTER ON DRUGS AND THERAPEUTICS 21(13):54-56, June 29, 1979.

Effects of oral contraceptives on nutritional status, by L. K. Massey, et al. AMERICAN FAMILY PHYSICIAN 19(1):119-123, January, 1979.

Effects of oral contraceptives on zinc and copper levels in human plasma and endometrium during the menstrual cycle, by E. J. Sing, et al. ARCHIVES OF GYNECOLOGY 226(4):303-306, December 29, 1978.

The effects on sexual response and mood after sterilization of women taking long-term oral contraception: results of a double-blind cross-over study, by J. Leeton, et al. AUSTRALIAN AND NEW ZEALAND JOURNAL OF OBSTETRICS AND GYNAECOLOGY 18(3):194-197, August, 1978.

Electronmicroscopic findings in a malignant hepatoma after oral contraceptives, by J. Hatzibujas, et al. ZEITSCHRIFT FUR GASTROENTEROLOGIE 16(10):616-624, October, 1978.

Enhanced retention of merits from nutritional supplementation in oral contraception users, by E. B. Dawson, et al.

AMERICAN JOURNAL OF CLINICAL NUTRITION
32:949, April, 1979.

An epidemiologic study of breast cancer and benign breast
neoplasias in relation to the oral contraceptive and estrogen use, by B. Ravnihar, et al. EUROPEAN JOURNAL
OF CANCER 15(4):395-405, April, 1979.

An epidemiological study of oral contraceptives and breast
cancer, by M. P. Vessey, et al. BRITISH MEDICAL
JOURNAL 1(6180):1757-1760, June 30, 1979.

Epidemiology of hepatocellular adenoma. The role of oral
contraceptive use, by J. B. Rooks, et al. JAMA 242(7):
644-648, August 17, 1979.

Estrogen and progestogen binding site concentrations in human endocretrium and cervix throughout the menstrual
cycle and in tissue from women taking oral contraceptives, by B. M. Sanborn, et al. JOURNAL OF STEROID
BIOCHEMISTRY 9(10):951-955, October, 1978.

Evaluation of the carcinogenic effects of estrogens, progestins
and oral contraceptives on cervix, uterus and ovary of
animals and man, by V. A. Drill. ARCHIVES OF TOXI-
COLOGY (2):59-84, 1979.

Evaluation of various liver function and blood coagulation
tests in early stages of treatment with oral contraceptives,
by C. Del Vecchio-Blanco, et al. CLINICA TERAPEU-
TICA 87(3):233-242, November 15, 1978.

Fetal loss, twinning and birth weight after oral contraceptive
use, by K. J. Rothman. NEW ENGLAND JOURNAL OF
MEDICINE 297:468-471, September 1, 1977.

Fibrocystic breast disease in oral contraceptive users: a his-
topathological evaluation of epithelial atypia. NEW
ENGLAND JOURNAL OF MEDICINE 299:381-385,

August 24, 1978.

Focal nodular hyperplasia of the liver and oral contraceptives, by R. Kinch, et al. AMERICAN JOURNAL OF OBSTETRICS AND GYNECOLOGY 132(7):717-727, December 1, 1978.

Further results about pregnancy and childbirth after use of oral contraceptives, by G. K. Döring, et al. GEBURTSHILFE UND FRAUENHEILKUNDE 39(5):369-371, May, 1979.

Galactorrhea and pituitary tumors in postpill and non-postpill secondary amenorrhea, by C. M. March, et al. AMERICAN JOURNAL OF OBSTETRICS AND GYNECOLOGY 134(1):45-48, May 1, 1979.

Gastrointestinal complications of oral hormonal contraceptives, by B. Braendli, et al. MEDIZINISCHE KLINIK 74(12):425-436, March 23, 1979.

Hepatic lesions by oral contraceptives, by M. Lopez. PATHOLOGICA 71(1012):253-258, March-April, 1979.

Hepatocarcinoma and oral contraceptives [letter], by R. Trias, et al. LANCET 1(8068):821, April 15, 1978.

High density lipoprotein cholesterole levels in peripheral vascular disease and in women on oral contraception, by J. M. Meerloo, et al. ATHEROSCLEROSIS 33(2): 267-269, June, 1979.

High hepatoma risk for women on pill four years or more. MEDICAL WORLD NEWS 19:13+, July 24, 1978.

Homocystinuria and oral contraceptives [letter], by H. Gröbe. LANCET 1(8056):158-159, January 21, 1978.

Hormonal content of plasma and endometrium of women

taking oral contraceptives, by H. Porias, et al. OBSTE-
TRICS AND GYNECOLOGY 52(6):703-707, December,
1978.

Hormonal tissue concentration and oral contraceptives: the
endometrium, by A. Carranco López, et al. GINE-
COLOGIA Y OBSTETRICIA DE MEXICO 45(270):329-
347, April, 1979.

How safe is the pill? by R. Gray. WORLD HEALTH pp. 12-
15, August, 1978.

Human cervical mucus. V. Oral contraceptives and mucus
rheologic properties, by D. P. Wolf, et al. FERTILITY
AND STERILITY 32(2):166-169, August, 1979.

Human hexosaminidase isozymes. IV. Effects of oral contra-
ceptive steroids on serum hexosaminidase activity, by H.
M. Nitowsky, et al. AMERICAN JOURNAL OF OB-
STETRICS AND GYNECOLOGY 134(6):642-647,
July 15, 1979.

Human platelet aggregation curve and oral contraception, by
C. M. Montanari, et al. ACTA HAEMATOLOGICA
61(4):230-232, 1979.

Hyperplastic changes and oral contraceptives in Anglo-Saxon
countries, by C. Markuszewski. POLSKI TYGODNIK
LEKARSKI 33(38):15191522, September 18, 1978.

IUD's and pelvic infection; FDA labeling revisions, by A.
Hecht. FDA CONSUMER 12:20-21, November, 1978.

Incidence of mycotic vaginitis in women using oral contraceptives, by A. Karwan-Plońska, et al. GINEKOLOGIA
POLSKA 49(12):1093-1094, December, 1978.

Increased platelet aggregation and decreased high-density
lipoprotein cholesterol in women on oral contraceptives,

by M. L. Bierenbaum, et al. AMERICAN JOURNAL OF
OBSTETRICS AND GYNECOLOGY 134(6):638-641,
July 15, 1979.

Increased risk of thrombosis due to oral contraceptives: a
further report, by M. G. Maguire, et al. AMERICAN
JOURNAL OF EPIDEMIOLOGY 110(2):188-195,
August, 1979.

Induction of hepatic drug metabolizing enzymes and pregnancy while taking oral contraceptives, by W. C. Buss.
JOURNAL OF ANTIMICROBIOL CHEMOTHERAPY
5(1):4-5, January, 1979.

The influence of age, sex, and the use of oral contraceptives
on the inhibitory effects of endothelial cells and PGI2
(prostacyclin) on platelet function, by A. Nordøy, et al.
SCANDINAVIAN JOURNAL OF HAEMATOLOGY
21(3):177-187, September, 1978.

Influence of mineral intake and use of oral contraceptives
before pregnancy on the mineral content of human colostrum and of more mature milk, by A. Kirksey, et al.
AMERICAN JOURNAL OF CLINICAL NUTRITION
32(1):30-39, January, 1979.

Influence of oral contraceptives on ascorbic acid and triglyceride status, by N. K. Hudiburgh, et al. JOURNAL OF
THE AMERICAN DIETETIC ASSOCIATION 75(1):19-
22, July, 1979.

Influence of oral contraceptives on blood clotting. (Results
after one year study), by S. Salahović, et al. LIJEC-
NICKI VJESNIK 100(9):525-529, September, 1978.

Influence of oral contraceptives on immediate postabortal
pituitary-ovarian function, by P. Lähteenmäki. ACTA
OBSTETRICIA ET GYNECOLOGICA SCANDINAVICA
76:1-43, 1978.

Jaundice by interaction of troleandomycin and contraceptive pills [letter], by R. Rollux, et al. NOUVELLE PRESSE MEDICALE 8(20):1694, May 5, 1979.

Liver adenoma, causing fetal abdominal hemorrhage, after prolonged administration of oral contraceptives, by J. Lukaćs, et al. MORPHOLOGIAI ES IGAZSAGUGYI ORVOSI SZEMLE 18(3):228-311, July, 1978.

Liver and the pill, by J. Eisenburg. NATURWISSENSCHAF-TEN 66(3):156, March, 1979.

Liver biopsy findings after intake of oral contraceptives, by K. Mölleken. ZENTRALBLATT FUER ALLGEMEINE PATHOLOGIE UND PATHOLOGISCHE ANATOMIE 123(3):195-201, 1979.

Liver cell adenoma associated with oral contraceptive hormone therapy, by N. J. Nicolaides. MEDICAL JOURNAL OF AUSTRALIA 2(6):274-276, September, 1978.

Liver tumor and prolonged oral contraception, by T. Espersen. UGESKRIFT FOR LAEGER 141(23):1581-1582, June 4, 1979.

Liver tumors and oral contraceptives, by J. J. Gonvers, et al. SCHWEIZERISCHE MEDIZINISCHE WOCHENSCHRIFT 108(48):1899-1901, December 2, 1978.

—: pathology and pathogenesis, by T. D. Gindhart. ANNALS OF CLINICAL AND LABORATORY SCIENCE 8(6):443-445, November-December, 1978.

—: a review of recent literature, by G. B. Feben. AUSTRALIAN FAMILY PHYSICIAN 8(6):641+, June, 1979.

Liver tumors associated with oral contraceptives, by W. J. Britton, et al. MEDICAL JOURNAL OF AUSTRALIA

2(6):223-227, September 9, 1978.

Malignant liver tumor after oral contraception, by H. Breining, et al. MEDIZINISCHE WELT 30(19):747-750, May 11, 1979.

Migraine attacks and increased platelet aggregability induced by oral contraceptives, by S. Mazal. AUSTRALIAN AND NEW ZEALAND JOURNAL OF MEDICINE 8(6): 646-648, December, 1978.

New evidence on pill side effects. SPOKESWOMAN 9(5):6, November, 1978.

New studies: pills don't increase diabetes danger: smoking multiples pill-associated stroke risk. FAMILY PLANNING PERSPECTIVES 11(2):120-122, March-April, 1979.

Nutrition during pregnancy, lactation, and oral contraception, by B. S. Worthington. NURSING CLINICS OF NORTH AMERICA 14(2):269-283, June, 1979.

OCs and resting blood flow [letter] , by A. Singer. ANGIOLOGY 30(2):129-130, February, 1979.

OCs—update on usage, safety, and side effects. POPULATION REPORTS (5):A133-A186, January, 1979.

Observations on the effect of some oral contraceptives on the ovary of rat, by P. Ghosh, et al. JOURNAL OF THE INDIAN MEDICAL ASSOCIATION 71(6):141-144, September 16, 1978.

Oral and intrauterine contraception: a 1978 risk assessment, by A. Rosenfield. AMERICAN JOURNAL OF OBSTETRICS AND GYNECOLOGY 132(1):92-106, September 1, 1978.

Oral contraception and the detection of carriers in haemophilia B, by E. Briët, et al. THROMBOSIS RESEARCH
13(3):379-388, September, 1978.

Oral contraception and the gingival mucosa, by C. Fruteau
de Laclos, et al. LIGAMENT 13(119):17-20, January-
March, 1976.

Oral contraception and multiple sclerosis, by A. Ghezzi, et
al. ARCHIVIO FER LE SCIENZE MEDICHE 136(1):
67-73, January-March, 1979.

Oral contraceptive pills and clinical ostosclerosis, by L. Podoshin, et al. INTERNATIONAL JOURNAL OF GYNAE-
COLOGY AND OBSTETRICS 15(6):554-555, 1978.

Oral contraceptive use alters the balance of platelet prostaglandin and thromboxane synthesis, by A. E. Schorer, et
al. PROSTAGLANDINS AND MEDICINE 1(1):5-11,
July, 1978.

Oral contraceptive use and fasting triglyceride, plasma cholesterol and HDL cholesterol, by C. H. Hennekens, et al.
CIRCULATION 60(3):486-489, September, 1979.

Oral contraceptive use and secondary amenorrhea, by M.
Kissi, et al. OBSTETRICS AND GYNECOLOGY 53(2):
241-244, February, 1979.

Oral-contraceptive use in relation to myocardial infarction,
by S. Shapiro, et al. LANCET 1(8119):743-747, April
7, 1979.

Oral contraceptives and birth defects [letter] , by I. D. Bross.
NEW ENGLAND JOURNAL OF MEDICINE 300(1):
47, January 4, 1979.

Oral contraceptives and cancer risk, by J. A. Gustafsson, et
al. LAKARTIDNINGEN 76(17):1625-1627, April 25,

1979.

Oral contraceptives and cervix uteri cancer [editorial] , by
B. I. Nesheim. TIDSSKRIFT FOR DEN NORSKE LAE-
GEFORENING 98(29):1422-1423, October 20, 1978.

Oral contraceptives and diabetes mellitus, by S. J. Wingrave,
et al. BRITISH MEDICAL JOURNAL 1(6155):23,
January 6, 1979.

Oral contraceptives and endometriosis, by K. J. Karnacky.
AMERICAN JOURNAL OF OBSTETRICS AND GYNE-
COLOGY 135(2):279-280, September 15, 1979.

Oral contraceptives and HDL cholesterol [editorial] , by O.
Frankman, et al. LAKARTIDNINGEN 76(1-2):15-16,
January 3, 1979.

Oral contraceptives and the liver, by A. G. de Pagter, et al.
NEDERLANDS TIJDSCHRIFT VOOR GENEESKUNDE
123(21):881-887, May 26, 1979.

Oral contraceptives and liver tumours [editorial] , by A. Marshall, et al. MEDICAL JOURNAL OF AUSTRALIA
2(6):240-241, September 9, 1978.

Oral contraceptives and myocardinal infarction, by P. Dillon,
et al. CARDIOVASCULAR NURSING 15(2):5-9,
March-April, 1979.

Oral contraceptives and neoplasia, by G. R. Huggins, et al.
FERTILITY AND STERILITY 32(1):1-23, July, 1979.

Oral contraceptives and the periodontium, by A. Fesseler.
ZAHNAERZTLICHE MITTEILUNGEN 69(10):634,
May 16, 1979.

Oral contraceptives and platelet aggregation, by N. Shevde,
et al. AMERICAN JOURNAL OF OBSTETRICS AND

GYNECOLOGY 132(3):303-306, October 1, 1978.

Oral contraceptives and the risk of neoplasms, by J. A. Gustafsson, et al. LAKARTIDNINGEN 76(17):1625-1627, April 25, 1979.

Oral contraceptives and stroke in young women: a clinicopathologic correlation, by N. S. Irey, et al. NEUROLOGY 28(12):1216-1219, December, 1978.

Oral contraceptives as a possible cause of cerebral vascular disorders, by M. Jarema. NEUROLOGIA I NEUROCHIRURGIA POLSKA 13(1):81-86, January-February, 1979.

Oral contraceptives, hyperlipoproteinemia and ischemic heart disease, by V. N. Titov, et al. TERAPEUTICHESKI ARKHIV 50(12):22-28, 1978.

Oral contraceptives, smoking, and other factors in relation to risk of venous thromboembolic disease, by D. B. Petitti, et al. AMERICAN JOURNAL OF EPIDEMIOLOGY 108(6):480-485, December, 1978.

Oral contraceptives, venous thrombosis, and varicose veins, by Royal College of General Practitioners' Oral Contraception Study. JOURNAL OF THE ROYAL COLLEGE OF GENERAL PRACTITIONERS 28(192):393-399, July, 1978.

Oral oestro-progestative contraception and cervical and vaginal cytology, by J. Favre, et al. SEMAINE DES HOPITAUX DE PARIS 55(7-8):384-388+, February, 1979.

Pathologic effects of oral contraceptives, by G. D. Hilliard, et al. RECENT RESULTS IN CANCER RESEARCH 66:49-71, 1979.

Patients treated for gynecologic cancer after use of oral con-

traceptives and IUD, by M. Szegvári, et al. ORVOSI
HETILAP 120(13):756-758, April 1, 1979.

The pill and amenorrhoea [editorial], by M. Katz. SOUTH
AFRICAN MEDICAL JOURNAL 54(12):465, September 16, 1978.

The pill and the breast, by A. Gregl, et al. MEDIZINISCHE
WELT 30(4):120-123, January 26, 1979.

The pill and circulatory disease, by V. Beral, et al. AMERI-
CAN HEART JOURNAL 97(2):263-246, February, 1979.

The pill and endocrine diseases, by I. Werner-Zodrow, et al.
GYNAEKOLOGISCHE RUNDSCHAU 18(3-4):246-252, 1978.

Pill and heart attacks: exaggerated? SCIENCE NEWS 115:
247, April 14, 1979.

The pill and mortality from cardiovascular disease: another
look, by C. Tietz. FAMILY PLANNING PERSPEC-
TIVES 11(2):80, March-April, 1979.

—. [United States], by C. Tietze. INTERNATIONAL
FAMILY PLANNING PERSPECTIVES 5:8-12, March, 1979.

The pill and other drugs, by E. S. Johnson. TRANSAC-
TIONS OF THE MEDICAL SOCIETY OF LONDON
92-93:131-134, 1975-1977.

The 'pill,' disease of civilization? by R. Veylon. NOUVELLE
PRESSE MEDICALE 7(44):4064+, December 9, 1978.

Pill linked to slight blood pressure rise; minor side effects
greater among underweight women. FAMILY PLAN-
NING PERSPECTIVES 10(5):300-301, September-

October, 1978.

The pill: a perspective for assessing risks and benefits, by F. S. Jaffe. NEW ENGLAND JOURNAL OF MEDICINE 297:612-614, September 17, 1977.

Pill raises blood pressure slightly; side effects vary with weight. FAMILY PLANNING PERSPECTIVES 10: 300-301, September-October, 1978.

Pituitary adenoma and oral contraceptives: a case-control study, by C. B. Coulam, et al. FERTILITY AND STE-RILITY 31(1):25-28, January, 1979.

Plasma and urine levels produced by an oral dose of ampicillin 0.5 G administered to women taking oral contraceptives, by A. Philipson. ACTA OBSTETRICIA ET GYNE-COLOGICA SCANDINAVICA 58(1):69-71, 1979.

Plasma bradykininogen levels before and after ovulation: studies in women and guinea pigs, with observations on oral contraceptives and menopause, by C. Smith, et al. AMERICAN JOURNAL OF OBSTETRICS AND GYNE-COLOGY 133(8):868-876, April 15, 1979.

Plasma levels of adrenocorticotropin and cortisol in women receiving oral contraceptive steroids treatment, by B. R. Carr, et al. JOURNAL OF CLINICAL ENDOCRINOLO-GY AND METABOLISM 49(3):346-349, September, 1979.

Plasminogen activator levels in plasma and urine during exercise and oral contraceptive use, by A. M. Hedlin, et al. THROMBOSIS AND HAEMOSTOSIS 39(3):743-750, June 30, 1978.

Possible hazards of oral contraceptive use, by W. B. Kannel. CIRCULATION 60(3):490-491, September, 1979.

Post-pill amenorrhea and menarche, by J. M. Wenderlein. FORTSCHRITTE DER MEDIZIN 96(44):2243-2248, November 23, 1978.

The pregnancy occuring during oral contraception or intra uterine device (i.u.d.), by A. Bremond, et al. JOURNAL DE GINECOLOGIE, OBSTETRIQUES, ET BIOLOGIE DE LA REPRODUCTION 7(3 Pt 2):581-589, April, 1978.

Pregnancy, oral contraceptives and multiple sclerosis, by S. Poser, et al. ACTA NEUROLOGICA SCANDINAVICA 59(2-3):108-118, March, 1979.

Primary malignant liver tumors: association with oral contraceptives, by J. Vana, et al. NEW YORK STATE JOURNAL OF MEDICINE 79(3):321-325, March, 1979.

Principle complications and contraindications of the use of oral contraceptives, by P. Mutti, et al. MINERVA GINECOLOGIA 31(5):363-375, May, 1979.

Problem of oral surgical interventions during pregnancy, menstruation and under the intake of hormonal contraceptives, by E. Stech. STOMALOLOGIE DER DDR 29(4):298-303, April, 1979.

Quantitative enhancement of dinitrochlorebenzene responsivity in women receiving oral contraceptives, by T. H. Rea. ARCHIVES OF DERMATOLOGY 115(3):361-362, March, 1979.

Reasonable surgical treatment for tumors of the liver associated with the use of oral contraceptives, by P. W. Catalano, et al. SURGERY, GYNECOLOGY, AND OBSTETRICS 148(5):759-763, May, 1979.

Recommendations arising out of the findings by the RCGP oral contraception study on the mortality risks of oral contraceptive users. From the Royal College of General Practitioners and the Royal College of Obstetricians and Gynaecologists. JOURNAL OF THE ROYAL COLLEGE OF GENERAL PRACTITIONERS 27(184):700, November, 1977.

Renal artery thrombosis in a young woman taking oral contraceptives, by s. M. Golbus, et al. ANNALS OF INTERNAL MEDICINE 90(6):939-940, June, 1979.

Reversible changes in the eye after long term use of oral contraceptive agents, by T. Pasanku, et al. MEDICINSKI PREGLED 31(11-12):493-496, 1978.

A review of the birth control pill and its relationship to thrombophlebitis, by M. E. Julsrud. JOURNAL OF THE AMERICAN PODIATRY ASSOCIATION 69(6): 376-382, June, 1979.

Rheumatoid arthritis and oral contraception [letter], by H. Berry. LANCET 1(8068):829, April 15, 1978.

Rheumatoid arthritis: pill users half as likely to develop the disease. FAMILY PLANNING PERSPECTIVES 10(4): 239-240, July-August, 1978.

Rise in female-initiated sexual activity at ovulation and its suppression by oral contraceptives, by D. B. Adams, et al. NEW ENGLAND JOURNAL OF MEDICINE 299(21): 1145-1150, November 23, 1978.

Rising cost of birth control pills, by D. Clayton. FINANCIAL POST 72:16, December 30, 1978.

Risk of cancer caused by the pill? MEDIZINISCHE KLINIK 73(43):4, October 27, 1978.

Risk of myocardial infarction in oral-contraceptive users [letter], by H. Jick. LANCET 1(8127):1187, June 2, 1979.

Risk of vascular disease in women. Smoking, oral contraceptives, noncontraceptive estrogens, and other factors, by D. B. Petitti, et al. JAMA 242(11):1150-1154, September 14, 1979.

The risks of oral contraception, by J. McEwan. BRITSIH JOURNAL OF HOSPITAL MEDICINE 21(2):144+, February, 1979.

Role of combined oral contraceptives in the pathogenesis of urodynamic disorders of the upper urinary tracts, by T. D. Catuashvili, et al. AKUSHERSTVO I GINEKOLOGIIA (2):13-15, 1979.

Role of oral contraception in congenital malformations of offspring, by M. B. Bracken, et al. INTERNATIONAL JOURNAL OF EPIDEMIOLOGY 7(4):309-317, December, 1978.

Role of oral contraceptive agents in the pathogenesis of liver tumors, by E. D. Nissen, et al. JOURNAL OF TOXICOLOGY AND ENVIRONMENTAL HEALTH 5(2-3): 231-254, March-May, 1979.

Serum level and 24hr. excretion pattern of potassium following the intake of combined oral contraceptives, by S. Kamyab, et al. ACTA MEDICA IRANICA 21(2):87-94, 1978.

Spontaneous rupture of a liver adenoma following many years' ingestion of an oral contraceptive, by H. Pollak. MMW 121(3):93-94, January 19, 1979.

Studies on liver function under the influence of oral contraceptives, by E. Brügmann, et al. INTERNATIONAL JOURNAL OF GYNAECOLOGY AND OBSTETRICS 16(5):394-397, March-April, 1979.

Studies show smoking raises pill risk. FDA CONSUMER

Studies show smoking raises pill risk. FDA CONSUMER 12:3, November, 1978.

Study confirms accentuated heart attack risk among pill users who are also heavy smokers. FAMILY PLANNING PERSPECTIVES 11:196-197, May-June, 1979.

Surveillance of women taking oral contraceptives by determination of antithrombin III [letter], by M. O. Benoit, et al. NOUVELLE PRESSE MEDICALE 8(7):528-529, February 10, 1979.

Survey of primary liver tumors and oral contraceptive use, by J. Vana, et al. JOURNAL OF TOXICOLOGY AND ENVIRONMENTAL HEALTH 5(2-3):255-273, March-May, 1979.

Symposium on nutrition. Nutrition during pregnancy, lactation, and oral contraception, by B. Worthington. NURSING CLINICS OF NORTH AMERICA 14:269-283, June, 1979.

A synthetic steroid (R2323) as a once-a-week oral contraceptive, by S. S. David, et al. FERTILITY AND STERILITY 31(3):278-281, March, 1979.

Thromboembolic accidents in patients on oral contraceptive treatment, by L. Pedrini, et al. ANGIOLOGIA 31(2): 51-56, March-April, 1979.

Thrombotic thrombocytopoenic purpura during oral contraceptive treatment [letter], by S. Vesconi, et al. THROMBOSIS AND HAEMOSTASIS 40(3):563-564, February 15, 1979.

Treatment possibilities of early stages of venous insufficiency caused by oral contraceptives, by S. Kalinski, et al. MEDIZINISCHE KLINIK 30(31-32):1169-1172, August 10, 979.

Tubal and uterine secretions; the possibilities for contraceptive attack, by R. J. Aitken. JOURNAL OF REPRODUCTION FERTILITY 55(1):247-254, January, 1979.

An unusual side-effect of the pill [letter] , by A. Barmania. SOUTH AFRICAN MEDICAL JOURNAL 54(5):181, July 29, 1978.

Using the pill can affect the gingiva and periodontium, by S. Bonner. DENTAL STUDENTS 56(4):54-60+, January, 1978.

What oral contraceptives do to migrane headache. NURSES DRUG ALERT 3:13 14, February, 1979.

When the pill causes a rise in blood pressure, by R. J. Weir. DRUGS 16(6):522-527, December, 1978.

Why aren't more pill-using blacks hypertensive? MEDICAL WORLD NEWS 20:50-52, February 5, 1979.

CONTRACEPTIVES: FEMALE: ORAL: COMPLICATIONS: PSYCHOLOGICAL
Depression and oral contraceptives: the role of pyridoxine. DRUG AND THERAPEUTICS BULLETIN 16(22):86-87, October 27, 1978.

Emotional distress in morning-after pill patients, by G. R. Huggins, et al. ACTA OBSTETRICIA ET GYNECOLOGICA SCANDINAVICA 58(1):65-68, 1979.

Hypertension and oral contraceptives [letter] , by M. G. Crane, et al. BRITISH MEDICAL JOURNAL 2(6145): 1165, October 21, 1978.

Oral contraception and depression, by J. L. Garrison. SOCIAL WORK 24:162-163, March, 1979.

—, by H. Warnes, et al. PSYCHOSOMATICS 20(3):187-

CONTRACEPTIVES: FEMALE: ORAL: COMPLICATIONS:
PSYCHOLOGICAL

189+, March, 1979.

Oral contraceptives and depressive symptomatology: biologic
mechanisms, by B. L. Parry, et al. COMPREHENSIVE
PSYCHIATRY 20(4):347-358, July-August, 1979.

CONTRACEPTIVES: FEMALE: ORAL: METABOLISM
The effect of oral contraceptives on vitamin B12 metabolism,
by A. M. Shojania, et al. AMERICAN JOURNAL OF
OBSTETRICS AND GYNECOLOGY 135(1):129-134,
September 1, 1979.

The effects of a once-a-week steroid contraceptive (R2323)
on lipid and carbohydrate metabolism in women during
three months of use, byW. N. Spellacy, et al. FERTILI-
TY AND STERILITY 30(3):289-292, September, 1978.

Implications of oral contraceptive use on vitamin nutritional
status, by M. S. Bamji. INDIAN JOURNAL OF MEDI-
CAL RESEARCH 68(Suppl):80-87, October, 1978.

Methionine metabolism and vitamin B6 status in women using
oral contraceptives, by L. T. Miller, et al. AMERICAN
JOURNAL OF CLINICAL NUTRITION 31:619-625,
April, 1978.

CONTRACEPTIVES: FEMALE: ORAL: RESEARCH
Research on male 'pill' intensifies, by T. Schultz. NEW
YORK TIMES pp. C-1, August 7, 1979.

CONTRACEPTIVES: FEMALE: ORAL: THERAPEUTIC USE
Chorea complicating oral contraceptive therapy. Case report
and review of the literature, by W. A. Pulsinelli, et al.
AMERICAN JOURNAL OF MEDICINE 65(3):557-559,
September, 1978.

The determination of antithrombin III. Comparison of six
methods. Effect of oral contraceptive therapy, by H.
Bounameaux, et al. THROMBOSIS AND HAEMOSTA-

SIS 39(3):607-615, June 30, 1978.

Effect of oral contraceptive therapy on gingival inflammation in humans, by K. L. Kalkwarf. JOURNAL OF PERIO-DONTOLOGY 49(11):560-563, November, 1978.

Failure of withdrawal bleeding during combined oral contraceptive therapy: 'amenorrhoea on the pill', by M. D. Gillmer, et al. CONTRACEPTION 18(5):507-515, November, 1978.

Therapy with oral contraceptive steroids and antibiotics, by M. L. Orme, et al. JOURNAL OF ANTIMICROBIOL CHEMOTHERAPY 5(2):124-126, March, 1979.

CONTRACEPTIVES: FEMALE: POST-COITAL
Postcoital copper IUD found to be effective in preventing pregnancy. FAMILY PLANNING PERSPECTIVES 11: 195, May-June, 1979.

CONTRACEPTIVES: FEMALE: POST-COITAL: COMPLICATIONS
An alternative to the use of high-dose estrogens for postcoital contraception, by L. H. Schilling. JOURNAL OF THE AMERICAN COLLEGE HEALTH ASSOCIATION 27(5): 247-249, April, 1979.

Carbohydrate metabolism in women receiving d-norgestrel for postcoital contraception, by F. Garmendia, et al. HORMONE AND METABOLIC RESEARCH 11(1):81-82, January, 1979.

CONTRACEPTIVES: FEMALE: SUPPOSITORY
Indian experience with a single long-acting vaginal suppository for the termination of pregnancies, by S. Tejuja, et al. CONTRACEPTION 19(2):191-196, February, 1979.

Treatment with a single vaginal suppository containing 15-methyl PGF2 alpha methyl ester at expected time of menstruation, by K. Kinoshita, et al. PROSTAGLAN-

DINS 17(3):469-481, March, 1979.

Uterine rupture with the use of vaginal prostaglandin E2 suppositories, by R. Z. Sandler, et al. AMERICAN JOURNAL OF OBSTETRICS AND GYNECOLOGY 134(3):348-349, June 1, 1979.

CONTRACEPTIVES: FEMALE: TOPICAL
Patentex-Oval—a contraceptive agent for topical use, by J. Higier, et al. WIADOMOSCI LEKARSKIE 31(19): 1349-1351, October 1, 1978.

CONTRACEPTIVES: LAWS
Constitutional law—the fundamental right of parents to care, custody, and nurture of their children requires that parents have notice and an opportunity to consult with their minor child before that minor may have access to contraceptives. UNIVERSITY OF DETROIT. JOURNAL OF URBAN LAW 56:268-288, Fall, 1978.

Constitutional law—substantive due process—children's rights —parents' right to be notified when their children are provided contraceptives by state funded family planning clinics. WAYNE LAW REVIEW 25:1135-1146, July, 1979.

Spain legalizes contraception, by M. Jones. POPULI 5:3-5, November 4, 1978.

CONTRACEPTIVES: MALE
Current efforts to develop male hormonal contraception, by S. B. Schearer. STUDIES IN FAMILY PLANNING 9(8):229-231, August, 1978.

An evaluation of male contraceptive acceptance in rural Ghana, by P. Lamptey, et al. STUDIES IN FAMILY PLANNING 9(8):222, August, 1978.

Male adolescent contraceptive utilization, by M. L. Finkel, et al. ADOLESCENCE 13:443-451, Fall, 1978.

Male contraception, by N. B. Attico. PUBLIC HEALTH RE-
VIEWS 7:55-81, January-June, 1978.

A plea for the condom, especially for teenagers. JAMA 241:
2517-2518, June 8, 1979.

Rate of "R" (increasing use of condoms). MOTHER JONES
3:11, June, 1978.

Remember your rubbers (condoms of the past). PLAYBOY
26:162+, February, 1979.

Some factors related to men's stated willingness to use a male
contraceptive pill, by H. G. Gough. JOURNAL OF SEX
RESEARCH 15:27-37, February, 1979.

Symposium on contraceptive technology, by L. Mastroianni,
Jr. FEDERATION PROCEEDINGS 37:2664-2665,
November, 1978.

CONTRACEPTIVES: MALE: ORAL
Chinese say their pill works for men. MEDICAL WORLD
NEWS 20:13+, February 5, 1979.

Chinese say their pill works for men [male contraceptive with
gossypol, a derivative of cottonseed]. MEDICAL WORLD
NEWS 20:13+, February 5, 1979.

From China: new pill for men; gossypol pill, by D. Fortino.
HARPER'S BAZAAR 112:129+, June, 1979.

Male pill. SCIENTIFIC AMERICAN 240(6):104A, June,
1979.

—, by J. Seligmann, et al. NEWSWEEK 93:84, January 22,
1979.

Male pill; gossypol. SCIENTIFIC AMERICAN 240:104,
June, 1979.

—; gossypol pill developed in China, by J. Seligmann, et al. NEWSWEEK 93:84, January 22, 1979.

Thousand try male "pill" in China, by W. Sullivan. NEW YORK TIMES pp. C-1, September 25, 1979.

CONTRACEPTIVES: MALE: ORAL: COMPLICATIONS
Gossypol—proposed contraceptive for men passes the Ames test [letter], by A. de Peyster, et al. NEW ENGLAND JOURNAL OF MEDICINE 301(5):275-276, August 2, 1979.

CONTRACEPTIVES: MORTALITY AND MORTALITY STATISTICS
Reproductive mortality [from contraceptives as well as pregnancy or abortion], by V. Beral. BRITISH MEDICAL JOURNAL 6191:632-634, September 15, 1979.

CONTRACEPTIVES: NASAL
Trials start for nasal-spray contraceptive [for women or men]. MEDICAL WORLD NEWS 19:58, August 21, 1978.

CONTRACEPTIVES: NATURAL
Who fills in natural contraceptive gap. NEW SCIENTIST 79: 622, August 31,1978.

CONTRACEPTIVES: ORAL
Antithrombin III and oral contraception with progestagen-only preparation [letter], by J. Conrad, et al. LANCET 2(1840):471, September 1, 1979.

Are there two types of postpill anovulation? by S. Harlap. FERTILITY AND STERILITY 31(5):486-491, May, 1979.

Artenal hypertension and oral contraceptives, by J. Lekief-fre. ANNALES DE CARDIOLOGIE ET D'ANGEIOLO-GIE 28(1):35-39, January-February, 1979.

Beneficial effects of nutrient supplementation in oral contraceptive usage, by E. B. Dawson, et al. AMERICAN JOURNAL

OF CLINICAL NUTRITION 32:950, April, 1979.

Beyond the pill, by E. Diozfalusy. WORLD HEALTH p. 22, August-September, 1978.

Capsules. . .a nosy contraceptive. TIME 114:68, August 20, 1979.

Caries prevalence and oral contraception, by S. Cebi, et al. COMMUNITY DENTISTRY AND ORAL EPIDEMIOLO-GY 7(3):183-184, June, 1979.

The choice of a combined oral contraceptive. DRUG AND THERAPEUTICS BULLETIN 17(1):1-14, January 5, 1979.

Choice of contraceptive pill, by P. Bergsjφ. TIDSSKRIFT FOR DEN NORSKE LAEGEFORENING 99(16):845-847, June 10, 1979.

Choice of oral contraceptives, by P. Bergsjφ. TIDSSKRIFT FOR DEN NORSKE LAEGEFORENING 99(16):845-847, June 10, 1979.

Classification of oral contraceptives and its practical application to choice of prescriptions, by M. Renaud, et al. JOURNAL DE GYNECOLOGIE, OBSTETRIQUE ET BIOLOGIE DE LA REPRODUCTION 7(7):1291-1302, October-November, 1978.

Considerations in the management of patients taking oral contraceptives, by S. Kennon, et al. JOURNAL OF THE AMERICAN DENTAL ASSOCIATION 97(4):641-643, October, 1978.

Continuous low-dose progestagen oral contraceptives. DRUG AND THERAPEUTICS BULLETIN 17(1):4, January 5, 1979.

Effects of contraceptive pills in the field of otorhinolaryngology, by H. A. Kley, et al. ARCHIVES OP OTO-RHINO-LARYNGOLOGY 219(2):475-476, November 22, 1978.

Endocrinologic aspects of oral contraception, by A. B. Little. JOURNAL OF REPRODUCTIVE MEDICINE 21(5 Suppl):247-249, November, 1978.

Endometrial adenocarcinoma: in estrogen, oral contraceptive and nonhormone users, by J. G. Blythe, et al. GYNECOLOGIC ONCOLOGY 7(2):199-205, April, 1979.

Experience with a new low dose oral contraceptive: norgestimate & ethinyl estradiol, by B. Rubio-Lotvin, et al. ACTA EUROPAEA FERTILITATIS 9(1):1-6, March, 1978.

The future of the pill, by M. Kenny. SPECTATOR p. 13, December 15, 1979.

Incidence of thyroid disease associated with oral contraceptives, by P. Frank, et al. BRITISH MEDICAL JOURNAL 2(6151):1531, December 2, 1978.

Megaloblastic anemia due to folic acid deficiency after oral contraceptives, by C. Barone, et al. HAEMATOLOGICA 64(2):190-195, April, 1979.

Metabolic repercussions of oral contraception, by U. Gaspard. JOURNAL DE PHARMACIE DE BELGIQUE 33(5):312-324, September-October, 1978.

Ministat: a new oral contraceptive of the combined type with low estrogen contents, by R. Demol, et al. BRUXELLES-MEDICALE 59(4):225-232, April, 1979.

Morphological and clinical liver changes after taking oral contraceptives, by K. Mölleken, et al. ZEITSCHRIFT FUR DIE GESAMTE INNERE MEDIZIN UND IHRE GRENZGEBIETE 34(2):79-81, January 15, 1979.

Oral contraceptives. POPULATION REPORTS (5):1, January, 1979.

—, by M. A. Barletta. AMERICAN DRUGGIST 178:35-36, August, 1978.

Oral contraceptives—an update, by D. Bartosik. AMERICAN FAMILY PHYSICIAN 19(5):149-150, May, 1979.

A radioimmunoassay for norethindrone (NET): measurement of serum NET concentrations following ingestion of NET-containing oral contraceptive steroids, by F. Z. Stanczyk, et al. CONTRACEPTION 18(6):615-633, December, 1978.

A randomized double-blind trial of two low dose combined oral contraceptives, by W. Bounds, et al. BRITISH JOURNAL OF OBSTETRICS AND GYNAECOLOGY 86(4):325-329, April, 1979.

Tryptophan and tyrosine availability and oral contraceptives [letter], by S. E. Møller. LANCET 2(8140):472, September 1, 1979.

25 years on the pill, by E. Shorter. WEEKEND MAGAZINE 29:14-16, August 18, 1979.

Vitamin A and oral contraceptives [letter], by J. Bohner. DEUTSCH MEDIZINISCHE WOCHENSCHRIFT 104(13):480, March 30, 1979.

The vitamin B6 requirement in oral contraceptive users. I. Assessment by pyridoxal level and transfease activity in erythrocytes, by T. R. Bossé, et al. AMERICAN JOURNAL OF CLINICAL NUTRITION 32(5):1015-1023, May, 1979.

—. II. Assessment by tryptophan metabolites, vitamin B6, and pyridoxic acid levels in urine, by E. A. Donald, et al.

AMERICAN JOURNAL OF CLINICAL NUTRITION
32(5):1024-1032, May, 1979.

What every woman should know...about "the pill" and other
forms of contraception, by J. P. Sauvage, et al. DIA-
BETES FORECAST 32:14, January-February, 1979.

CONTRACEPTIVES: ORAL: COMPLICATIONS
Benign liver-cell-tumors and oral contraceptives, by W. Fa-
bian, et al. MEDIZINISCHE KLINIK 74(17):662-666,
April 27, 1979.

Benign liver tumors and oral contraceptives, by C. W. Aungst.
NEW YORK STATE JOURNAL OF MEDICINE 78(12):
1933-1934, October, 1978.

beta-thromboglobulin levels and oral contraception [letter],
by M. Aranda, et al. LANCET 2(8137):308-309, August
11, 1979.

Bigne eating associated with oral contraceptives, by R. A.
Moskovitz, et al. AMERICAN JOURNAL OF PSYCHIA-
TRY 136(5):721-722, May, 1979.

CONTRACEPTIVES: ORAL: RESEARCH
Biochemical changes in the uterus & uterine fluid of mated
rats treated with embelin—a non-steroidal oral contraceptive, by C. Seshadri, et al. INDIAN JOURNAL OF
EXPERIMENTAL BIOLOGY 16(11):1187-1188, November, 1978.

Clinical experience with a low dose oral contraceptive con-
taining norethisterone and ethinyl oestradiol, by E. M.
Morigi, et al. CURRENT MEDICAL RESEARCH AND
OPINION 5(8):655-662, 1978.

Clinical pharmacology of the steroidal oral contraceptives, by
J. L. Durand, et al. ADVANCES IN INTERNAL MEDI-
CINE 24:97-126, 1979.

Comparative clinical investigation of oral contraceptives with different doses, by M. Mall-Haefeli, et al. GEBURT-SHILFE UND FRAUENHEILKUNDE 39(7):553-557, July, 1979.

Comparative electron-microscopic studies of benign hepatoma and icterus in patients on oral contraceptives, by M. Balázs. VIRCHOWS ARCHIV. ABT. A. PATHOLO-GISCHE ANATOMIE-PATHOLOGY 381(1):97-109, December 12, 1978.

Comparative studies on two combination oral contraceptives, one containing synthetic estrogen, the other 'natural' estrogens, by D. M. Saunders, et al. CONTRACEPTION 18(5):527-534, November, 1978.

Comparison of effects of different combined oral-contraceptive formulations on carbohydrate and oral metabolism, by V. Wynn, et al. LANCET 1(8125):1045-1049, May 19, 1979.

CONTRACEPTIVES: PARENTERAL
Injectable contraception. STOREFRONT 5(6):4, February, 1978.

The monthly injectable contraceptive: a two-year clinical trial, by S. Koetsawang, et al. INTERNATIONAL JOURNAL OF GYNAECOLOGY AND OBSTETRICS 16(1): 61-64, 1978.

Multinational comparative clinical evaluation of two long-acting injectable contraceptive steroids: northisterone oenanthate and medroxyprogesterone acetate, by G. Benagiano, et al. CONTRACEPTION 17(5):395, May, 1978.

A new principle of injectable depot contraceptives. I. Drug selection and studies in monkeys, by M. Hümpel, et al. CONTRACEPTION 19(4):411-419, April, 1979.

CONTRACEPTIVES: RESEARCH
   Comparative clinical trial of the progestins R-2323 and levon-
      orgestrel administered by subdermal implants, by F.
      Alvarez, et al. CONTRACEPTION 18(2):151-162,
      1978.

   The present and future of immunologic approaches to con-
      traception, by G. P. Talwar. INTERNATIONAL JOUR-
      NAL OF GYNAECOLOGY AND OBSTETRICS 15(5):
      410-414, 1978.

   Problem-solving skills, locus of control, and the contraceptive
      effectiveness of young women, by B. Steinlauf. CHILD
      DEVELOPMENT 50:268-271, March, 1979.

   Progestagen and contraceptive activity of a 16alpha-methy-
      lene derivative of progesterone, by G. V. Nikitina.
      PROBLEMY ENDOKRINOLOGII I GORMONOTERA-
      PII 25(1):68-71, January-February, 1979.

   Specific prophylaxis of enzootic chlamydial ovine abortion,
      by G. Sorodoc, et al. VIROLOGIE 30(2):131-134,
      April-June, 1979.

   Spermatozoa repellent as a contraceptive, by W. W. Tso, et al.
      CONTRACEPTION 19(3):207-212, March, 1979.

CONTRACEPTIVES: STATISTICS
   Two million ever-married women are IUD users; Lippes Loop
      most popular, followed by Copper 7. FAMILY PLAN-
      NING PERSPECTIVES 11:119-120, March-April, 1979.

CONTRACEPTIVES: TECHNIQUES
   Accumulation of norethindrone and individual metabolities
      in human plasma during short- and long-term administra-
      tion of a contraceptive dosage, by W. E. Braselton, Jr., et
      al. AMERICAN JOURNAL OF OBSTETRICS AND
      GYNECOLOGY 133(2):154-160, 1979.

A comparison of metal and plastic cannulae for vacuum aspiration, by M. R. Narvekar, et al. INTERNATIONAL JOURNAL OF GYNAECOLOGY AND OBSTETRICS 15(5):433-435, 1978.

Premarital contraceptive use: a test of two models, by J. Delamater, et al. JOURNAL OF MARRIAGE AND THE FAMILY 40:235-247, May, 1978.

Use of the bicoagulaton technic in irreversible contraception, by O. Havemann, et al. ZENTRALBLATT FUR GYNAEKOLOGIE 101(2):100-106, 1979.

The use of a contraceptive vaginal ring governed by the pattern of individual uterine bleeding, by J. Toivonen, et al. CONTRACEPTION 19(4):401-409, April, 1979.

CONTRACEPTIVES AND ADVERTISING
The application of market research in contraceptive social marketing in a rural area of Kenya, by T. R. L. Black, et al. MARKET RESEARCH SOCIETY. JOURNAL 21: 30-43, January, 1979.

CONTRACEPTIVES AND COLLEGE STUDENTS
Affective, attitudinal, and normative determinants of contraceptive behavior among university men, by W. A. Fisher. DISSERTATION ABSTRACTS INTERNATIONAL 39(9-B):4613-4614, March, 1979.

Personality and the use of oral contraceptives in British university students, by R. Priestnall, et al. SOCIAL SCIENCE AND MEDICINE 12(5A):403-407, September, 1978.

The relationship betwen first sexual intercourse and ways of handling contraception among college students, by R. H. Needle. JOURNAL OF THE AMERICAN COLLEGE HEALTH ASSOCIATION 24(2):106-111, December, 1975.

Reproductive and contraceptive knowledge among undergraduate university students, by D. S. Godbole, et al.
JOURNAL OF FAMILY WELFARE 24:27-31, December, 1977.

Sex-role attitudes and the anticipated timing of the initial
stages of family formation among Catholic university
students, by J. W. Wicks, et al. JOURNAL OF MAR-
RIAGE AND THE FAMILY 40(3):505-514, August,
1978.

Sex role attitudes and contraceptive practices among never-
married university students, by M. Hedin-Pourghasemi.
DISSERTATION ABSTRACTS INTERNATIONAL
38(10-A):6344-6345, April, 1978.

Sexual behaviour and contraceptive practice of undergraduates at Oxford University, by P. Anderson, et al. JOUR-
NAL OF BIOSOCIAL SCIENCE 10(3):277-286, July,
1978.

Sexual contraceptive attitudes and behaviour of high school
and college females, by E. S. Herold, et al. CANADIAN
JOURNAL OF PUBLIC HEALTH 69(4):311-314, July-
August, 1978.

CONTRACEPTIVES AND ECONOMICS
Contraceptive research funding: eroded by inflation, increas-
ingly dependent upon government support. DRAPER
FUND REPORT pp. 16-17, Summer, 1978.

UK women plot suits in US over pill ills, by J. H. Miller.
BUSINESS INSURANCE 13:4, May 28, 1979.

CONTRACEPTIVES AND EDUCATION
Community linkages and outreach services in adolescent con-
traceptive clinic programs, by J. G. Greer, et al. PUB-
LIC HEALTH REPORTS 94:415-419, September-
October, 1979.

Contraception in the adolescent. Educational programmes, by K. Dunn. AUSTRALIAN FAMILY PHYSICIAN 7(Spec No):21-24, August, 1978.

Contraceptive counseling for young girls, by A. Huber. FORTSCHRITTE DU MEDIZIN 96(33):1638-1642, September 7, 1978.

Everything you've always wanted to know about contraceptives; excerpt from Ms. medical guide to a woman's health, by C. W. Cooke, et al. MS MAGAZINE 8:84+, September, 1979.

Preventing unwanted adolescent pregnancy. Cognitive behavioral approach, by S. P. Schinke, et al. AMERICAN JOURNAL OF ORTHOPSYCHIATRY 49:81-88, January, 1979.

Reproductive and contraceptive knowledge among undergraduate university students, by D. S. Godbole, et al. JOURNAL OF FAMILY WELFARE 24:27-31, December, 1977.

Teaching successful use of the diaphragm, by L. L. Corline. AMERICAN JOURNAL OF NURSING 79:1732-1735, October, 1979.

A test of knowledge of contraceptive methods: pharmacists and pharmacy students, by M. Smith, et al. AMERICAN JOURNAL OF PHARMACEUTICAL EDUCATION 43(1):19-21, February, 1979.

CONTRACEPTIVES AND HORMONES
Choice of hormonal contraception, by P. J. Keller. PRAXIS 68(13):408-411, March 27, 1979.

Contraceptive hormones, vascular risk and abnormal precipitation of serum gamma-globulins, by V. Beaumont, et al. SEMAINE DES HOPITAUX DE PARIS 55(1112):

585-591+, March, 1979.

Examination of hormonal contraceptives by enzyme induction, by G. Klinger, et al. ZENTRALBLATT FUR GYNAEKOLOGIE 101(5):302-305, 1979.

Hormonal steroid contraceptives: a further review of adverse reactions, by E. G. McQueen. DRUGS 16(4):322-357, October, 1978.

Immune reactivity of women on hormonal contraceptives: dinitrochlorobenzene sensitization test and skin reactivity to irritants, by G. Gerretsen, et al. CONTRACEPTION 19(1):83-89, January, 1979.

Investigation of hydroxyproline by hormonal contraception, by G. Klinger, et al. ZENTRALBLATT FUER GYNAEKOLOGIE 101(5):306-308, 1979.

Liver cell adenoma associated with oral contraceptive hormone therapy, by N. J. Nicolaides. MEDICAL JOURNAL OF AUSTRALIA 2(6):274-276, September 9, 1978.

Liver function studies under the effect of 4 sequential hormonal contraceptives, by E. Brügmann, et al. ZEITSCHRIFT FUR DIE GESAMTE INNERE MEDIZIN UND IHRE GRENZGEBIETE 33(22):826-829, November 15, 1978.

Liver function studies under the influence of hormonal contraceptives (sequential preparations), by E. Brügmann, et al. DEUTSCHE ZEITSCHRIFT FUER VERDAUUNGSUND STOFFWECHSELKRANKHEITEN 39(2):69-74, 1979.

Low-level, progestogen-releasing vaginal contraceptive devices, by F. G. Burton, et al. CONTRACEPTION 19(5):507-516, May, 1979.

CONTRACEPTIVES AND HORMONES

Natural oestrogens for oral contraception [letter], by J.
Serup, et al. LANCET 2(8140):471-472, September 1,
1979.

Neuro-ophthalmologic accidents caused by hormonal con-
traception, by M. Ardouin, et al. BULLETINS ET
MEMOIRES DE LA SOCIETE FRASCAISE D'OPH-
THALMOLOGIE 90:261-267, 1978.

A new long-acting injectable microcapsule system for the administration of progesterone, by L. R. Beck, et al. FER-
TILITY AND STERILITY 31(5):545-551, May, 1979.

Optimum dosage of an oral contraceptive. A report from the
study of seven combinations of norgestimate and ethinyl
estradiol, by J. S. Lawson, et al. AMERICAN JOURNAL
OF OBSTETRICS AND GYNECOLOGY 134(3):315-
320, June 1, 1979.

Oral contraceptive estrogen and plasma lipid levels, by A.
Hedlin, et al. OBSTETRICS AND GYNECOLOGY
52(4):430-435, October, 1978.

Oral contraceptive use alters the balance of platelet prost-
glandin and thromboxane synthesis, by A. E. Schorer, et
al. PROSTAGLANDINS AND MEDICINE 1(1):5-11,
July, 1978.

Ovulation recovery after hormonal contraception, by J. A.
Portuondo, et al. ENDOSCOPY 11(2):114-115, May,
1979.

Patterns of serum LH and FSH in response to 4-hour infusions of luteinizing hormone releasing hormone in normal
women during menstrul cycle, on oral contraceptives, and
in postmenopausal state, by D. M. de Kretser, et al.
JOURNAL OF CLINICAL ENDOCRINOLOGY AND
METABOLISM 46(2):227-235, February, 1978.

413

Peptide agents may spark contraceptive revolution. MEDI-
CAL WORLD NEWS 20:4-6, September 17, 1979.

Peptide contraception:—antifertility properties of LH-RH
analogues, by A. Corbin, et al. INTERNATIONAL
JOURNAL OF GYNAECOLOGY AND OBSTETRICS
16(5):359-372, March-April, 1979.

A rare obstetric contraindication to the use of vaginal prosta-
glandins for fetal demise, by S. J. Waszak. JOURNAL
OF REPRODUCTIVE MEDICINE 22(4):204-206,
April, 1979.

Secondary effects of hormonal contraception on the breast,
by J. Bonte. GYNAEKOLOGISCHE RUNDSCHAU
18(3-4):220-245, 1978.

Serious liver diseases in women on hormonal contraceptives,
by M. Brodanová, et al. CASOPIS LEKARU CESKYCH
118(1):22-27, January 5, 1979.

Severe liver diseases in women using hormonal contracep-
tion, by M. Brodanová, et al. CESKOSLOVENSKA
GASTROENTEROLOGIE A VYZIVA 32(8):515-516,
December, 1978.

Sex hormone binding globulin capacity as an index of oestrogenicity or androgenicity in women on oral contraceptive
steroids, by M. N. El Makhzangy, et al. CLINICAL EN-
DOCRINOLOGY 10(1):39-45, January, 1979.

Swedish contraceptive uses brain hormone. BRAIN/MIND
3(17):3, July 17, 1978.

Toxic liver diseases after hormonal contraception, by C. W.
Schmidt, et al. ZEITSCHRIFT FUR AERZTLICHE
FORTBILDUNG 72(22):1097-1099, November 15,
1978.

Treatment with a single vaginal suppository containing 15-methyl PGF2 alpha methyl ester et expected time of menstruation, by K. Kinoshita, et al. PROSTAGLANDINS 17(3):469-481, March, 1979.

Vaginal progesterone for contraception, by A. Victor, et al. FERTILITY AND STERILITY 30(6):631-635, December, 1978.

The value of the gingival cytogram for the evaluation of hormonal contraceptives, by G. Klinger, et al. STOMATOLOGIE DER DDR 29(1):11-15, January, 1979.

Vitamin A transporting plasma proteins and female sex hormones, by A. Vahlquist, et al. AMERICAN JOURNAL OF CLINICAL NUTRITION 32(7):1433-1438, July, 1979.

CONTRACEPTIVES AND HOSPITALS
Sterilization and contraceptive services in Catholic hospitals, by J. M. O'Lane. AMERICAN JOURNAL OF GYNAECOLOGY AND OBSTETRICS 133(4):355-357, February 15, 1979.

CONTRACEPTIVES AND MENSTRUATION
A comparison of spontaneous and contraceptive menstrual cycles on a visual discrimination task, by J. Friedman, et al. AUSTRALIAN AND NEW ZEALAND JOURNAL OF PSYCHIATRY 12:233-240, December, 1978.

CONTRACEPTIVES AND THE MENTALLY RETARDED
Use of contraceptive methods by the mentally retarded, by N. Rundeau-Wallace. MENTAL RETARDATION 26(3): 59-61, July, 1976.

CONTRACEPTIVES AND NURSES
Contraceptive supply to single young persons, by D. Wills. NEW ZEALAND NURSING FORUM 7(1):5-6, 1979.

Contraceptive supply to single young persons. . .nurses attitudes, by D. Wills. NEW ZEALAND NURSING FORUM 7:5-6, June-July, 1979.

Legal aspects: the nurse and contraceptive practices among adolescents, by C. L. Sklar. INFIRMIERE CANADIENNE 21(1):16-19, January, 1979.

CONTRACEPTIVES AND PHYSICIANS
Prescribing—is a second opinion required? [letter] , by N. Chisholm. BRITISH MEDICAL JOURNAL 1(6158): 272-273, January 27, 1979.

Spell back phoned-in Rxs. DRUG TOPICS 122:79, November 7, 1978.

Training physicians of developing nations in female surgical contraception, by V. Benchakan, et al. INTERNATIONAL JOURNAL OF GYNAECOLOGY AND OBSTETRICS 15(5):459-461, 1978.

CONTRACEPTIVES AND RELIGION
Contraception and the Christian institution, by R. Slesinski. LINACRE QUARTERLY 46:264-278, August, 1979.

Religion & contraception, by B. Delatiner. McCALLS 106: 70, October, 1978.

Sterilization and contraceptive services in Catholic hospitals, by J. M. O'Lane. AMERICAN JOURNAL OF OBSTETRICS AND GYNECOLOGY 133(4):355-357, February 15, 1979.

CONTRACEPTIVES AND YOUTH
Adolescent contraceptive use: current status of practice and research, by E. W. Freeman, et al. OBSTETRICS AND GYNECOLOGY 53(3):388-394, March, 1979.

Changes in sexual behaviour among unmarried teenage wo-

men utilizing oral contraception, by P. A. Reichelt.
JOURNAL OF POPULATION 1(1):57-68, Spring,
1978.

Coital and contraceptive behavior of female adolescents, by
P. A. Reichelt. ARCHIVES OF SEXUAL BEHAVIOR
8(2):159-172, March, 1979.

Community linkages and outreach services in adolescent contraceptive clinic programs, by J. G. Greer, et al. PUBLIC
HEALTH REPORTS 94:415-419, September-October,
1979.

Condom ads aim at the youth market, by T. Thompson.
MARKETING 83:18, November 27, 1978.

Contraception and the adolescent female, by C. Poole.
JOURNAL OF SCHOOL HEALTH 46(8):475-479,
October, 1976.

Contraception for teenagers, by N. Louden. MIDWIFE
AND HEALTH VISITOR COMMUNITY NURSE 15:
356+, September, 1979.

Contraception for the unmarried, by B. Bhasin. JOURNAL
OF FAMILY WELFARE 25:35-43, December, 1978.

Contraception in the adolescent. Alternative methods, by
G. Betheras. AUSTRALIAN FAMILY PHYSICIAN
7(Spec No):37-38, August, 978.

—. Educational programmes, by K. Dunn. AUSTRALIAN
FAMILY PHYSICIAN 7(Spec No):21-24, August, 1978.

—. Introduction, by J. Leeton. AUSTRALIAN FAMILY
PHYSICIAN 7(Spec No):3-5, August, 1978.

—. Proceedings of a seminar held in Melbourne, March 10,
1978, by the Family Planning Association of Victoria.

AUSTRALIAN FAMILY PHYSICIAN 7(Spec No):3-38, August, 1978.

—. Psychological aspects, by E. Koadlow. AUSTRALIAN FAMILY PHYSICIAN 7(Spec No):16-20, August, 1978.

—. Steps towards a situational ethic, by P. J. Hollingworth. AUSTRALIAN FAMILY PHYSICIAN 7(Spec No):6-11, August, 1978.

Contraceptive counseling for young girls, by A. Huber. FORTSCHRITTE DER MEDEZIN 96(33):1638-1642, September 7, 1978.

Contraceptive use-effectiveness and the American adolescent, by K. C. Lyle, et al. JOURNAL OF REPRODUCTIVE MEDICINE 22(5):225-232, May, 1979.

Middle-class Americans frown on premarital sex but think teens should be offered contraception. FAMILY PLANNING PERSPECTIVES 10(5):301-302, September-October, 1978.

Oral contraception in the adolescent, by E. Weisberg. AUSTRALIAN FAMILY PHYSICIAN 7(Spec No):32-36, August, 1978.

Oral contraceptives and stroke in young women: a clinico-pathologic correlation, by N. S. Irey, et al. NEUROLOGY 28(12):1216-1219, December, 1978.

Problems of teaching sex education—a survey of Ontario Secondary Schools, by E. S. Herold, et al. FAMILY COORDINATOR 28(2):199-203, April, 1979.

Reasons for nonuse of contraception by sexually active women aged 15-19, by M. Zelnik, et al. FAMILY PLANNING PERSPECTIVES 11:289-296, September-October, 1979.

Schoolchildren and contraception. Knowledge, attitudes and behavior, by L. Bernsted, et al. UGESKRIFT FOR LAEGER 141(6):397-399, February 5, 1979.

Self-esteem, locus of control, and adolescent contraception, by E. S. Herold, et al. JOURNAL OF PSYCHOLOGY 101:83-88, January, 1979.

Sexual contraceptive attitudes and behaviour of high school and college females, by E. S. Herold, et al. CANADIAN JOURNAL OF PUBLIC HEALTH 69(4):311-314, July-August, 1978.

Survey of contraceptive services available to college students, by B. E. Pruitt. RESEARCH QUARTERLY 48:489-491, May, 1977.

Use and abuse of the minipill in adolescence, by A. Maranzana. MINERVA MEDICA 69(46):3180-3182, September 30, 1978.

DR. WILLIAM WADDILL
Abortionist strangles baby (Dr. Wm. B. Wadill on trial for allegedly strangling baby after aborting it), by L. Jeffries. CATHOLIC DIGEST 4:16+, June, 1978.

Waddill strangled infant, says witness in murder trial of California abortionist, by K. Granville. OUR SUNDAY VISITOR 67:2, April 1, 1979.

FAMILY PLANNING (GENERAL)
The choice of childlessness: a workshop model, by M. G. Russell, et al. FAMILY COORDINATOR 27:179-184, April, 1978.

Classical approaches to population and family planning, by L. P. Wilkinson. POPULATION AND DEVELOPMENT REVIEW 4(3):439, September, 1978.

Conception control—a growing awareness. AMERICAN
PHARMACY 19(8):14-15, July, 1979.

Concepts of family planning, by C. W. Hubbard. CURRENT
PRACTICE IN OBSTETRIC AND GYNECOLOGIC
NURSING 2:3-23, 1978.

An extension of the waiting time distribution of first conceptions, by K. B. Pathak. JOURNAL OF BIOSOCIAL SCI-
ENCE 10:231-234, July, 1978.

Family planning, by H. Dutly. KRANKENPFLEGE 71(7):
296-305, July, 1979.

Family planning and contraception. NOT MAN APART
8(6):11, April, 1978.

Family planning and family health, by J. F. Martin. INTER-
NATIONAL NURSING REVIEW 25(6):172-174, November-December, 1978.

Family planning availability and contraceptive practice, by
G. Rodríguez. FAMILY PLANNING PERSPECTIVES
11(1):51-70, January-February, 1979.

Family planning: a crucial programme, by A. B. Wadia.
JOURNAL OF FAMILY WELFARE 24:58-65, December, 1977.

Family planning in big town conditions depending on the
birthplace of the parents, by I. Dimitrov. FOLIA MEDI-
CA 20(1):35-41, 1978.

Family planning policies: a 1979 people wallchart, by N.
Fincancioglu, et al. PEOPLE 6:1 folded sheet insert
no 2, 1979.

The family planning success story, by M. Potts. PEOPLE
6(2):14, 1979.

Fertility effects of family planning programs: a methodological review, by J. D. Forrest, et al. SOCIAL BIOLOGY 25:145-163, Summer, 1978.

Filling family planning gaps, by B. Stokes. POPULATION REPORTS (20):J369-J389, September, 1978.

How many children do couples really want; by L. C. Coombs. FAMILY PLANNING PERSPECTIVES 10(5):303, September-October, 1978.

Improving management through evaluation: techniques and strategies for family planning programs, by M. E. Gorosh. STUDIES IN FAMILY PLANNING 9(6):163-168, June, 1978.

Intentionally childless couple, by D. E. Bensen. U.S.A. TODAY 107:45-46, January, 1979.

Lactation for delaying re-establishment of menstruation and its possible role in family planning, by S. Rathee, et al. JOURNAL OF THE INDIAN MEDICAL ASSOCIATION 71(2):30-33, July 16, 1978.

A look at community based planning, by E. Trainer. POPULI 6(2):9, 1979.

Management issues in the organization and delivery of family planning services, by R. A. Loddengaard, et al. PUBLIC HEALTH REPORTS 94:459-465, September-October, 1979.

Motivation and family planning: incentives and disincentives in the delivery system, by F. O. Bicknell, et al. SOCIAL SCIENCE AND MEDICINE 10(11-12):579-583, November-December, 1976.

Must you have more than one child? by T. B. Brazelton. REDBOOK 152(5):58, March, 1979.

New issues, new options: a management perspective on population and family planning, by D. C. Korten. STUDIES IN FAMILY PLANNING 10(1):3, January, 1979.

On drawing policy conclusions from multiple regressions: some queries and dilemmas, by R. B. Dixon. STUDIES IN FAMILY PLANNING 9(10-11):286-288, October-November, 1978.

Planned childbirth, by S. Maehara. KANGO 30(12):18-24, December, 1978.

Planning for sex, marriage, contraception, and pregnancy, by A. L. Graber, et al. DIABETES CARE 1(3):202-203, May-June, 1978.

Prescribing and family planning [letter], by N. Chisholm. BRITISH MEDICAL JOURNAL 2(6145):1167-1168, October 21, 1978.

The role of medical factors in the failure to achieve desired family size, by C. M. Young. JOURNAL OF BIOSOCIAL SCIENCE 11(2):159-171, April, 1979.

Sex differences in adolescent family communication and media use about occupations and family planning, by P. V. Miller. DISSERTATION ABSTRACTS INTERNATIONAL 38(6-A):3123, December, 1977.

Subjective expected utility and the prediction of birth-planning decisions, by L. R. Beach, et al. ORGANIZATIONAL BEHAVIOR AND HUMAN PERFORMANCE 24:18-28, August, 1979.

Underlying family-size preferences and reproductive behavior, by L. C. Coombs. STUDIES IN FAMILY PLANNING 10(1):25-36, January, 1979.

Unmet needs. PEOPLE 5(3):25, 1978.

We quit, bishop tells United Way: Planned Parenthood won't play in Peoria. OUR SUNDAY VISITOR 68:1, August 12, 1979.

Where are the deaths? [editorial] . FAMILY PLANNING PERSPECTIVES 11(2):78+, March-April, 1979.

Why family planning is failing, by M. A. Qadeer. SOCIAL POLICY 6(3):19-23, November-December, 1975.

Why infertility services should be provided by family planning agencies, by R. S. Atlas, et al. JOURNAL OF NURSE MIDWIFERY 24:33-35, July-August, 1978.

World leaders declaration on population. STUDIES IN FAMILY PLANNING 9(7):180-181, July, 1978.

AUSTRALIA
　　Attitudes towards family planning among the women of a Northern Australian Aboriginal community, by J. Reid, et al. MEDICAL JOURNAL OF AUSTRALIA 1(2 Suppl):5-7, February 24, 1979.

　　Cultural factors affecting the use of family planning services in an Aboriginal community, by J. Reid. MEDICAL JOURNAL OF AUSTRALIA 1(2 Suppl):1-4, February 24, 1979.

BANGLADESH
　　Integration of health, nutrition, and family planning: the Companiganj project in Bangladesh, by C. McCord. FOOD RESEARCH INSTITUTE STUDIES 16(2): 91-105, 1977.

CANADA
　　After initial risk-taking, most Canadian students use effective methods. FAMILY PLANNING PERSPECTIVES 11(1):44, January-February, 1979.

CANADA

The British Columbia Conference on the family—process and outcomes, by J. D. Friesen, et al. FAMILY CO-ORDINATOR 28(2):260-263, April, 1979.

CHILI

Family allowance and family planning in Chile, by S. J. Plank. AMERICAN JOURNAL OF PUBLIC HEALTH 68(10):989-994, October, 1978.

CHINA

Birth planning in China, by M. Chen. FAMILY PLAN-NING PERSPECTIVES 5:92-100, September, 1979.

The Chinese experience, by P. Chen. PEOPLE 6(2):17, 1979.

The Chinese experience [some of the ways in which China has established the small family norm, provided nation-wide birth planning services and measured the results], by P. Chen. PEOPLE 6:17-20, November 2, 1979.

Planned fertility and fertility socialization in Kwangtung province, by P. P. T. Ng. CHINA QUARTERLY (78):351-359, June, 1979.

COLOMBIA

The differential evaluation of "large" and "small" families in rural Colombia: implications for family planning, by M. Micklin, et al. SOCIAL BIOLOGY 22(1):44-59, Spring, 1975.

An economic model of contraceptive choice: analysis of family planning acceptors in Bogotá, by W. J. Kahley, et al. SOCIAL BIOLOGY 24(2):135-143, Summer, 1977.

COSTA RICA
Public policies in conflict: land reform and family planning in Costa Rica, by M. A. Seligson. COMPARATIVE POLITICS 12:49-62, October, 1979.

DENMARK
Sex and family planning in Denmark and in Danish Communes, by T. H. Shey. INTERNATIONAL JOURNAL OF SOCIOLOGY OF THE FAMILY 7(1):15-24, January-June, 1977.

EAST ASIA
East Asia review, 1976-7: an overview, by S. M. Keeny. STUDIES IN FAMILY PLANNING 9(9):253-254, September, 1978.

GHANA
AECT's international window; Ghana national family planning program, by R. E. Wileman. AUDIO-VISUAL INSTRUCTION 24:48-49, February, 1979.

Impact of family planning information on acceptance at a Ghanaian rural health post, by W. B. Ward, et al. INTERNATIONAL JOURNAL OF HEALTH EDUCATION 21(4):273-281, 1978.

GREAT BRITAIN
Comparisons: the United States and Britain, by E. F. Jones. FAMILY PLANNING PERSPECTIVES 11(2):136-137, March-April, 1979.

Family planning in the practice of midwifery in England and Wales, by S. M. Clark. JOURNAL OF NURSE-MIDWIFERY 24:11-17, May-June, 1979.

Family planning nursing in Britain, by M. Pollock. IPPF MEDICAL BULLETIN 12:1-2, October, 1978.

The family, sex and marriage in England 1500-1800

GREAT BRITAIN
[critique of Lawrence Stone] , by A. MacFarlane.
HISTORY AND THEORY 18(1):103-126, 1979.

Family size, contraceptive practice and fertility intentions in England and Wales, 1967-1975, by A. Cartwright. FAMILY PLANNING PERSPECTIVES 11:
128-131+, March-April, 1979.

GUATEMALA
Ethnic differences in family planning acceptance in rural
Guatemala, by J. T. Bertrand, et al. STUDIES IN
FAMILY PLANNING 10:238-245, August-Septem-
ber, 1979.

HONG KONG
East Asia review, 1976-7: Hong Kong, by P. Lam, et al.
STUDIES IN FAMILY PLANNING 9(9):234-235,
September, 1978.

INDIA
Awareness of unmarried girls regarding population problem, human reproduction and family planning, by P.
Rasheed, et al. INDIAN PEDIATRICS 15(9):735-
745, September, 1978.

Effect of family planning programme on reduction in
fertility in Haryana, 1965-75, by P. A. Kataraki.
JOURNAL OF FAMILY WELFARE 25:20-27, December, 1978.

Family planning campaign halted; India, by A. S. Abraham. TIMES EDUCATIONAL SUPPLEMENT
3305:15, November 3, 1978.

Family planning in India: living with frustration, by J.
Rowley. POPULI 5(4):7, 1978.

From one generation to the next: changes in fertility,

INDIA
>   family size preferences, and family planning in an
>   Indian state between 1951 and 1975, by K. Sriniva-
>   san, et al. STUDIES IN FAMILY PLANNING
>   9(10-11):258-271, October-November, 1978.

>   Is there an alternative to the family planning programme
>   in India? by S. Mukerji. JOURNAL OF FAMILY
>   WELFARE 25:19-33, September 1978.

>   Learning about the population problem: children's atti-
>   tudes toward family planning in India, by S. Iyengar.
>   YOUTH AND SOCIETY 10(3):275-295, March,
>   1979.

>   Political will and family planning: the implications of
>   India's emergency experience [under the former Prime
>   minister Indira Gandhi, during 1975 and 1976], by
>   D. R. Gwatkin. POPULATION AND DEVELOP-
>   MENT REVIEW 5:29-59, March, 1979.

INDONESIA
>   East Asia review, 1976-7: Indonesia, by S. Surjaningrat,
>   et al. STUDIES IN FAMILY PLANNING 9(9):235-
>   237, September, 1978.

>   Where population planning makes a dent: Indonesia's
>   growth rate is 1.9%—and going down, by J. W. McCul-
>   la. AGENDA 2:2-5, March, 1979.

IRAN
>   Family type, family resources, and fertility among Iran-
>   ian peasant women, by A. Aghajanian. SOCIAL
>   BIOLOGY 25:205-209, Fall, 1978.

>   Toward an assessment of the social role of rural midwives
>   and its implication for the family program: an Iranian
>   case study, by W. O. Beeman, et al. HUMAN OR-
>   GANIZATION 37:295-300, Fall, 1978.

IRELAND
  Family planning: the Irish solution, by C. Walker. SPEC-
  TATOR p. 12, March 31, 1979.

ISRAEL
  Mother and comforter [family planning in Israel] , by A.
  Sablosky. NEW DIRECTIONS FOR WOMEN 7:12,
  August, 1978.

JAPAN
  Family planning in Japan: a comparison between success-
  ful and unsuccessful couples, by C. M. Lu, et al.
  INTERNATIONAL JOURNAL OF HEALTH EDU-
  CATION 21(3):174-182, 1978.

KOREA
  East Asia review, 1976-7: Korea (South), by D. W. Han,
  et al. STUDIES IN FAMILY PLANNING 9(9):238-
  241, September, 1978.

  Effect of infant death on subsequent fertility in Korea
  and the role of family planning, by C. B. Park, et al.
  AMERICAN JOURNAL OF PUBLIC HEALTH 69:
  557-565, June, 1979.

  Family planning program in Korea, by J. M. Yang.
  YONSEI MEDICAL JOURNAL 18(1):64-74, 1977.

LATIN AMERICA
  Family planning in four Latin American countries—
  knowledge, use and unmet need: some findings from
  the world fertility survey, by J. W. Brackett. INTER-
  NATIONAL FAMILY PLANNING PERSPECTIVES
  AND DIGEST 4:116-123, Winter, 1978.

  Politics of Latin America: family-planning policy, by J.
  L. Weaver. JOURNAL OF DEVELOPING AREAS
  415:37, July, 1978.

MALAYSIA
  East Asia review, 1976-7: Malaysia, by N. L. Aziz.
    STUDIES IN FAMILY PLANNING 9(9):41-42, Sep-
    tember, 1978.

  Impact of the Malaysian family planning program on
    births: a comparison of matched acceptor and non-
    acceptor birth rates, by J. T. Johnson, et al. POPU-
    LATION STUDIES 32(2):215, July, 1978.

  Influences on family planning acceptance: an analysis of
    background and program factors in Malaysia, by J.
    T. Johnson. STUDIES IN FAMILY PLANNING
    10(1):15-24, January, 1979.

MEXICO
  Characteristics of women participating in the family plan-
    ning program of the Direccion General de Atencion
    Medica Materna Infantil y Planificacion Familiar de la
    SSA, by S. Correu Azcona, et al. SPM 20(3):275-
    285, May-June, 1978.

  Efficiency in the use of contraception in the voluntary
    family planning program of the Institute Mexicana
    del Seguro Social, by J. Garcia Geña, et al. SPM
    20(4):425-434, July-August, 1978.

  Knowledge about family planning in the urban area of
    Merida, Yucatan. Restricting factors, by T. E.
    Cando de Cetina, et al. SPM 20(3):355-360, May-
    June, 1978.

NIGERIA
  Birth intervals, survival and growth in a Nigerian village,
    by P. Doyle, et al. JOURNAL OF BIOSOCIAL SCI-
    ENCE 10(1):81-94, January, 1978.

PAKISTAN
  Communications channels and family planning in Pakis-

PAKISTAN
> tan, by S. H. Syed. STUDIES IN FAMILY PLAN-
> NING 10(2):53-60, February, 1979.

PERU
> Behavior of the male population with respect to family
> planning in Trujillo, Peru, by V. Villanueva Montoya,
> et al. BOLETIN DE LA OFICINA SANITARIA
> PAN AMERICANA 85(4):290-299, October, 1978.

THE PHILIPPINES
> Continued use of contraception among Philippine family
> planning acceptors. A multivariate analysis, by J. F.
> Phillips. STUDIES IN FAMILY PLANNING 9:182-
> 197, July, 1978.

> East Asia review, 1976-7: Philippines, by M. B. Concep-
> ción. STUDIES IN FAMILY PLANNING 9(9):243-
> 245, September, 1978.

> Family planning course for nurses and midwives in the
> Philippines, by A. Cerdinio. IPPF MEDICAL BUL-
> LETIN 12(5):2-3, October, 1978.

> Maternal and child health/family planning. STUDIES
> IN FAMILY PLANNING 10(6-7): , June-July,
> 1979.

SINGAPORE
> East Asia review, 1976-7: Singapore, by M. Loh. STUD-
> IES IN FAMILY PLANNING 9(9):246-247, Septem-
> ber, 1978.

SOUTH AFRICA
> Planning families or checking population? by T. Lukk.
> AFRICA REPORT 23:35-38, November, 1978.

TAIWAN
> Do intentions predict fertility? the experience in Taiwan,

TAIWAN
> 1967-74, by A. I. Hermalin, et al. STUDIES IN
> FAMILY PLANNING 10:75-95, March, 1979.

> East Asia review, 1976-7: Taiwan, by C. M. Wang, et al.
> STUDIES IN FAMILY PLANNING 9(9):247-250,
> September, 1978.

> The transition from natural to controlled fertility in Tai-
> wan: a cross-sectional analysis of demand and supply
> factors, by S. J. Jajeebhoy. STUDIES IN FAMILY
> PLANNING 9:206-211, August, 1978.

THAILAND
> Abortion in rural Thailand: a survey of practitioners, by
> T. Narkavonnakit. STUDIES IN FAMILY PLAN-
> NING 10:223-229, August-September, 1979.

> East Asia review, 1976-7: Thailand, by W. Kolasartsenee,
> et al. STUDIES IN FAMILY PLANNING 9(9):251-
> 252, September, 1978.

> The influence of traditional values and beliefs on family
> planning decisions in Thailand, by D. M. Ebnet.
> DISSERTATION ABSTRACTS INTERNATIONAL
> 38(10-A):6343, April, 1978.

> The McCormick Family Planning Program in Chiang Mai,
> Thailand, by G. B. Baldwin. STUDIES IN FAMILY
> PLANNING 9(12):300-313, December, 1978.

> Measuring the Thai family planning program's impact on
> fertility rates: a comparison of computer models, by
> S. E. Khoo. STUDIES IN FAMILY PLANNING
> 10(4):137-145, April, 1979.

TURKEY
> Cost-effectiveness evaluation of a home visiting triage
> program for family planning in Turkey, by R. L.

TURKEY
Bertera, et al. AMERICAN JOURNAL OF PUB-
LIC HEALTH 69(9):950-953, September, 1979.

The effects of husband and wife education on family
planning in rural Turkey, by N. H. Fisek, et al.
STUDIES IN FAMILY PLANNING 9(10-11):280-
285, October-November, 1978.

UNITED STATES
Comparisons: the United States and Britain, by E. F.
Jones. FAMILY PLANNING PERSPECTIVES
11(2):136-137, March-April, 1979.

Comparisons: the United States and Britain. . .fertility
patterns, by E. F. Jones. FAMILY PLANNING
PERSPECTIVES 11:136-137, March-April, 1979.

Factors related to the intention to have additional children in the United States: a reanalysis of data from
the 1965 and 1970 national fertility studies, by C.
Lee, et al. DEMOGRAPHY 15:337-344, August,
1978.

Family planning and abortion policy in the United
States, by K. H. Gould. SOCIAL SERVICE RE-
VIEW 53:452-463, September, 1979.

Family planning in Virginia: the role of public health,
by H. D. Gabel. VIRGINIA MEDICINE 106(5):
393-394+, May, 1979.

Fertility control and family planning in the United
States of America, by R. W. Rochat, et al. BOLETIN
DE LA OFICINA SANITARIN PANAMERICANA
85(2):115-127, August, 1978.

Nurse-midwifery and family planning in the United
States: data from the 1976-1977 American College

UNITED STATES
of Nurse-Midwives' study, by S. H. Fischman, et al. ADVANCES IN PLANNED PARENTHOOD 13(3-4):78-86, 1978.

Rural and urban family planning services in the United States, by A. Torres. FAMILY PLANNING PERSPECTIVES 11:109-114, March-April, 1979.

Toward greater reproductive freedom: Wisconsin's new family planning act. WISCONSIN LAW REVIEW 1979:509-536, 1979.

FAMILY PLANNING: ATTITUDES
Changing approaches to population assistance [since 1974; on the part of donor agencies, chiefly], by M. Wolfson. PEOPLE 6:11-13, November 2, 1979.

Hierarchy of birth planning values: an aid in genetic counseling, by B. D. Townes, et al. JOURNAL OF PSYCHIATRIC NURSING 17:37-41, September, 1979.

To have—or not to have—another child: family planning attitudes, intentions, and behavior, by D. Vinokur-Kaplan. JOURNAL OF APPLIED SOCIAL PSYCHOLOGY 8(1):29-46, January-March, 1978.

FAMILY PLANNING: DEVELOPING COUNTRIES
The role of family planning in recent rapid fertility declines in developing countries, by J. W. Brackett, et al. STUDIES IN FAMILY PLANNING 9(12):314-323, December, 1978.

FAMILY PLANNING: ECONOMICS
AID investment of $1 billion in family planning/population is resulting in sharp birthrate declines. FAMILY PLANNING PERSPECTIVES 11(1):45-46, January-February, 1979.

The cost per unit of family planning services, by W. C. Robinson. JOURNAL OF BIOSOCIAL SCIENCE 11(1):93-103, January, 1979.

Natural family planning; in the U.S. the fight goes on for government funding, by F. Franzonia. OUR SUNDAY VISITOR 68:2, August 19, 1979.

FAMILY PLANNING: HISTORY
Family Planning Association, by B. Górnicki. PEDIATRIA POLSKA 54(6):633-637, June, 1979.

The family, sex and marriage in England 1500-1800 [critique of Lawrence Stone], by A. MacFarlane. HISTORY AND THEORY 18(1):103-126, 1979.

FAMILY PLANNING: LAWS AND LEGISLATION
Constitutional law—substantive due process—children's rights—parents' right to be notified when their children are provided contraceptives by state funded family planning clinics. WAYNE LAW REVIEW 25:1135-1146, July, 1979.

Family planning democratized, by M. Manisoff. AMERICAN JOURNAL OF NURSING 75(10):1660-1666, October, 1975.

Health (family planning) bill 1978. IRISH MEDICAL JOURNAL 72(1):1-2, January 12, 1979.

Senate passage: family planning, crib death fund authorized, by L. B. Weiss. CONGRESSIONAL QUARTERLY WEEKLY REPORT 36:2063-2065, August 5, 1978.

FAMILY PLANNING: NATURAL
Natural family planning: the contribution of fertility awareness to body-person integration, by H. Klaus. SOCIAL THOUGHT 5:35-42, Winter, 1979.

—: Father Bernard Haring's position: an essay review, by W. May. SOCIAL THOUGHT 5:67-71, Summer, 1979.

—: in the U.S. the fight goes on for government funding, by F. Franzonia. OUR SUNDAY VISITOR 68:2, August 19, 1979.

—: the ovulation method, by N. Elder. JOURNAL OF NURSE-MIDWIFERY 23:25-30, Fall, 1978.

Natural family planning teachers, inc. WELL-BEING 33:5, June 15, 1978.

A randomized prospective study of the use-effectiveness of two methods of natural family planning: an interim report, by M. E. Wade, et al. AMERICAN JOURNAL OF OBSTETRICS AND GYNECOLOGY 134(6):628-631, July 15, 1979.

WHO study finds natural family planning to be 'relatively ineffective' even with careful teaching. FAMILY PLANNING PERSPECTIVES 1(1):40-41, January-February, 1979.

FAMILY PLANNING: RURAL
Knowledge, attitude and practice of family planning in a rural Ceylonese community, by P. L. R. Dias, et al. JOURNAL OF FAMILY WELFARE 25:28-34, December, 1978.

Rural and urban family planning services in the United States, by A. Torres. FAMILY PLANNING PERSPECTIVES 11:109-114, March-April, 1979.

Utilization of paramedical personnel in family planning services in rural areas: an experimental study, by R. Rivera Damm, et al. SPM 20(2):177-194, March-April, 1978.

FAMILY PLANNING: STATISTICS
Factors related to the intention to have additional children in the United States: a reanalysis of data from the 1965 and 1970 national fertility studies, by C. F. Lee, et al. DEMOGRAPHY 15(3):337-344, August, 1978.

FAMILY PLANNING AND ADOLESCENTS
The needs of adolescent women utilizing family planning services, by J. Cahn. JOURNAL OF SEX RESEARCH 13(3):210-222, August, 1977.

FAMILY PLANNING AND ADVERTISING
Sex differences in adolescent family communication and media use about occupations and family planning, by P. V. Miller. DISSERTATION ABSTRACTS INTERNATIONAL 38(6-A):3123, December, 1977.

FAMILY PLANNING AND COLLEGE STUDENTS
After initial risk-taking, most Canadian students use effective methods. FAMILY PLANNING PERSPECTIVES 11(1):44, January-February, 1979.

Attitudes related to the number of children wanted and expected by college students in three countries, by H. G. Gough, et al. JOURNAL OF CROSS-CULTURAL PSYCHOLOGY 7:413-424, December, 1976.

FAMILY PLANNING AND THE MILITARY
Pronatalism and fertility: the case of the military, by C. S. Stokes, et al. SOCIAL BIOLOGY 25:259-271, Winter, 1978.

FAMILY PLANNING AND NURSES
The contribution of nurse practitioners to service delivery in family planning, by M. Flynn. LAMP 35:14-16, October, 1978.

Family planning course for nurses and midwives in the Philippines, by A. Cerdinio. IPPF MEDICAL BULLETIN

12(5):2-3, October, 1978.

Family planning. Current problems with special reference to the preparation and education of obstetrical nursing staff, by L. B. Sassi. PROFESSIONI INFERMIERISTICHE 32(2):65-66, April-June, 1979.

Family planning nursing in Britain, by M. Pollock. IPPF MEDICAL BULLETIN 12(5):1-2, October, 1978.

Impact of family planning nurse practitioners, by M. Manisoff. JOGN 8(2):73-77, March-April, 1979.

Nurse specialists in family planning: the results of a 3-year study, by J. Newton, et al. CONTRACEPTION 18(6): 577-592, December, 1978.

Visit with a practicing midwife: Ms. Sazuki Suzuki who is active as a public health nurse at the town office of Tsukui-machi, Kanagawa Pref.—a promoter of regional health care and family planning, by M. Fujiwara. JO-SANPU ZASSHI 32(7):450-453, July, 1978.

Why it is right for family planning nurses to prescribe the pill, by S. Thompson. NURSING MIRROR AND MID-WIVE'S JOURNAL 147(16):9, October 19, 1978.

FAMILY PLANNING AND PHYSICIANS
The effectiveness of non-physicians as providers of family planning services, by B. N Bibb. JOGN 8(3):137-143, May-June, 1979.

Family health and family planning in medical education, by J. F. Martin. TROPICAL DOCTOR 9(2):85-88+, April, 1979.

Family planning and the private primary care physician, by P. Tschetter. FAMILY PLANNING PERSPECTIVES 10(6):350-353, November-December, 1978.

Family planning visits to private physicians, by B. K. Cypress. FAMILY PLANNING PERSPECTIVES 11:234-236, July-August, 1979.

The psychiatrist in a family planning center, by G. Maruani, et al. ANNALES MEDICO-PSYCHOLOGIQUES 136(6-8):879-891, June-October, 1978.

FAMILY PLANNING AND THE RETARDED
Family planning agencies and the mentally retarded, by J. L. Cohen. THE JOURNAL FOR SPECIAL EDUCATORS 15:3-9+, Fall, 1978+.

Family planning for the mentally ill [letter], by H. Grunebaum. AMERICAN JOURNAL OF PSYCHIATRY 136(4A):461-462, April, 1979.

FAMILY PLANNING AND YOUTH
Adolescent sexuality: legal aspects, by L. Vick. AUSTRALIAN FAMILY PHYSICIAN 7(Spec No):12-15, August, 1978.

Adolescents and knowledge of population dynamics and family planning, by V. Gupta, et al. JOURNAL OF FAMILY WELFARE 25:33-40, March, 1979.

Adolescents' knowledge of childbearing, by J. Walter, et al. FAMILY COORDINATOR 28(2):163-171, April, 1979.

Family planning services for indigent women and girls, by K. T. Sung. HEALTH AND SOCIAL WORK 3(4):152-172, November, 1978.

Teenage sexual behavior: perceptive and behavioural outcomes associated with receipt of family planning services, by C. A. Akpom, et al. JOURNAL OF BIOSOCIAL SCIENCE 11:85-92, January, 1979.

FAMILY PLANNING CLINICS
  Birth control: clinics are major source of care for poor teen-
     agers, and for more affluent, too. FAMILY PLANNING
     PERSPECTIVES 11:197-198, May-June, 1979.

  Contraceptive practice after clinic discontinuation, by P. S.
     Cosgrove, et al. FAMILY PLANNING PERSPECTIVES
     10:337-341, November-December, 1978.

  Contraceptive risk taking among women entering a family
     planning clinic, by E. E. Hall. DISSERTATION AB-
     STRACTS INTERNATIONAL 38(1-0B):5017, April,
     1978.

  Effectiveness of sex information dissemination by selected
     planned parenthood clinics, by G. D. Pippin. DISSER-
     TATION ABSTRACTS INTERNATIONAL 39(7-A):
     4070, January, 1979.

  An exploration of factors affecting referral of adolescent girls
     to a planned parenthood clinic, by S. E. Osterbusch.
     DISSERTATION ABSTRACTS INTERNATIONAL
     38(11-A):6943, May, 1978.

  Extent of demand for exclusive private family planning
     clinics among urban middle classes, by G. Narayana.
     JOURNAL OF FAMILY WELFARE 24:52-57, Decem-
     ber, 1977.

  Nutrition counseling at planned parenthood centers, by H.
     Smiciklas-Wright, et al. PUBLIC HEALTH REPORTS
     94(3):239-242, June, 1979.

  Planned parenthood fights back. NATIONAL NOW 11(8):
     12, July, 1978.

  Planned parenthood: a port in the storm (problem pregnancy
     a lonely experience), by R. K. Rein. NEW JERSEY
     MONTHLY 3:49, July, 1979.

The record of family planning programs, by R. Freedman, et al. STUDIES IN FAMILY PLANNING 7(1):40, January, 1976.

Voluntary agencies in transition: changing patterns of relationships in countries with governmental family planning programs, by S. M. Keeny. JOURNAL OF VOLUNTARY ACTION RESEARCH 2(1):16-23, January, 1973.

FAMILY PLANNING COUNSELING
Age structure, unwanted fertility, and the association between racial composition and family planning programs: a comment on Wright, by M. Hout. SOCIAL FORCES 57(4):1387-1392, June, 1979.

Awareness of unmarried girls regarding population problem, human reproduction and family planning, by P. Rasheed, et al. INDIAN PEDIATRICS 15(9):735-745, September, 1978.

Counseling clients in natural methods of family planning, by M. T. Curry. MARYLAND NURSE :26-29, February, 1979.

Nutrition counseling at planned parenthood centers, by H. Smiciklas-Wright, et al. PUBLIC HEALTH REPORTS 94:239-242, May-June, 1979.

Tasks of family and maternal counseling. ORVOSI HETILAP 120(6):341, February 11, 1979.

Why it is right for family planning nurses to prescribe the pill, by S. Thompson. NURSING MIRROR AND MIDWIVE'S JOURNAL 147(16):9, October 19, 1978.

FAMILY PLANNING EDUCATION
Communicating population and family planning, by R. R. Worrall. POPULATION BULLETIN 31(5):3-40, February, 1977.

Continued education course of the Swiss Society for Family
Planning, Basel, 13-14 May 1977. Current contraception.
GYNAEKOLOGISCHE RUNDSCHAU 18(3-4):157-266,
1978.

Family health and family planning in medical education, by
J. F. Martin. TROPICAL DOCTOR 9(2):85-88+, April,
1979.

Family planning and sex education: the Chinese approach,
by S. E. Fraser. COMPARATIVE EDUCATION 13:15-
28, March, 1977.

Family planning training: a network program and sample instructional materials, by K. Finseth, et al. IMPROVING
HUMAN PERFORMANCE QUARTERLY 7(1):217-
225, Spring, 1978.

Sex education for teenagers, by J. H. Ford. WESTERN
JOURNAL OF MEDICINE 130(3):273-276, March,
1979.

Survey on knowledge and interest on family planning, by
Y. Sakamoto, et al. JOSANPU ZASSHI 33(3):143-
146, March, 1979.

FAMILY PLANNING RESEARCH
The correspondence of data gathered from husband and
wife: implications for family planning studies, by J. J.
Card. SOCIAL BIOLOGY 25(3):196-204, Fall, 1978.

Research in family planning; symposium. WORLD HEALTH
pp. 2-37, August, 1978.

FERTILITY
Consistency between fertility attitudes and behaviour: a conceptual model, by S. B. Kar. POPULATION STUDIES
32:173-186, March, 1978.

Consistencey of reporting fertility planning status, by N. B. Ryder. STUDIES IN FAMILY PLANNING 10(4):115-128, April, 1979.

Psychiatric aspects of infertility, by H. E. Walker. UROLO-GIC CLINICS OF NORTH AMERICA 5(3):481-488, October, 1978.

FERTILITY CONTROL
Assistance to fertility regulation projects within the United States system, by R. K. Som. POPULATION BULLE-TIN (10):36-62, 1977.

The biocultural pattern of Japanese-American fertility, by D. L. Leonetti. SOCIAL BIOLOGY 25:38-51, Spring, 1978.

A conceptual model for the identification, organization, and measure of influence of fertility policies and programs, by B. F. Pendleton. SOCIAL BIOLOGY 23(4):326-340, Winter, 1976.

Fertility and demographic structures—hypothesis on evolution of fertility since 1940, by H. Leridon. POPULA-TION 33:441-447, March-April, 1978.

Fertility control and family planning in the United States of America, by R. W. Rochat, et al. BOLETIN DE LA OFICINA SANITARIA PANAMERICANA 85(2):115-127, August, 1978.

Fertility control: what's ahead?—symposium, by G. Celso-Ramon, et al. CONTEMPORARY OB/GYN 13(1):54, January, 1979.

Fertility in psychiatric outpatients, by W. A. Burr, et al. HOSPITAL AND COMMUNITY PSYCHIATRY 30:527-531, August, 1979.

Fertility preferences and social exchange theory, by L. J. Beckman. JOURNAL OF APPLIED SOCIAL PSYCHOLOGY 9:147-169, March-April, 1979.

Fertility regulating agents from plants. WHO CHRONICLES 33(2):58-59, February, 1979.

Fertility regulation in the male, by D. M. de Kretser. WHO BULLETIN 56(3):353-360, 1978.

Fertility related attitudes of minority mothers with large and small families, by M. W. Linn, et al. JOURNAL OF APPLIED SOCIAL PSYCHOLOGY 8:1-14, January-March, 1978.

Genetic causes and workup of male and female infertility. 1. Prenatal reproductive loss, by J. M. Opitz, et al. POSTGRADUATE MEDICINE 65(5):247-252+, May, 1979.

Immunological procedure to regulate fertility, by V. C. Stevens. BOLETIN DE LA OFICINA SANITARIA PANAMERICANA 86(1):63-76, January, 1979.

Informed consent for fertility control services [United States], by E. W. Paul, et al. FAMILY PLANNING PERSPECTIVES 11:159-163+, May-June, 1979.

Intergenerational occupational mobility and fertility: a reassessment, by F. D. Bean, et al. AMERICAN SOCIOLOGICAL REVIEW 44:608-619, August, 1979.

Malleability of fertility-related attitudes and behaviour in a Filipino migrant sample, by J. J. Card. DEMOBRAPHY 15:459-476, November, 1978.

Mediosocial reasons for limiting the birth rate, by I. V. Poliakov, et al. ZDRAVOOKHRANENIYE ROSSIISKOI FEDERATZII (3):17-21, 1979.

Model of fertility by planning status, by N. B. Ryder. DE-MOGRAPHY 15:433-458, November, 1978.

Multivariate analysis of interstate variation in fertility of teenage girls, by E. A. Brann. AMERICAN JOURNAL OF PUBLIC HEALTH 69:661-666, July, 1979.

On social norms and fertility decline, by N. R. Crook. JOUR-NAL OF DEVELOPMENT STUDIES 14:198-210, July, 1978.

Ova harvest with in vivo fertilization, by L. B. Shettles. AMERICAN JOURNAL OF OBSTETRICS AND GYNE-COLOGY 133(7):845, April 1, 1979.

Pathological aspects of the infertile testis, by T. W. Wang, et al. UROLOGIE CLINICS OF NORTH AMERICA 5(3): 503-530, October, 1978.

Prospects and programs of fertility reduction: what? where?, by B. Berelson. POPULATION AND DEVELOPMENT REVIEW 4:579-616, December, 1978.

Recent advances in the pharmacologic regulation of fertility in men, by B. N. Barwin. CANADIAN MEDICAL ASSOCIATION JOURNAL 119(7):757-759, October 7, 1978.

Status of women and fertility in India, by J. C. Bhatia. JOURNAL OF FAMILY WELFARE 25:20-32, March, 1979.

Study of attitudes of women attending an immunization clinic towards fertility regulations and fertility regulating methods, by M. Karkal, et al. JOURNAL OF FAMILY WELFARE 24:17-25, June, 1978.

Theory of rapid fertility decline in homogeneous popula-tions, by R. D. Retherford. STUDIES IN FAMILY

PLANNING 10:61, February, 1979.

The transition from natural to controlled fertility in Taiwan: a cross-sectional analysis of demand and supply factors, by S. J. Jejeebhoy. STUDIES IN FAMILY PLANNING 9(8):206, August, 1978.

2 countries, 2 approaches to controlling populations, by J. Thomas. NEW YORK TIMES p. 16E, September 2, 1979.

Women's work and fertility. An inquiry in Quebec in 1971, by E. LaPierre-Adamcyk. POPULATION 33:609-632, May-June, 1978.

INDIA
Fertility, schooling, and the economic contribution of children in rural India: an econometric analysis, by M. R. Rosenzweig, et al. ECONOMETRICA 45: 1065-1079, July, 1977.

ISRAEL
Immigration, social change and cohort fertility in Israel, by D. Friedlander, et al. POPULATION STUDIES 32:299-318, July, 1978.

HYSTERECTOMY
Effect of surveillance on the number of hysterectomies in the province of Saskatchewan, by F. J. Dyck, et al. HYSTE-RECTOMY 296:1326+, June 9, 1977.

The psychological effects of hysterectomy, by S. Meikle. CANADIAN PSYCHOLOGICAL REVIEW 18:128-141, April, 1977.

Relationship between nurse counseling and sexual adjustment after hysterectomy, by J. C. Krueger, et al. HYSTEREC-TOMY 28:145-150, May-June, 1979.

10-year survey of 485 sterilisations. Part I—Sterilisation or hysterectomy? by R. G. Whitelaw. BRITISH MEDICAL JOURNAL 1(6155):32-33, January 6, 1979.

Vaginal hysterectomy for elective sterilization, by W. C. Daniell, et al. MILITARY MEDICINE 143(12):864-865, December, 1978.

Vaginal hysterectomy in a community hospital: study of 491 cases, by B. A. Harris. NEW YORK STATE JOURNAL OF MEDICINE 76:1304-1307, August, 1976.

MARRIAGE AND THE FAMILY
Alternative marital and family forms: their relative attractiveness to college students and correlates of willingness to participate in nontraditional forms, by L. D. Strong. JOURNAL OF MARRIAGE AND THE FAMILY 40(3): 493-503, August, 1978.

Changing family roles: women and divorce, by P. Brown, et al. JOURNAL OF DIVORCE 1(4):315-328, Summer, 1978.

Childfree marriage—a theological view, by D. Dohety. CHICAGO STUDIES 18:137-145, Summer, 1979.

Child-parents: can we ignore the facts any longer? by M. Lalonde. INFIRMIERE CANADIENNE 21(1):10-11, January, 1978.

Children, magic, and choices, by D. Bisenieks. MYTHLORE 6(1):12-16, 1979.

Child's reaction to mother's abortion: case report, by J. O. Cavenar, Jr., et al. MILITARY MEDICINE 144(6): 412-413, June, 1979.

Cohabitation: its impact on marital success, by J. M. Jacques, et al. FAMILY COORDINATOR 28(1):35-39, January,

1979.

Contraception for the unmarried, by B. Bhasin. JOURNAL OF FAMILY WELFARE 25:35-43, December, 1978.

Couples want fewer children. SCIENTIFIC AMERICAN 241(4):72A, October, 1979.

Dealing in divorce: is birth control to blame? by R. T. Michael. HUMAN BEHAVIOR 7:37, November, 1978.

The decision to parent or not: normative and structural components, by M. G. Ory. JOURNAL OF MARRIAGE AND THE FAMILY 40(3):531-539, August, 1978.

The desire to have children, by W. Maier. GEBURTSHILFE UND FRAUENHEILKUNDE 38(12):1091-1092, December, 1978.

Diagnosing marital and family systems: a training model, by R. E. Cromwell, et al. FAMILY COORDINATOR 28(1):101-108, January, 1979.

Differences in U.S. marital fertility, 1970-73, by planning status of births, by J. E. Anderson. PUBLIC HEALTH REPORTS 94(4):319-325, July-August, 1979.

Differential fertility by intelligence: the role of birth planning, by J. R. Udry. SOCIAL BIOLOGY 25:10-14, Spring, 1978.

The effects of student practice on several types of learning in a functional marriage course, by M. R. Jensen, et al. FAMILY COORDINATOR 28(2):217-227, April, 1979.

The family, sex and marriage in England 1500-1800 [critique of Lawrence Stone], by A. MacFarlane. HISTORY AND THEORY 18(1):103-126, 1979.

Family violence explored in newly-released books, by J. R.
Nash. LAW ENFORCEMENT NEWS 4(22):9, Decem-
ber 25, 1978.

The fractured conjugal family: a comparison of married and
divorce dyads, by P. C. McKenry, et al. JOURNAL OF
DIVORCE 1(4):329-339, Summer, 1978.

Healthy family systems, by L. R. Barnhill. FAMILY CO-
ORDINATOR 28(1):94-100, January, 1979.

The impact of physical disability on marital adjustment: a
literature review, by Y. Peterson. FAMILY COORDINA-
TOR 28(1):47-51, January, 1979.

Is adultery biological? by M. North, et al. NEW SOCIETY
41(772):125-126, July 21, 1977.

Late marriage and non-marriage as demographic responses:
are they similar? by R. B. Dixon. POPULATION STUD-
IES 32:449-466, November, 1978.

Marriage and family enrichment: a new professional area, by
R. M. Smith, et al. FAMILY COORDINATOR 28(1):
87-93, January, 1979.

Marriage and family in a tudor elite: familial patterns of
Elizabethan Bishops, by J. Berlatsky. JOURNAL OF
FAMILY HISTORY 3(1):6-22, Spring, 1978.

Marriage and fertility in the developed countries, by C. F.
Westoff. SCIENTIFIC AMERICAN 239(6):51, December, 1978.

Marriage and parenting: our daughter's happiness depends
on her being steril, by N. Mills. NEW HORIZONS
11(4):7-11, Summer, 1977.

Mormon demographic history. I. Nuptiality and fertility of

once-married couples, by M. Skolnick, et al. POPULA-TION STUDIES 32:5-20, March, 1978.

Perceived contribution of children to marriage and its effects on family planning behavior, by P. L. Tobin. SOCIAL BIOLOGY 22(1):75-85, Spring, 1975.

Role experiences of young women: a longitudinal test of the role hiatus hypothesis, by G. D. Spitze. JOURNAL OF MARRIAGE AND THE FAMILY 40(3):471-479, August, 1978.

Seasons of birth and marriage in two Chinese localities, by B. Pasternak. HUMAN ECOLOGY 6(3):299, September, 1978.

Sex-role attitudes and the anticipated timing of the initial stages of family formation among Catholic university students, by J. W. Wicks, et al. JOURNAL OF MARRIAGE AND THE FAMILY 40(3):505-514, August, 1978.

Sexual enhancement groups for dysfunctional women: an evaluation, by S. R. Leiblum, et al. JOURNAL OF SEX AND MARITAL THERAPY 3(2):139-152, Summer, 1977.

The small, healthy family project, by H. Suyono, et al. STUDIES IN FAMILY PLANNING 9(7):201-202, July, 1978.

Some consequences of premarital heterosexual cohabitation for marriage, by D. E. Olday. DISSERTATION AB-STRACTS INTERNATIONAL 38(9-A):5745-5746, March, 1978.

Teaching family relations to dating couples versus non-couples: who learns better? by A. W. Avery, et al. FAMILY COORDINATOR 28(1):41-45, January, 1979.

A test and reformulation of reference group and role correlates of premarital sexual permissiveness theory, by R. W. Libby, et al. JOURNAL OF MARRIAGE AND THE FAMILY 40(1):79-92, February, 1978.

There just wasn't room in our lives for another baby, by L. B. Francke. FAMILY CIRCLE 91:54+, March 27, 1978.

A typology of intimate relationships, by C. J. Sager. JOURNAL OF SEX AND MARITAL THERAPY 3(2):83-112, Summer, 1977.

The use of simulation games in teaching family sociology, by M. W. Osmond. FAMILY COORDINATOR 28(2):205-216, April, 1979.

MISCARRIAGES

Ablactation after a major miscarriagd and delivery, by M. Bulajić, et al. SRPSKI ARHIV ZA CELOKUPNO LEKARSTVO 105(11):985-988, November, 1977.

A comparison of the predictive value of the pregnanediol/ creatinine ratio and the human chorionic gonadatrophin titre in threatened miscarriage, by N. France. NEW ZEALAND JOURNAL OF LABORATORY TECHNOLOGY 32:85-86+, November, 1978.

Coping with miscarriage, by M. Newton. FAMILY HEALTH 10:12+, October, 1978.

Current theories on the causes of miscarriage (review of the literature), by N. G. Kosheleva. VOPROSY OKHRANY MATERINSTVA I DETSTVA 24(1):65-68, January, 1979.

Familial dicentric translocation t(13;18)(p13;p11.2) ascertained by recurrent miscarriages, by A. Daniel, et al. JOURNAL OF MEDICAL GENETICS 16(1):73-75, February, 1979.

Karolinska Hospital-study of laboratory personnel: every fifth pregnancy ends in miscarriage, by B. Kolmodin-Hedman, et al. VARDFACKET 3(5):54-55, March 8, 1979.

Miscarriage or premature birth: additional thoughts on Exodus 21:22-25, by H. Wayne House. WESTMINSTER THEOLOGICAL JOURNAL 41:105-123, Fall, 1978.

Natural prevention of genetic defects: spontaneous abortion or miscarriage in Down's syndrome. SCIENCE NEWS 114:379, November 25, 1978.

Prophylactic medication to prevent miscarriage in pregnant women with a history of sterility, by K. Philipp, et al. WIENER MEDIZINISHCE WOCHENSCHRIFT 90(18): 670-672, September 29, 1978.

Repeated abortions increase risk of miscarriage, premature births and low-birth-weight babies. FAMILY PLANNING PERSPECTIVES 11:39-40, January-February, 1979.

Undiagnosed Wilson's disease as cause of unexplained miscarriage [letter], by J. G. Klee. LANCET 2(8139):423, August 25, 1979.

Use of morphogram in the prognosis of miscarriage, by L. V. Timoshenko, et al. VOPROSY OKHRANY MATERINSTVA I DETSTVA 23(11):81, November, 1978.

Woman, wife, mother: coping with miscarriage, by M. Newton. FAMILY HEALTH 10:12+, October, 1978.

MORTALITY
Infections and perinatal mortality, by J. Pryse-Davis, et al. JOURNAL OF ANTIMICROBIOL CHEMOTHERAPY 5(A):59-70, May, 1979.

PREGNANCY
Drugs and pregnancy, by S. J. Yaffe. CLINICAL TOXI-
COLOGY 13(4):523-534, 1978.

PREGNANCY: ADOLESCENT
Adolescent fertility: epidemic or endemic problem, by J. F.
Jekel, et al. STUDIES IN FAMILY PLANNING 10:
107-109, March, 1979.

Adolescent pregnancy: a review of the literature, by P. C.
McKenry, et al. FAMILY COORDINATOR 28(1):
17-28, January, 1979.

Adolescent pregnancy revisited, by J. E. Fielding. NEW
ENGLAND JOURNAL OF MEDICINE 299:893-896,
October 19, 1978.

Adolescent pregnancy: a study of pregnant teenagers in a
suburban community on Ontario, by D. E. Guyatt.
DISSERTATION ABSTRACTS INTERNATIONAL
39(4-A):2549, October, 1978.

Is pregnancy good for teenagers? by R. Lincoln. U.S.A. TO-
DAY 107(2398):34-37, July, 1978.

PROSTAGLANDINS
see: Abortion and Hormones

PSYCHOLOGY OF ABORTION
Abortion and intimacy, by M. F. Rousseau. AMERICA
140:429-432, May 26, 1979.

Abortion: some observations on the contraceptive practice
of women referred for psychiatric assessment in Dunedin, by D. J. Lord. NEW ZEALAND MEDICAL JOUR-
NAL 88(626):487-489, December 27, 1978.

SEX AND SEXUALITY
The acquisition of basic sex information, by P. H. Gebhard.

THE JOURNAL OF SEX RESEARCH 13(3):148-169, August, 1977.

Age and sexual culture among homosexuality oriented males, by J. Harry, et al. ARCHIVES OF SEXUAL BEHAVIOR 7(3):199-209, May, 1978.

Are there really any gay male athletes? An empirical survey, by B. Garner, et al. THE JOURNAL OF SEX RE-SEARCH 13(1):22-34, February, 1977.

Attitudes and experiences of sexual relations, by A. Lundstrom. INTERNATIONAL JOURNAL OF SOCIOLOGY OF THE FAMILY 8(2):231-234, July-December, 1978.

Attitudes of asolescent males toward abortion, contraception, and sexuality, by E. Vadies, et al. SOCIAL WORK IN HEALTH CARE 3(2):169-174, Winter, 1977.

A call to responsible ecumenical debate on abortion and homosexuality, by National Council of Churches. EN-GAGE/SOCIAL ACTION 7:41-44, October, 1979.

Coming out: similarities and differences for lesbians and gay men, by C. de Monteflores, et al. THE JOURNAL OF SOCIAL ISSUES 34(3):59-72, 1978.

The crime of precocious sexuality: female juvenile delinquency in the Progressive Era, by S. Schlossman, et al. HARVARD EDUCATIONAL REVIEW 48:65-94, February, 1978.

A critique of anthropological research on homosexuality, by T. K. Fitzgerald. JOURNAL OF HOMOSEXUALITY 2(4):385-397, Summer, 1977.

Cruising the truckers: sexual encounters in a highway rest area, by J. Corzine, et al. URBAN LIFE 6(2):171-192, July, 1977.

Curriculum and other choices: relationships with men's sex-role beliefs, by M. J. la Plante. DISSERTATION ABSTRACTS INTERNATIONAL 38(9-B):4537-4538, March, 1978.

Development of masturbation in college women, by R. Clifford. ARCHIVES OF SEXUAL BEHAVIOR 7(6):559-573, November, 1978.

The evaluation of sexual health services in a medical setting, by J. P. Held, et al. JOURNAL OF SEX AND MARITAL THERAPY 3(4):256-264, Winter, 1977.

Female sexual attitudes and the rise of illegitimacy: a case study, by C. Fairchilds. JOURNAL OF INTERDISCIPLINARY HISTORY 8:627-668, Spring, 1978.

Fertility awareness and sexuality, by W. May. LINACRE QUARTERLY 46:20-26, February, 1979.

Going public: a study in the sociology of homosexual liberation, by J. A. Lee. JOURNAL OF HOMOSEXUALITY 3(1):49-78, Fall, 1977.

Guidelines for ecumenical debate on abortion and homosexuality; Faith and Order Commission of the National Council of Churches. ORIGINS 8:517-519, February 1, 1979.

Heterosexual experience, marital status, and orientation of homosexual males, by N. McConaghy. ARCHIVES OF SEXUAL BEHAVIOR 7(6):575-581, November, 1978.

The high court, privacy and teenage sexuality, by G. L. Beiswinger. FAMILY COORDINATOR 28(2):191-198, April, 1979.

Loving women: attachment and autonomy in lesbian relationships, by L. A. Peplau, et al. THE JOURNAL OF

SOCIAL ISSUES 34(3):7-27, 1978.

Media mating I: newspaper "personals" ads of homosexual men, by M. R. Laner, et al. JOURNAL OF HOMO-SEXUALITY 3(2):149-162, Winter, 1977.

Parental rights and teen-age sexuality counseling, by M. Schwartz. OUR SUNDAY VISITOR 67:4+, April 29, 1979.

Perception of parental sex guilt and sexual behavior and arousal of college students, by P. R. Abramson, et al. PERCEPTUAL AND MOTOR SKILLS 45(1):337-338, August, 1977.

Perils of personhood, by R. Weiss. ETHICS 89:66-75, October, 1978.

Personality, sexuality, and demographic differences between volunteers and nonvolunteers for a laboratory study of male sexual behavior, by G. M. Farkas, et al. ARCHIVES OF SEXUAL BEHAVIOR 7(6):513-520, November, 1978.

The philosophy of existentialism and a psychology of irreversible homosexuality, by J. P. Cangemi, et al. COLLEGE STUDENT JOURNAL MONOGRAPH 8(3):1-11, September-October, 1974.

Premarital coitus and the Southern black: a comparative view, by H. T. Christensen, et al. JOURNAL OF MARRIAGE AND THE FAMILY 40(4):721-731, November, 1978.

Premarital sex: no, teen contraception: yes. FAMILY PLANNING PERSPECTIVES 10:301-302, September-October, 1978.

Premarital sexual attitudes and behavior, by J. P. Hornick.

SOCIOLOGICAL QUARTERLY 19:534-544, Autumn, 1978.

Projected extramarital sexual involvement in unmarried college students, by L. H. Buckstel, et al. JOURNAL OF MARRIAGE AND THE FAMILY 40(2):337-340, May, 1978.

Prostaglandins: physiology, biochemistry, pharmacology and clinical applications, by T. M. Elattar. JOURNAL OF ORAL PATHOLOGY 7(5):253-282, October, 1978.

Psychiatry and sexuality (preliminary reports), by P. A. Gloor. SCHWEIZER ARCHIV FUER NEUROLOGIE, NEUROCHIRUGIE UND PSYCHIATRIE 122(1):87-89, 1978.

Recent work on the history of sexuality, by R. P. Neuman. JOURNAL OF SOCIAL HISTORY 11(3):419-425, Spring, 1978.

Relationship between contraceptive sex role sterotyping and attitudes toward contraception among males, by S. A. Weinstein, et al. JOURNAL OF SEX RESEARCH 15: 235-242, August, 1979.

The relationship of creativity variables to sex role types for males and females, by C. H. Crawford. DISSERTATION ABSTRACTS INTERNATIONAL 39(3-A):1432-1433, September, 1978.

Romantic love and sexual expression, by M. L. Wilkinson. THE FAMILY COORDINATOR 27(2):141-148, April, 1978.

Sex and adaptation to the environment, by D. Ferembach. LA RECHERCHE 9(85):14-19, January, 1978.

Sex and cancer prevention, by C. SerVaas. SATURDAY

EVENING POST 251(2):86, March, 1979.

Sex and confinement, by A. Neier. CIVIL LIBERTIES RE-VIEW 5:6-16, July-August, 1978.

Sex and family planning in Denmark and in Danish Communes, by T. H. Shey. INTERNATIONAL JOURNAL OF SOCIOLOGY OF THE FAMILY 7(1):15-24, January-June, 1977.

Sex and Jewish teenagers, by A. S. Maller. JEWISH DIGEST 23:60-64, June, 1978.

Sex and the single punk. MOTHER JONES 3(9):8, November, 1978.

Sex films, by R. T. Francoeur. SOCIETY 14(5):33-37, July-August, 1977.

Sex guilt and contraceptive use, by M. L. Upchurch. JOURNAL OF SEX EDUCATION AND THERAPY 4:27-31, Spring-Summer, 1978.

Sex role attitudes and contraceptive practices among never-married university students, by M. Hedin-Pourghasemi. DISSERTATION ABSTRACTS INTERNATIONAL 38(10-A):6344-6345, April, 1978.

Sex-role identification and success, by C. Katz, et al. CONTEMPORARY PSYCHOANALYSIS 12(2):251-257, April, 1976.

Sexology in West Germany, by B. Meyenburg, et al. THE JOURNAL OF SEX RESEARCH 13(3):197-209, August, 1977.

Sexual attitude and sexual behavior among college students, by M. C. McBride, et al. JOURNAL OF COLLEGE STUDENT PERSONNEL 18:183-187, May, 1977.

Sexual attitudes among British and Japanese students, by S. Iwawaki, et al. JOURNAL OF PSYCHOLOGY 98: 289-298, March, 1978.

The sexual attitudes of aggressive sexual offenders, by K. Howells, et al. THE BRITISH JOURNAL OF CRIM- INOLOGY 18(2):170-174, April, 1978.

Sexual behaviour and contraceptive practice of undergradu- ates at Oxford University, by P. Anderson, et al. JOUR- NAL OF BIOSOCIAL SCIENCE 10:277-286, July, 1978.

Sexual behavior in adolescence, by J. R. Hopkins. JOUR- NAL OF SOCIAL ISSUES 33(2):67-85, 1977.

Sexual correlates of homosexual experience: an exploratory study of college women, by E. Goode, et al. THE JOUR- NAL OF SEX RESEARCH 13(1):12-21, February, 1977.

Sexual permissiveness: evidence for a theory, by J. Kelley. JOURNAL OF MARRIAGE AND THE FAMILY 40(3): 455-468, August, 1978.

Sexual preference, sex role appropriateness, and restriction of social access, by J. Millham, et al. JOURNAL OF HOMOSEXUALITY 2(4):343-357, Summer, 1977.

Sexuality—the mature or childbearing year and the effect of gynecologic surgery, by J. D. Chapman. JAOA 78(7): 509-514, March, 1979.

Sexuality of youth: attempt at forming a theory, by C. J. Straver. SOZIOLOGENKORRESPONDENZ 4:121-150, May, 1977.

Sixth session: the women's movement; presentation, by L. Chanin, et al. CONGRESSIONAL MONITOR 45:34-38,

March-April, 1978.

The social context of rape: sexual scripts and motivation, by S. Jackson. WOMEN'S STUDIES INTERNATIONAL QUARTERLY 1(1):27-38, 1978.

Some consequences of premarital heterosexual cohabitation for marriage, by D. E. Olday. DISSERTATION ABSTRACTS INTERNATIONAL 38(9-A):5745-5746, March, 1978.

Sources of sex bias in evaluations of performance, by J. C. Foress. DISSERTATION ABSTRACTS INTERNATIONAL 38(12-B):6148, June, 1978.

Sources of sex information and premarital sexual behavior, by G. B. Spanier. JOURNAL OF SEX RESEARCH 13: 73-88, May, 1977.

Styles of sexual expression in women: clinical implications of multivariate analyses, by E. F. Hoon, et al. ARCHIVES OF SEXUAL BEHAVIOR 7(2):105-116, March, 1978.

Subjective sexual experience in college women, by R. E. Clifford. ARCHIVES OF SEXUAL BEHAVIOR 7:183-197, May, 1978.

Substantive and methodological issues in replication research: Reiss' proposition one of the theory of premarital sexual permissiveness as a case in point, by R. Walsh, et al. INTERNATIONAL JOURNAL OF SOCIOLOGY OF THE FAMILY 6(2):211-223, 1976.

SEX EDUCATION AND NURSES
Providing holistic patient care as a sex educator, by B. Henshaw. NURSING 9(6):78-80, June, 1979.

STERILIZATION (GENERAL)
Compulsory sterilization practices, by S. Tessler. FRON-
TIERS 1(2):52-66, 1975.

Current status of sterilization, by C. Wood. AUSTRALIAN
FAMILY PHYSICIAN 8(5):486-490, May, 1979.

Happiness is never having to say it's permanent, by S. Henry.
MACLEAN'S 92:39-40, April 30, 1979.

Late complications of laparoscopic sterilization, II., by W. D.
Edgerton. JOURNAL OF REPRODUCTIVE MEDICINE
21(1):41-44, July, 1978.

Non-therapeutic sterilization—malpractice, and the issues of
"wrongful birth" and "wrongful life" in Quebec law, by
R. P. Kouri. CANADIAN BUSINESS REVIEW 57:89-
105, March, 1979.

On the concept of the article 'test of sterility', by J. Sagáth,
et al. CESKOSLOVENSKA FARMACIE 27(4):196-200,
June, 1978.

Psychiatric aspects of sterilization, by I. C. Bernstein. JOUR-
NAL OF REPRODUCTIVE MEDICINE 22(2):97-100,
February, 1979.

Reversibility as a consideration in laparoscopic sterilization,
by R. Palmer. JOURNAL OF REPRODUCTIVE MEDI-
CINE 21(1):57-58, July, 1978.

The saga of positive culture—ETO sterilization, by M. S. Fox.
HOSPITAL TOPICS 57:18-20+, May-June, 1979.

Sexual profile of women requesting laparoscopical sterilization, by M. Samsula, et al. CESKOSLOVENSKA GYNE-
KOLOGIE 44(4):253-256, May, 1979.

Sterilisation des arrieres mentaux, by D. J. Roy. RELA-

TIONS 39:35, February, 1979.

Sterilization and its importance, by C. Trifan. VIATA MEDI-CALA 26(5):111-114, May, 1978.

Sterilization and laparoscopy [editorial]. SOUTH AFRICAN MEDICAL JOURNAL 54(7):260-261, August 12, 1978.

Sterilization and sterile preparations in pharmacy. XI. Aseptic procedures, by A. Burelová, et al. CESKOSLOVEN-SKA FARMACIE 27(9):412-418, November, 1978.

Sterilization as a contraception method, by S. Ivanov, et al. AKUSHERSTVO I GINEKOLOGIIA 17(5):366-370, 1978.

— [letter], by N. S. Louw. SOUTH AFRICAN MEDICAL JOURNAL 54(14):555, September 30, 1978.

Sterilization: a conference and a report, by B. Dillingham. AMERICAN INDIAN JOURNAL 4(1):13-16, January, 1978.

Sterilization in 1977, by S. C. Christensen, et al. UGE-SKRIFT FOR LAEGER 141(4):260, January 22, 1979.

Sterilization—judge who granted petition to sterilize a "somewhat retarded" minor held immune from liability because he had not acted in "clear absence of all jurisdiction," despite the lack of a specific statute granting jurisdiction and despite procedural errors. JOURNAL OF FAMILY LAW 17:611-616, May, 1979.

Sterilization of a non-scrotal mammal (Suncus murinus L.) by intratesticular injection of cadmium chloride, by S. K. Singh, et al. ACTA EUROPAEA FERTILITATIS 9(1): 65-70, March, 1978.

Stop sterilization abuse, by B. Ehrenreich. HERESIES 6:45,

1978.

10-year survey of 485 sterilizations. Part II: patients' views on their sterilization, by R. G. Whitelaw. BRITISH MEDICAL JOURNAL 1(6155):34-35, January 6, 1979.

Uterotubal implantation and obstetric outcome after previous sterilization [proceedings], by E. P. Peterson, et al. INTERNATIONAL JOURNAL OF FERTILITY 23(4): 254, 1978.

INDIA
Factors involved in the acceptance of voluntary female sterilization among Indians in Natal, by M. E. Hampson. SOUTH AFRICAN MEDICAL JOURNAL 55(18):719-721, April 28, 1979.

Impact of laparoscopic sterilization on birth prevention in Nepal, by B. R. Pande, et al. JOURNAL OF FAMILY WELFARE 25:13-19, December, 1978.

Indian woman's sterilization suite starts, by P. Moore. NATIONAL CATHOLIC REPORTER 15:1+, January 19, 1979.

MEXICO
Cultural cross fires; study by Carols Velez of Mexican American women sterilized without consent at Los Angeles County-USC Medical Center, by D. Ainsworth. HUMAN BEHAVIOR 8:52-55, March, 1979.

PANAMA
Sterilization in Panama: in Panama, one-third of women who want no more children have been sterilized; sterilization now prevents almost one unwanted birth per woman over her reproductive career, by C. F. Westoff, et al. INTERNATIONAL FAMILY PLANNING PERSPECTIVES 5:111-117, September, 1979.

UNITED STATES
HEW sets sterilization funding rules. ARIZONA NURSE 32:4,March-April, 1979.

Native American peoples on the trail of tears once more; Indian Health Service and coerced sterilization, by M. Miller, et al. AMERICA 139:422-425, December 9, 1978.

Number of Americans choosing sterilization. SPOKES-WOMAN 9(4):6, October, 1978.

Sterilization and pill top U.S. birth control methods. SPOKESWOMAN 9(5):6, November, 1978.

Sterilization in the United States, by C. F. Westoff, et al. FAMILY PLANNING PERSPECTIVES 11(3):147, May-June, 1979.

STERILIZATION: ATTITUDES
Emotional reaction in interval and postpartum sterilization, by A. Aribarg, et al. INTERNATIONAL JOURNAL OF GYNAECOLOGY AND OBSTETRICS 16(1):40-41, 1978.

Menstrual patterns and women's attitudes following steriliza-tion by Falope rings, by L. M. Rubinstein, et al. FER-TILITY AND STERILITY 31(6):641-646, June, 1979.

STERILIZATION: COMPLICATIONS
Automatic sterilizer replaces autoclaves for ASTM humid-age test [urethane foams]. PLASTICS WORLD 37:35, September, 1979.

Complications and psychosomatic problems after tubal sterilization, by B. M. Bric, et al. FORTSCHRITTE DU MEDIZIN 97(7):304-306, February 15, 1979.

Complications of laparoscopic sterilization. Comparison of

2 methods, by M.S. Baggish, et al. OBSTETRICS AND GYNECOLOGY 54(1):54-59, July, 1979.

Control of infection, sterilisation and bacteriology: the role of the microbiologist, by M. Thomas. NATIONAL NEWS 16(2):6-8, February, 1979.

Ectopic pregnancy by transmigration of sperm after sterilisation with Hulka-Clemens clips, by G. A. Clarke, et al. BRITISH MEDICAL JOURNAL 1(6164):659-660, March 10, 1979.

Sciatic nerve injury in a patient undergoing laparoscopy, by F. D. Loffer, et al. JOURNAL OF REPRODUCTIVE MEDICINE 21(6):371-372, December, 1978.

Technical problems and early complications of laparoscopic sterilization done on a day-case basis, by E. J. Coetzee, et al. SOUTH AFRICAN MEDICAL JOURNAL 54(27): 1132-1134, December 30, 1978.

Thermal injury to the bowel as a complication of laparoscopic sterilization, by R. F. Maudsley, et al. CANADIAN JOURNAL OF SURGERY 22(3):232-234, May, 1979.

Ultra-flash sterilization of fluid food by friction, by C. Alais, et al. ANNALES DE LA NUTRITION ET DE L'ALIMENTATION 32(2-3):511-521, 1978.

STERILIZATION: ECONOMICS
HEW sets sterilization funding rules. ARIZONA NURSE 32:4, March-April, 1979.

New regulations governing DHEW sterilization funding now in effect; stress informed consent. FAMILY PLANNING PERSPECTIVES 11(1):46-47, January-February, 1979.

STERILIZATION: FAILURE
  Civil liability arising from "wrongful birth" following an unsuccessful sterilization operation, by G. B. Robertson.
  AMERICAN JOURNAL OF LAW AND MEDICINE
  4(2):131-156, Summer, 1978.

  Compensation for damages in unsuccessful sterilization with-
  out occurring pregnancy, by H. J. Rieger. DEUTSCH
  MEDIZINISCHE WOCHENSCHRIFT 104(26):932-933,
  June 29, 1979.

  Failure of laparoscopic sterilization [letter], by H. Puder.
  GEBURTSHILFE UND FRAUENHEILKUNDE 38(12):
  1099, December, 1978.

  Uchida tubal sterilization failure: a report of four cases, by
  T. J. Benedetti, et al. AMERICAN JOURNAL OF OB-
  STETRICS AND GYNECOLOGY 132(1):116-117,
  September 1, 1978.

STERILIZATION: FEMALE
  Bipolar coagulation. Technic of female sterilization by
  laporoscopy. Preliminary report of 100 cases, by L. C.
  Uribe Ramírez, et al. GINECOLOGIA Y OBSTETRICIA
  DE MEXICO 43(258):243-249, April, 1978.

  The decision for male versus female sterilization, by M. P.
  Clark, et al. FAMILY COORDINATOR 28(2):250-254,
  April, 1979.

  The effects on sexual response and mood after sterilization of
  women taking long-term oral contraception: results of a
  double-blind cross-over study, by J. Leeton, et al. AUS-
  TRALIAN AND NEW ZEALAND JOURNAL OF OB-
  STETRICS AND GYNAECOLOGY 18(3):194-197,
  August, 1978.

  Female sterilization, by J. F. Hulka. SOUTH AFRICAN
  MEDICAL JOURNAL 55(4):118-124, January 27, 1979.

Female sterilization in small camp settings in rural India, by R. Bhatt, et al. STUDIES IN FAMILY PLANNING 9: 39-43, February-March, 1978.

Minilaparotomy for female sterilization, by A. J. Penfield. OBSTETRICS AND GYNECOLOGY 54(2):184-188, August, 1979.

Post-partum sterilization, by M. Kubica, et al. CESKOSLO-VENSKA GYNEKOLOGIE 43(9):713-714, November, 1978.

Sterilization of the woman, by E. V. van Hall. NEDER-LANDS TIJDSCHRIFT VOOR GENEESKUNDE 122(52):2052-2055, December 30, 1978.

Sterilization of women through a minilaparotomy, by M. Rabøl, et al. DANISH MEDICAL BULLETIN 25(4): 177-178, August, 1978.

Sterilization of young women [letter] , by D. K. Quinlan. SOUTH AFRICAN MEDICAL JOURNAL 54(17):688, October 21, 1978.

Sterilization reversal for women. STOREFRONT 6(3):4, August, 1978.

Timing of female sterilisation, by J. M. Emens, et al. BRITISH MEDICAL JOURNAL 2(6145):1126, October 21, 1978.

STERILIZATION: FEMALE: COMPLICATIONS
Cyanamid attacked over sterilization of female workers. CHEMICAL MARKETING REPORTER 215:3+, January 8, 1979.

Immediate and early postoperative complications and various psychosomatic problems following laparoscopic sterilization of women, by B. M. Berić, et al. JUGOSLAVENSKA GINEKOLOGIJA I OPSTETRICIJA 17(4):225-

231, July-August, 1977.

Late complications following sterilization in women, by T. Sørensen, et al. UGESKRIFT FOR LAEGER 141(15): 998-999, April 9, 1979.

Post-partum sterilisation—an anaesthetic hazard? by A. L. Rennie, et al. ANAESTHESIA 34(3):267-269, March, 1979.

Risks and benefits of culdoscopic female sterilization, by M. F. McCann, et al. INTERNATIONAL JOURNAL OF GYNAECOLOGY AND OBSTETRICS 16(3):242-247, 1978-1979.

STERILIZATION: FEMALE: COMPLICATIONS: PSYCHO-LOGICAL
Immediate and early postoperative complications and various psychosomatic problems following laparoscopic sterilization of women, by B. M. Berić, et al. JUGOSLAVEN-SKA GINEKOLOGIJA I OPSTETRICIJA 17(4):225-231, July-August, 1977

STERILIZATION: FEMALE: REVERSAL
Reliability and reversibility of female sterilisation [editorial]. BRITISH MEDICAL JOURNAL 2(6154):1734-1735, December, 1978.

STERILIZATION: FEMALE: TECHNIQUES
A comparison of the clip and ring techniques for laparoscopic sterilization of postabortion and postpartum patients, by T. H. Lean, et al. INTERNATIONAL JOURNL OF GYNAECOLOGY AND OBSTETRICS 16(2):150-156, 1978-1979.

A comparison of the socio-demographic and fertility characteristics of women sterilized in hospitals and camps, by S. Pachauri. INTERNATIONAL JOURNAL OF GYNAECOLOGY AND OBSTETRICS 16(2):132-136,

1978-1979.

Female sterilization using an elasticated silicone ring, by D. G. Cave. MEDICAL JOURNAL OF AUSTRALIA 1(12): 577-578, June 16, 1979.

STERILIZATION: HISTORY
Compulsory sterilization in the Breshau district in 1934-1944, by S. Kusperek. PRZEGLAD LEKARSKI 36(1): 50-60, 1979.

STERILIZATION: INVOLUNTARY
Involuntary sterilization: recent developments, by S. J. Vietello. MENTAL RETARDATION 16:405-409, December, 1978.

Women claim Cyanamid forced sterilization. CHEMICAL AND ENGINEERING NEWS 57:6, January 8, 1979.

Women to appeal decision on forced sterilization suit. NATIONAL NOW 11(10):9, September, 1978.

STERILIZATION: LAWS AND LEGISLATION
Final sterilization rules issued. SPOKESWOMAN 9(6):5, December, 1978.

Five submit to sterilization to avoid losing their jobs, by P. Kassel. NEW DIRECTIONS FOR WOMEN 8:1+, January, 1979.

HEW sets new sterilization rules. SPOKESWOMAN 8(7&8): 8, January, 1978.

High court orders complex sterilization case to trail [forced sterilization of a deaf-mute woman]. MEDICAL WORLD NEWS 19:52+, October 13, 1978.

Judicial immunity—tort liability of a state court judge in granting the sterilization of a minor without due process.

HOWARD LAW JOURNAL 22:129-141, 1979.

Legal implications of sterilization of the mentally retarded, by C. Dowben, et al. AMERICAN JOURNAL OF DISEASES OF CHILDREN 133(7):697-699, July, 1979.

Reproduction, ethics, and public policy: the federal sterilization regulations, by R. P. Petchesky. HASTINGS CENTER REPORT 9:29-41, October, 1979.

Sort of dampens your spirits; suit against Dr. C. H. Pierce for sterilizing welfare patients, by S. Derks. NATION 227: 675-676, December 16, 1978.

Sterilization regulation: government efforts to guarantee informed consent. SANTA CLARA LAW REVIEW 18: 971-996, Fall, 1978.

Torts—cause of action on behalf of parents for the negligent sterilization of mother resulting in the birth of an unwanted child held sufficiently supported by case law to warrant denial of motion for summry judgment and to allow claimant-parents to prove all items of damage, including the anticipated cost of rearing the child, less any benefit conferred by the birth. DRAKE LAW REVIEW 28:503-512, 1978-1979.

STERILIZATION: MALE
Acceptability of male sterilization in Bangladesh: its problems and perspectives, by A. R. Khan, et al. BANGLADESH DEVELOPMENT STUDIES 6:201-212, Summer, 1978.

Chemosterilization of dermacentor variabilis say (acari: ixodidae); effects of metepa on the cytology and fertility of males treated as unfed adults, by R. L. Osburn, et al. JOURNAL OF PARASITOLOGY 64:719-726, August, 1978.

Condoms. CONSUMER REPORTS 44(10:583, October, 1979.

The decision for male versus female sterilization, by M. P. Clark, et al. FAMILY COORDINATOR 28:250-254, April, 1979.

STERILIZATION: MALE: TECHNIQUES
Chemical sterilization of males—successful inhibition of spermatogenesis in langurs (Presbytis entellus entellus dufresne) after metopiron (SU-4885, Ciba) administration, by V. P. Dixit. ENDOKRINOLOGIE 72(3):291-298, November, 1978.

STERILIZATION: OUTPATIENT
Ongoing program of outpatient sterilizations, by R. E. Hassler. WISCONSIN MEDICAL JOURNAL 77(11):113-114, November, 1978.

STERILIZATION: PSYCHOLOGY
Consequences and psychological interactions associated with salpingoclasis, by E. Shapiro Ackerman, et al. GINECOLOGIA Y OBSTETRICA DE MEXICO 43(259):333-338, May, 1978.

Sterilization, by G. H. Holtzhausen. SOUTH AFRICAN MEDICAL JOURNAL 54(5):182, July 29, 1978.

STERILIZATION: REVERSAL
Acceptability of reversible versus permanent tubal sterilization: an analysis of preliminary data, by R. N. Shain. FERTILITY AND STERILITY 31(1):13-17, January, 1979.

It is now possible to reverse surgical sterilization of women. NATIONAL NOW 11(8):2, July, 1978.

Normal intrauterine pregnancy after sterilization reversal in wife and husband [letter], by S. J. Silber, et al. FER-

TILITY AND STERILITY 31(1):90, January, 1979.

The reversibility of sterilisation, by S. Whitehead. NURSING TIMES 75(25):1048-1049, June 21, 1979.

—, by R. M. L. Winston. IPPF MEDICAL BULLETIN 12(6):1, December, 1978.

Reversible sterilization, by A. Ingelman-Sundberg, et al. INTERNATIONAL JOURNAL OF FERTILITY 23(2): 156-157, 1978.

—, by G. Largey. SOCIETY 14(5):57-59, July-August, 1977.

—: socio-ethical considerations, by G. Largey. SOCIAL BIOLOGY 25(2):135-144, Summer, 1978.

Reversible sterilization technique shows promise, JAMA 242(1):16, July 6, 1979.

A simple solution to five of the major problems of the micro-surgical reversal of sterilization, by J. J. Hoffman. FER-TILITY AND STERILITY 30(4):480-481, October, 1978.

Workshop on reversal of sterilization, 1977. Reversal of sterilization. HARPERS' BAZAAR 1978.

STERILIZATION: TECHNIQUES
Application of steril technic. AUXILIAIRE 52(2):21-28, June, 1979.

The choice of sterilizing procedure according to its potential reversibility with microsurgery, by B. Cantor, et al. FERTILITY AND STERILITY 31(1):9-12, January, 1979.

Early assessment of a tubal plastic (Bleier) clip, by L. Craft, et al. FERTILITY AND STERILITY 32(1):28-30, July, 1979.

Gamma sterilization moves up, by W. C. Simms. MODERN PACKAGING 52:50-52, May, 1979.

Gynecologic microsurgery: a déja vu of laparoscopy, by J. M. Phillips. JOURNAL OF REPRODUCTIVE MEDICINE 22(3):135-143, March, 1979.

Hulka-Clemens clips [letter], by B. A. Lieberman. BRITISH MEDICAL JOURNAL 1(6171):1148, April 28, 1979.

Influence of sterilization and temperature changes on the in vitro characteristics of the pH electrode, by H. Rüttgers, et al. ARCHIVES OF GYNECOLOGY 226(1-2):25-30, September 1, 1978.

Laparoscopic sterilization with the band. JOURNAL OF THE KENTUCKY MEDICAL ASSOCIATION 76(10): 505, October, 1978.

Laparoscopic sterilization with electrocautery: complications and reliability, by U. Bänninger, et al. GEBURTSHILFE UND FRAUENHEILKUNDE 39(5):393-400, May, 1979.

Laparoscopy before insemination stirs debate. MEDICAL WORLD NEWS 20:11+, February 5, 1979.

Laparoscopy for the general surgeon, by T. C. Dickinson, et al. SURGERY CLiNICS OF NORTH AMERICA 59(3):449-457, June, 1979.

Microsurgery: a new dimension in gynecology, by M. M. Oliphant, Jr. THE SURGICAL TECHNOLOGISTS 11:9-13, September-October, 1979.

Microsurgery of the fallopian tubes, by M. C. Ferreira. REVISTA PAULISTA DE MEDICINA 92(3-4):64-65,

September-October, 1978.

Microsurgical techniques in reconstructive surgery of the fallopian tube, by J. F. Daniel. SOUTHERN MEDICAL JOURNAL 72(5):585-587, May, 1979.

Microsurgical techniques of anastomosis of the fallopian tubes, by R. N. Smith, et al. TRANSACTIONS OF THE PACIFIC COAST OBSTETRICAL AND GYNECOLOGI-CAL SOCIETY 45:111-115, 1978.

Nursing care study. Surgical female sterilisation: it's all done with tubes and clips, by A. Bennett. NURSING MIR-ROR AND MIDWIVES' JOURNAL 148(10):42-44, March 8, 1979.

Reanastomosis of fallopian tubes [letter], by V. Gomel. FERTILITY AND STERILITY 30(4):483-484, October, 1978.

Regeneration of the fallopian tubes following sterilization, by K. Semm, et al. GEBURTSHILFE UND FRAUEN-HEILKUNDE 39(1):14-19, January, 1979.

Reversible sterilization technque shows promise. JAMA 242(1):16, July 6, 1979.

Safety to alparoscopy [editorial]. LANCET 1(8068):807, April 15, 1978.

Shoulder-hand syndrome after laparoscopic sterilisation, by L. C. Low, et al. BRITISH MEDICAL JOURNAL 2(6144):1059-1060, October 14, 1978.

Silicone band sterilization with radiographic and laparoscopic evaluation, by P. Beck, et al. OBSTETRICS AND GYNE-COLOGY 53(6):698-702, June, 1979.

Statistical survey of gynecological laparoscopy/pelviscopy in

Germany till 1977, by K. Semm. ENDOSCOPY 11(2): 101-106, May, 1979.

Sterility in oxygen humidifiers, by T. P. Meehan. RESPIRA-TORY TECHNOLOGY 14:14-15+, Summer, 1978.

A sterilization technique [letter] , by W. D. Marais. SOUTH AFRICAN MEDICAL JOURNAL 54(20):809, Noember 11, 1978.

Sterilization technqiues, by J. Kagan. McCALLS 106:69, October, 1978.

Surgical female sterilisation: it's all done with tubes and clips, by A. BEnnett. NURSING MIRROR AND MID-WIVES' JOURNAL 148:42-44, March 8, 1979.

Surgical sterilisation in a New Twon practice, by A. F. Wright. HEALTH BULLETIN 36(5):229-234, September, 1978.

Surgical sterilization of women. Personal experience with Pomeroy's method, by P. Guccione. MINERVA GINE-COLOGIA 31(1-2):61-65, January-February, 1979.

STERILIZATION: TUBAL
A comparative study of rural and urban population under-going tubal ligation, by N. N. Wig, et al. JOURNAL OF FAMILY WELFARE 24:34-43, June, 1978.

Complications and psychosomatic problems after tubal sterilization, by B. M. Berić, et al. FORTSCHRITTE DU MEDIZIN 97(7):304-306, February 15, 1979.

Continued pregnancy after curettage and incidental tubal fulguration by laparoscopy: a case report, by L. E. Savel, et al. INTERNATIONAL JOURNAL OF GYNAECOL-OGY AND OBSTETRICS 16(1):38-39, 1978.

Cytohormonal assessment of ovarian function following tubal ligation, by S. Khanna, et al. INTERNATIONAL JOURNAL OF GYNAECOLOGY AND OBSTETRICS 16(5):373-376, March-April, 1979.

Ectopic pregnancy following tubal sterilization, by T. A. Athari, et al. WEST VIRGINIA MEDICAL JOURNAL 74(9):229-232, September, 1978.

A histological study of a microsurgical tubal to anastomosis, by E. Cornier, et al. JOURNAL DE GYNECOLOGIA, OBSTETRIQUE ET BIOLOGIE DE LA REPRODUC- TION 7(8):1441-1446, December, 1978.

Initial results of laparoscopic tubal sterilization, by R. Bur- mucic, et al. WIENER MEDIZINISCHE WOCHEN- SCHRIFT 128(23):724-726, December 15, 1978.

Laparoscopic electrocoagulation and tubal ring techniques for sterilization: a comparative study, by S. Koetsawang, et al. INTERNATIONAL JOURNAL OF GYNAECOLO- GY AND OBSTETRICS 15(5):455-458, 1978.

Laparoscopic sterilization with spring-loaded clip and tubal ring in postabortal cases—one-year follow-up, by S. D. Khandwala, et al. INTERNATIONAL JOURNAL OF GYNAECOLOGY AND OBSTETRICS 16(2):115-118, 1978-1979.

Laparoscopic tubal occlusion with silicone rubber bands, by T. Kumarasamy, et al. AUSTRALIAN AND NEW ZEA- LAND JOURNAL OF OBSTETRICS AND GYNAE- COLOGY 18(3):190-193, August, 1978.

Laparoscopic tubal sterilization in unselected outpatients, by M. H. saidi, et al. TEXAS MEDICINE 74(9):55-57, September, 1978.

Luteal deficiencey among women with noraml menstrual

cycles, requesting reversla of tubal sterilization, by E. Radwanska, et al. OBSTETRICS AND GYNECOLOGY 54(2):189-192, August, 1979.

Microsurgery after tubal ligation, by R. Henrion. NOU-VELLE PRESSE MEDICALE 8(13):1089-1090, March 17, 1979.

A new approach to tubal sterilization by laparoscopy, by R. F. Valle, et al. FERTILITY AND STERILITY 30(4): 415-422, October, 1978.

Peruvian experience of the practice of tubal ligation, by J. O. Dalrymple, et al. TROPICAL DOCTOR 8(4):198-200, October, 1978.

Possible ovulatory deficiency after tubal ligation, by G. S. Berger, et al. AMERICAN JOURNAL OF OBSTETRICS AND GYNECOLOGY 132(6):699-700, November 15, 1978.

Radiographic appearance of laparoscopic tubal ring, by M. L. McJunkin, et al. AJA INFORMATION 132(2):297-298, February, 1979.

Reconstructive tubal surgery after surgical sterilization, by J. Anselmo. REVISTA CHILENA DE OBSTETRICIA Y GINECOLOGIA 42(4):256-260, 1977.

Silicone band technique for laparoscopic tubal sterilization in the gravid and nongravid patient, by P. Beck, et al. OBSTETRICS AND GYNECOLOGY 53(5):653-656, May, 1979.

A sruvey of tubal ectopic pregnancy, with particular reference to cases following sterilization, by S. M. Walton. AUSTRALIAN AND NEW ZEALAND JOURNAL OF OBSTETRICS AND GYNAECOLOGY 18(4):266-267, November, 1978.

Tubal ligation by colpotomy incision, by C. F. Whitaker, Jr. AMERICAN JOURNAL OF OBSTETRICS AND GYNECOLOGY 134(8):885-888, August 15, 1979.

Tubal microsurgery—a review, by P. Paterson. AUSTRALIAN AND NEW ZEALAND JOURNAL OF OBSTETRICS AND GYNAECOLOGY 18(3):182-184, August, 1978.

Tubal pregnancy subsequent to transperitoneal migration of spermatozoa, by K. G. Metz, et al. OBSTETRICAL AND GYNECOLOGICAL SURVEY 34(7):554-560, July, 1979.

Tubal reanastomosis using absorbable stent, by A. H. Ansari. INTERNATIONAL JOURNAL OF FERTILITY 23(4): 242-243, 1978.

Tubal repermeabilisation after sterilization. Techniques and results, by R. Henrion, et al. NOUVELLE PRESSE MEDICALE 8(13):1091-1094, March 17, 1979.

Tubal sterilization, by E. Bolob. WIENER MEDIZINISCHE WOCHENSHRIFT 91(4):130-133, February 16, 1979.

Tubal sterilization and ovarian perfusion: selective arteriography in vivo and in vitro, by R. Manzanilla-Sevilla, et al. INTERNATIONAL JOURNAL OF GYNECOLOGY AND OBSTETRICS 16(2):137-143, 1978-1979.

Tubal sterilization with the tupla-clip per laparoscopiam, by J. Babenerd, et al. MEDIZINISCHE KLINIK 74(20): 769-773, May 18, 1979.

Uchida tubal sterilization failure: a report of four cases, by T. J. Benedetti, et al. AMERICAN JOURNAL OF OBSTETRICS AND GYNECOLOGY 132(1):116-117, September 1, 1978.

STERILIZATION: VOLUNTARY
Fourth international converence on voluntary sterilization, by L. C. Landman. FAMILY PLANNING PERSPEC-TIVES 11:241-247, July-August, 1979.

Voluntary steriliazation: USA and China, by J. Presl. CE-SKOSLOVENSKA GYNEKOLOGIE 43(8):626, September, 1978.

—: world's leading contraceptive method, by C. P. Green. POPULATION REPORTS (2):1, March, 1978.

World-wide spread of voluntary sterilization. MEDIZINI-SCHE WELT 30(5):20, February 2, 1979.

STERILIZATION AND CRIMINALS
'Asexualization' proposed for convicted child molesters. JUVENILE JUSTICE DIGEST 7(1):5, January 12, 1979.

STERILIZATION AND THE HANDICAPPED
Indications for the sterilisation of the handicapped adolescent, by A. Animashaun. NIGERIAN MEDICAL JOURNAL 8(3):253-254, May, 1978.

STERILIZATION AND HOSPITALS
Sterilization and contraceptive services in Catholic hospitals, by J. M. O'Lane. AMERICAN JOURNAL OF GYNAECOLOGY AND OBSTETRICS 133(4):355-357, February 15, 1979.

STERILIZATION AND THE MENTALLY RETARDED
Addressing the consent issue involved in the sterilization of mentally incompetent females. ALBANY LAW REVIEW 43:322-338, Winter, 1979.

For whose benefit are mentally retarded people being sterilized? by D. Robillard. CANADIAN MEDICAL ASSOCIATION JOURNAL 120(11):1433-1434+, June 9,

1979.

Issues and opinions. I. Sterilization of the mentally retarded minor, by C. Cooper. JOURNAL OF NURSE-MID-WIFERY 23:14-15, Spring-Summer, 1978.

—. II. Sterilization of the mentally retarded: HEW's new regulations, by P. Urbanus. JOURNAL OF NURSE-MIDWIFERY 23:16, Spring-Summer, 1978.

Legal implications of sterilization of the mentally retarded, by C. Dowben, et al. AMERICAN JOURNAL OF DISEASES OF CHILDREN 133(7):697-699, July, 1979.

Should the mentally handicapped be sterilized? by D. Robillard. CANADIAN MEDICAL ASSOCIATION JOURNAL 120(6):756-757, March 17, 1979.

STERILIZATION AND PHYSICIANS
Medics; Dr. I. Lubell of the Association for Voluntary Sterilization, by P. Burstein. PEOPLE 10:71-72, December 11, 1978.

Sort of dampens your spirits; suite against Dr. C. H. Pierce for sterilizing welfare patients, by S. Derks. NATION 227:675-676, December 16, 1978.

STERILIZATION AND RELIGION
Sterilization and contraceptive services in Catholic hospitals, by J. M. O'Lane. AMERICAN JOURNAL OF GYNAECOLOGY AND OBSTETRICS 133(4):355-357, February 15, 1979.

STERILIZATION AND YOUTH
Indications for the sterilisation of the handicapped adolescent, by A. Animashaun. NIGERIAN MEDICAL JOURNAL 8(3):253-254, May, 1978.

STERILIZATION RESEARCH
Boll weevil; chemosterilization by fumigation and dipping, by
A. B. Borkovec, et al. JOURNAL OF ECONOMIC
ENTOMOLOGY 71:862-866, December, 1978.

VASECTOMY
Clinical study of 425 couples soliciting vasectomies, by M.
Díaz, et al. GINECOLOGICA Y OBSTETRICIA DE
MEXICO 43(259):317-323, May, 1978.

Epididymal extravasation following vasectomy as a cause
for failure of vasectomy reversal, by S. J. Silber. FER-
TILITY AND STERILITY 31(3):309-315, March, 1979.

Follow-up of vasectomy using medical record linkage, by M.
J. Goldacre, et al. AMERICAN JOURNAL OF EPI-
DEMIOLOGY 108(3):177-180, 1978.

Immediate sterility after vasectomy with the use of 0.1%
ethacridine lactate, by D. S. Kamat, et al. JOURNAL OF
POSTGRADUATE MEDICINE 24(4):218-220, October,
1978.

Is the low fertility rate after vasovasostomy caused by nerve
resection druing vasectomy? by R. Pabst, et al. FER-
TILITY AND STERILITY 31(3):316-320, March, 1979.

A plea to all vasectomists [letter], by W. K. Yeates. BRITISH
MEDICAL JOURNAL 1(6155):55, January 6, 1979.

Psychologic effects of vasectomy in voluntarily childless
men, by R. A. Brown, et al. UROLOGY 14(1):55-58,
July, 1979.

Recanalisation of vas after vasectomy. Evaluation of various
techniques in dogs, by O. P. Taneja, et al. BRITISH
JOURNAL OF UROLOGY 50(5):342-347, August,
1978.

Vasectomy. AMERICAN JOURNAL OF NURSING 79: 447+, March, 1979.

— [letter], by E. R. Owen. MEDICAL JOURNAL OF AUSTRALIA 1(5):184, March 10, 1978.

Vasectomy and its microsurgical reversal, by S. J. Silber. UROLOGIC CLINICS OF NORTH AMERICA 5(3).573-584, October, 1978.

Vasectomy news. STOREFRONT 5(6):4, February, 1978.

Vasectomy: operative procedures and sterility tests not standardized. FAMILY PLANNING PERSPECTIVES 11: 122-125, March-April, 1979.

Vasectomy reversal, by R. D. Amelar, et al. JOURNAL OF UROLOGY 121(5):547-550, May, 1979.

VASOVASOSTOMY

Experience with vasovasostomy: operative technique and results, by I. L. Jenkins, et al. BRITISH JOURNAL OF UROLOGY 51(1):43-45, February, 1979.

Microsurgical vasovasostomy clamp, by F. F. Marshall. UROLOGY 13(4):419, April, 1979.

Modified technique for microsurgical vasovasostomy, by A. Hamidinia, et al. INVESTIGATIVE UROLOGY 17(1): 42-45, July, 1979.

A technical aid for vasovasostomy, by F. J. Leary, et al. UROLOGY 13(3):256, March, 1979.

Vasovasostomy, by S. S. Schmidt. UROLOGIC CLINICS OF NORTH AMERICA 5(3):585-592, October, 1978.

Vasovasostomy and vas occlusion: preliminary observations using artificial devices in guinea pigs, by K. L. Mohr, et al.

FERTILITY AND STERILITY 30(6):696-701, December, 1978.

Vasovasostomy: evaluation of success, by R. Wicklund, et al. UROLOGY 13(5):531-534, May, 1979.

AUTHOR INDEX

484

487

Gunby, P. 67
Gupta, V. 21
Gupte, B. 170
Gustafsson, J. A. 143, 144
Guyatt, D. E. 21
Gwatkin, D. R. 154

Hacker, A. 140
Hale, R. W. 140
Haliburton, J. 170
Halimi, G. 4
Hall, A. K. 95
Hall, E. D. 56
Haller, U. 109
Hamidinia, A. 132
Hampson, M. E. 84
Han, D. W. 70
Hansen, H. 34, 62, 177
Hanson, M. S. 16
Hansson, R. O. 55
Harari, H. 56
Harlap, S. 27, 41
Harmon, J. D. 4
Harmon, K. 4
Harper, M. J. 56
Harris, B. A. 55, 209
Harris, F. W. 78
Harry, J. 22
Hart, M. A. 126
Hartwig, W. 82
Hassler, R. E. 141
Hassold, T. 145
Hassouna, T. 4
Hatcher, R. A. 30
Hatzibujas, J. 77
Hauser, G. A. 57
Havemann, O. 207, 210
Havránek, F. 17, 27, 90, 112
Hayler, B. 10
Hecht, A. 104
Hedin-Pourghasemi, M. 181

Hedlin, A. M. 142, 154
Heilmann, E. 144
Heissmeyer, H. 123
Held, J. P. 81
Helms, J. 215
Hennekens, C. H. 142
Henrion, R. 130, 203
Henry, P. 112
Henry, S. 98
Henshaw, B. 163
Hermalin, A. I. 68
Herold, E. S. 178, 182
Higier, J. 147
Hilliard, G. D. 147
Himmelberger, D. U. 41-42
Hinz, E. J. 193
Hoffman, J. J. 184
Holland, D. 43
Hollingworth, P. J. 53
Holtzhausen, G. H.
Hong, S. B. 194
Honorof, I. 213
Hoon, E. F. 192
Hopkins, J. R. 182
Horan, D. V. 24, 211
Hornick, J. P. 158, 159
Horowitz, A. J. 131
Horowitz, N. H. 21
Horton, K. C. 17
Horwitz R. I. 36
House, H. W. 132
Hout, M. 22
Howells, K. 182
Hoyos, M. D. 54
Hoyt, R. G. 106
Hubbard, C. W. 49
Huber, A. 54
Huber, D. H. 55
Hudiburgh, N. K. 110
Huggins, G. R. 59, 78, 144
Hulka, J. F. 89
Hume, K. 10

494